BRITAIN AND PORTUGUESE TIMOR

1941-1976

BRITAIN AND PORTUGUESE TIMOR 1941-1976

Nicholas Tarling

MONASH University
Publishing

© Copyright 2013
All rights reserved. Apart from any uses permitted by Australia's Copyright Act 1968, no part of this book may be reproduced by any process without prior written permission from the copyright owners. Inquiries should be directed to the publisher.

Monash University Publishing
Building 4, Monash University
Clayton, Victoria 3800, Australia
www.publishing.monash.edu
www.publishing.monash.edu/books/bpt-9781921867347.html

Monash University Publishing brings to the world publications which advance the best traditions of humane and enlightened thought. Monash University Publishing titles pass through a rigorous process of independent peer review.

Design: Les Thomas
Cover image: A small party of Australian troops in Dili, Portuguese Timor, 1945. Image courtesy of the Australian War Memorial. Image ID number: 119632.

The Monash Asia Series comprises works that make a significant contribution to our understanding of one or more Asian nations or regions. The individual works that make up this multi-disciplinary series are selected on the basis of their contemporary relevance. The Monash Asia Series of the Monash Asia Institute replaces Monash University's MAI Press imprint, which, from the early 1970s, has demonstrated this University's strong interest and expertise in Asian studies.

Monash Asia Series Editorial Board
Professor Marika Vicziany, Chair, Professor of Asian Political Economy, Monash Asia Institute, Faculty of Arts
Professor Greg Barton, School of Political and Social Inquiry, Faculty of Arts
Associate Professor Gloria Davies, School of Languages, Cultures and Linguistics, Faculty of Arts
Dr Julian Millie, School of Political and Social Inquiry, Faculty of Arts
Dr Jagjit Plahe, Department of Management, Faculty of Business and Economics
Dr David Templeman, School of Philosophical, Historical and International Studies, Faculty of Arts

National Library of Australia Cataloguing-in-Publication entry:
  Author: Tarling, Nicholas.
  Title: Britain and Portuguese Timor 1941–1976 / Nicholas Tarling.
  ISBN: 9781921867347 (pbk.)
  Series: Monash Asia Series.
  Notes: Includes bibliographical references and index.
  Subjects: Portugal--Colonies--History; Timor-Leste--Foreign relations--Great Britain; Great Britain--Foreign relations--Timor-Leste; Indonesia--Foreign relations--Timor-Leste.
  Dewey Number: 325.32095987

Printed in Australia by Griffin Press an Accredited ISO AS/NZS 14001:2004 Environmental Management System printer.

The paper this book is printed on is certified by the Programme for the Endorsement of Forest Certification scheme. Griffin Press holds PEFC chain of custody SGS - PEFC/COC-0594. PEFC promotes environmentally responsible, socially beneficial and economically viable management of the world's forests.

For Hugh Whittaker

Contents

Map of East Timor viii

Acknowledgements ix

Introduction xi

Chapter One
The Second World War 1

Chapter Two
The Japanese Occupation 37

Chapter Three
Wartime Negotiations 79

Chapter Four
The Re-establishment Of Portuguese Rule 109

Chapter Five
Confrontation 139

Chapter Six
The Carnation Revolution 175

Chapter Seven
Timorese Conflicts 217

Chapter Eight
The Incorporation of Timor 259

Epilogue 303

Bibliography 307

Index 311

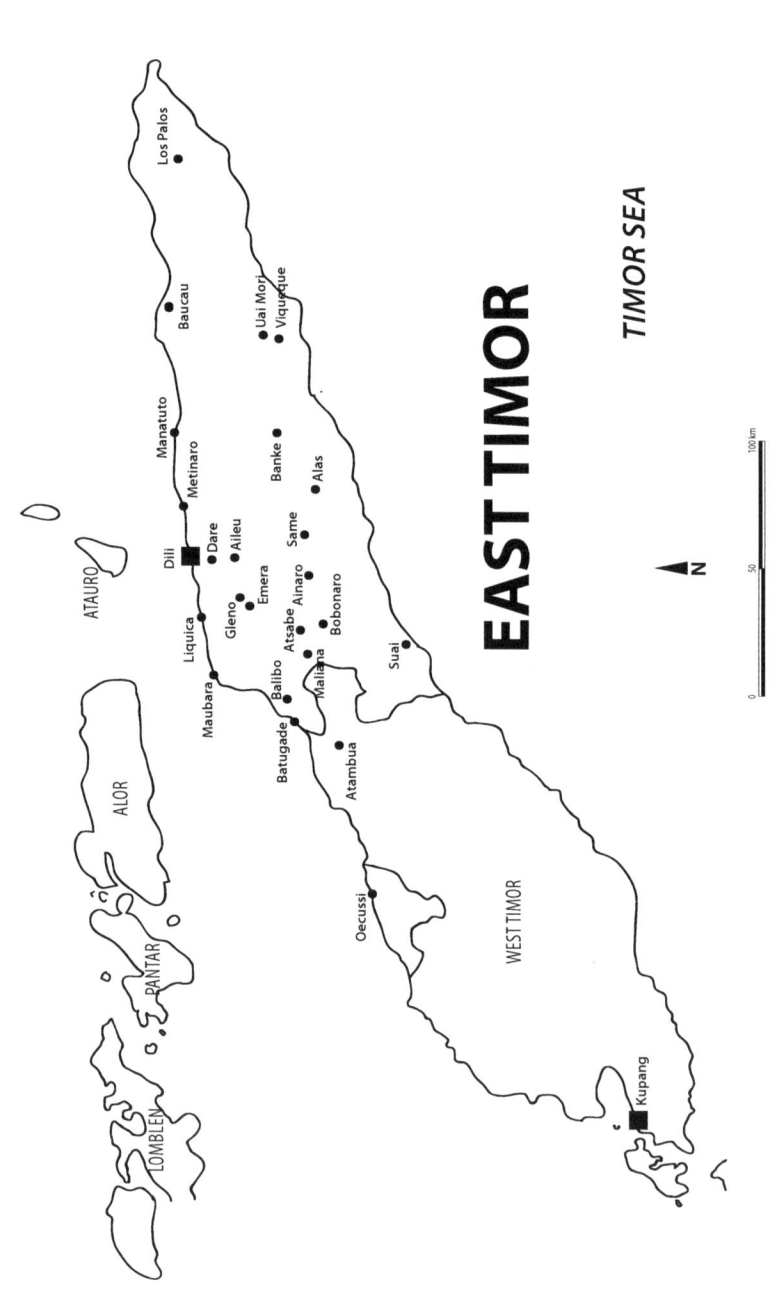

Acknowledgements

The author is grateful for the assistance afforded by The National Archives in London, by the staff of the General Library at The University of Auckland, and by the New Zealand Asia Institute. He is also grateful to Dr Brook Barrington for his helpful criticism and to Fiona and Rupert Wheeler for their generous hospitality.

Introduction

The emergence of an independent state of Timor Leste was a largely unexpected event of the last years of the 20th century, though it might be regarded as part of the process of decolonisation that had been a prime feature of the whole post-Second World War period. In Timor's chequered history, many other states were involved. The prime purpose of this book is to examine the role of the British. Timor was neither a part of their empire nor important to their commerce. But their approach to it was affected by their relationship with all the powers that were, the Portuguese, the Dutch, the Australians, the Japanese, the Indonesians, the Americans. The longest relationship was that with Portugal, with which, indeed, Timor had its longest relationship. Britain's interest was thus largely indirect. It had two peaks, marked by the Second World War and the decolonisation of Southeast Asia. Those are recognised in the book, one the concern of the first four chapters, the other the focus of the last four. But there are links between them, in memory and in history.

The book is not a history of the Timorese. To that it can but make a contribution. But the resources and the strategic position of the island have made it a focus of interest for outsiders, who have played a large part in determining its fate. Even so, in such a book as this we may read of the role of the Timorese in the guerrilla struggle led by Australian soldiers in the Pacific War and of the punishment that the Japanese forces meted out. And after the Carnation Revolution overthrew the Salazar system, we find in Timor a new generation of educated politicians who sought to play a decisive role in its future. The book ends with an account of the Indonesian incorporation of the territory that frustrated them. Britain's reportage was still copious and perceptive, but Britain, which had finally withdrawn from Singapore, now adopted only a very limited policy-making role. Though its interest was more indirect than ever, it was not without implications for the independence that the Timorese finally secured, which affirmed the rule that postcolonial states were successor states of empire.

The period on which this book focuses covers the Japanese interregnum and the decolonisation that followed. Other aspects of British policy in that period have been covered in other books by the author, most recently in his *Britain and the West New Guinea Dispute* (Tarling 2008) and *Britain and the*

Neutralisation of Laos (Tarling 2011). But it has, of course, been the subject of many other works, in particular those that have been concerned with the 'Emergency' in Malaya, the creation of Malaysia, 'confrontation' with Indonesia and the end of Britain's 'East of Suez' policy. Many of them have been able to draw on the rich resources of The National Archives in London, now largely open to readers for the whole of the period in which Britain played a substantial role. Those relating to Portuguese Timor, however, have not so far been fully utilised. They are the main source for the present author.

Though ostensibly a limited topic, British policy towards Portuguese Timor may be placed in several larger contexts. The first is that of the long-term relationship between Europe and Asia. From the 16th century CE, the contestation among the European states had extended into other parts of the world where they might gather wealth and power to use in their internecine struggle. But what is now called 'homeland security' came first. If an alliance was sought or a compromise needed, the basis of it might be found in the overseas empires that the Europeans acquired. That was particularly evident in the case of the British. Secure in Europe after the defeat of Napoleonic France in the early 19th century and uniquely advantaged as the first industrial power, they acquired a vast empire and an even larger commercial influence. When other powers industrialised later in the century and challenged its hegemony, Britain had to stake out its claims, but it also compromised. The First World War showed that that was not enough. In 1914 Britain's own security was at stake. The same was true in the Second World War.

Putting the topic in a long-term context has another advantage. The Portuguese were after all the first of the European powers to seek wealth and security by adventure outside Europe, seeking African gold, then rounding the Cape to compete in the intra-Asian trade, extending their enterprise to China and Japan in the East as well as to Brazil in the West. Much of this empire had been lost by the inter-war period, but by no means all. Brazil had gone its own way in the 1820s, initially as an empire under one of the Bragança monarchs, then as a republic. Much earlier, in 1641, the Dutch had displaced the Portuguese from their key stronghold at Melaka and built their own commercial empire in the Malay world. But the Portuguese retained a foothold in Timor and the Lesser Sunda islands, and in Macau, the settlement on the coast of China they had made in the 1550s and still held. Like the French, they also retained a foothold in India—at Goa—even after Britain became the paramount power on the subcontinent. But their prime possessions were those in Africa, where their claims were indeed so large that greater powers were anxious to challenge them in the late 19th century in the process developing a firmer criterion for the recognition of imperial rights. The loss of empire was not, however, something that a minor European state with a long history of overseas enterprise was ready to contemplate. In the inter-war period, the Salazar regime tied the empire into the ideology of the 'New State' and that regime lasted well beyond the end of the Second World War.

Successful retention of the remnants of empire could not, however, depend merely on Portugal's obstinacy or Salazar's subtlety. It had to depend—with as little humiliation as possible—on the support of other powers, in particular Britain, the world's prime naval power until the First World War. The two states often invoked their ancient treaties of alliance. Those had been made in the very different circumstances of earlier centuries, but there was an enduring common interest. For the British, Portugal was one of those minor European states whose continued independence helped to prevent any one major power so dominating the continent as to threaten Britain's own security. That issue was more important than any colonial interest or rivalry. Not admirers of Portuguese rule, the British were never going to be its destroyers.

Britain's capacity to act, even in that negative way, was diminished by the decline in its power evident after the First World War and then by the Depression and the rise of Nazi Germany. In East Asia, furthermore, its erstwhile ally, Japan, shifted away from the relatively moderate policies of the Taisho democracy of the 1920s, though its expansionist ventures were initially focused on Manchuria and then on northern China, and not on Southeast Asia. With the opening of the war in Europe in 1939, however, the Japanese took the opportunity to exert pressure on the European colonial powers in Southeast Asia, France, the Netherlands and Britain, and when the United States frustrated them, they invaded the region with striking success, securing the prompt surrender of Britain's strategic base, Singapore, in February 1942.

It was in this phase that Portuguese Timor, 'a periphery of a peripheral… empire' (Telkamp 1979:82), occasionally mentioned in negotiations among the other powers in earlier periods, became the object and site of military operations, and it is with this phase that the main part of this book opens. Always unhappy with the continued existence of what seemed an enclave in Netherlands India, the Dutch were anxious to intervene and the Australians were concerned at the prospect of Japanese expansion southwards, which gave Timor a new strategic importance. Their interposition was vain, but the Japanese invasion was followed by Australian guerrilla operations in

1942 and 1943. No fighting took place at the end of the war, however. The Japanese surrender in August 1945 preceded any Allied military venture, though Salazar had, of course, been anxious that Portugal should play a part in any operations that took place, if not itself receiving the Japanese surrender.

That did not mean that Timor simply returned to the pre-war status quo. Soon, for example, it found itself alongside not a more or less antagonistic Netherlands India but an independent Indonesia. Under Sukarno Indonesia made the acquisition of West New Guinea a priority on the argument that it had been part of Netherlands India. It could not make that claim in respect of Portuguese Timor. But might it not claim it even so? The chances were increased when independent India moved on Goa in 1961 and the winds of change reached the Portuguese territories in Africa as well as the United Nations. Australia, arguing for self-determination there, was in a quandary so far as Timor was concerned. It wanted good relations with its large new neighbour, Indonesia, and it was generally thought that Timor could not survive on its own. It seemed that it ought to become part of Indonesia, but not as a result of Indonesian aggression. By the late 1960s Britain had withdrawn from a strategic stance in Southeast Asia and wanted to avoid a key role in this affair. But rather more than onlookers, British diplomats saw much of the game and their reports give another perspective on the Indonesian incorporation of Timor, often as it has been discussed. They also add to accounts of the policy-making of other powers, too, whether or not their archives have been opened.

Over the period this book covers there were continuities and changes in the world at large—the decline of British power, the Cold War, the establishment of the Peoples Republic of China, decolonisation—and in the region—Indonesia's acquisition of West New Guinea, its confrontation of Malaysia, the war in Vietnam and its reunification—and Timor was placed in that shifting context. But various episodes in its history suggest continuity as well as change. The Portuguese, for example, did not forget the Dutch–Australian intervention of 1941 when, at the end of the war, the Australians sought a say in the Japanese surrender and, it seemed, a stake in the future. Nor was their role forgotten when Timor's incorporation into Indonesia came into view, nor, indeed, though this is beyond the scope of the book, when the Australians played a role in the de-incorporation of Timor after the fall of Suharto.

In Britain's own policy-making itself there were changes and continuities. Throughout, of course, it retained a parliamentary system, but foreign policy rarely figured in debates. It figured rather more in Cabinet discussions and in those of Cabinet committees. Officials played a substantial role in committees and, of course, in government departments. Of those the most important in international relations was the Foreign Office (FO), though the defence departments and the Chiefs of Staff (COS) were especially significant in wartime, and the Dominions Office (DO), later the Commonwealth Relations Office (CRO), also figured until it was combined with the FO in the late 1960s to become the Foreign and Commonwealth Office (FCO). The FO dealt with the all-important relationship with the United States, as well as with Britain's oldest ally, and for a while it acted in Lisbon for Australia, which had limited diplomatic representation in the 1940s. The FO/FCO was itself divided into departments, initially mostly of a regional nature, Portugal thus being dealt with in one of the European departments and Timor in one of the Asian departments. Reconciling the priorities Britain had was one of the prime tasks, undertaken by co-ordinating under-secretaries and ultimately by the Secretary of State, the Foreign Secretary, as the foreign minister was called. One of the means of policy-formulation was the preparation of minutes on incoming material or forthcoming meetings and conferences. Another was the exchange of 'private' correspondence alongside 'official' telegrams and despatches. That was a by-product of the parliamentary system; private correspondence might not be laid before Parliament when numbered telegrams or despatches were presented and were difficult for members to cite and call for. Their content helps to sustain the narrative of this book. To work out how people made judgments or chose options is a fundamental interest of the historian.

Chapter One

The Second World War

Portugal was for centuries an ally of the British and its retention of an empire in the 19th century depended on their pre-eminence. After Brazil proclaimed its independence, most of Portugal's empire was in Africa, though in Asia it retained Goa, Macau and part of Timor. Portugal's political and economic weakness put the empire at risk, but also, particularly under the inter-war dictatorship of Salazar, made it more determined to retain it. When the Second World War began in Europe, Portugal remained neutral. Britain accepted that, although it was concerned lest Germany obtained the Azores as a base for attacks on Atlantic shipping. The opening of the Pacific War brought Timor into question. For the Dutch, it was a kind of enclave in Netherlands India. For the Australians, it was a kind of strategic outlier of the northern part of their vast territory. As with the Azores, so with Timor, Salazar was unwilling to prejudice Portugal's neutrality by making agreements in advance of actual attack. Japan began the war before an agreement was made. The Dutch and the Australians sent a force into Portuguese Timor. The action aroused bitter protest. It was long remembered.

The English alliance and the Portuguese Empire

Portuguese Timor was indeed part of a once widespread empire, of which significant elements yet remained even in the late 19th and early 20th centuries, including islands in the Atlantic besides the Azores, the Cape Verde islands, São Tomé and Príncipe, colonies in Africa, Guinea-Bissau, Angola and Moçambique, Goa on the Indian subcontinent and Macau on the Chinese coast. Widespread empires, as the British also realised, were a source of weakness as well as strength; unfortunate examples might be set or followed, even if alien forces might be usefully deployed. The Portuguese hold on Timor had indeed been tenuous for much of the 17th and 18th centuries. Factions among the 'Black Portuguese' disputed with each other and with the Governor, and the trade in sandalwood, taken to Macau, was exhausted. The 19th century saw the introduction of coffee from Java, while the government came to terms with the Timorese chiefs, the *liurai* and the heads of the *sucos*, playing them off if necessary (Andaya 2010:391–420; Disney 2009:347–350; Esteves Fuelgas 1956:208,474).

In the early years the Portuguese contended with the Dutch who had driven them from Melaka in 1641 and made themselves dominant among the Europeans in the Indonesian archipelago. Arguably, indeed, the distrust between them continued throughout the colonial period. The Dutch drove the Portuguese from Kupang in 1653 and they then focused on Lifau in Oé-kussi, moving their main base to Dili only in 1769. In April 1859 the two states concluded a treaty of exchange and demarcation, allowing the Dutch to consolidate the 'Netherlands India' realm in the Lesser Sundas and the Portuguese to retain part of Timor. The Portuguese abandoned their claims in the neighbouring islands of Flores and Solor, while the Dutch transferred the 'kingdom' of Maubara, a coffee region. A small Dutch enclave remained within the Portuguese territory and the Portuguese retained Oé-kussi as an enclave in Dutch territory.[1]

In a convention of June 1893 the two powers expressed a desire to demarcate their possessions more exactly and to eliminate the enclaves and, in a declaration the following month, they agreed that in the case of cession of all or part of the territories or rights of sovereignty in question they would offer each other the first option.[2] Most of the boundary was settled by a commission in 1898–9, the rest referred to a conference in The Hague in 1902. The result was the convention of 1904. The Dutch withdrew from their enclave in Portuguese territory, but, though they gained Noimuti, the Portuguese retained most of Oé-kussi. Its boundaries remained in dispute, however. Attempts to determine them failed and they were finally made the subject of an arbitral award in June 1914 (Krieger 1997:6–17). The Portuguese, as Peter Hastings later wrote, were subject to 'perennial fears that the Dutch harboured annexationist designs' (Hastings 1975:193).

Both states were by this time minor contenders in the age of imperialism. For both the key relationship was with the greatest imperial power, Britain. It too had contended with the Dutch, but, though successful, had contented itself with securing the Straits Settlements under the treaty of 17 March

---

[1] The treaty is in Krieger (1997:1–2); see also Pélissier (1996:39).
[2] The convention and the declaration are found in Krieger (1997:2–3).

1824 and later northern Borneo, where it placed Sarawak, Brunei and North Borneo (Sabah) under its protection in 1888. Elsewhere the Dutch, provided they offered commercial opportunity, could be allowed political predominance. They continued to construct 'Netherlands India'.

Portugal was Britain's oldest ally. The connection dated back to the late 14th century, but, though the continuities were not quite legendary, both its context and its purpose had changed over time. In face of the ambitions of medieval Castile, backed by France, England had sided with Portugal, and in 1373 Edward III had made an agreement with Dom Fernando, 'a true, constant and mutual and perpetual Friendship, Alliance, Union of sincere affection', the two parties undertaking to be 'Friends to Friends, Enemies to Enemies'.[3] The alliance was not one-sided. Castile then had a major fleet of galleys that was more than a match for England's naval forces and in the late 1370s they were able to dominate the Channel and to attack some English coastal cities (Russell 1955:239ff). João I signed a perpetual alliance in 1386, the treaty of Windsor, ratified by Richard II early in 1387. John of Lancaster, who had claims to the throne of Castile, led an expedition to the Peninsula, but it proved 'a tremendous fiasco' (Russell 1955:486).

The alliance, however, was to be 'the bedrock of Portuguese diplomacy until well into the twentieth century' (Birmingham 1993:21). It was reaffirmed in 1642 when Portugal regained the independence that, after the death of King Sebastião in 1578, it had lost to the Spanish monarchy that had united the other Iberian kingdoms, and again in 1661 when Charles II married Catherine of Bragança. The marriage treaty of that year engaged the English king to effect a peace between the Portuguese and the Dutch, to guarantee the defence of the Portuguese Indies in the event of warfare and to supply 10,000 auxiliaries for defence against Spain. In return he was ceded Bombay and Tangier (Ogg 1963:I,186–187). In the face of the ambitions of Louis XIV England not only fought in the Netherlands but also attempted to put a Habsburg on the Spanish throne in opposition to his Bourbon candidate. Under the Methuen Treaty of 1703 Portugal broke with France as part of this vain strategy (Coward 2003:410). In the Peninsular wars of the Napoleonic period, a century later, Portugal and the United Kingdom fought together—amid some tension—against French-dominated Spain.

In general the two parties shared an antagonism to France and Spain. There was some continuity in the commercial connection as well as the political.

---

[3] FO 972/8: Memorandum, The Anglo–Portuguese Alliance 1373–1973 (Foreign Policy Documents No. 8).

Back in the late 14th century, trade with Lisbon and Oporto had substituted for England's trade with Castile (Russell 1955:202). The 1642 treaty offered commercial privileges to English merchants. In 1703 the Methuen brothers covered commercial as well as political matters (Birmingham 1993:62). The discontinuity is found in the relative power of the two states. Portugal had created a worldwide empire in the 16th and 17th centuries—in Asia, America and Africa—but the Dutch had undermined its trade and taken some of its key holdings. By contrast Britain built a new empire to replace its lost American colonies. Even more important, it finally defeated France and, becoming in addition the first industrial power, became the predominant state of the mid-19th century. If Portugal wished to retain the remains of its empire, the longstanding alliance had a new significance. But then, as the industrial revolution spread, Britain faced new challenges, initially overseas, and then in Europe itself.

The Anglo–Portuguese connection was at first damaged and then reaffirmed in the age of imperialism. The Berlin Africa conference of 1884–5 deemed that the doctrine of effective occupation, rather than prior discovery, was the indicator of sovereignty that other states should accept, at least for coastal regions. That was designed to deal with a dispute that Germany had raised when Bismarck began his colonial policy; he had challenged Britain's claims to Southwest Africa (Namibia) and then the treaty it made with Portugal in February 1884 in order to stem France's advance in the Congo basin (Mommsen 1988:157–161). But a dispute between the old allies followed the conference when Portugal signed agreements with France and Germany for support in linking the colonies of Angola and Moçambique, thus threatening Britain's expansion from the Cape Colony. In 1890 Britain demanded the evacuation of the disputed territories and Portugal, backing down, had to sign the treaty of 1891 amidst 'great bitterness and popular indignation'.[4] The resulting riots gave a fillip to the republican movement in Portugal (Birmingham 1993:146).

The German Kaiser's actions prompted a renewal of good relations. In 1897 Portugal appeared to be on the verge of bankruptcy. A group of financiers in London suggested that Britain should arrange a loan and that, in return, Portugal would grant Britain practical control of Delagoa Bay in Moçambique, important because it granted the Boer Transvaal Republic an access to the outside world not under British control. The Portuguese Government feared that this would provoke Germany into seizing some other portion of its empire

---

[4] FO 972/8: Memorandum, The Anglo–Portuguese Alliance 1373–1973 (Foreign Policy Documents No. 8), p.15.

and no agreement was reached. The Kaiser's seizure of Jiaozhou in November alarmed the Portuguese, however. In June 1898 Ambassador Soveral proposed the renewal of the loan negotiations on condition that Britain reaffirmed the alliance treaties of 1661, 1703 and 1710. Getting wind of this, Germany sought 'compensation'; Timor was on Ambassador Hatzfeldt's list (Grenville 1964:191). The Portuguese decided they could do without a loan. But some members of the British Cabinet wanted to improve relations with Germany and two Anglo–German agreements were signed in August 1898. One laid down the conditions on which Britain and Germany would furnish a loan, spelling out the territories from which the revenues would form the security; those of Timor would form part of the security of the German loan. The other, which was secret, provided for the contingency of 'its unfortunately not being found possible to maintain the integrity of the African possessions of Portugal south of the Equator, as well as those of Timor'. The colonies would be partitioned on the basis of the spheres of influence defined in the first convention (Grenville 1964:194–195). Portugal survived and no colonial carve-up ensued.

That, as Langhorne says, was fortunate for Britain, for it did not want Germany to benefit and the Boer War made a new agreement necessary (Langhorne 1977:309). Before it began, Lord Salisbury, British Prime Minister and Foreign Secretary, had pressed the Portuguese Government to stop the supply of arms going through Delagoa Bay to Pretoria, the Transvaal capital. He appealed to the old alliance in vain. He also tried blackmail; if arms supplies continued, Britain might have to 'raise the question of the Portuguese position in Africa under the Anglo–German agreement' (quoted in Grenville 1964:260). The French and German ministers in Lisbon pressed Portugal not to agree, but on 14 October 1899 it concluded an agreement in which Britain reaffirmed the treaties of 1642 and 1661, so binding itself to defend Portugal and its colonies, and Portugal undertook not to allow arms to pass into Transvaal once war had been declared (Grenville 1964:262). The convention was, Grenville argues, not at odds with the Anglo–German convention of the previous year. It was kept secret at the wish of the Portuguese Government (Grenville 1964:262–263).

The renewal of good relations between Britain and Portugal was affirmed by royal visits. Edward VII went to Lisbon the year before his famous visit to Paris. In 1904 the King of Portugal made a state visit in return. When he was overthrown in 1910 in a revolution initiated by junior army officers, Britain recognised the new republic.

There were, however, further discussions with Germany over the future of the Portuguese colonies. They began late in 1911 as a result of the desire to reduce tension after the Agadir crisis. Sir Edward Grey, now the British Foreign Secretary, considered the agreements of 1898 and 1899 contradictory and disliked their secrecy. He also thought the Portuguese colonies were 'sinks of iniquity', and that it would be well if Portugal sold them.

> *But* how can we of all people put pressure on Portugal to sell: we who are bound by an alliance to protect and preserve her colonies for Portugal—an alliance renewed secretly for value received during the Boer War? And Portugal won't part with her colonies…for when nations have gone down hill until they are at their last gasp, their pride remains undiminished if indeed it is not increased.[5]

A new convention was initialled in October 1913 in which Germany would gain more of Angola, while agreeing to substitute São Tomé and Príncipe for Timor (Stone 1994:182)—'a shady transaction', as AJP Taylor (1954:502) puts it. But Grey wanted it published, along with those of 1898 and 1899, and that was unacceptable to the Germans. The German Ambassador thought Grey was assuming the position of medical adviser to the Portuguese empire, 'while what Germany contemplated was rather that of being the heir' (Taylor 1954:504). The convention had not been signed when the First World War broke out.

The Portuguese feared that their colonies would be used to buy the Germans out of Belgium and wished to enter the war. Grey told them that their intervention was unnecessary 'for the moment' (Taylor 1954:532). Early in 1917, however, Portugal concluded a military convention with its old ally. Twenty-five thousand men embarked for France and Flanders and they fought heroically at Lys in 1918 when the brunt of the German attack fell on them.[6]

Post-war the republic confronted Portugal's financial crisis with 'austere realism'. Budget savings were, however, against the interests of senior cadres in the army (Birmingham 1993:151–152). An army coup ensued on 18 May 1926, though the Estado Novo (New State) was not firmly established until the ex-academic Dr António de Oliveira Salazar, the finance minister from 1928, became Prime Minister in 1932, remaining as head of an authoritarian regime by relying strongly on political police until 1968. His aims were to

---

[5] Grey to Goschen, Ambassador to Berlin, 29 December 1911, quoted in Langhorne (1977:311).
[6] FO 972/8: Memorandum, The Anglo–Portuguese Alliance 1373–1973 (Foreign Policy Documents No. 8), p.18.

preserve his régime from revolutionary republicans at home and communists abroad, to defend Portugal from the 'Spanish danger', and to protect its empire from the great powers (Rosas 2002:269). Indeed 'the fact of empire was cemented in the whole historical definition of Portugal as an independent country'. Under Salazar, Portugal 'would find its definition increasingly in its colonial vocation' (Bruneau 1984:22–23). Others would contest the economic value of the colonies, but the political and intellectual elite 'unanimously' considered them 'an essential precondition for the maintenance of Portuguese independence in the face of the traditional annexationist intentions of its powerful Spanish neighbour' (Rosas 2002:269).

In the inter-war world, and especially in the 1930s, the colonies were by no means secure. Salazar's policy made them pay for themselves, though at the cost of development. But the Japanese acquisition of Manchuria and Italian intervention in Ethiopia were alarming. The alliance with Britain remained essential. At times, indeed, Britain contemplated a colonial deal with Nazi Germany as part of a policy of appeasement. In the event, however, it did not renew what Robert Vansittart called 'this ancient and dirty game' (quoted in Stone 1994:87). The day after Kristallnacht, the British Government declared that it was no longer bound by the secret convention of 1898 and reaffirmed its commitment to the Anglo–Portuguese treaties (Stone 1994:111).

The opening of the Second World War

At the outset of war in September 1939, Salazar announced Portugal's intention, with Britain's approval, to remain neutral; it was on both sides 'accepted and understood within the framework of the alliance' (Rosas 2002:272). 'Britain', he told the National Assembly in October,

> asked nothing in the name of our centuries old alliance and friendship which could oblige us to join in the conflict. However, our conscience would be unhappy if—as friends who do not reject their friends in adversity—we did not immediately reaffirm our full fidelity to our alliance with Britain. The National Assembly knows how much Britain welcomes our neutrality declaration. The attitude we assumed was best calculated to serve the interests of the two nations.[7]

---

[7] Quoted in FO 972/8: Memorandum, The Anglo–Portuguese Alliance 1373–1973 (Foreign Policy Documents No. 8), p.19..

The British Chiefs of Staff (COS) were aware of the poor condition of Portugal's forces and considered its participation would be a commitment rather than as asset. Moreover, its entry into the war might convert Spanish neutrality into hostility (Stone 1994:129). But they did want Portuguese neutrality to be as benevolent as possible.

Hitler's triumphs in 1940 brought him to the Pyrenees. Would he enter Spain? 'Portugal conceded significant political and economic favours to Hitler's Germany', seen also, after all, as a barrier against Bolshevism, 'but was careful not to put at risk the essential terms of its old alliance with Britain' (Rosas 2002:274). The Atlantic islands, particularly the Azores, were a test for its policy. Hitler had hopes, discounted by German naval leaders, of using them as advanced bases for attacking shipping and as stepping stones to the Western hemisphere. Salazar was more worried about their possible occupation by the British, and especially by the Americans; he was unwilling to grant any facilities until the Germans had actually violated Portuguese neutrality, whereas the United States and the United Kingdom wanted him to accept their protection if Germany entered Spain or when there was imminent danger of its so doing (Toynbee 1956:328,331–332).

In May 1941 the prospect that defeated France might make Dakar available to the Germans led Roosevelt to declare that the Nazi occupation of any of the Atlantic islands jeopardised the ultimate safety of the United States and to extend the range of naval patrols. Portugal emphasised its determination to defend its neutrality and sought reassurance over the maintenance of its sovereignty. Salazar remained unwilling to accept war material from the United States unless it was unobtainable from the United Kingdom (Toynbee 1956:331–332; Stone 1994:175,177–178).

In the meantime Japan had taken advantage of Hitler's victories. Frustrated in its war on China, it used the defeat of France to move into northern Indochina. Would it move further south? Would the Salazar regime, 'obliged to walk warily owing to Japanese retaliation against Macao', as Dr Teixeira de Sampayo, Secretary-General of the Foreign Ministry in Lisbon had put it,[8] stand up to Japanese penetration in Timor? And what could its forces do if the Japanese openly attacked? The Salazar regime was determined to retain the empire, a core part of its nationalist appeal. But how would it go about it?

In these questions the Australians, too, were of course interested. Their longstanding apprehensions over the security of the 'Near North' were

---

[8] FO 371/27792 [F1149/222/61]: Telegram from Campbell, 14 February 1941, 53.

increased by the threat of Japan and Britain's involvement in the European war, both of which undermined the security the colonial pattern of Southeast Asia had provided. Japan's interest in Portuguese Timor had attracted their attention. They competed for oil concessions (Stone 1994:183); both established air services, QANTAS from Darwin, in 1935 and Dai Nippon Airways from Kobe and Palau in 1938 (Frei 1991:158–159). David Ross of the Civil Aviation Department was sent to administer the air service, but also to report, and FJ Whittaker, his assistant, was in fact a 'spy' (Jolliffe 1978:242). When the Japanese sent a consul, Kuroki Tokitaro, Australia followed Britain's advice and made Ross British Consul (Frei 1991:159). In the Allies' conversations in Singapore earlier in the year the Australians had also undertaken to send troops to Dutch Timor in the event of hostilities (Tarling 1996:310). Though the Dutch were not anxious to see them in such numbers as to diminish their own standing with the local people, the Foreign Minister, Eelco van Kleffens, had admitted that Timor was 'one of the weakest and most vulnerable spots' (quoted in Tarling 1996:223). Presumably he had the Portuguese in mind.

Pre-empting the Japanese

Following the German invasion of the Soviet Union, the Japanese moved into southern Indochina and the Americans reacted with economic embargoes designed to stop them in their tracks. Implemented with severity, the embargoes in fact provoked them, while the Americans offered the British or the Dutch no reassurances till the last minute. The Australian Government again brought up the question of Portuguese Timor; 'undue Japanese penetration' had been prevented, but it might be occupied by the Japanese, with or without Portuguese assent, whether a war had begun or not. The United Kingdom, Australia and the Netherlands should 'agree beforehand on what preventive action is feasible'.[9] A Japanese landing would 'constitute a most serious threat to our communications', SH Hebblethwaite minuted in the Far Eastern Department at the Foreign Office (FO) in London; presumably, LH Foulds added, the idea of sending an Australian force to Kupang was connected to some extent with the possible need to occupy Portuguese Timor.[10]

---

[9] FO 371/27794 [F9212/222/61]: Telegram, Commonwealth/DO, 8 September 1941, p. 558; also *Documents on Australian Foreign Policy* (AFPD):V,102–103.
[10] FO 371/27794 [F9212/222/61]: Minutes 13, 15 September 1941.

The Chiefs of Staff in London agreed that Britain should concert measures with the Dutch as an additional Australian commitment and the FO decided to approach the Portuguese.[11] The Dominions Office (DO) suggested to the Australian Government that they should be asked if they would accept 'outside help' if 'the military authorities on the spot' found it necessary, and that they and the Dutch should be asked to agree to discussions with the Australians about preventive action and about action to be taken 'if a threat should actually eventuate'.[12] The Australians' response was positive; they would be ready to send additional forces to Kupang for the purpose. The Dutch should accept advance parties in Ambon and Kupang immediately.[13] They did.[14]

In the Central Department of the FO, however, Frank Roberts questioned bringing the Dutch into the discussions before the matter had been raised with the Portuguese. It was not clear how they would react even to the Australians and it was important not to scare them off staff talks over the Atlantic that had been arranged with great difficulty. The British must not appear to rush the Portuguese.

> The latter clearly take the line that they have only granted commercial facilities to the Japanese and are fully alive to the dangers of Japanese infiltration. They will not therefore readily agree even to discuss the hypothesis of Japanese attack, and still less to go beyond this and entrust the defence of Timor to outside parties.[15]

In reference to the Azores, they always said they did not need outside help. They were 'so susceptible and touchy' about their empire that the British should not say they were discussing it with the Dutch. They were opposed to the Americans' showing an interest in the Atlantic islands.

The Foreign Secretary, Anthony Eden, was nevertheless 'ready to break the ground' with the Portuguese Ambassador, Dr Monteiro, who, it was thought, 'will surely take the line that Timor is in no danger and will have Macao in mind'.[16] In opening the conversation on 4 November Eden raised

---

[11] FO F9212: Minutes by Hebblethwaite and Makins, 23 September 1941.
[12] FO 371/27794 [F10787/222/61]: Telegram from the DO, 13 October 1941, 689; also AFPD:V,136–137.
[13] FO 371/27794 [F10890/222/61]: Telegram, 17 October 1941, 683; also AFPD:V,147.
[14] Cranborne to Curtin, 27 November 1941, 786, in AFPD:V,231–232.
[15] F0371/27794 [F10890/222/61]: Minutes, 20, 23 October 1941.
[16] FO 371/27794 [F10890/222/61]: Minute, 29 October 1941.

the question of infiltration, then moved on to that of a possible attack. He presumed the Portuguese Government intended to resist. Monteiro confirmed that. That being so, Eden wondered whether, under the Anglo–Portuguese alliance it would ask Britain's help in such an eventuality, and suggested that, if so, secret staff discussions might take place. Perhaps Colonel Barros Rodrigues could take them up, suggested Eden, referring to the Portuguese officer who, with Commandant Susa Viva, was engaged in talks about Anglo–Portuguese collaboration in the event of an attack on Portugal with Colonel JYE Myrtle, Wing Commander RE de T Vintras and Commander W Evershed. Monteiro said he would refer the matter to his government. If it agreed to Eden's suggestion, it would probably want to use an officer more informed about Timor. In the Portuguese mind, he added, the problems of Macau and Timor were 'closely linked, one being dependent on the other'. Macau presented special problems, said Eden, as did Hong Kong, 'but this factor should not prevent us from considering together what action, if any, could be taken in respect of Timor'.[17]

When he saw the Permanent Under-Secretary at the FO, Sir Alexander Cadogan, on 10 November, Monteiro had no reply from his government. He was, however, certain his government would resist an attack and welcome British help. The Portuguese staff officers currently in London had been told by their British counterparts that Timor could not be covered in their talks, but would have to be covered in the Far East. He thought there could nevertheless be preliminary talks in London and on his own responsibility would authorise the Portuguese officers to extend their stay for the purpose.[18] Those took place on 12 November.[19] Myrtle urged that advance planning was needed to meet the Japanese threat and Vintras pointed out the risk of infiltration.[20]

The reply of the Portuguese Government was delivered the following day. It was resolved to defend all its territories against aggression and in particular to defend Timor against any aggression from Japan. Its forces in Timor were, however, 'very slender, amounting to hardly more than a police force', and it considered it would be a mistake to disperse its forces by sending troops from Portugal or elsewhere. It would seek Britain's assistance

---

[17] FO 371/27795 [F11814/222/61]: Eden to Campbell, 4 November 1941, 453; cf Monteiro to MFA, 5 November 1941, 641, and Telegram, 6 November 1941, 324, in *Dez anos de política externa* (DAPE) 1974:X,14–15,18–19.
[18] FO 371/27796 [F12104/222/61]: Conversation, 10 November 1941.
[19] FO 371/27796 [F12289/222/61]: Eden to Campbell, 15 November 1941, 465.
[20] Minutes, 12 November 1941, in DAPE:X,75–76.

and indeed expect it under the alliance. It would be useful, it thought, to open conversations in London 'on the possibility of establishing a joint plan of action in case of need'. If, Monteiro added, the British considered it would be more convenient to exchange views in more detail, locally, say in Singapore, they could suggest that.[21]

Eelco van Kleffens, in London with the Dutch Government exiled after the German conquest of his country in 1940, told Eden that the Netherlands chargé in Lisbon (Pallandt) had expressed its concern to Dr Sampayo over possible Japanese infiltration in Timor, 'adding that we were sure that Portugal would live up to her proud tradition and would withstand any Japanese attempts to this effect'. The Netherlands Indies Government, van Kleffens also told Eden, had sent advance parties to West Timor and Ambon. Eden recapitulated his exchanges with Monteiro. Van Kleffens said that, if staff talks were held, his government would like to send experts too. Eden reminded him 'that the Portuguese were our allies', and said that on that basis 'they were ready to have secret talks with us, but that they might see difficulties about admitting Netherlands representatives'. He would, however, 'throw a fly over the Portuguese Ambassador…and see whether he looked like rising to it'. Van Kleffens observed 'that it was inconceivable that, if the Australians moved, the Dutch would not move too'.[22]

Roberts thought 'the progress already achieved…very satisfactory, having regard to Portuguese caution'. Should the British now try to persuade the Portuguese to join in discussions with the Dutch and the Australians as well as themselves? Given their favourable reaction to the British approach and the fact that the Dutch had raised the matter in Lisbon, Roberts saw no objection, 'but if the Portuguese show any signs of taking fright, we should at once offer to restrict the conversation to the Portuguese and ourselves. We could then keep the Dutch and Australians informed of what was happening'. The United States had acquiesced in such a process over Atlantic islands.[23] When the Portuguese had found a suitable representative, Eden told van Kleffens on 17 November, the British might suggest the Dutch should appoint one; 'but this proposal would have to be made with caution'.[24]

Britain's Commander-in-Chief Far East, Sir Robert Brooke-Popham, wanted to assure the Dutch that the British recognised their direct interest

---

[21] FO 371/27796 [F12289/222/61]: Memorandum by Cadogan, 13 November 1941.
[22] FO 371/27796 [F12142/222/61]: Eden to Bland, 6 November 1941, 97.
[23] FO 371/27796 [F12142/222/61]: Minute, 14 November 1941.
[24] FO 371/27781 [F12472/54/61]: Eden to Bland, 17 November 1941, 100.

in Timor. A Dutch representative had to take part in any discussions. 'They are working closely with Singapore and Australia in the matter. Some regret has been expressed in N.E.I. of omission of any reference to them in recent speeches', and it was most important to maintain their full co-operation.[25] It was, as Ashley Clarke put it, 'a question of handling the Portuguese delicately'.[26]

The FO prepared an aide-mémoire for the Portuguese Ambassador, formally suggesting talks in Singapore, including Australian representatives and associating Dutch ones. Given the 'present conditions in the Far East and the consequent urgency of this matter', an 'early expression' of the Portuguese Government's views would be 'greatly appreciated'.[27] Cadogan handed the aide-mémoire to Monteiro on 2 December. He said there might be some difficulty in authorising conversations with the Netherlands authorities. Cadogan replied 'that in any event we should be in conversation with the latter, who were our Allies and if we could get into contact with the Portuguese there would then effectively be consultation between the three Powers'.[28]

The Dutch representative in Lisbon had appealed to Salazar to consult with his government over the defence of Timor, the Dutch Ambassador in London, E Michiels van Verduynen, told Cadogan on the afternoon of 4 December. The Portuguese, Cadogan commented, 'had shown some hesitation about discussing the defence of Portuguese Timor with a belligerent with whom they were not allied'. Sir Ronald Campbell, the British Ambassador in Lisbon, should be instructed to support the representations. The Dutch Government was meanwhile telegraphing its Governor-General, AWL Tjarda van Starkenborgh-Stachouwer, 'to hold his hand pending the result of the representations in Lisbon. If, however, war breaks out in the Far East, it is fairly evident that the Dutch will act without waiting on Dr Salazar'.[29]

No telegram was sent to Lisbon, however, for on 5 December Monteiro presented an aide-mémoire from his government.[30] That indicated that it had no objection to sending an officer to Singapore to discuss with a representative of the British High Command 'the question of the defence of Timor in the event of a Japanese attack against that Colony arising out of the existence

---

25   FO 371/27796 [F12731/222/61]: Telegram, 21 November 1941, 21916.
26   FO 371/27796 [F12732]: Minute, 26 November 1941.
27   FO 371/27796 [F12732]: Aide-mémoire, 28 November 1941; also in DAPE:X,166.
28   FO 371/27796 [F13304/222/61]: Memorandum by Cadogan, 3 December 1941; cf Monteiro to MFA, Telegrams, 2 December 1941, 359, 360, in DAPE:X,155–156.
29   FO 371/27796 [F13305/222/61]: Minute by Makins, 4 December 1941.
30   FO 371/27796 [F13283/222/61]: Telegram to Campbell, 6 December 1941, 2007.

of a state of war between Japan and Great Britain or the United States'. It presumed that, 'should such an eventuality materialise', the operations would be 'predominantly naval' and so it would send a naval officer:

> There is nothing to prevent this officer from being informed, through the intermediary of the British High Command, of the point of view of the Netherlands authorities; nor do the Portuguese Government see any objection to his being permitted to exchange views with a representative of the Netherlands East Indies on the eventualities which might affect that part of Timor belonging to the Netherlands and which, in consequence, would be matters of interest to the defence of Portuguese Timor.[31]

Chargé Pallandt saw Salazar, who told him

> that while it was natural that Portugal should have staff talks locally with her ally, it seemed preferable as no such reason existed in the case of the Netherlands, that the Dutch expert should not directly participate. Since he agreed, however, that close contact was necessary he was very willing that the Dutch expert should be kept informed through the British representative. In any matter affecting exclusively Portugal and the Netherlands their respective experts could of course talk together direct.

This 'typically Portuguese arrangement' seemed to meet the case, Campbell commented, and Pallandt seemed satisfied. He did not therefore intervene himself.[32]

The landing of Dutch and Australian troops

The Japanese went to war on 7 December 1941. The Dutch should move into Portuguese Timor, Duff Cooper, Chancellor of the Duchy of Lancaster and soon to be appointed Resident Minister in the Far East, proposed on 10 December.[33] 'We have to go carefully with the Portuguese in view of

---

[31] Telegram, 4 December 41, 313, in DAPE:X,169–170; Aide-mémoire, 5 December 1941, in DAPE:X,179–180; also FO 371/27796 [F13306/222/61].
[32] FO 371/27796 [F13315/222/61]: Telegram from Campbell, 6 December 1941, 1570; Telegram from Lisbon, 6 December 1941, 314, in DAPE:X,182–183.
[33] FO 371/27797 [F13517/222/61]: Telegram, 10 December 1941.

important discussions now proceeding with them regarding other parts of the Portuguese Empire', he was told. The FO was trying to get them to agree to immediate occupation under Britain's auspices.[34]

Pallandt had suggested, Campbell reported, that, in the event of an attack, Dutch and Australian forces should immediately be called in. The Secretary-General had told him that the Portuguese did not desire to prejudice the Singapore conversations and wished to consult their British ally.[35] Sir Orme Sargent and Ashley Clarke asked Monteiro if the proposal would be easier if it came from Australia. A further idea was that it would be a British proposal, implemented by Dutch and Australian forces.[36] He reported home that he had expressed his anxiety that assistance should be based on the British alliance, so that the United Kingdom would feel obliged to return Portuguese Timor if it were lost. Getting into a war for the sake of the Dutch and Australians was 'absolument inconveniente'.[37]

An interdepartmental meeting at the War Office on 11 December considered ways of forestalling a Japanese move. The Australians had been asked if they could send a force immediately but had not yet replied. The FO representatives proposed invoking the ancient treaty. 'It is hoped that the Portuguese Government agreement may be received in 24 hours though it is possible that they will prove reluctant to countenance any such defence measures on account of the reactions of the Axis powers.' Such action would probably precipitate the occupation of Macau. Should the Portuguese reaction be unfavourable, the matter would have to be reconsidered, perhaps by the COS, 'for our actions in Portuguese Timor might have an important bearing on the negotiations which have been in progress about the Atlantic Islands'. The Portuguese would object if Netherlands Indies troops played a major part. At least a token Australian detachment should be involved.[38]

Sargent put it to Monteiro that, in virtue of the Anglo–Portuguese alliance, Britain should go to the help of Portuguese Timor in the event of a Japanese attack, assistance being furnished by Australian and Dutch troops who would evacuate when the emergency had passed. The Japanese might act at any moment, Sargent added, so that the local authorities should be given 'wide latitude so as to ensure that the assistance contemplated was in

---

[34] FO 371/27797 [F13517/222/61]: Telegram, 11 December 1941, 35.
[35] FO 371/27797 [F13468/222/61]: Telegram, 9 December 1941, 1581.
[36] FO 371/27797 [F13468/222/61]: Telegram, 10 December 1941, 2044.
[37] Telegrams, 10 December 1941, 378, 379, in DAPE:X,224–226.
[38] WO 208/852: Minute by FC Scott, 11 December 1941.

good time'.[39] Britain, Campbell was told, wanted the Portuguese Governor, Ferreira de Carvalho, to invite assistance well before the attack developed.[40] That might be difficult to secure, given the way the Portuguese had reacted in the European talks—they proffered collaboration after an attack; the British wanted to anticipate one (Stone 1994:180).

It was unlikely that the Portuguese representative could reach Singapore before Christmas, Lord Cranborne, the Secretary of State for the Dominions, had telegraphed to Prime Minister John Curtin in Canberra. Some 'immediate provision against the possibility of Japanese attack on Portuguese Timor' seemed very important. Discussion with Monteiro indicated that the Portuguese Government would not admit Allied troops at that stage 'without further evidence of Japanese designs on their territory, but we think they might be prepared to authorise the Governor to make a local request for Australian military assistance without reference to Lisbon if and when he has reason to apprehend that a Japanese attack may be threatening'. Would it be in accord with the wishes of the Australian Government that the Portuguese Government should be asked 'if they would issue such authorisation immediately'? If so, could the British say that Australian forces would be ready to help? The British hoped to arrange for Portugal to give a similar authority to the Dutch. The arrangement, though not precise, should do. 'It is designed to take account of Portuguese difficulties as a neutral.'[41] Canberra agreed. Portugal might well be requested to invite Allied troops 'to protect her possession even at this stage'.[42]

The Dutch Governor-General had authority 'to take necessary action for liquidating of Japanese in Portuguese Timor', Cranborne telegraphed the Australian Government on 11 December. In view of that, and of the 'increasing urgency' of the situation—the sinking of the *Repulse* and *Prince of Wales* occurred on 10 December—the British Government was endeavouring to eliminate the delays that were possible if the Governor hesitated. The Portuguese Government was being 'invited' to instruct the Governor he should facilitate the task of the Dutch and Australian troops. The British Government attached importance to sending 'even a very small token force of Australians'.[43] Again Canberra agreed. The move should be made 'without

---

[39] FO 371/27797 [F13579/222/61]: Minute by Sargent, 11 December 1941; cf Telegram, 11 December 1941, 381, in DAPE:X,238.
[40] FO 371/27797 [F13579/222/61]: Telegram, 11 December 1941, 2056.
[41] Telegram, 10 December 1941, 812, in AFPD:V, 296; also FO 371/27797 [F13576/222/61].
[42] Telegram, 11 December 1941, 791, in AFPD:V, 298; also FO 371/27797 [F13578/222/61].
[43] Telegram, 11 December 1941, 819, in AFPD:V, 304; also FO 371/27797 [F13601/222/61].

delay'. Forces were being sent to Kupang that day. An independent company was 'earmarked' for Portuguese Timor.[44]

The Portuguese Government, Campbell telegraphed on 12 December, accepted the British proposals and would instruct the Governor.[45] Clarke and his colleagues at the War Office and Dominions Office welcomed 'this very satisfactory development'. The way was now open 'for arrangements to be made on the spot between the Dutch and the Australians on one side and the Governor of Timor on the other … the best plan would be to arrange for a Dutch officer and the senior Australian officer at Koepang to go at once to Dili to talk matters over with the Governor'. Holmes agreed to draft a telegram to Canberra, recommending that the senior officer should be empowered to make arrangements on the spot. The FO also informed the Netherlands Minister, who undertook to have instructions sent to the Governor-General. In view of 'Portuguese susceptibilities' and 'the importance of doing nothing to prejudice arrangements with the Portuguese Government in other parts of the world', he was told, the assistance had 'ostensibly' to come from Britain. The Minister read parts of the Dutch Government's telegram to Clarke. At its conclusion, it stated 'that in case of the local authorities' being certain of imminent danger of attack which brooks of no delay, they may take any measures which they consider necessary'. Clarke thought that it must be allowed to include that passage, since there might be a sudden attack before a final arrangement had been made with the Governor. So he agreed, 'but asked that some phrase should be inserted to show that action without full agreement with the Portuguese local authorities should *not* be taken except in the case of a sudden and imminent danger'.[46] The DO, Sargent added, should ask the Australian Government to tell its officer-in-charge in Timor 'to give every consideration to Portuguese susceptibilities and to ensure that the Dutch do likewise'.[47]

On 13 December the DO told the Australian Government that the Portuguese Government had accepted that, 'in virtue of their alliance with us', assistance should be provided in the event of a Japanese attack by Dutch and Australian troops, and would instruct the Governor invite or accept assistance accordingly. He was being instructed to get in touch with the Governor of Dutch Timor to discuss matters of common interest. It was

---

[44] Telegram, 12 December 1941, 797, in AFPD:V,305; also F13601.
[45] FO 371/27797 [F13607/222/61]: Telegram, 12 December 1941, 1608.
[46] FO 371/27797 [F13607/222/61]: Minute by Clarke, 13 December 1941.
[47] FO 371/27797 [F13607/222/61]: Minute, 14 December 1941.

impressed on the Portuguese Ambassador that the local authorities should have 'wide latitude' so that assistance was 'in good time'. The Portuguese wanted discussions in Singapore and a representative would leave on 17 December. 'They have also been given to understand that there is no question of continued presence of Australian and Dutch forces in Portuguese Timor once the emergency is over.' The Portuguese wanted to 'give prominence to the ancient alliance', so the Australian role should be 'substantial and conspicuous'.[48] The FO telegraphed Duff Cooper on 14 December. It was essential to respect Portuguese susceptibilities, he was told, in view of repercussions elsewhere in the Portuguese empire.[49]

On 15 December the British sent a formal note on to Monteiro. That welcomed the readiness of the Portuguese Government to send an officer to Singapore to discuss the defence of Timor. But the outbreak of war suggested the need for 'some immediate precautionary measures'; 'in virtue of the ancient alliance by which they are bound to Portugal', the British Government was prepared to arrange for immediate assistance, furnished by Australian forces in West Timor and by Dutch forces. The Governor should be authorised to call for them 'if the occasion arises' or to acquiesce in their assistance if there were no time to make a request. Any troops would be withdrawn as soon as the emergency that required was past.[50]

The Dutch Government had meanwhile telegraphed its Governor-General as agreed.[51] Tjarda replied at once that Japanese submarines were reportedly off Timor and that it was dangerous to delay. A request from the Portuguese Governor was the only solution.[52] A Japanese coup was feared, he cabled two days later (15 December). Two officers would go to Dili on 17 December and seek a request from the Governor. Whether or not he agreed, the *Soerabaja* would land 230 Dutch and 120 Australian troops.[53] Prime Minister Gerbrandy agreed.[54]

The Australian Government told the DO that it was advised that the Dutch Governor-General had decided on immediate action. There would

---

[48] Telegram, 13 December 1941, 829, in AFPD:V,309–310; also FO 371/27797 [F13785/222/61].
[49] Telegram, 14 December 1941, 55, in AFPD:V,309–310.
[50] Note, 15 December 1941, in DAPE:X:268–269; also in F13607.
[51] Telegram from Gerbrandy, 13 December 1941, in *Documenten betreffende de buitenlandse politiek van Nederland 1919–45. Periode C* (DBPN):IV,22.
[52] Telegram, 13 December 1941, in DBPN:IV,24–25.
[53] Telegram, 15 December 1941, in DBPN:IV,27–28.
[54] Telegram, 15 December 1941, in DBPN:IV,28n.

be consultation with the Governor, including the Australian commander, Lieutenant Colonel WW Leggatt, at 7 am on 17 December and the Dutch and Australian forces would arrive at Dili at 9 am in anticipation of an invitation to land and would land even if the Governor hesitated. The Australian Government agreed with the Dutch proposals. In view of 'urgency', the conference at Singapore was 'superseded'. But the Australian Government pressed on the British the desirability of instructing the Governor to invite or acquiesce in the presence of the troops, intended solely to protect Portuguese Timor against Japanese aggression.[55]

The DO suggested that 'if possible rather longer interval should be allowed to elapse between time when Conference at Dili begins and time when combined force arrives in order to give greater appearance of Portuguese concurrence and indeed of compliance on our part with an invitation from them'. As a result of the representations made to the Portuguese Government, it hoped that the Governor had been instructed as the Australian Government wished. It would be desirable for no public statement to be made, but the FO wanted to work out with the Portuguese one that might be held in readiness. That would allude to reports of Japanese aggression, as a result of which Portugal had invoked its ancient treaties of alliance and sought Britain's help, and a combined Australian–Dutch force was proceeding to Timor to co-operate with the local Portuguese authorities in securing the territory.[56]

The FO cabled Campbell in Lisbon two hours later:

> We would have liked to see the principle of consultation with the Portuguese more closely followed than the two hours delay now provided for and we are therefore trying to get it extended. But delays in telegraphing and difference between Greenwich and local time may well make this impossible. In that case we hope that the Portuguese Government will realise that we had no alternative and that our hand was forced by the suddenness of the emergency.

It had accepted proposals that included the acquiescence of the Governor if there were no time for him to issue an invitation. It was left to Campbell to

---

[55] Telegram, 16.December 1941, 798, in AFPD:V,315; also, dated 15 December, in FO 371/27797 [F13785].
[56] FO 371/27797 [F13785]: Telegram, 16 December 1941, 833; summarised in AFPD:V,315–316n.

decide whether to inform the Portuguese Government in advance, bearing in mind that at most the arrival of the force could be postponed for a few hours. The Dutch envoy would have instructions and Campbell should discuss the matter with him before saying anything to the Portuguese. It was hoped to issue a statement, if possible agreed with them.[57] If that could not refer to their agreement with the move, it might say that it was done in virtue of Britain's obligations to them.[58]

In Lisbon Campbell called on the Ministry of Foreign Affairs with telegrams from his government indicating that Australian planes had seen Japanese submarines near Timor and that a Dutch force was moving towards Dili to prevent a landing. The Portuguese feared that their neutrality would be destroyed.[59] Dr Sampayo objected to a premature landing; it would make Portugal a belligerent and lose it Macau.[60] Pallandt saw him after Campbell: 'stap zeer slecht ontvangen [move very badly received]'. It might destroy Portugal's neutrality[61] and lead to a declaration of war by Japan and possibly by Germany and Italy. Dr Salazar was reportedly 'very much upset', Campbell reported. If it were too late to alter instructions and the Commanders insisted on landing, a declaration should be issued, giving the reasons and stating that it was done in face of the Governor's protest. Such a declaration ought to come from the Dutch and the Australians; invoking the British alliance would 'increase the possibility of Portugal being drawn into the war'. The Portuguese Government would certainly not endorse the declarations the FO had drafted.[62] That Sampayo reaffirmed.[63]

The DO urged the Australian Government to make every effort to reach agreement with the Governor before the landings.[64] Campbell was instructed to urge the Portuguese Government to acquiesce.[65] 'After Pearl Harbour and the events of the past ten days it must surely be obvious that assistance will be too late if delayed until attack has materialised'. That was why the FO had insisted that the Governor should be given 'wide latitude…

---

[57] FO 371/27797 [F13607/222/61]: Telegram, 16 December 1941, 2093.
[58] FO 371/27797 [F13807/222/61]: Telegram, 16 December 1941, 2097.
[59] Telegrams from Salazar, 16 December 1941, 356, 357, in DAPE:X,273–274.
[60] FO 371/27797 [F13808/222/61]: Telegram, 16 December 1941, 1644.
[61] Telegram, 16 December 1941, 255–257 in DBPN:IV,36–37; also Pallandt to van Kleffens, 16 December 1941, in DBPN:IV,38–39.
[62] FO 371/27797 [F13808/222/61]: Telegram, 16 December 1941, 1648.
[63] Memorandum and conversation, 17 December 1941, in DAPE:X,279–281.
[64] Telegram, 16 December 1941, 834 summarised in AFPD:V,332n.
[65] FO 371/27797 [F13808/222/61]: Telegram, 16 December 1941, 2109.

to ensure assistance well before the development of any attack'. It seemed clear, however, that the Portuguese Government had 'effected complete volte-face' and desired that their hand should be forced. 'We must accept this position.' The FO contemplated a post-landing announcement that the Portuguese, wishing to preserve their neutrality, had protested, that their sovereignty was intact, and that the Allied force would be withdrawn 'as soon as the threat from the enemy is removed'.[66]

Sargent had seen Monteiro. 'I am afraid action has already been taken', he said.[67] Campbell reported on 17 December,

> Dr Sampayo was unable to believe that a landing would be forced in opposition to the wishes of the Portuguese Governor who had no authority to permit it in advance of a definite Japanese movement against his territory. When he at length grasped that it might already have occurred…he said 'then you will have reversed the roles and have done the very thing your avoidance of which hitherto had given you the high moral authority which you enjoy among all decent people.[68]

Sampayo insisted that the agreement had related to 'attack' and had not mentioned 'threat of attack'. Now, at a few hours' notice,

> the Portuguese Government had been confronted with demand for admission of foreign troops, because of the appearance of submarines, which might well be in those waters in the normal course of their patrols. Such action could have no further unpleasant consequences for the countries that were already at war, but it was quite another matter when it involved another country which was not yet at war, and was struggling to preserve its neutrality. If Japan wanted a pretext to seize Macao, we could not have given her a better one.

All Campbell's arguments failed to shake the Secretary-General. 'I do not think', the Ambassador remarked, 'that the Portuguese *wanted* to have their hand forced. They are much too afraid that war with Japan may involve them in war with Germany and Italy.' If there were no time to hold up

---

[66] FO 371/27797 [F13808/222/61]:Telegrams, 17 December 1941, 2114, 2115.
[67] Telegram from Monteiro, 16 December 1941, in DAPE:X,276–277.
[68] FO 371/27797 [F13860/222/61]: Telegram, 17 December 1941, 1659; the last sentence does not appear in the account in DAPE:X,276–281.

the landing, 'the next best thing we could do was to show that it had been effected in face of Portuguese [protest]'. He was glad the FO was following that course.[69]

Its telegram to Washington described Portugal's policy as a *volte face*, though it was hardly that. The Portuguese, the FO added, wanted to claim that they gave way to *force majeure*.[70] In other words, they did not want their hand forced but they certainly wanted to show the Axis powers that they had been trying to be neutral. As in their discussions over Spain, they had drawn a line between attack and threat of attack.

The Australian forces had reached Kupang on 13 December—the 2/40th Australian Battalion and the 2/2nd Independent Company, a commando force, as well as a battery of coast artillery and a flight of Hudson bombers (Frei 1996:285). Ross was at a meeting on 16 December between the Australian officers, Lieutenant Colonels Leggatt and W Detiger, and the Netherlands Indian Army commander NLW van Straaten. He then went back to Dili to prepare Governor Ferreira de Carvalho for their arrival. The Governor contacted Lisbon and was told not to allow the troops to land (Frei 1996:285–286). He thus declined to accept the proffered help, 'because the position with regard to the conflict is one of strict neutrality, and because no aggression of any sort has taken place in our territory, the last-mentioned being the sole condition under which the Government of Portugal could accept the help of Australian and Dutch forces for the Defence of the Colony'. Every disembarkation would be considered 'a breach of the neutrality of our territory'.[71] One hundred and fifty-five Australian commandos and 260 Dutch troops landed on the afternoon of 17 December and occupied town and airfield (Frei 1996:286). The Governor had stipulated 'that the landing should take place down the coast and not in the harbour itself, otherwise he would feel it necessary to provide all the opposition within his power' (Callinan 1953:13).

He also telegraphed Curtin.[72] The Commonwealth Government replied with a message to Ross. Portugal's sovereignty would not be impaired; Australia was defending it. 'Commonwealth Government desire to assist in every way possible regarding administration and economic life of the colony'[73]—not really what Salazar wanted to hear.

---

[69] FO 371/27797 [F13862/222/61]: Telegram, 17 December 1941, 1662.
[70] FO 371/27797 [F13808/222/61]: Telegram to Washington, 17 December 1941, 6992.
[71] Governor to Leggatt and Detiger, 17 December 1941, in AFPD:V,320–321.
[72] Telegram, 18 December 1941, in AFPD:V,321n.
[73] Message, 18 December 1941, in AFPD:V,321.

On 17 December he told his ambassador in Tokyo to inform the Japanese Government that the move was an act of force unauthorised by the Government or by the local authorities.[74] In forwarding his government's reply to the note of 15 December, Monteiro reminded Sargent that it was its policy 'to maintain the country's neutrality until the last possible moment'. An 'overhasty act' in the Far East might have 'grave repercussions elsewhere'.[75]

Salazar was beside himself, Campbell told Pallandt.[76] He demanded an explanation: had the local commanders taken the law into their own hands?; had the British Government been a full and willing party?[77] The Ambassador drafted a reply, including an historical introduction.[78] The FO suggested some additions. It had been too late for the British government to modify the action taken, but it had hoped that the Portuguese would accept the help sent. 'The war with Germany had provided abundant evidence of the danger of belated action and the speed of Japanese movements... showed that if effective assistance was to be rendered it would be futile to await attack.' The line should be to express regret that circumstances compelled the Allies to act 'in a manner which proved unwelcome to the Portuguese Government', but stress that the strategic importance of Timor and 'its defenceless state' made it a military necessity in the war Japan had forced on them. Campbell could repeat the undertaking of 15 December that the troops would be withdrawn when the emergency had passed. He could also add that the position would be reconsidered as soon as the Portuguese Government could itself 'make military dispositions which will ensure the effective protection of Portuguese Timor against Japanese aggression'.[79]

The latter addition was a Dutch idea. Van Kleffens had suggested it to Pallandt[80] and he had suggested the Portuguese might send troops from Africa.[81] Sargent thanked Michiels for the suggestion,[82] which was put forward in a conversation about issuing a communiqué. Pending his meeting

---

[74] Telegram, 17 December 1941, 68, in DAPE:X,289.
[75] Monteiro to Sargent, 17 December 1941, in DAPE:X,295–296; also FO 371/27798 [F13974/222/61].
[76] Pallandt to van Kleffens, 18 December 1941, 291, in DBPN:IV,48.
[77] FO 371/27798 [F13866/222/61]: Telegram, 17 December 1941, 1672.
[78] FO 371/27798 [F13908/222/61]: Telegram, 18 December 1941, 1675.
[79] FO 371/27798 [F13909/222/61]: Telegram, 18 December 1941, 2142.
[80] Van Kleffens to Pallandt, 18 December 1941, telegrams 352–353, in DBPN:IV,47.
[81] Pallandt to van Kleffens, 18 December 1941, 291, in DBPN:IV,48.
[82] FO 371/27797 [F13807/222/61]: Sargent to Michiels, 18 December 1941.

with Salazar, Campbell had asked that the FO make no public statement.[83] Sargent and John Sterndale Bennett of the Far East Department at the FO had discussed their draft with van Kleffens and Michiels on 17 December, mentioning Campbell's view that it should emanate from the Dutch and the Australians and not from the British. Returning to approve the final draft, Michiels argued that it should be issued by all three governments; it was taken in their joint interests. 'A very delicate situation had arisen vis-à-vis the Portuguese Government', the British officials responded, 'and we had to handle the latter gently…for tactical reasons it was essential that we should not appear in the forefront.' Michiels was 'clearly much upset by this attitude which he characterized as backing out on our part and placing the onus upon the Dutch'.[84]

The effect on the Dutch Minister, Bennett wrote, was 'definitely bad'. The situation needed 'the most careful handling' lest it wrecked relations with Portugal. But there was 'a definite conflict of interest' between those and relations with Australia and Netherlands India. The situation in the Far East was

> most critical, and we cannot afford to be half-hearted in the prosecution of the war against Japan or to take risks which endanger the safety of the Netherlands East Indies and Australia. Portuguese Timor may be a miserable island a long way away, but it is of vital importance to Port Darwin.

Bennett feared the danger of

> falling between two stools…by endeavouring to placate the Portuguese we may produce the worst effect on the Dutch, on whose help we may be greatly dependent in saving our position in Malaya. Our hesitation also is likely to produce an extremely bad impression in Australia.[85]

In the event, however, the communiqué, issued in Batavia, was on the lines the FO had agreed. It included recognition of Portuguese sovereignty and a promise of withdrawal when the enemy threat was over (DBPN:IV,40n).

---

[83] FO 371/27798 [F13865/222/61]: Telegram, 17 December 1941, 1671.
[84] FO 371/27798 [F14046/222/61]: Minute by Bennett, 19 December 1941; also in DBPN:IV,59–60.
[85] FO 371/27798 [F14050/222/61] Minute by Bennett, 18 December 1941; also DBPN:IV,52.

Campbell delivered his historical account and the undertaking to withdraw to Sampayo on 19 December. Britain renewed the undertaking of 15 December. The Alllied troops would be withdrawn 'as soon as the emergency with which they came to deal is past', the statement declared; it also expressed regret and trusted that the Portuguese Government would accept the 'urgent military necessity' of the action.[86] Authorised by van Kleffens, Pallandt also put the idea of sending sufficient Portuguese forces.[87] Perhaps, the Dutch chargé suggested, these approaches moderated the speech Salazar made in the Assembly, also broadcast, on 19 December.[88] It was bitter enough.

The attempts to restore relations with Salazar

On Campbell's advice the British Government made a public statement on 21 December.[89] Once it was made, he suggested, it would be possible to consider 'what can be done to restore the former relationship'. Most members of the National Assembly in Lisbon had reportedly expected Salazar to announce that he was breaking off relations with Britain. It was hard to believe that he had contemplated that, but that the impression existed showed how seriously the matter was viewed. 'Injury to Portuguese pride will take time to heal.' Salazar had indicated that steps had to be taken to clear up the situation. An apology? If so, the memorandum to the Secretary-General would suffice. Immediate withdrawal of the troops? That should not be done until it was clear that Portuguese defences were 'adequate. Apart from anything else we should merely look ridiculous and lose face in Portuguese eyes.' If approached along those lines, 'we should re-state our readiness to withdraw immediately we are satisfied that the Portuguese have so strengthened their own forces there as to have a reasonable chance of defending themselves successfully'.[90]

Sampayo called Campbell in on the evening of 22 December. The Ambassador feared he would ask for early withdrawal and planned to

---

[86] FO 371/27798 [F14001,14002/222/61]: Telegrams, 19 December 1941, 1692, 1693; also DAPE:X,342–345 and DBPN:IV,65–68.
[87] Van Kleffens to Pallandt, 18 December 1941, telegrams 352–353, in DBPN:IV,47; Pallandt to van Kleffens, 19 December 1941, 294–296, in DBPN:IV,56.
[88] Pallandt to van Kleffens, 21 December 1941, in DBPN:IV,62–65; FO 3171/27798 [F14004/222/61]: .Telegram from Campbell, 19 December 1941, 1704.
[89] FO 371/27798 [F14037/222/61]: Telegrams from Campbell, 21 December 1941, 1726, 1727; to Campbell, undated, 2180.
[90] FO 371/27798 [F14031/222/61]: Telegram, 20 December 1941, 1722.

tell him it might be considered as soon as 'adequate' Portuguese forces had reached Timor.[91] In the event the Secretary-General gave him a note seeking withdrawal 'without loss of time' and another note indicating that Portuguese forces could arrive only late in January.[92] The first note responded to the memorandum earlier given to the Secretary-General. It entered

> the most energetic protest against the action.…The days which have elapsed since the threat of an imminent attack was invoked have demonstrated the lack of foundation, not indeed for the landing, for which there could never be any basis in the absence of agreement with the Portuguese Government, but for invoking the threat referred to.

The Portuguese Government was preparing to send forces to raise the forces to double the number landed.[93]

In face of all Campbell's arguments, Sampayo stuck to his 'juridical standpoint'. If there had been a Japanese landing, the Ambassador asked, would the Portuguese not have commended the Allies for anticipating it? Did they want to feel responsible for making their ally's position in the Far East even more difficult? The Secretary-General 'always came back to the contention that we were in effect seeking to justify our action on the ground that under stress of military exigency everything was permissible'. Threats of force had always been resented, he said; 'the British ultimatum of 1890 had even yet not been forgotten'. Campbell believed that Salazar wanted to find a solution and that, if the Allies announced that they would leave, he would not press for naming a date. That was 'quite inacceptable'. The problem 'then becomes' one of 'bridging the gap between now and late January'. If no bridge were found, Campbell now thought, Salazar might break off relations.[94]

The FO also received a copy of the notes. Given the longstanding relationship, Monteiro said, 'a harsh word from Great Britain tended to have more effect in Portugal than a grave act on the part of some other Power. The feelings of his country had been deeply wounded', and he hoped for a formula that would close 'the unhappy incident'. Standing in for Eden, Sir John Anderson, Lord President of the Council, said that the expedition had

---

[91] FO 371/27798 [F14082/222/61]: Telegram, 22 December 1941, 1736.
[92] FO 371/27798 [F14082/222/61]: Telegram, 23 December 1941, 1742.
[93] FO 371/27799 [F14162/222/61]; Notes in Anderson to Campbell, 22 December 1941, 503; also DAPE:X,362–363 and DBPN:IV,87–88.
[94] FO 371/27798 [F14083/222/61]:Telegram, 23 December 1941, 1747.

already sailed when the British Government heard of it, but that in any case it would not have been 'justified in overriding the discretion of the local military and naval authorities as to the imminence of the peril against which they were seeking to guard'. It would be prepared to consider any suggestion over a formula, 'but it would have to be a prerequisite of any accommodation that the presence in Timor of a force sufficient to deal with any sudden aggression should be assured'.[95]

A note to Pallandt repeated the energetic protest. Portugal was sending troops. The presence of Dutch troops was incompatible with correct and friendly relations.[96] The note, Pallandt thought, had the displeasing tone of an ultimatum.[97] The whole tenor of the document was 'stiffer' than the protest made to the British, Campbell commented.[98] The Portuguese Government might be 'seeking to drive a wedge between ourselves and the Dutch', he speculated, perhaps ignoring the longstanding tension between the two states in Timor, or even 'under strong Axis pressure...manoeuvring for a break in relations with the Netherlands Government while remaining in relations with ourselves'. If it was 'attempting to have presence of Netherlands troops regarded in a different light from that of Australian troops', that seemed 'inadmissible', given that it had earlier accepted that help would come from both.[99] If Salazar were making a manoeuvre—inducing Britain to throw its Dutch ally to the wolves, posing as having imposed his will on the British, appeasing the Axis—it would be 'intolerable'. The time had come for 'plain speaking', but not so as to 'bang the door'.[100]

He spoke to Sampayo, not Salazar. The Secretary-General replied with 'a laboured and involved rigmarole which passed my understanding but which appeared to be based on (a) the fact that the Netherlands are neighbouring power in Timor and (b) obligations which Portugal had towards us but not towards the Netherlands'. Campbell indicated that 'the English public' would not be disposed to be disassociated from its valiant Dutch ally. If Portugal pressed its demands on the Netherlands, he went on, the 'logical sequence' was to press them on Britain, and no government 'engaged in a life and death struggle' could withdraw its troops until the emergency had passed. A rupture with Britain would remove the 'counterpoise of alliance' and 'it

---

[95] FO 371/27799 [F14162/222/61]: Anderson to Campbell, 22 December 1941, 503.
[96] Note, 22 December 1941, in DBPN:IV,79–80 and DAPE:X,365–366.
[97] Pallandt to van Kleffens, 23 December 1941, 4274, in DBPN:IV.79.
[98] FO 371/27799 [F14163/222/61]: Telegram, 23 December 1941, 1749.
[99] FO 371/27799 [F14164/222/61]: Telegram, 23 December 1941, 1750.
[100] FO 371/27799 [F14166/222/61]: Telegram, 23 December 1941, 1752.

would not be long before German submarines were based on Portuguese ports and bombers on Portuguese aerodromes'. Could the two parties not find a way out? The Portuguese 'had submitted to force majeure when forces had been landed. They would be doing the same if they acquiesced in forces remaining until they could be replaced…honour was satisfied'.[101]

The only suggestion Campbell could make—put into a telegram to the FO—was an offer to put the Allied forces under Portuguese command.[102] The FO had its own suggestion: that the defence of Timor should devolve on troops from the British Empire alone.[103] This suggestion, accepted by the Dutch provided it did not appear to be the result of the Portuguese note,[104] was put to the Australians on 25 December,[105] though Campbell doubted if Salazar would accept it unless his own suggestion were also followed.[106]

It was proposed, the DO explained, that only Australian forces should act until adequate Portuguese forces arrived, that the Dutch should leave when the Australians were reinforced, and the Australians when the Portuguese reinforcements arrived. The proposal would get the Portuguese out of the 'impasse' into which they had put themselves by their 'virtual ultimatum' to the Dutch, get the Dutch out of the difficulty into which the ultimatum had put them, give Salazar 'a diplomatic victory' over one of the two parties with which he was in dispute, 'go a long way to soothe Portuguese pride', and restore Anglo–Portuguese relations. Campbell suggested an oral communication to Sampayo first. The written one should not refer to the British alliance, though it would refer to British troops. The proposal had little to recommend it logically, 'but…we are dealing with an emotional problem'.[107]

The attempts to put matters right with Portugal, however, aroused Australian resentment. The Commonwealth Government recapitulated what had in its view happened. Britain had approved its course. At Britain's request the plan had been amended to allow the Governor more than two

---

[101] FO 371/27799 [F14168/222/61]: Telegram, 23 December 1941, 1763; Sampayo's account of the conversation is in DAPE:X,381–382.
[102] FO 371/27799 [F14174/222/61]: Telegram, 23 December 1941, 1765.
[103] FO 371/27799 [F14169/222/61]: Telegrams to Campbell, 24 December 1941, 2220, 2221.
[104] Memorandum by van Kleffens, 24 December 1941, in DBPN:IV,85–87.
[105] FO 371/27799 [F14254/222/61]: Telegram, 25 December 1941, 887.
[106] FO 371/27799 [F14238/222/61]: Telegram, 25 December 1941, 1786.
[107] Telegram, 26 December 1941, 905, in AFPD:V,366–367; also FO 371/27800 [F14361/222/61].

hours to respond. The Portuguese Government had 'suddenly become hostile and lost its nerve'. Now it was urged that the British connection should not be mentioned and the British Government had expressed its regret over the action taken by military authorities on the spot, 'the suggestion being that you were not a party to the plan'. The Governor was organising troops to harass the Allied troops and complained that the Allied commanders in Dili were acting 'high-handedly'. Now it was suggested that Dutch forces should leave and only the Australians act, but Australia had no more troops available. Portugal should have been told from the beginning that the occupation was based on 'military necessity' and that Japanese infiltration and invasion could not otherwise be prevented. Subsequent difficulties were aggravated by Britain's failure to take 'a strong line' with the Portuguese Government. The defence of Timor was crucial to the Netherlands and to the whole British position in the Far East, 'and there should be no retreat. Faith of Australian public would be shaken if, having regard to what has already happened, a further withdrawal of occupying forces were to take place at the very door of Australia', Curtin concluded, presumably in reference to what was happening in Malaya.[108]

Bruce, the Australian High Commissioner in London, saw the draft of the DO's reply. It went at length into the sequence of events and attempted to 'justify bad case. The hard facts are that the Portuguese reaction to the landing without the previous consent of the Portuguese before actual attack by the Japanese was misjudged and the sooner this is admitted the better.' Bruce urged that the argumentative part of the draft should be 'scrapped' and the 'hard facts' put to Curtin, inviting him to co-operate in finding a way out. Probably it would not be scrapped, but find its way into a separate telegram.

The facts, Bruce suggested, were:

(a) Portuguese Timor had to be occupied; (b) this was done by Australian and Dutch Forces with the agreement of the United Kingdom Government; (c) the desirability of Portuguese acquiescence recognised, and believed that as a result of the United Kingdom–Portuguese conversations this would be forthcoming; (d) this anticipation was wrong and the Portuguese have reacted violently with the possibility if solution not found of breach of relations, almost certainly with the Dutch and probably with the United Kingdom; (e) such a breach most undesirable at the present time particularly in view of the secret

---

[108] Telegram, 26 December 1941, 831, in AFPD:V,360–362; also in FO 371/27800 [F14392/222/61].

conversations in regard to Portuguese Atlantic Islands in the event of German invasion of Iberian Peninsula; (f) suggested possible solution Australian troops to replace the Dutch in Portuguese Timor.

Could Australia provide the troops either by switching with the Dutch or sending more? Did the Netherlands Indies Government share the Dutch Government's view on the matter? Would the Portuguese Government accept? The United Kingdom authorities thought it was possible. An alternative view was that the United Kingdom should not put up solutions, but say that Japan's enemies had to protect themselves and appeal to the Portuguese for a solution.[109]

Unless there were an 'amicable' solution to the Timor question, Salazar might break off relations, ran the United Kingdom's 'hard facts' response, and then the Axis might penetrate the Iberian Peninsula, Gibraltar become unusable and the islands in the Atlantic become unavailable. Sea and air communication to Asia and Australia would be endangered, as well as that in the Atlantic. Secret talks, designed to safeguard Britain's position in the Atlantic islands in the event of Axis action on the peninsula, were 'in jeopardy'. While Timor was 'vital to our Far Eastern defences' and 'there could be no withdrawal until adequate arrangements' were made for its protection, it was necessary to do everything possible to avoid a rupture with the Portuguese. In the light of the report on the Governor's behaviour, the British Government did not wish to suggest joint command should be vested in him. But could the Australians send to Portuguese Timor sufficient Australian troops from those in Dutch Timor to replace the Dutch troops that had gone there? That might, though it was not certain, 'offer the best if not the only chance of solving our present difficulties with the Portuguese'.[110]

As Bruce anticipated, a separate telegram covered the 'history' of the episode. The 'misunderstandings', Cranborne wrote, were mainly due to the rapidity of developments and the impossibility of conveying the full correspondence with Lisbon and the conversations with the ambassadors in London. The British Government had hoped the Portuguese would see 'imminent threat of an attack as tantamount to an actual attack'. In fact they interpreted the agreement strictly literally. Their response to the action was violently unfavourable. Campbell argued that the only way to get them to

---

[109] Telegram from Bruce, 27 December 1941, 240, in AFPD, pp. 373–374.
[110] Telegram, 27 December 1941, 913, in AFPD:V,374–376; also FO 371/27800 [F14431/222/61].

retain 'any vestige of confidence in us' was to present it in such a way as would enable them to plead *force majeure*. He suggested a draft statement omitting any reference to the alliance and emanating from the Australian and Dutch governments, or preferably from the Dutch alone. Eventually the Dutch agreed to issue theirs alone. In its expression of regret, the United Kingdom deplored the 'military exigency'. At no time had it attached 'any blame' to the Allied military authorities. Britain was bound to take the Portuguese attitude into account, but it remained 'absolutely firm' that Portuguese Timor had to be denied to the enemy and that prerequisite to any solution was the presence of a force 'sufficient to deal with sudden aggression'.[111]

Hard facts or historical explanation or both produced Australian assent. On 29 December Curtin indicated he was ready to send Australian troops from Dutch Timor into Portuguese Timor to replace the Dutch troops there. If the Dutch would not agree, but withdrew their troops from Portuguese Timor, no further Australians would go there, leaving just the one Australian Infantry Force company.[112]

The Dutch, as van Kleffens had indicated, were prepared to agree to the replacement of their troops with Australian troops, provided it did not appear to be done under threat as a result of the Portuguese note of 22 December. On 27 December he showed Sargent the draft of a reply. The latter thought it might induce Salazar to implement his threat rather than withdraw it. At present there were 'difficulties' with the Australians, but, if it became possible to put the suggestion forward, it might be done 'orally and without committing the Dutch in the first instance'. If the Portuguese Government agreed, a Dutch note could form one of the documents constituting a settlement.[113]

In face of the Australian doubts, the FO had also checked with the Chiefs of Staff on 27 December. Should Britain persist with the proposal, or abandon it and simply take the stand that it was necessary to take all the steps necessary to guard against Japanese aggression until adequate Portuguese forces were available and that when they were it would be prepared to withdraw? That might mean, as Bennett put it, a 'rupture of relations with Portugal'. The COS should advise on 'the consequences of this as compared with the importance of Portuguese Timor in the scheme of

---

[111] Telegram, 28 December 1941, 915, in AFPD:V,376–378; also F14431.
[112] Telegram, 29 December 1941, 837, in AFPD:V,379; also FO 371/27800 [F14394/222/61].
[113] FO 371/27800 [F14375/222/61]: Minute by Bennett, 27 December 1941; Minute by van Kleffens, undated, in DBPN:IV,97–98.

Far Eastern defence'.[114] Bennett pressed the COS Secretary, Colonel Price, for a preliminary answer before the COS met. The COS felt, he said, that there must be 'no abandonment of Portuguese Timor, which they regard as vital for Far Eastern defence, and...they can only look to the Foreign Office to do their best to prevent untoward repercussions on the Atlantic'.[115] The meeting agreed that the defence of Portuguese Timor was 'crucial both to the Netherlands and to our position in the Far East'; there should be 'no retreat'.[116]

When the Australian agreement came through, Bennett, after consulting Price and the DO, told Teixeira de Mattos, the Dutch Counsellor in London. The Dutch Government, he understood, had given Tjarda discretionary power to take over the administration of Portuguese Timor, but to be as 'circumspect' as possible. Perhaps it could reiterate the importance of avoiding any incident while a solution was under discussion.[117]

In the meantime Campbell had contemplated the reverse solution— that Dutch troops should remain pending the arrival of Portuguese and Australian troops withdraw. That would give Salazar a diplomatic victory that the National Assembly could applaud. It would also be an *amende honorable*, uphold the contention that the action had been necessary, restore amicable relations, and ease Portugal's relations with the Axis. The disadvantages would be that it would give Salazar 'a greater victory...than he is entitled to expect', that it would diminish Britain's prestige, that it would represent a victory for the Axis, that it would create an 'anomalous situation', and that it would encourage Salazar to think 'that we would always give way'. It was a solution that Campbell would himself 'detest' to put forward.[118]

The FO had not been in favour. It was pursuing the Australian option, though the reports that the Governor was organising the harassment of Allied troops made it unlikely that he could be given command.[119] The position, according to reports the Commonwealth Government received from Kupang, was deteriorating, 'due largely to the suggestions of early withdrawal by the Dutch forces because of Portugal's protest'. A number of Japanese were at large and should be interned. Unless the Governor co-operated, the Australian COS considered that military action should

---

[114] FO 371/27800 [F14393/222/61]: Minute by Bennett, 27 December 1941.
[115] FO 371/27800 [F14393/222/61]: Minute by Bennett, undated.
[116] CAB 79/16: COS (41) 436th, 27 December 1941, 11.
[117] FO 371/27780 [F14394/222/61]: Minute, 29 December 1941; also in DBPN:IV,11–13.
[118] FO 371/27800 [F14308/222/61]: Telegram, 26 December 1941, 1795.
[119] FO 371/27800 [F14308/222/61]: Telegram, 28 December 1941, 2251.

be taken.[120] That made it more necessary, as the Australian Government was told, that Campbell should be able to offer a face-saving proposal, but he might also communicate its concerns to the Portuguese Government, stopping short of suggesting military takeover.[121]

Campbell thought that the Portuguese Government might have instructed the Governor to make a show of obstruction 'in order to [enable?] themselves to plead force majeure'. If they were seen to be co-operating, they would have the Japanese 'down on them in a moment'. That they had always to have in their mind, 'just as we must bear in mind that we are up against a concerted Axis plot to secure a break between Great Britain and Portugal, the success of which would give the Germans a free run in this country'. The Portuguese Government was 'bound to seek a solution which will give the appearance, at least, of a rift in Anglo–Portuguese relations'. He would see Sampayo again.[122]

His decision to act, he told the FO, was 'tactical'. The Portuguese Government could not in fact have Japanese subjects arrested. He continued:

> It is precisely what the Axis is playing for. The Japanese Government would at once say that Portugal had abandoned her neutrality and must be regarded as ally of Great Britain and therefore the enemy of Japan, Germany and Italy and would then get to work.

Germany would not need to occupy Portugal by force; that would in any case be 'an embarrassment to her on account of Spain'. It would 'operate by diplomatic pressure' demanding a rupture of relations with Britain, then facilities for submarines on the Tagus. 'If plot comes off will Salazar resist?' Campbell was now no longer so sure as he had been. Salazar had been 'faithful to the alliance on sternly practical grounds', but might now feel it was not worth what he thought, 'especially if the outcome of the Timor affair were to involve him in loss of prestige'. Did the Dutch and Australian governments fully understand 'complexities and wider implications'?[123]

He saw Sampayo late in the morning of 29 December. He began by saying that the FO had approved 'the idea of putting my head together with him in a purely informal way in an attempt to find the basis of a solution' and also

---

[120] FO 371/27800 [F14343/222/61]: Telegram, 28 December 1941, 2253.
[121] FO 371/27800 [F14343/222/61]: Telegram, 28 December 1941, 2254.
[122] FO 371/27800 [F14329/222/61]: Telegram, 28 December 1941, 1802.
[123] FO 371/27800 [F14352/222/61]: Telegram, 29 December 1941, 1809.

endorsed what he said about Britain's solidarity with the Netherlands and the impossibility of withdrawing before 'the emergency could be regarded as past'. It was 'unthinkable', he went on, that 'an irreparable breach' should develop. Sampayo interrupted to say 'that there could be no question of that'. Salazar had told him that Portuguese troops would be ready to sail next day, 30 December. He suggested that his Government should be informed that the Australian-Dutch force would be withdrawn when the force, numbering 700, had arrived. That seemed to Campbell, as he reported, so complete a surrender that he could not help 'suspecting something behind it'. He checked that the Portuguese would accept identic notes from the British and the Dutch and did not intend to stand on their note to the Dutch. He told Sampayo he was disposed to put it to the FO 'as a personal suggestion' of his own—'he was clearly fishing for this'. After thinking it over, he now did so and told Sampayo he was sufficiently sure of a positive reply to suggest that the Portuguese expedition could leave next day.[124]

He was, as he reported, 'taken by surprise by the suddenness and seeming completeness of this surrender'. Perhaps Britain had succeeded in 'thoroughly frightening' Salazar; perhaps after his speech he had found his people 'not so solidly behind him as he had thought'. The solution seemed to suit Britain, which had always been ready to withdraw when adequate forces were available. It should suit the Netherlands, since it by-passed the ultimatum and allowed their forces to remain for the meantime; it was a 'climb-down' by the Portuguese and spelled a total failure for the Axis manoeuvres.[125]

The Dutch, Bennett thought, could not object to the proposal, since they were committed to withdrawing when an equivalent Portuguese force arrived, though they might be difficult over the form of the settlement, given the note of 22 December. 'We may however have difficulty with the Australians and must not lose sight of the realities of the situation.' Inadequately defended, Portuguese Timor would be a danger to Darwin. The Japanese, it was known, were in touch with the Portuguese Government and some Japanese were at large in Timor. 'Can we afford to withdraw…until this Japanese influence has been somehow removed?' Could 700 Portuguese troops be regarded as adequate defence? Only 350 Allied troops were there, 'but we can count on them and they would not necessarily remain unreinforced'. Britain, Bennett suggested, should close with the Portuguese offer, but, pointing out that there were 'no easily available reinforcements', stipulate for the renewal of

---

[124] FO 371/27780 [F14377/222/61]: Telegram, 29 December 1941, 1812.
[125] FO 371/27780 [F14377/222/61]: Telegram, 30 December 1941, 1822.

the conversations 'with a view to an understanding that the Portuguese forces would accept British assistance (or British and Dutch assistance) at once in the event of either an attack or a plain threat of attack'.[126]

The telegram to Lisbon, sent on 30 December, followed Bennett's suggestion. Britain would recommend to Australia and the Netherlands agreeing to withdraw on the arrival of the Portuguese forces. 'But we must ask in the meantime that there may be joint consultation to consider whether the Portuguese troops now in question would be adequate to deal with a Japanese attack'. Account would have to be taken of their equipment in relation to the situation in the Far East. The telegram added in parenthesis that the British Government had always considered the Dutch and Australian force 'insufficient in present circumstances'. The Portuguese Government should arrange as soon as possible for a qualified officer to meet the British and Dutch military authorities in the Far East, with a view to an understanding that it would agree 'to invite or accept the assistance of Netherlands and Australian troops in the event of an attack or a threat of an attack by Japan'. Was it likely to accept such a proposition?, the telegram asked Campbell. It would also be necessary for it to instruct the Governor to co-operate and it was not clear how the Japanese internees could be dealt with.[127]

In the meantime Campbell had prepared a draft indicating that Allied troops would be withdrawn when Portuguese reinforcements arrived.[128] The draft, he explained, did not refer to the offer of withdrawal when equivalent forces arrived. That was because when the Dutch made it, it was considered insulting since it imposed a specific condition and it had enabled the Portuguese Government to draw a distinction between them and the British. It should not be referred to again. 'Indeed its appearance in note under discussion would destroy basis of solution in sight.'[129]

That made the FO 'a little disturbed'. Given the line Campbell could now see it was taking, it was 'clearly important that there should be no confusion'. The Dutch chargé had offered to withdraw when 'equivalent' forces had arrived. The FO had never taken that line, either in the telegram of 18 December or in the discussion Anderson had with Monteiro, and Campbell had himself used the word 'adequate'.[130] Pallandt had in fact used the word 'sufficient'.

---

[126] FO 371/27780 [F14377/222/61]: Minute, 30 December 1941.
[127] FO 371/27800 [F14402/222/61]: Telegram, 30 December 1941, 2285.
[128] FO 371/27800 [F14416/222/61]: Telegrams, 30 December 1941, 1830, 1831.
[129] FO 371/27800 [F14417/222/61]: Telegram, 30 December 1941, 1834.
[130] FO 371/27800 [F14417/222/61]: Telegram, 31 December 1941, 2288.

Aware from the Azores negotiations that Salazar would not want military intervention until an attack occurred, the British had arranged talks in Singapore and when war began they had hoped to induce a local request for help. Neither proved feasible. It seems clear that the Dutch precipitated the intervention, though there may have been a Japanese submarine in the area. Australians do not need to see it as, in David Scott's phrase, their first betrayal of the Timorese (Scott 2005:2,329). Once it had taken place, however, they were not anxious to leave and even the British had some second thoughts on Salazar's undertaking to send in Portuguese forces to replace those of the Allies. The interchanges were not at an end.

Chapter Two

The Japanese Occupation

On account of their interest in the Azores, the British sought to restore relations with Salazar after the Dutch and Australian troops had been sent to Timor and negotiated for their replacement by Portuguese forces. But, given Japanese successes in Malaya, Australia doubted whether its troops should be withdrawn. Again the British faced the question of priorities. They sought to attach to the withdrawal a provision for the renewal of staff conversations, but they met the same difficulty as before: could action follow the threat of attack or only an actual attack? The conversations had not been completed by the time the Japanese attacked Portuguese Timor on 18 February 1942, three days after the fall of Singapore. Salazar again protested, but less firmly than the British hoped; he was apprehensive lest the Japanese forces in China should invade Macau. Famously the Australian troops took to guerrilla warfare for the remainder of 1942. They were helped by Timorese.

Portuguese reinforcements

Would the Allied troops leave when the Portuguese arrived? 'I may be wrong', Campbell had cabled, 'but I have an uncomfortable feeling that the Commonwealth Government are hoping for a situation which they would consider to justify them in taking over Portuguese Timor completely for the duration of the war'. That would give 'the knock-out blow' to Britain's relations with Portugal. Moreover, it could not go back on its offer to withdraw when the emergency was past, 'which we have interpreted to mean when the Portuguese force arrives'.[1] Earlier the Ambassador had been 'aghast' at the offer in the Australian message to the Governor to assist in

---

[1] FO 371/27800 [F14412/222/61]: Telegram, 30 December 1941, 1825.

the administration and economic life of Timor; it would be taken to indicate 'more than a passing interest'.[2] 'There may be something in Sir R. Campbell's uneasy feeling', Clarke thought. 'It would not be unnatural for Australia to feel like that', Bennett commented.[3]

Tjarda did not like the idea of a Portuguese takeover; fifth column activities would be unchecked, the Portuguese too weak.[4] Van Kleffens told Eden on 31 December that the Governor-General did not see Portuguese troops as affording the same degree of security as Dutch and Australian troops; their reliability was doubtful. 'Owing to the unfortunate turn of events in the war in the Far East it has become more difficult than before to make available the necessary forces, which would eventually have to restore a situation in Timor that had got out of control'. Eden said that it would be weeks before the troops arrived, but once they did, 'it seemed that we were in honour bound to withdraw'. Van Kleffens and the Dutch Minister agreed, but the latter 'was sceptical about their even starting, and there was no doubt in any of our minds that Timor must remain a source of anxiety'. Van Kleffens added that the Portuguese had no anti-aircraft guns.[5]

Campbell was anxious that Britain should accept Salazar's proposal without arguing the point as Bennett had suggested. With it, the Ambassador urged, he in fact accepted what the British had put to him. 'In doing so he has made a big gesture. If we throw this back in his teeth I cannot say what he might not do under stress of righteous indignation. This time moreover he would have his public behind him.' The Allied troops numbered 350. To be sure that the British would not 'quibble' about their 'relative value'—as Sampayo made clear—he was proposing to send double the number of Portuguese with full equipment, and they were ready to go:

> [I]f before accepting a solution which must have cost his pride a lot to make we now embark on a discussion as regards adequacy of the Portuguese force it seems to me that in the light of these past assurances we give him every reason to question our good faith.

There could be secret staff talks, though only after Allied troops had left. They could not, however, cover 'appeal for help in advance of attack. If Dr

---

[2] FO 371/27798 [F14031/222/61]: Telegram, 20 December 1941, 1722.
[3] F14412: Minutes, 31 December 1941.
[4] Tjarda to Gerbrandy, telegram, 22 December 1941 in DBPN:IV,73–74.
[5] FO 371/31727 [F100/2/61]: Eden to Bland, 31 December 1941, 118.

Salazar could not agree to this before, still less could he agree in the present circumstances.'⁶ The Portuguese force would not leave, Sampayo indicated, until Salazar knew the matter could be settled along the suggested lines. 'Until then he could not indeed be certain that the Portuguese would be allowed by the Allied force to land.'⁷

Salazar had been angry, Campbell telegraphed, because he thought 'he had not had a square deal (ie that while we were still negotiating mixed force was landed in circumstances which he had never admitted and which constituted a violation of Portugal's neutrality)'. Now he was 'in the mood to climb down if we allow him to save his face'. But he would not admit that any other government but the Portuguese could interpret what forces were required to defend Portuguese territory. Campbell sympathised with the Australian Government, 'but do they also realise wider issues at stake and that Axis powers are watching Dr Salazar as a cat watches a mouse, ready to pounce if he makes a false move[?]'⁸ There was no hope that the Governor would be instructed to co-operate with the Allied forces. If he were, the Portuguese Government would be open to Axis accusations that it had abandoned neutrality, and there would be reprisals.⁹ The Ambassador suggested he might come home to consult. The FO agreed, provided he was not away when Monteiro was in Lisbon.¹⁰

Before he left Monteiro saw Eden. He explained that Allied action had hurt Portuguese opinion. The Allies had not put their case in the right way. 'Portugal had once been a great imperial Power and…every Portuguese was conscious of this. Though Portuguese strength was sadly diminished, the memory of the past was always present in Portuguese minds and determined their reactions.' They were sensitive to any suggestion that an action, even by an ally, was one of charity and would have understood what was done better 'if we had explained that we wanted Portugal to help us and not merely that we wanted ourselves to help Portugal'. Monteiro suspected that it was the Dutch rather than the British who had been responsible for the despatch of troops. 'This in itself was a sore point…A good deal of the Netherlands East Indies had once been Portuguese, and wars had been fought for the sake of these possessions.' Eden said he was sure the Dutch did not intend

---

6   FO 371/31727 [F8/2/61]: Telegram, 31 December 1941, 1843.
7   FO 371/31727 [F9/2/61]: Telegram, 31 December 1941, 1844.
8   FO 371/31727 [F12/2/61]: Telegram, 1 January 1942, 1.
9   FO 371/31727 [F11/2/61]: Telegram, 31 December 1941, 1852.
10 FO 371/31727 [F13/2/61]: Telegram, 1 January 1942, 2.

to retain Portuguese Timor. '[T]he only basis for our action had been the necessity of providing for the defence of Timor as an outpost for the defence of Australia.' Now the problem was to find a solution acceptable to Portugal that denied the territory to the Japanese. 'Meanwhile, it was unthinkable that incidents of this kind at the other end of the world should seriously affect relations between Portugal and Great Britain. Statesmanship would be required on both sides.'[11]

Eden told the Cabinet later the same day that the Dutch were prepared to withdraw on the arrival of the Portuguese. Earle Page, then attending the British Cabinet, said the Australian Government was not prepared to say unconditionally that it would do the same. 'Could 700 Portuguese be regarded as an adequate garrison in all contingencies?' The Chief of the Imperial General Staff said that, once they were withdrawn, it would take 'some time' for the Dutch and Australian forces to return. Eden doubted whether Australia had fully appreciated the practical disadvantages of a rupture with Portugal. The Cabinet invited Page, the Dominions Secretary (Cranborne), and a FO representative to confer on the point.[12]

At the Central Department in the FO, Roger Makins had argued that the occupation had struck 'a heavy blow' at Anglo–Portuguese relations. If the British or Australians now prevaricated over withdrawing once equivalent Portuguese forces arrived, the effect would be 'irreparable', and it was pretty certain that diplomatic relations would be broken. The pro-Axis minority would get the upper hand. That would mean the cancellation of the results of the military conversations: 'instead of obtaining the use of the Azores and Cape Verde in the event of a German occupation of Portugal, the Islands will be denied to use and facilities may be given to our enemies'; and the islands would be lost as a refuelling base, which would make it impossible for escort vessels to take convoys to Freetown, and as a source of intelligence. Communications through Lisbon to Africa, Asia and the United States would also be interrupted. Portugal's wolfram—the source of tungsten used in armour-piercing projectiles, also a catalyst for synthetic oil production (Stone 1994:142)—would be lost and the alternative source was Burma. The Portuguese were unlikely to be able to resist German demands for facilities and Britain's relations with Spain would deteriorate, threatening the supply of iron ore and the use of Gibraltar. Securing Timor was important and in the eyes of the Australians 'vital'. But it was unlikely that the Allies had

---

[11] FO 371/31727 [F83/2/61]: Eden to Campbell, 1 January 1942, 6.
[12] CAB 65/25: WM (42) 1st, 1 January 1942, 3.

the forces to defend it. 'It would be merely foolish to terminate the Anglo–Portuguese connexion, and then fail to hold Portuguese Timor.'[13]

In the Far Eastern Department, Bennett saw the force of this. He would have preferred that Australia and the DO should put the other side, since they could do it more strongly:

> The plain facts are that we and the Netherlands and Australia have got our backs to the wall in the Far East, that Timor is at Australia's front door and that there can be no doubt about the threat to it from Japan except to those who wilfully shut their eyes to it. Australia is faced with the possibility of the Netherlands East Indies being overrun and of her communications being cut—in fact of being completely isolated. She is unlikely to be impressed, therefore, if, when she takes what seems to her to be an essential defence measure, we squeal about the Iberian Peninsula being overrun and our communications via Lisbon being cut.

The forces on Timor might not be able to defend it, but they could fight a delaying action, and it had yet to be shown that reinforcements could not be sent 'in the last resort'. The Australians might think it better to have some of their own troops there to deny the Japanese the airfield as long as possible, rather than leave it to Portuguese who might make common cause with the Japanese. If Britain ignored the 'Australian angle', it might run into 'far worse dangers' than those Makins enumerated. '[P]lain speaking' might secure a solution based on reality:

> What is Portugal going to gain by pushing matters to the extreme of a rupture with us? What will then become of Timor, of Mozambique and other Portuguese territories? Moreover, if Japan and German were to win this war, what would become of Portuguese colonies or, indeed, of Portugal herself, even if she had been Germany's 'ally'?[14]

William Strang, the Assistant Under-Secretary, thought it might be possible to avoid the break. One reason was indeed that it would be serious for Portugal as well as for Britain. Portugal would have to expect that Britain would seize the Atlantic islands and cut off its commerce with the outside world. Although the Portuguese could dispose of their products in

---

[13] FO 371/31728 [F472/2/61]: Minute, 31 December 1941.
[14] FO 371/31728 [F472/2/61]: Minute, 31 December 1941.

Germany, it was not clear that Germany could spare enough oil to keep the Portuguese economy going.[15]

Campbell's efforts, and those of the Central Department, were 'very naturally concentrated on finding a formula to save Dr Salazar's face', wrote Bennett on 1 January. A formula could indeed dress up a solution, but the solution must be based on realities. Avoiding 'irreparable harm' to Anglo–Portuguese relations was indeed one of Britain's preoccupations. But relations with Australia and the conduct of the Far Eastern campaign were equally important. Over the provision of troops it was not a question of quibbling, but 'a severely practical question. Are the Portuguese troops likely to oppose a Japanese landing? Are they likely to be properly equipped to do so? And if they do so, can they be reinforced in time?'

Campbell, Bennett continued, suggested that the question of an agreement can be left till the Portuguese had arrived and the allies departed. 'Even then he thinks that Dr Salazar could not agree to accept assistance in advance of an attack and that it would be unreasonable to press him to do so.' He had understood neither the urgency of the matter nor the nature of the war in the Far East. Salazar, he also reported, refused to admit that any but his government could decide what forces were required to defend Timor. 'This is the crux of the whole matter. The question is not one which concerns Portugal alone. Australia cannot afford to allow any uncertainty to persist about the defence of a territory at her front door now that the war is rapidly sweeping towards her.'

Was Britain going to bring pressure on the Portuguese Government to 'face realities and accept a perfectly reasonable condition (which will not be made public)'? Or was it going to press the Australians to withdraw unconditionally at the risk of a serious dispute with them and serious practical danger to Australia? Bennett was not convinced that pressure on Portugal would result in a rupture, as Campbell advised; he could not help feeling that, rash though it might seem, 'straight speaking' to Dr Salazar might yet overcome the crisis without one.

> The Portuguese would never have kept their colonies so long if it had not been for ourselves. They will not keep them now except for us. Is the alliance then to fail us at the hour of *our* greatest need, more particularly when what we have done has been done as friends and not as enemies?[16]

---

[15] FO 371/31728 [F472/2/61]: Minute, 31 December 1941.
[16] FO 371/31727 [F13/2/61]: Minute, 1 January 1942.

The FO set out the issues for the Chiefs of Staff. The Portuguese Government might not agree to resuming the conversations with a view to discussing the adequacy of the Portuguese forces and reaching an agreement whereby it would invite or accept the assistance of Dutch and Australian forces in the event of an attack or a threat of attack. The Australian Government might not accept the Portuguese solution even with these conditions.

> The question is whether the importance of retaining Australian and Netherlands troops in Portuguese Timor is such as to warrant the risk of a rupture of relations with Portugal; or whether the repercussions of a breach with Portugal on our position and plans in other theatres of operations make it desirable to insist on the withdrawal of allied forces in Portuguese Timor on the arrival of a Portuguese force, at the risk of a possibly serious dispute with the Commonwealth Government.[17]

Failure to reach a solution could endanger Britain's position in the Atlantic islands, for example its refuelling facilities in the Azores, its communications through Lisbon, and its supplies of wolfram and cork, and there would be 'no prospect of an unopposed occupation of the Atlantic islands in the future'. Axis influence in Portugal would increase and relations with Spain deteriorate. But, if the solution were unacceptable to Australia, it would 'throw a further strain' on the relationship. 'The worst result would be to accept a breach of relations with Portugal and still fail to protect Portuguese Timor.' It was therefore desirable to consider 'both the imminence of the threat to that territory and the adequacy of the forces available to protect it'. The views of the COS were sought.[18]

At the COS on 2 January, Vice-Admiral Moore pointed to the strategic importance of Timor: it was a base from which to control 'one of the most important passages in the Malay Barrier'. He also pointed to the threat to Darwin that the enemy occupation of Timor would present. Nevertheless, 'we were not justified, in our attempts to add to the security of Timor, in maintaining an attitude which might lead to a rupture of our relations with the Portuguese, thereby losing the chance of being able to use the Azores'. Sir Alan Brooke agreed that 'for military reasons' the British could not risk alienating the Portuguese.[19]

---

[17] FO 371/31727 [F13/2/61]: further minute by Bennett, 1 January 1942.
[18] FO 371/31727 [F62/2/61]: Memorandum, 1 January 1942.
[19] FO 371/31727 [F82/2/61]: COS (42) 2nd, 2 January 1942, 7.

Bennett doubted that this, which went back on the earlier COS opinion, was right. The case for it was 'overwhelming', but only on two assumptions, 'namely (a) that we cannot in any case hold Portuguese Timor and (b) that we should remain passive, or have not the means wherewith to seize the Azores, in the event of a rupture with Portugal'. The worst result, as the FO memorandum had suggested, was to accept a breach with Portugal and then fail to protect Timor 'or at all events to put up a prolonged resistance there'. The COS apparently did not consider the question the FO had put in its final paragraph, the imminence of the threat and the adequacy of the forces available. As for a rupture with Portugal, 'all that has been done is to recognise the dangers and inconveniences'; no consideration had been given to the question 'whether and how we meet them'. It would be argued, Bennett continued,

> that Portuguese Timor is a miserable place whose retention cannot possibly compare with the other issues involved. But it happens to be in the Far East that our danger is greatest at present; and it happens that Portuguese Timor is in that chain of territory whose denial to the Japanese has just been ruled to be the prime object of our Far Eastern strategy. The idea of making the Portuguese definitely responsible for its defence obviously has great attraction, though it is the kind of solution which savours rather of the old Geneva days than of the stern realities of today. If we return the place to Portugal without a firm understanding that we shall return in the event of an attack or a threat of attack, we shall be running a graver risk than…is now realised, even by the Chiefs of Staff.[20]

Again a different view was offered in the Central Department. Roberts thought the COS decision 'entirely right'. A good deal depended on assumption (a), but he could not help feeling 'that the answer must be that we cannot hold Portuguese Timor in the face of a determined Japanese attack unless we are prepared to send there far greater forces than seem at present to be available'. That was, however, 'a matter for the experts', and High Commissioner Bruce had himself suggested that it required careful consideration and that the answer 'should go far to determine our decision'. As for assumption (b), 'we could no doubt have seized the Azores and could probably still do so to-day in spite of the Portuguese reinforcements which,

---

[20] FO 371/31727 [F82/2/61]: Minute, 3 January 1942.

with our full approval, have been poured into the island in recent months'. But the seizure of the Azores would result in 'a German entry into Spain and Portugal', resulting in a denial of important supplies and of the use of Gibraltar as a naval base and in the use of Portuguese and Spanish ports as German naval and air bases. 'There is also the further possibility that our action would accelerate a German entry into Morocco.' Roberts also suggested—surely more dubiously—that it was 'highly unlikely' that Japan would attack Timor, given that the Portuguese would then call on Britain and bring the alliance into operation in the Far East and elsewhere. 'Such a result must obviously be entirely contrary to German desires, and their influence with the Japanese must surely be sufficient to prevent such a development.'[21]

At the DO it had been agreed that Bruce would ask for an appreciation from the Australian Staff; if it concluded that it was unlikely that Timor could be held, Bruce thought that 'it would be foolish to provoke a rupture with Portugal with the consequences which would be likely to follow in the Atlantic'. Noting that, Strang suggested that the COS opinion did not 'absolve us from the duty of trying to secure our own position to the maximum possible extent in Timor, short of provoking a rupture with Portugal'. Campbell had, Strang thought,

> rather overestimated the danger of a breach from the Portuguese side. It rather looks as though most of those concerned (the Dutch, ourselves, and even some of the Australians, as well as the Portuguese) now realise that, unless the effects of the Timor incident are circumscribed and a solution found, we shall be driven into a dangerous situation which everyone will regret.[22]

Campbell joined a meeting in Cadogan's room on 4 January, and then met Bruce and Page at the DO. They outlined the reasons the Commonwealth Government was unlikely to agree to withdrawal from Portuguese Timor, but agreed to ask its views on what was in mind in London. On the assumption that it would co-operate, a further meeting at the FO on 5 January further considered the approach to the Portuguese Government. Canberra was unlikely to accept an unconditional undertaking to withdraw, followed by a subsequent approach for staff conversations. Campbell therefore proposed

---

[21] FO 371/31727 [F82/2/61]: Minute by Roberts, 3 January 1942.
[22] FO 371/31727 [F82/2/61]: Minute, 3 January 1942.

that, on returning to Lisbon, he would renew his informal contact with Sampayo.

> He would then say that we were prepared to withdraw and to make a formal statement to this effect which could be used publicly without qualification. In return for this, however, we should ask that staff conversations should be renewed at once to consider the making of arrangements for the allied forces to be called in again in the event of a Japanese attack.

That would not formally be presented as a condition, but the Portuguese Government's consent would be 'a *sine qua non* of our formally declaring our intention to withdraw'. If a preliminary agreement along these lines could be reached with Sampayo, Campbell would put the matter 'more formally' to Salazar. He thought there was a good chance Salazar would accept. If he remained 'obdurate', the meeting considered, 'we should have no alternative but to say flatly that…we had entered the territory in our vital interests and would stay there until it suited us to go'.[23]

Salazar, John Balfour reported from Lisbon, was 'still very angry', partly 'because he had not got over the shock which the occupation caused to his pride as the statesman who restored Portugal to its rightful position', partly because he had been proved wrong in overruling the reinforcement of Timor the Minister of Colonies had proposed, and partly because he had rejected the Minister's objections to the granting of air facilities to the Japanese in 1941. Monteiro was very critical of Salazar's handling of the affair.[24] His recall to Lisbon had been an indication of Salazar's displeasure. The interview, Balfour reported, was indeed difficult. Apparently Monteiro went so far as to say that it was owing to the Royal Navy that the Portuguese Empire was intact. But Salazar insisted that a wrong must be righted. The British, he told his Colonial Minister, were determined to force the Portuguese to abandon their neutrality.[25]

Monteiro, Balfour reported in the evening, was, however, 'reasonably hopeful of a solution'. President Carmona had apparently persuaded Prime Minister Salazar that it would be 'a grave mistake to persist in treating the Timor affair on the basis of abstract principle which admitted of no

---

[23] FO 371/31727 [F137/2/61]: Minutes of meeting, 5 January 1942.
[24] FO 371/31727 [F186/2/61]: Telegram, 6 January 1942, 62.
[25] FO 371/31728 [F260/2/61]: Telegrams, 8 January 1942, 70, 71.

compromise on points of practical detail'. After a second interview with Salazar, Monteiro enlarged on the adequacy of the reinforcements at Moçambique—'he reminded me that the Dutch contingent included a large number of Portuguese deserters and maintained that the Australians were alone capable of meeting any attack'—and that suggested that discussion was still possible. He also sought to minimise the categorical tone of the note sent to the Dutch, saying it had specified no time limit. 'He did not demur when I suggested to him that the Dutch and Australian Governments must be increasingly pre-occupied about the defence of Timor as a result of the rapidly deteriorating situation in the Western Pacific.' Those were 'hopeful indications', Balfour thought, but the 'utmost care' was needed lest Salazar should 'relapse into his earlier mood of cold anger'.[26]

Axis propaganda designed to exploit Anglo–Portuguese differences had 'fallen entirely flat', Monteiro said. Salazar's strictures on Britain in the Assembly, Balfour reported on 10 January, were 'the subject of very bitter comment both by the man in the street and by educated opponents of the regime', who 'angrily tax him with being as pro-German as some of his supporters'. The Minister of Public Works lamented 'the blow to Portuguese moral position', but when Balfour alluded to the attacks on Britain in the Assembly, he 'piteously remarked that His Majesty's Government should not be too hard on his impulsive countrymen', and should do nothing to lower Salazar in their esteem. He expressed distress at the delay over a settlement, 'declaring that the Japanese were bombarding the Portuguese Government with ugly threats'.[27]

On 11 January the Portuguese Ambassador to Madrid told the United States Naval Attaché, who was on leave in Lisbon, that Salazar hoped for 'an immediate agreement' on the basis of allied withdrawal on the arrival of Portuguese forces from Moçambique and Macau. The Allied troops could return 'once an Axis attack develops or is imminent'. Balfour's own sources, however, indicated that, in his latest interview with Monteiro, Salazar had 'harped upon the fact that he could not send his troops from Moçambique until he learnt whether the Allied forces would retire from Portuguese Timor on their arrival'. He was 'still in a very difficult mood' and 'suspected Great Britain of wishing to drive him from power'.[28] At the

---

[26] FO 371/31728 [F257/2/61]: Telegram, 8 January 1942, 72.
[27] FO 371/31728 [F344/2/61]: Telegram, 10 January 1942, 85.
[28] FO 371/31728 [F412/2/61]: Telegram, 12 January 1942, 97.

FO, however, Ashley Clarke thought the atmosphere now more propitious than when Campbell left.[29]

He had, as Eden told the Cabinet, stayed in London till Australia's reply arrived.[30] On 6 January the Australian Chiefs of Staff had commented on the proposal put to Campbell on 30 December. It seemed 'dangerous'. Japanese occupation of Timor would prejudice the defence of Darwin. Seven hundred Portuguese troops would not constitute 'an adequate protection', even if the Dutch and Australian troops were retained as well. They could keep out only 'small nibbles', but not withstand any serious Japanese attempts to seize the island unless 'very considerable air forces' were brought in immediately, and they were 'unlikely to be available in the near future'. The defence problem, it was added, would be 'very much facilitated' if the road from Dili to the Dutch border were converted to a motor road. The opinion of Wavell, now with overall responsibility in Southeast Asia, should be obtained.[31] What Campbell was waiting for was the reply to the next DO telegram.

That was sent on 8 January and, while de-stressing the Atlantic factors, outlined the discussions held with Campbell, with whom, it said, Page and Bruce had been taken into consultation. The Ambassador had described Salazar's position: an autocrat, but reliant on a Nationalist bloc susceptible to Axis influence; probably ready to take action that would demonstrate that Portugal could take its own line; 'subject to constant reminders by the Axis'; and having 'increasing difficulty' in holding the balance between Axis and Allies. Campbell had done everything possible to represent Australia's position, but had been able to make little impression on Salazar, 'who maintained that he had at no time thought or spoken in terms of Allied assistance being accepted unless and until a Japanese attack had actually been made'.

A rupture with the Portuguese could have very serious consequences, 'since the operation of the route to the Cape is largely dependent upon refuelling facilities provided by the Portuguese who do in fact diverge in our favour in various matters from strict neutrality, to which otherwise they would cling tenaciously'. The supplies of wolfram and cork would also be cut off. Any additional difficulty for convoys on the Cape route would embarrass South Africa and affect the despatch of reinforcements to the Middle East and Far East. 'It would thus have, if for this reason alone, serious repercussions on Australia.'

---

[29] FO 371/31728 [F412/2/61]: Minute, 14 January 1942.
[30] CAB 65/25: WM (42) 2nd, 5 January 1942.
[31] FO 371/31727 [F181/2/61]: Telegram, 6 January 1942, 13; also in AFPD:V, 415–416.

There was too little time to seek Wavell's view, as the Australian COS had suggested, since he would not yet have been able to obtain 'a general conspectus of the problem that confronts him'. In all the circumstances, it seemed 'essential to concentrate on some middle course between the extremes of (a) agreeing unconditionally that the Allied Forces should be withdrawn on the arrival of Portuguese reinforcements, and (b) refusing altogether to withdraw'. Campbell considered that the Portuguese Government would not openly accept any conditions, but that it might be possible 'to secure a private and secret undertaking…that a formal agreement that Allied Forces would be withdrawn as soon as the Portuguese troops arrive should be understood to carry with it the institution at once of Staff conversations on the lines which had previously been contemplated'. Campbell held out no hope that Salazar would agree that such discussions would be on the basis of assistance before an actual attack.

> It might be possible, however, that once discussions had been initiated in a favourable atmosphere they might, if skilfully handled, be widened to cover the acceptance of Allied help in advance of an attack, ie in other words it might be possible to persuade the Portuguese military representatives to ensure that Allied help was invoked in good time.

The Allied commanders now in Timor might explore the improvement of the road from West Timor in advance of any conversations.

If a Japanese attack took the form of only a small raid, the 800 additional Portuguese, plus immediate Allied reinforcements, could prevent its success. If, 'probably to the detriment of their operations elsewhere', the Japanese chose to deliver a major attack, it was unlikely that the territory could be held. 'In that case we should have quarrelled with the Portuguese, have lost the territory and, in short, have got the worst of both worlds'. The Commonwealth Government might like to know that the United Kingdom COS considered 'that the importance of retaining Allied troops in Portuguese Timor would not justify from the point of view of the war as a whole the risk of rupture in our relations with Portugal'.[32]

By the time the Portuguese troops arrived, the Australian Government replied, United States naval and air reinforcements might have improved the position at Darwin and repelling an attack on Timor might have become more feasible. It therefore agreed to the British proposal provided that the

---

[32] FO 371/31728 [F290/2/61]: Telegram, 8 January 1942, 25.

road to Dutch border were improved.[33] The positive outcome of Curtin's famous appeal to the United States, conveyed in Casey's telegram of 2 January (AFPD:V,406), had made Canberra more confident.

Campbell returned to Lisbon with appropriate instructions, though the manner of his approach to the Portuguese government was left to his discretion. The staff conversations sought might be held in London, Singapore, Darwin, or at Wavell's headquarters in Netherlands Indies. 'We confidently hope that in our hour of need we can count on the same measure of assistance from Portugal as we have given Portugal in the past'.[34]

The Ambassador saw Sampayo on 15 January 1942, following his instructions 'closely'. The Secretary-General mostly 'contented himself with listening'. There was, however, clearly no difficulty over an assurance that Portugal would summon Allied help in the event of an attack. Nor was there any difficulty about staff conversations, but

> he looked down his nose when I said that the point we should like to reach was an understanding that help would be summoned in advance of an attack at any time one appeared to be imminent. When I insisted he said this was the crux of the whole difficulty.

Campbell argued that 'surely it was only common prudence to give the Portuguese commander discretion to summon help if he himself were convinced that attack was about to be launched'. Sampayo did not dispute it, 'but gave me no indication that the Portuguese Government could modify their attitude on this point'. Campbell argued that Wavell's headquarters should be the venue for the conversations. 'Dr Sampayo thought that Dutch territory might present difficulty.' He did not demur when Campbell said that it would be necessary for Australian and Dutch representatives to be 'associated' in staff discussions. Campbell doubted he would be able to secure 'participation'.[35]

On 16 January Sampayo told Campbell that Salazar was ready to accept the conditions and was ready to nominate an officer to go to Wavell's HQ to discuss the manner in which 'British help' would be forthcoming in the event of a Japanese attack. That officer, and also the Portuguese Timor authorities, would be 'instructed in the sense that such help will be invited the moment

---

[33] FO 371/31728 [F290/2/61]: Telegram, 10 January 1942, 37.
[34] FO 371/31728 [F474/2/61]: Eden to Campbell, 14 January 1942, 19.
[35] FO 371/31728 [F532/2/61]: Telegram, 16 January 1942, 117.

an attack begins'. Instructions had already been for the improvement of the West Timor road.³⁶ When Campbell reminded Sampayo of the British desire for an understanding over the threat of an attack, he again said it was the crux of the whole matter. 'He admitted, however, that judgment as to when an attack had already begun was a military matter and that the Portuguese commander would presumably not necessarily wait until a landing had been effected. This was the best I could obtain', Campbell added. He had not reverted to the 'association' of the Dutch and Australians in the talks, but would continue to press for 'participation'. That was, however, 'another point of principle, arising out of the Portuguese Government's main consideration which is not to compromise their neutrality'. The reference to 'British' help did not, however, controvert the understanding that Dutch and Australian troops would be used.³⁷

Sampayo said that Salazar wanted to make two separate announcements. The first, presumably an official statement in the press, would merely state that, as a result of conversations with the British government, orders had been given for the immediate departure from Lourenço Marques (Maputo) of the forces already prepared for the defence of Portuguese Timor. The second announcement, made after the changeover, would indicate that the Portuguese troops had taken the place of the mixed force and that the incident was closed. 'Before the first announcement was made public, an exchange of secret documents (of an informal character) would take place.' The British document would state that the mixed force would be withdrawn on the arrival of the Portuguese. The Portuguese document would offer the assurance required, stating that it was 'in harmony with the conversations… in December last'. The reason for the procedure was that Salazar felt 'unable to show publicly or in official records that he has negotiated an agreement sanctioning the remaining on Portuguese soil for a specified period…of foreign troops against whose incursion he made a formal protest'. It would also help him in answer to any Axis enquiries to repudiate any charge that he was 'collaborating' with opponents of Axis powers.

Campbell 'discountenanced' the procedure 'on the ground (the only one I could give)' that obtaining agreement from London would involve delay and finally induced Sampayo to go back to Salazar and try to persuade him 'to telescope his announcement into one'. He failed, saying later that Salazar, though anxious to avoid delay, 'adhered rigidly to his juridical standpoint'.

---

[36] FO 371/31728 [F544/2/61]: Telegram, 17 January 1942, 124.
[37] FO 371/31728 [F544/2/61]: Telegram, 17 January 1942, 125.

Campbell did, however, succeed in getting Sampayo to say there would be no objection to the British government's 'announcing, whenever they wished to do so, that they had offered to withdraw the Allied force as soon as [the] Portuguese contingent arrived'. That would be 'a unilateral statement and not imply that there had been a bargain (ie collaboration)'.[38]

Campbell commented:

> As Doctor Salazar has in fact negotiated in private an agreement which he does not wish to appear in public to have negotiated, it must be presumed that apart from his juridical argument he realizes that his proposed procedure, 'typical of his character', is the best way of presenting the matter to his public.

He thought Britain should acquiesce. It was not in its interests to humiliate Salazar publicly. It would not 'regain his confidence and collaboration'. His position was 'already becoming weaker owing to economic reasons', and it was in Britain's interest to strengthen it not weaken it further. 'There is no alternative to Doctor Salazar.' Britain did after all undertake to withdraw when the emergency was passed, subsequently interpreted to mean when Portuguese troops arrived, and was not strictly entitled to impose conditions. 'We have in fact imposed them and Doctor Salazar has swallowed them in private.' Campbell hoped that the FO would agree that the British objective had been attained; 'nor must we forget in the first instance we were technically in the wrong'.[39]

At the FO Ashley Clarke thought proposals and procedure acceptable. He wanted to add 'immediate' to the reference to the departure of the Portuguese officer. He saw 'no insuperable objection' to there being two announcements. Indeed there was some advantage in not announcing the withdrawal until it had taken place, though it was necessary to know the terms and exact time of the announcement. The DO was not planning again to consult the Australian Government, but would like to show Bruce the draft of the telegram to Campbell. Clarke had given Michiels a summary of the telegrams.[40] Eden authorised a telegram approving in principle, but seeking the modifications Clarke suggested.[41]

---

[38] FO 371/31729 [F585/2/61]: Telegram, 17 January 1942, 126.
[39] FO 371/31729 [F585/2/61]: Telegram, 17 January 1942, 127.
[40] FO 371/31729 [F585/2/61]: Minute, 17 January 1942.
[41] FO 371/31729 [F585/2/61]: Telegram, 17 January 1942, 131.

Sampayo, Campbell commented, made no difficulty over the urgency of the staff talks; transport for the Portuguese officer had to be arranged by the British. The two-stage procedure Campbell thought the FO might have considered made things '*too* easy' for Salazar. 'On second thoughts I am not sure there is much in it.' In private he had had to swallow a number of pills: he had 'dislodged us at the time of our choice rather than his'; he had failed to divide the British from the Dutch; they would have ignored his virtual ultimatum; he had agreed to talks while the Allied troops were still in Timor. 'We shall have kept him for more than a fortnight on tenterhooks (we know many of his Ministers have been making no secret of their anxiety).' All that was 'more than enough to make him realise that he must treat us with greater respect in future'.[42]

Campbell's draft of the letter to Salazar alluded to the note of 19 December 1941, in which the British Government undertook that the Australian and Dutch forces would be withdrawn as soon as the emergency was past. It also alluded to Salazar's statement in the National Assembly on 19 December that his government was proceeding with adequate reinforcements and noted that they were now ready to sail. In these circumstances Britain, in agreement with the Australian and Dutch governments, offered formal assurances that the forces would be immediately withdrawn on the arrival of the reinforcements.[43] Campbell also sent a translation of Salazar's letter: 'In harmony with conversations…in December last', the Portuguese Government would, 'as soon as transport is available', send an officer to discuss 'conditions under which British help was to be 'effected, in case of attack by the Japanese'. The Portuguese Government 'consider it as agreed… that assistance…will be requested without delay, in Timor, as soon as any attack shall begin'.[44]

Ashley Clarke doubted whether the British note should take up the statement of 19 December. As part of the face-saving arrangement, the FO was earlier prepared to consider that the emergency would be past when Portuguese reinforcements reached Timor. 'But in fact we know that the emergency will not have passed until the Japanese have been defeated.' It would be better to put something like: 'they have always made it clear that their primary concern was the denial of this territory to their enemy'.[45]

---

[42] FO 371/31729 [F605/2/61]: Telegram, 18 January 1942, 142.
[43] FO 371/31729 [F606/2/61]: Telegram, 18 January 1942, 143.
[44] FO 371/31729 [F607/2/61]: Telegram, 18 January 1942, 144.
[45] FO 371/31729 [F608/2/61]: Minute, 19 January 1942.

Wavell had meanwhile telegraphed after receiving the War Office's account of the negotiations[46] and discussing them with Governor-General Tjarda.

> We are all deeply concerned at prospect of withdrawal of allied troops since we feel no confidence that any Portuguese troops would resist Japanese aggression and are sure that Japanese intrigue and pressure will be resumed in Timor…the moment allied troops are withdrawn. Japanese force established in Timor would be very serious threat to communications between Australia and N.E.I. Fighter aircraft cannot be flown from Australia without landing at Timor.[47]

Churchill and Eden were concerned by the telegram. The COS, the Foreign Secretary told the Prime Minister, had been consulted throughout and had concluded that the importance of retaining troops in Timor would not justify a rupture with Portugal:

> I am at all times ready to play the diplomatic hand in accordance with military requirements for the conduct of the war. But at this late stage when we have largely committed ourselves to the Portuguese Government, I am bound to say that it would be dangerous to put our policy into reverse.

Though it was 'outside my province', Eden added that 380 Dutch and Australian troops would hardly suffice to prevent the Japanese capturing the whole territory if they chose to attack in force.[48]

'We should say to the Portuguese Government that we are guarding Timor until their reinforcements arrive', Churchill wrote.

> Nevertheless when they do arrive we should not go. We should leave our troops, the Dutch troops and their troops all on the spot. The Portuguese are obviously not capable of protecting their neutrality, and Timor is a key-point. General Wavell should be authorized to take all necessary steps for the military security of Timor regardless of the effects produced on Portuguese pride. There is no need to raise

---

[46] FO 371/31728 [F520/2/61]: WO telegram, 13 January 1942.
[47] FO 371/31729 [F589/2/61]: Telegram, 15 January 1942, 00058.
[48] FO 371/31729 [F745/2/61]: Minute for Prime Minister, 18 January 1942.

the question yet with the Portuguese Government, as we have several weeks (how many?) before the Portuguese troops can arrive.[49]

Eden sought to discuss the matter further. If there were any question that the Allied forces would not be withdrawn when the Portuguese contingent arrived, 'we must carefully consider the consequences on our wider strategic interests of a definite break with Portugal'. Having called Salazar to order once, it would be delusion to think that 'we could get away with it a second time' (quoted in Stone 1994:198). At the Cabinet meeting on 19 January members were informed of the negotiations that led the Portuguese to think that the withdrawal would be immediate. Indeed such was the commitment that they would be 'greatly affronted' if that did not happen. It was agreed that for the time being the question must continue to be dealt with along the lines already approved, but that the position should be reviewed in two to three weeks.[50]

After the Cabinet meeting Eden asked the FO to prepare instructions to Campbell and also to consider whether the British should press the Portuguese to cover the threat of an attack. That, Clarke said, the FO had concluded it could not secure, hoping instead that the staff officer could be brought round in discussion. Clarke had now had long discussions with the DO and with Michiels, who feared lest the Portuguese forces should arrive before the staff conversations had reached definite conclusions; a worse incident would follow. The Central Department felt it would be wrong to raise the question now.[51] In the end two telegrams were sent to Campbell.

One put some amendments forward. The Consul at Lourenço Marques spoke of the preparation of 450 troops.[52] The telegram proposed to insert the number of reinforcements, 700 or 800, since it was 'very desirable to hold the Portuguese to the number which they originally told us would be going'. The other main amendment was on the lines of Clarke's suggestion, presumably reinforced by the Cabinet discussion: 'We do not wish to commit ourselves even by implication to the view that when the Portuguese troops have arrived the emergency will have passed. In fact this is unlikely to be the case.' The passage should be replaced by a sentence indicating that the

---

[49] FO 371/31729 [F745/2/61]: Minute, 19 January 1942.
[50] CAB 65/25: WM (42) 9th, 19 January 1942, 6.
[51] F607: Minute, 20 January 1942.
[52] FO 371/31729 [F678/2/61]: Minute by Bromley, 18 January 1942.

British Government had made it clear that its main concern was 'the defence of the vital interests of the Allied nations by the denial of this territory to the enemy'.[53]

In the second telegram Campbell was reminded that 'we have always held the view that a threat of attack and not merely an attack should be provided for'. He had advised that the Portuguese Government was unlikely to agree, but the FO looked for a further attempt. If, however, he thought that would do more harm than good, he was once more to emphasise

> that, in our view, to defer a call for assistance until attack has actually developed is, as has been many times demonstrated, not enough. It is important that we should have gone on record with the Portuguese Government to this effect, so that if by the time the Portuguese troops reach Timor the situation has become so imminently menacing that it will not be possible for us to withdraw our troops, our moral position with the Portuguese Government will be to that extent improved.

Ambon had been bombed, the FO added.[54] A third telegram took up Michiels' point: the staff officer must be instructed to work rapidly and effectively.[55]

Campbell saw Sampayo on the evening of 21 January. He did not like the removal of the paragraph on the end of the emergency. 'He evidently suspected at first that it implied some retraction from our previous attitude', but 'eventually' recalled that the words were already on record and added that their suppression could not 'invalidate' the last part of the note. After discussion of the other amendments, Campbell reminded Sampayo that the British Government had wished the Portuguese Government 'to admit the desirability of not waiting till an attack had developed'. The Secretary-General replied that that had from the start been 'a fundamental point of principle' from which his government could not depart. 'An attack had seemed imminent when the allied force had gone in but had not materialised.' Campbell reminded him

> that he had recently recognised that judgment when an attack could be said with certainty to be coming was a military matter, and that the Portuguese Commander would not necessarily wait until the enemy

---

[53] FO 371/31729 [F608/2/61]: Telegram, 20 January 1942, 152.
[54] FO 371/31729 [F608/2/61]: Telegram, 20 January 1942, 151.
[55] FO 371/31729 [F608/2/61]: Telegram, 21 January 1942, 157.

was on Portuguese soil. Could he not devise some formula which would express this in suitable terms? He said that he would see what could be done.[56]

Then the two diplomats discussed the size of the Portuguese reinforcements. The FO had asked Campbell about it on receiving the information from Lourenço Marques.[57] It transpired in a conversation he then had with Sampayo that the troops numbered 500, not 700. The issue raised 'another fundamental principle', that the Portuguese Government alone determined the troops required to defend its territory. Campbell therefore took it up only when he received the FO's final instructions on the negotiations, indicating that it was 'a paramount factor in the case'. All the exchanges had been on the basis of 700 troops. Unless the number could be made up to that, the whole question might have to be reopened.[58] 'Notwithstanding the way I put it, my appeal [on troop numbers] amounted to something very little removed from a condition violating one of [Salazar's] sacred principles.'[59]

Finally Campbell urged Sampayo to appeal to Salazar to accept the amendments and conclude the business, using an approach the Secretary-General had suggested earlier. 'In the lifetime of every friendship—and this applied to the Anglo–Portuguese Alliance—it was sometimes one and sometimes the other party which had need of help and understanding of the other', he said. 'To-day it was the British who were appealing to the Portuguese partner.' He thought Sampayo felt that would be 'helpful in securing Doctor Salazar's willingness not only to conclude the negotiations but to do everything on his side to bury the hatchet'.[60]

Salazar accepted the modifications the FO wanted in the draft agreement, Sampayo told Campbell on 22 January, and agreed to augment the force due to leave Lourenço Marques to 700. Had the Secretary-General been able to find 'a formula shewing that the appeal for help in the event of attack appearing imminent was not entirely excluded'? The 'furthest limit' to which his government could agree, he replied, 'was to agree to contact being maintained between the Portuguese Commandant and the Allied

---

[56] FO 371/31729 [F759/2/61]: Telegram, 22 January 1942, 162.
[57] FO 371/31729 [F589/2/61]: Telegram, 18 January 1942, 138.
[58] FO 371/31728 [F760/2/61]: Telegram, 22 January 1942, 165.
[59] FO 371/31729 [F762/2/61]: Telegram, 22 January 1942, 167.
[60] FO 371/31729 [F759/2/61]: Telegram, 22 January 1942, 162.

Commanders in the neighbouring territory. This seems better than nothing', Campbell commented. He urged that the British representatives in the staff discussions should not try to improve on it. The Portuguese officer would have 'no authority to discuss anything beyond it' and the attempt to do so would raise suspicion and perhaps prejudice the conversations.

The remaining issue, Campbell concluded, was Dutch and Australian participation in the conversations. Sampayo confirmed that representatives could be 'associated' and Campbell had thought it better not to ask if that could be interpreted as 'direct participation. I suggest that when the time comes it should be assumed that it does.' If the Portuguese representative formally objected, it would be best to accept it and for the British representative 'to act as connecting link'. But he was inclined to think that no objection would be raised.[61]

Campbell was 'relieved' when agreement was reached 'after one of the stickiest negotiations it has come my way to take part in'. What would happen next—assuming no Japanese attack in the meantime—was causing him 'some worry'. Telegrams received since he returned seemed to indicate 'that we are attempting to fortify our moral position in case by the time the Portuguese contingent arrives the situation may have developed in such a way as to make it undesirable to withdraw the Allied force'. He would not quarrel with such a decision 'on any ground save that of our general strategic interests'. Again the problem would 'become one of balance of advantage'.

Campbell thought it would be 'rash' to think that it could be resolved in as satisfactory manner as the problem just resolved. Salazar was, he wrote,

> capable of flying into a black rage, from which he is slow to recover…If we gave him cause to feel that we had let him down a second time,…he would either have done with us for good and all and throw himself on the mercy of Germany, or (perhaps more probably) throw in his hand and make way for another Government; which…could only result in chaos from which no one but our enemies would benefit.

The Ambassador concluded

> that if there is any question of the Allied force not being withdrawn when the Portuguese contingent arrives (thereby obliging it to turn

---

[61] FO 371/31729 [F761/2/61]: Telegram, 22 January 1942, 166.

round and sail home again) we *must* carefully consider the consequences on our wider strategic interests of a definite break with Portugal.[62]

The despatch provoked a minor renewal of the dispute between the FO's Central and Far Eastern departments. Bennett insisted that the matter had been considered in its 'wider' aspect. Makins denied that it had been before 2 January, and then the COS had reached the right answer.[63] The dispute reflected, of course, the difficulty in determining priorities between Europe and Asia, though in general, and especially in times of crisis, the British chose Europe, which was fundamental to their security. What seems obvious in retrospect does not necessarily seem so to contemporaries. The same observation may apply to Campbell's assessments of Salazar and of his likely reactions. Rosas (2002:280–281) is able to write as an historian that the dissension between the United Kingdom and Portugal 'never assumed such proportions as to jeopardise either the existence of the alliance or Portugal's policy of neutrality' and that disputes were always 'in the end and despite Salazar's penchant for bargaining, resolved in the Allies' favour'. The Ambassador could hardly assume that.

The Japanese attack

On 8 February 1942 Consul Ross reported that two Japanese fighter planes had attacked Dili with machine guns that morning. The Australian Government argued that this was a violation of neutrality, that it portended a general attack which would warrant a call for Allied help, and that troops should therefore remain. In what it saw as a new situation, it wanted the Portuguese Government to issue appropriate instructions to the representative about to start conversations at Wavell's headquarters.[64]

The FO doubted that it could be claimed that a new situation had arisen, 'since, when belligerent troops are on neutral territory, it cannot be regarded as a violation of the neutrality of the territory if an attack is made on ground occupied by belligerent troops'. In any case, 'the Portuguese Government would not admit that a new situation had arisen warranting an immediate call for Allied assistance and would argue that only the presence of Allied troops

---

[62] FO 371/31730 [F1162/2/61]: Campbell to Eden, 23 January 1942, personal communication, circulated to Cabinet as WP (42) 47, 29 January 1942.
[63] FO 371/31730 [F1162/2/61]: Minutes, 4 February.1942.
[64] FO 371/31730 [F1367/2/61]: Telegram from Commonwealth of Australia, 8 February 1942, 109.

was responsible for the attack'. In fact Salazar instructed his ambassador in Tokyo, Esteves Fernandes, to protest, also indicating that the enemy forces in Timor would soon be replaced.

The FO doubted, moreover, whether anything would be gained by trying to retain the Allied troops in Timor. They consisted, it understood, of a company of Australians and 300 Netherlands troops, while there was an Australian battalion and 200 Netherlands troops at Kupang. It was for the military authorities to decide if the force at Dili were strong enough to resist a Japanese attack or if it could be reinforced for that purpose. Unless the answers were affirmative,

> it appears unsound to insist on the retention of a force which may only serve as a provocation to Japan at the expense of a further dispute with Portugal. An attempt on our side to go back on the arrangement made for the relief of Allied by Portuguese troops would have an irremediable effect on our relations with Portugal.[65]

Major Nogueiro arrived at the Allied headquarters in Batavia on 14 February, where conversations resulted in a text forwarded on 17 February, two days after the fall of Singapore to the Japanese. It was agreed that Allied troops would be withdrawn 'as soon as possible' after the arrival of the Portuguese reinforcements. 'The evacuation by sea is difficult while by air impracticable.' Nogueiro agreed that it might have to be by road and agreed 'urgently to represent to his Government the need to provide as much assistance as possible in the matter of transport for equipment and supplies of the Allied troops as far as the border'. He recognised the time taken for withdrawal would depend on that assistance and on the condition of the road, the improvement of which the Portuguese Government had previously agreed upon. It was agreed that the Governor would ask the Allied commander at Kupang for assistance 'immediately it is clear that the Japanese intend to attack' and that the Governor would be guided by the opinion of Colonel Antunes, the commander of the Portuguese forces. Nogueiro undertook to ask his Government to instruct the Governor accordingly 'in order that Allied reinforcements despatched from Koepang may arrive in time'.[66] After

---

[65] FO 371/31731 [F1532/2/61]: Memorandum, 10 February 1942; Telegram to Tokyo, 10 February 1942, 13, in DAPE:X,546–547.
[66] FO 371/31731 [F1589/2/61]: Telegram from GHQ Batavia, 17 February 1942, OPX 1860; also in AFPD:V,529–530.

consulting the Dutch government, the FO endorsed the text on 20 February, although events appeared to have overtaken it.[67] The Japanese had arrived.

The Japanese armed forces had planned an attack only on West Timor, fearing that an attack on Portuguese Timor would prompt neutral Portugal to side with the Allies and that the Axis would lose the capacity to collect information at Lisbon. The stationing of Allied forces, Ken'ichi Goto (2003:33) tells us, 'brought an abrupt change in Japanese policy', the argument being 'that the presence of these forces in itself constituted a breach of neutrality, irrespective of possible Portuguese protests, and fully justified counteraction by Japan'.

On 5 January Southern Forces headquarters had alerted Tokyo that there were about 1,000 Australian and Dutch troops in Portuguese Timor. Should enemy troops be using the territory when Japan invaded West Timor, they would have to be attacked, argued Sugiyama Hajime, the Army Chief of Staff. A debate followed at the Liaison Committee. Sugiyama argued that Portugal would have to be asked to expel the troops and that, if need be, Japan should attack; he was supported by Nagano Osami, the Chief of Naval Staff. The Foreign Ministry argued for warning Portugal to take action. Togo Shigenori hoped to secure the co-operation of the Portuguese as of Thais. Finally it was decided that Portuguese Timor would be invaded as well as Dutch (West) Timor and without prior warning (Goto 2003:33–34; Frei 1996:288–291).

What should follow? Prime Minister Tojo Hideki advocated 'speedy withdrawal', but the navy insisted that Japan should retain Portuguese Timor, which in any case could not sustain its neutrality, as 'a base for operations for Australia'. On 2 February at a liaison meeting it was agreed that 'the Imperial troops will evacuate the Portuguese territory as long as Portugal can maintain her neutral stand; however, depending on Portugal's attitude and the overall war situation, Portuguese Timor may be made use of as a base'. The Germans were notified. The naval authorities were discouraging: if Japan occupied Timor, the Allies would probably occupy the Azores and Cape Verde. But the Wilhelmstrasse thought that they would not act, for fear of provoking Germany to occupy the Iberian Peninsula, and Hitler decided in favour of the Foreign Ministry.

The attack went ahead, designed to precede attacks on eastern Java, so as to take the enemy from behind and to be coupled with an air attack on Darwin. Instructions were issued to the Southern Forces on 7 February and the operation began on 18 February. The 228th Infantry Regiment under

---

[67] FO 371/31731 [F 1589/2/61]: Telegram to Campbell, 20 February 1942, 320.

Major-General Ito Takeo attacked East and West Timor simultaneously (Farram 2004:167). The Japanese Government announced that the object was to eliminate Allied forces, that the operations did not violate Portuguese sovereignty and that the Japanese forces would speedily withdraw so long as Portugal maintained neutrality ((Goto 2003:34–35; Frei 1996:292–296, 1991:170).

The Japanese minister delivered the message to Sampayo on the evening of 19 February, adding the Portuguese Government had nothing to fear at Macau. Sampayo had protested that it was 'incomprehensible' that Japan should take such action after congratulating his government on 'the happy solution of the Timor incident'. At his request a written statement followed, though only three hours later, which replaced the word 'sovereignty', used in the oral statement, with the phrase 'territorial integrity'.[68] Esteves Fernandes was instructed to protest in Tokyo.[69] He pointed the Japanese Vice-Minister to the accord under which the British agreed to withdraw on the arrival of Portuguese troops.[70]

It was clear to Campbell that the Portuguese Government would do its utmost 'to avoid being drawn into a state of war with Japan'. He refrained from saying 'anything committal' until he had heard from the FO. He merely reminded Sampayo

> that at the outset I had said that the Japanese would or would not attack Timor according to whether or not the operation responded to some strategic exigency and that if it did they would have no scruples for Portuguese neutrality[.] (This was when the Portuguese Government were attempting to make out that our action might compromise their neutrality).

The Japanese, he had added, 'would play the usual Axis game by claiming to save Portugal from her friends and so on' and he hoped that the Portuguese Government would not lend itself to 'such manoeuvres'.[71]

The FO forwarded an announcement by the Japanese headquarters, which referred to the 'invasion' by British and Dutch troops on 17 December

---

[68] FO 371/31731 [F1703/2/61]: Telegram, 20 February 1942, 335; Conversation, 19 February 1942; Aide-memoire, 19 February 1942, in DAPE:XI,15–19.
[69] Telegram, 19 February 1942, 20, in DAPE:X,577–578.
[70] Telegram, 20 February 1942, 25, in DAPE:X,587.
[71] FO 371/31731 [F1704/2/61]: Telegram, 20 February 1942, 356.

1941, the Portuguese protest and subsequent negotiations for their removal. 'The Portuguese Government have, it seems, endeavoured to bring about an improvement of the situation which, however, has remained without any improvement until now.' Given the progress of Japan's operations in Dutch Timor, it was now 'confronted with the necessity in self-defence of expelling the British and Dutch troops' from Portuguese Timor. The Japanese Government understood the position of Portugal, embarrassed by actions committed by the British and Dutch 'in disregard of international faith'. It was 'prepared to assure the territorial integrity of Portuguese Timor' and would withdraw its forces 'on the attainment of the objectives pursued in self-defence, as long as the Portuguese Government maintain a neutral attitude. Japan is harbouring no design on Portugal'.[72]

The British countered with an immediate announcement. Japan had agents in Timor at the outset of the war and its threat to the 'virtually undefended' territory, and to Allied communications and to Darwin, could not be ignored. When submarine activity portended an attack, Allied troops were sent in. The Allies had 'readily agreed' to withdraw them when informed that Salazar intended to send reinforcements. The Japanese Government knew that the reinforcements were nearing their destination, but 'with their customary hypocrisy the Japanese pretend that no solution had been reached in order to justify their attempt to seize the territory before the Portuguese troops arrive. Japan's plea of self-defence is clearly ridiculous.' It had always intended to occupy Portuguese Timor at the moment it found suitable.[73] The announcement was not without some hypocrisy on the part of the British, especially in view of their ambivalent attitude to withdrawal.

Later that evening Campbell handed over the text of the note just received from London, commenting on the 'characteristic and treacherous falsity' of the announcement from the Japanese Headquarters. Sampayo said that he had 'vigorously disputed' with the Japanese Minister 'the passage stating that no improvement had been reached up to date of the situation created by the entry of Allied forces'. Campbell told Sampayo that he assumed the Portuguese would protest at least as vigorously as they had when Allied forces entered Timor 'in very different circumstances and for a very different purpose'. Sampayo replied that a protest had been telegraphed to Tokyo, accompanied by a demand for further explanations. 'He said that situation was a perilously

---

[72] FO 371/31731 [F1723/2/61]: Telegram, 20 February 1942, 321.
[73] FO 371/31731 [F1723/2/61]: Telegram, 20 February 1942, 322; copy in Portuguese, transmitted by Monteiro, 20 February 1942, 70, in DAPE:X,583–584.

difficult one for the Portuguese Government.' What would it do about the reinforcements? 'If, when they arrive Japanese were still in possession they could not land and appear to be co-operating with them. If they attempted to evict the Japanese, which would mean, of course, war with Japan, they would promptly be sent to the bottom.' The Portuguese Government, Campbell replied, 'would cut a very sorry figure if they recalled expedition', and it would be 'tantamount to acquiescing in Japanese occupation'. Sampayo did not demur. Campbell did not think he would 'get anything more out of [these?] frightened people' until they heard from Tokyo.[74]

The Portuguese convoy was still on its way from Lourenço Marques. On 16 February the Portuguese counsellor in London told his Dutch counterpart that the sloop *Gonçalves Zarco* would probably be calling at Colombo to refuel. The SS *João Belo*, the troopship it was escorting, would not call there, but proceed on its way to Timor.[75]

At the FO Ashley Clarke wondered if the British could assist over the convoy. Campbell produced arguments against a recall. The troops 'would certainly be an embarrassment to us in British or Dutch territory (eg Ceylon or Java)'. The first step, from the Portuguese point of view, was no doubt to demand that the Japanese should agree to withdraw when the troops arrive. 'Even if operations in Portuguese territory are completed, the Japanese are perhaps unlikely to agree to this, and the problem will then remain in a somewhat more acute form.' Should Britain 'simply allow the problem to develop'? Or, 'considering that we to some extent got them into this mess', should it 'offer to harbour the troops until the problem has been solved'? The decision perhaps turned on 'whether, if something happens to the convoy, the fury of the Portuguese will be turned on the Japanese as the direct cause or on ourselves as the more remote'. Subject to the views of the Central Department, Clarke was 'inclined to let the situation develop a bit further before jumping in with any offers'. The Japanese, there was reason to think, were 'very anxious not to oblige Portugal to abandon her neutrality'. That put the Portuguese 'in a strong position' to press its views with the Japanese government.

Eden had discussed the position with the United States Ambassador, Winant. He had suggested that it might be useful to offer the Portuguese Government 'some assurance' that Timor would be restored at the end of the war. The Japanese had stated that they would withdraw their troops when their 'objectives of self-defence' had been attained. That vague phrase might

---

[74] FO 371/31731 [F1705/2/61]: Telegram, 20 February 1942, 339.
[75] Portuguese Counsellor to Dutch Counsellor, 16 February 1942, in DAPE:X,566–567.

mean anything at all, but if the Japanese succeed in installing themselves in Dutch Timor they may be content to withdraw from Portuguese Timor long before the war is over, more especially as until we can challenge their command of the sea the strategic importance of Portuguese Timor is considerably reduced.

An assurance along the lines Winant suggested appeared not to go as far as the Japanese promise and might not 'cut much ice' with the Portuguese. When Japan's intentions and the military situation became clearer, 'an opportunity for a statement of this kind may occur'. Clarke suggested waiting.[76]

A reference to the idea—which would require 'very careful consideration' in consultation with the Dutch and the Australians—was cut out of the draft telegram to Campbell. He was instructed to encourage the Portuguese to take 'as stiff a line' with the Japanese as they had with the British. He was to give 'no lead' on the convoy, but to assure the Portuguese Government that if it required any facilities for the convoy, 'we shall of course be glad to do anything in our power'. Were there any ways in which Britain might 'exploit the situation…to promote an attitude of more benevolent neutrality in connexion with current negotiations'?[77]

On the morning of 21 February Campbell learned that Salazar intended to make a statement in the Assembly that afternoon. He asked Sampayo what the Prime Minister intended to say, expressing regret that he felt unable to wait till there had been an exchange of views with the British. He was going to protest, the Secretary-General replied, and state that the incident was not closed; he was not going to say anything at present 'which might make a rupture with Japan, and the consequent seizure of Macao inevitable'. Campbell hoped for a 'vigorous' protest:

> What sort of figure would Portugal cut before the world if, after the violent protest made when Allied forces, although admittedly committing a technical breach of neutrality, went in to help Portugal defend her own colony, she made only a timid protest when Japanese forces went in to use it as a base for offensive operations against Portugal's Ally[?]

Sampayo 'interposed to say that the strength of feeling [a]roused on the former occasion was due to the fact that the act had been committed by a

---

[76] FO 371/31731 [F1705/2/61]: Minute, 21 February 1942.
[77] FO 371/31731 [F1705/2/61]: Telegram, 21 February 1942, 339.

friend and an Ally from whom such things were not expected'. Campbell 'expostulated', then went on to say that Japan and other Axis powers would exploit any sign of weakness, 'all of whom would think they had only to show their teeth for Portugal to turn tail'.[78]

Salazar's speech recounted the earlier episode, paying a tribute to the British for recognising Portugal's right to protest and for working for a formula. Unfortunately one month passed before Portugal received a guarantee of withdrawal on the arrival of reinforcements and meanwhile they did not leave Lourenço Marques. Before they arrived in Timor, and so achieved 'the complete reinstatement of our sovereignty and the definite closing of a painful incident', the Japanese made the statement of 19 February. That Salazar quoted in his speech, saying it must have preceded the attack that began 'the new calvary' in Timor. The 'correct' terms of the Japanese communication did not 'diminish the extreme gravity of the facts'. Neither the dictates of strategy, nor the previous violation of Portuguese rights, justified a further violation, against which the Government had put in an energetic protest. It was 'useless violence from the point of view of the sequence of operations of the war and entirely superfluous, because the early arrival of the Portuguese troops in Timor would have as a consequence the withdrawal of the forces considered hostile'. The Japanese Government knew of the arrangements and had indicated its satisfaction. It 'could not even invoke, like England, obligations of assistance derived from existing treaties, well or badly interpreted at the moment'.[79]

'This milk-and-water statement is the measure of Portuguese fear of Japan—and of losing Macau', Sterndale Bennett commented. It implied that the Japanese attack was no worse than the Allied 'violation' and also inferred that the Allies were responsible for the delay in sending the reinforcements. There was cause for dissatisfaction with it, therefore, but it was for the Central Department to consider whether it could be turned to account. Bennett added it seemed likely that the Japanese attack preceded the Japanese communication.[80]

In the Central Department, Makins took quite a different view. The statement was 'eminently satisfactory' in that it contained 'a re-affirmation, both express and implied', of the treaty relationship with Britain, and contrasted British actions with Japanese. He did not think Salazar could be

---

[78] FO 371/31731 [F1743/2/61]: Telegram, 21 February 1942, 346.
[79] FO 371/31731 [F1744/2/61]: Telegram from Campbell, 21 February 1942, 351.
[80] FO 371/31731 [F1744/2/61]: Minute, 22 February 1942.

blamed for delaying the departure of troops, given the attitude of the Dutch and the Australians. 'After all, he had just had a signal demonstration of our inability to control the actions of our Allies.' The further delay was partly due to Britain's insistence that the number be made up to 800. The statement certainly tailed off

> rather feebly … but as we have hopelessly failed to defend Portuguese territory in the Far East, and the Portuguese can do nothing in the matter, we cannot expect bold demonstrations of defiance … especially at a time when to the timorous Latin the British military situation does not look particularly bright.

The Portuguese Government might, however, 'adopt a more benevolent attitude in a number of matters under current negotiation between our two Governments'. If, Makins concluded, Britain had

> insisted on the withdrawal of the Dutch–Australian expedition, either Timor would not have been attacked, or the Japanese would have been the sole aggressors and we should have been in a very strong position ourselves in Portugal. As it is, we may count ourselves lucky not to have suffered more damage than we have done as a result of this business.[81]

There might have been a sharper reaction against the Japanese than ourselves, the Permanent Under-Secretary, Sir Alexander Cadogan, commented. But the Portuguese were dominated by fear, and they had more to fear from the Japanese.[82] Indeed Eden told Monteiro that he was disappointed that Salazar used milder language about the Japanese than he had about the Allies.[83]

The notion that Britain could have insisted on Dutch/Australian withdrawal seems in retrospect quite unrealistic, whatever Makins thought. He was, however, surely right to suggest uncertainty about the Japanese reaction. Frei (1996:301) has suggested that Japan would have respected the neutrality of Portuguese Timor, as they respected that of Macau, but it seems far from certain.

---

[81] FO 371/31731 [F1744/2/61]: Minute, 22 February 1942.
[82] FO 371/31731 [F1744/2/61]: Minute, 22 February 1942.
[83] FO 31732 [F1923/261]: Telegram, 25 February 1942, 363; cf Telegram, 23 February 1942, 75, in DAPE:XI,23–24.

Salazar, Campbell noted, drew some distinction between the Allied and Japanese actions: 'although there was implicit suggestion that two wrongs do not make a right there was no attempt to assert that it was the original allied action which had brought this new blow on Portugal's head'. Indeed Salazar made it clear that the Japanese did not have the pretext of the offer of assistance that the Allied Commanders had given. Compared with those of 19 December, the Assembly's proceedings were 'listless', Campbell added, which was 'probably largely due to the fact that on the earlier occasion Dr Salazar found it necessary to whip up indignation against the Allies lest indignation might not have been forthcoming'.[84]

Clarke found it disappointing that Salazar was on this occasion so careful to avoid an excessive display of feelings. It would have promoted distrust between Japan and Germany and probably have strengthened the Portuguese position. He feared to lose Timor and Macau altogether, Roberts commented: 'Our experiences in the Far East are hardly calculated to inspire the Portuguese with reckless courage!'[85]

It was premature to think of exploiting the Japanese action—as the FO had suggested—until the crisis was over, Campbell thought. What were the prospects? In the short time before the *João Belo* arrived at Dili, the Portuguese would 'use every endeavour', including perhaps appeal to other Axis governments, to secure an undertaking that the Japanese would then withdraw. If meanwhile the Allied forces had been overwhelmed, the Japanese might 'give and implement' such an undertaking 'in order to avoid pushing Portugal into the Allied camp and in the knowledge of ample opportunities to come, of creating fresh trouble between her and Great Britain'. Whether or not they obtained the undertaking, the Portuguese could not recall their forces 'without intolerable loss of face'. If when the *João Belo* arrived, fighting was still going on, Campbell could not imagine what would happen. If, on the other hand, Allied forces had been overwhelmed and the Japanese did not withdraw, the Portuguese forces must 'either land with Japanese assent or be [prevented?]'. In the former case, 'Portugal would virtually become the ally of Japan'. In the latter case, it could hardly do less than break off relations with Japan.

'A more hideous situation for Dr Salazar, whose primary pre-occupation is still to preserve his rather shop-soiled neutrality, it is difficult to conceive.' During the crisis, he would not be 'responsive to any attempt to push him a

---

[84] FO 371/31732 [F1754/2/61]: Telegram, 22 February 1942, 357.
[85] FO 371/31732 [F1754/2/61]: Minutes, 14, 25 February 1942.

little further along the road we wish him to go…He has not yet fully realised that the Axis Powers do not know the meaning of good faith. When he has, we may find him more amenable'. Meanwhile Campbell could not suggest 'any concrete steps' that Britain could counsel the Portuguese Government to undertake.[86]

He returned to the topic two days later. Three things could happen if there had been no agreement by the time the *João Belo* arrived: the Japanese refused to allow the Portuguese to land; the Japanese allowed them to land, but themselves refused to leave; the Japanese agreed to move to West Timor. The first and second cases would probably lead to a rupture of relations. 'Is it to our interest to try to push the Portuguese Government to go further and declare a state of war?' Campbell was doubtful. Britain's 'moral standpoint' was, in Portuguese eyes, 'not unassailable. Fear of consequences would render most Portuguese sufficiently blind to claim that "none of this would have happened" if allied troops had not gone in originally.' Salazar would think Britain wanted to drag Portugal into war for its own ends. Other Allied powers would threaten Portugal, which would increase Britain's difficulties in Lisbon. And it would 'serve no practical purpose'. The third hypothesis would 'enable the Japanese to make play with having ousted Allied forces and restored Portuguese sovereignty', but, after Salazar's declaration in the Assembly, 'this would not get them very far. A more valid objection is perhaps the difficulties which it might create for us during subsequent operations.'

All these considerations were based on the assumption that if fighting were still in progress when the Portuguese contingent arrived, it would, even if prepared to give battle, be 'unable to turn the scale'. There was thus, Campbell thought, 'no forcible reason to press this, that or the other course on the Portuguese Government', and there was 'much to be said for leaving them to make their own choice rather than expose ourselves later to the charge of having led them to make the wrong one'. Salazar would in any case be unlikely 'to listen to us against his own judgment unless we made it the occasion for formally invoking alliance with all the consequences which that might entail'.[87]

Later the same day Campbell learned from Sampayo that so far Portugal had failed to secure any assurance from the Japanese Government: what happened when the *João Belo* arrived had, it declared, to be in the hands of the Commander on the spot. It had warned that, owing to the extent of

---

[86] FO 371/31732 [F1807/2/61]: Telegram, 23 February 1942, 361.
[87] FO 371/31732 [F1895/2/61]: Telegram, 25 February 1942, 370.

the battle, the convoy should not pass the 90th degree of longitude. It had already done so, Sampayo said, but the Minister of Marine had ordered it not to approach within 300 miles of Sumatra. That meant a diversion southward and would retard its arrival. No approach had been made to other Axis governments, Sampayo said.[88]

Campbell did not mention the possibility, the FO pointed out, that Portuguese troops might land while the Japanese were still there and that the Portuguese Government might desire or be compelled to negotiate and its troops to collaborate.[89] The reason, the Ambassador replied, was that Sampayo had said that his government was reluctant 'to do anything which might savour of collaboration with the Japanese'. He had, however, come to doubt if it could be relied upon; in every conversation with the Secretary-General, the word 'Macau' cropped up.

Now Campbell told him that the British Government, while not wishing to press any particular course on Portugal, was 'following the course of events with grave preoccupation' and hoping that it would 'stoutly uphold' its neutrality and honour. It would 'create a most unpleasant impression if the Portuguese force were to land and remain side by side with the Japanese'. The Japanese commander might invite them to do so, and to encourage the Portuguese commander to agree 'might well say that although Japanese forces must remain for a few days for the purposes of clearing up they would be withdrawn very shortly'. Once he had walked into the trap, the Japanese forces would remain on one pretext or another and 'Portugal would give the appearance, if nothing worse, of collaborating with Japanese in defence of the colony' against its ally. No doubt the Japanese Government wanted to bring such a situation about. 'There was no limit to its dangers; it was not impossible for instance to imagine British bombs destined for the Japanese, falling on Portuguese troops.' Had the Portuguese Government reflected on the possibilities?

It had indeed, Sampayo replied, pointing out that he had earlier mentioned the necessity of avoiding anything like collaboration. On 26 February the Japanese Minister Chiba Shinichi, had, he said, 'murmured…something' that prompted the reply that, if he were suggesting 'a division of sovereignty', he was 'making a serious mistake if he thought that Portuguese Government would entertain it for a moment'. The Minister hastily replied that he was

---

[88] FO 371/31732 [F1876/2/61]: Telegram, 25 February 1942, 372. In fact the Germans had been informed (Salazar to Ambassador in Berlin, 26 February 1942, in DAPE:XI,29–30).
[89] FO 371/31732 [F1876/2/61]: Telegram, 27 February 1942, 370.

speaking without instructions. 'Quoi? Un partage de souveraineté?' Sampayo's own record runs. 'Mais ce serait impossible, Monsieur le Ministre'. Once Java was occupied, how could Japan retain what was Portugal's? The episode, Campbell commented, confirmed his fears. 'Surely firm and plain words were called for.' Speaking 'quite unofficially', he suggested that 'a warning of rupture of relations' could alone make the Japanese realise that the Portuguese Government 'was not to be trifled with'.[90] 'Sir R Campbell spoke well', Eden commented, and wondered if he himself or Cadogan should take the matter up with Monteiro.[91]

The Portuguese convoy, it was reported on 2 March, had been instructed to return to Colombo. 'If it had continued the voyage, Portuguese force owing to exhaustion of fuel and water would have been obliged on arrival either to attempt to land in the teeth of Japanese opposition or to land with Japanese consent and thus appear to be collaborating.' That averted the eventuality that had especially concerned the FO. 'What next?' Presumably the Portuguese Government was hoping that by the time the *João Belo* and its escort had refuelled, 'battle may have developed in such a way as to permit the Japanese to withdraw from Portuguese Timor'. There might therefore be 'a considerable and indeterminate period' before any firm decision were taken, during which the Portuguese Government would 'continue to lose face'. Britain, Campbell thought, could only warn it against 'drifting into an unbearably humiliating position (with consequent loss of British and American sympathy)'; stress the contrast between their attitude to the Allies and to the Japanese; 'and generally endeavour to instil some spirit'.[92] '[W]e have nothing new to suggest', Ashley Clarke minuted.[93]

Campbell saw Salazar on the evening of 4 March. He referred to the 'vigorous protest' in Tokyo. Obviously, he said, the convoy could not proceed while fighting was continuing 'and without knowing what would happen on her arrival'. He was still seeking 'some definite assurance, for what it might be worth, in regard to Japanese intentions'. Campbell asked if he thought the Japanese would ever leave. 'He shrugged his shoulders'. Did he intend to give the Japanese a time limit for a clear reply? He did not think that was realistic, inasmuch as the Japanese could not be expected to say when the

---

[90] FO 371/31732 [F1960/2/61]: Telegram, 28 February 1942, 393; conversation between Sampayo and Chiba, 26 February 1942, in DAPE:XI,32; conversation between Sampayo and Campbell, 28 February 1942, in DAPE:XI,34–35.
[91] Note on FO 371/31732 [F1960/2/61].
[92] FO 371/31732 [F2018/2/61]: Telegram, 2 March 1942, 399.
[93] FO 371/31732 [F2018/2/61]: Minute, 5 March 1942.

war position would allow it. It had taken the best part of a month for Britain and Portugal to reach an agreement over the Allied forces, he recalled.

Campbell decided not to take Salazar up on this or other points: 'atmosphere was not appropriate'. Instead he reminded the Prime Minister that the British Government

> had a close interest…For one thing they would take it amiss if Portuguese Government after taking a very strong line with their ally were to end by taking a feeble one with their ally's enemy. For another thing a display of weakness towards Japan would undoubtedly encourage her partners to think that they had only got to bang on the table for Portugal to succumb.

Salazar said he intended to be firm.[94]

The Australian guerrillas

The Allied troops had withdrawn, Salazar said, but some resistance was being put up by Australian guerrillas to the south and east of Dili.[95] Indeed such resistance, aided by the co-operation of Timorese *criados*, continued into 1943. Had Leggatt moved his troops to West Timor by the time the Japanese arrived, they would not have aborted their landing, but, Frei (1996:298) suggests, Portuguese Timor would have been spared much suffering. It was hard, however, to contemplate withdrawing a determined force, the endeavours of which seemed to show a determination not shown elsewhere in Southeast Asia. In any case much of the suffering was the result of bombing rather than the guerrilla campaign. The Japanese garrison force reported late in 1942 that the remnants of the Allied troops were 'hiding and moving about in the deep mountains of the central part', but they were 'nothing' compared with the aerial attacks launched from Australia. Nevertheless they wanted to get rid of the opposition and the Portuguese government seems to have hoped that they might leave Timor if the guerrilla struggle were abandoned (Goto 2003:35).

Late in May 1942 Monteiro had called at the FO with a report from the Portuguese authorities in Timor which he thought might interest the British Service Departments. According to the report, there were no longer

---

[94] FO 371/31733 [F2113/2/61]: Telegram, 5 March 1942, 419.
[95] FO 371/31733 [F2114/2/61]: Telegram, 5 March 1942, 420.

any Dutch or Australian forces in Dutch Timor. The remnants had joined the 'small groups' that maintained 'a nucleus of resistance' in Portuguese Timor. In Dutch Timor, the Japanese had won over 'a large proportion of the native tribes', but not in Portuguese Timor, where the Portuguese authorities had tried to 'prevent contact'. The Japanese had abandoned work on the aerodrome and left it unguarded.[96]

Early in June Sampayo told Campbell that the Governor had been approached by David Ross, the Consul. He seemed to think that the 'handful of Australians… still holding out in the hills' were 'suffering uselessly (if they are not caught by the Japanese they must eventually die of starvation or sickness) and that if they gave themselves up and submitted to internment in Dutch Timor Japanese would withdraw altogether from Portuguese part of the island'. That, Sampayo said, 'would of course suit Portuguese Government', since the Japanese were requisitioning food supplies and generally behaving intolerably. Campbell interposed, 'perhaps rather hastily': if that were 'a suggestion that we should ease the difficulties of the Portuguese Government by ordering the surrender of a band of brave men determined to hold out to the last', it would not be sympathetically received in London. Sampayo said Campbell had misunderstood him: the initiative came from Ross, not from the Portuguese Government. 'On receiving his approach, the Governor had succeeded in getting into touch with the Australian commander who said that he had no means of soliciting or receiving orders but beyond that had been non-committal.' That put 'a somewhat different aspect on the matter', Campbell admitted, but Sampayo should realise that Timor was 'a rather sore subject in London', given the 'feeble reaction' of the Portuguese to the Japanese invasion. Their hands were 'tied by the fear of reprisals against Macau', Sampayo sadly replied. After more 'fencing', he said that, if the Australians gave themselves up, the Portuguese Government would demand the immediate withdrawal of the Japanese forces.[97]

Ross told the Governor that he had been approached by Consul Koroki. The Japanese took him to Liquiça, then pointed him in the direction of the guerrilla group. He informed its commanders that the Netherlands Indies Government had surrendered and suggested that they might also. They declined; they took orders from the headquarters in Melbourne, not from the Indies, and would prefer to fight on rather than become prisoners-of-

---

[96] FO 371/31733 [F3891/2/61]: Eden to Campbell, 24 May 1942, 167.
[97] FO 371/31733 [F4226/2/61]: Telegram, 6 June 1942, 972; repeated in Attlee to Commonwealth of Australia, 9 June 1942, 455, in AFPD:V,838–840.

war. Ross suggested to the Governor that he reach an agreement with the Japanese, providing for the withdrawal of their forces simultaneously with the internment of the Australian forces by the Portuguese administration. 'I think that the Australian commander would agree to this procedure which after all is in accordance with international law for combatants forced into neutral territory.'[98]

Sampayo's version was all the FO had to go on and to P Broad it sounded 'rather fishy'. Other information suggested that some 400 Australians were still resisting in Portuguese Timor and 200 Dutch in West Timor. There was also some kind of communication between Australia and the Australian forces. It was 'odd' that Ross could pass on such a message without being in contact with the Australian commander and 'curious' that he seemed to be able to contact the Governor without the knowledge of the Japanese. 'It is transparent that the object is to get us to agree to terminate hostilities in the Portuguese colony and thus give the Portuguese a chance of once more establishing their sovereignty there.' Possibly the Japanese themselves encouraged the approach. Broad had discussed it with the Dominions Office, the War Office and the Admiralty. The consensus of opinion was to ignore any such suggestion of an armistice, 'first since the Japanese would have far more to gain than ourselves and secondly because any message passed on to the Australian forces, through the channel of the Portuguese authorities, could not be authoritative'.[99]

Monteiro called on Cadogan on 8 June and relayed a message similar to the one Campbell had reported. He commented on the air raids, which did not do a great deal of damage, but had a considerable effect on the morale of the population. 'A state of lawlessness was growing up which was made still worse by the economic situation.' Essential goods were lacking. 'At the same time the hatred of the Japanese was growing which might at any moment lead to grave incidents, rendering the position of the local authorities extremely difficult.'

There were some Australian forces in the hills, apparently still disciplined under an Australian commander. They seemed to possess 'fairly adequate armament' and apparently received some help from the white Portuguese population. They were, however, short of supplies, in particular of drugs, and had no chance of early reinforcement.

The Japanese, Monteiro continued, had insufficient forces to establish themselves.

---

[98] Ross to Governor, 21 May 1942, in DAPE:XI,104–105; Callinan (1953:70–71).
[99] FO 371/31733 [F4226/2/61]: Minute, 8 June 1942.

Their discipline was not good. They were apt to indulge in acts of violence, and they showed a growing indignation against the Portuguese, because they were inclined to attribute to the latter their lack of success against the remaining Australian forces.

But they had sufficient war material and could be readily reinforced.

The ambassador then gave an account of Ross's letter to the Governor. The Portuguese Government, he said, had taken no action, 'as they did not consider that any initiative rested with them'. The Governor had taken 'soundings', but the results were not encouraging. 'On the one hand the Australians indicated that they were not disposed to surrender, and on the other hand the Japanese claimed that it was only a matter of time before they reduced the whole island.' A further note had now been received from Ross, repeating his proposal, and on 5 June the Governor asked for instructions.

His Government, Monteiro said, was anxious to know the views of the British Government. '[I]f the situation were allowed to drift the prospect was hopeless'. Life in Timor would become 'more disorganised' and the Australians could not hold out 'indefinitely'. If the British Government was prepared to approve, 'the Portuguese Government would be prepared to do what might be possible with the Japanese Government'. It could suggest 'a suspension of hostilities (which would of course include suspension of our air raids on the island)' and withdrawal of Japanese troops from Dili.

> At the same time they would endeavour to arrange that the Japanese should withdraw to Dutch Timor, and the Australians be handed over for internment. He added that if the Portuguese troops at present in Timor were not sufficient, his Government would be ready to reinforce them, provided that hostilities were suspended.[100]

Eden saw 'little advantage' in the proposals, but thought it mainly a matter for the military authorities and for the Australians.[101] The DO told the Australian Government that the Portuguese were clearly trying to make an arrangement at Allied expense in the hope of getting rid of the Japanese. Its sources suggested that Ross, 'evidently in Japanese hands', was not a free agent. What reply should be sent? The DO could offer no comment, but

---

[100] FO 371/31733 [F4298/2/61]: Minute by Cadogan, 8 June 1942.
[101] FO 371/31733 [F4298/2/61]: Note on Cadogan's minute, 9 June 1942

expressed 'admiration for the determined resistance' the Australian force was offering.[102]

The Portuguese proposal was discussed with General Douglas MacArthur (Supreme Allied Commander South-West Pacific) and the Australian Chiefs of Staff, the Australian Government replied. There were some 400 Australians and 200 Dutch in Portuguese Timor; they had sufficient food and plenty of drugs; they had help from Portuguese subjects and 'the natives, the majority of whom are loyal to the Allies'; and they had secret means of communication with Australia. Ross was in Japanese hands. In March the Japanese, misleading him as to the state of the troops, sent him to convey a request for surrender. It was unlikely, whatever arrangements were made, that the Japanese would withdraw and it would be 'undesirable to make any arrangement which would or might be understood to preclude the Allies from using Portuguese Timor now or in the future for operations against the Japanese'. MacArthur had considered both plans to attack Timor and plans to withdraw Allied forces. The former proved 'impracticable', but there were 'manifold advantages' in the presence of the Allied forces. They would be supplied in the hope that they could continue their activities until an attack was launched. If not, it was likely that they could be evacuated. The Australian Government was therefore not prepared to negotiate.[103]

The British COS concurred with this view. The FO was not certain that Ross was in Japanese hands,[104] but in replying to the Portuguese Ambassador it seemed suitable to say so.[105] That made it easier to suggest that his statements on the position of the Australian troops could not be relied upon. Australian and Dutch forces appeared indeed to be offering 'a gallant and valuable resistance'. Even if the Japanese did agree to withdraw, 'there would be no guarantee that they would refrain from a new invasion after a short period'. Britain shared Portugal's desire to see law and order restored, but that could not be brought about until Japan was defeated.[106] Cadogan spoke to Monteiro along those lines on 29 June.[107]

Ross was in fact confined to his residence. A new Japanese Consul summoned him and said the Japanese commander had decided to give the

---

[102] FO 371/31733 [F4298/2/61]: Telegram, 10 June.1942, 456.
[103] FO 371/31734 [F4519/2/61]: Telegram, 18 June 1942, 335; also in CAB 121/772.
[104] FO 371/31734 [F4459/2/61]: Minute by Foulds, 18 June 1942.
[105] FO 371/31734 [F4519/2/61]: Minute by Broad, 24 June 1942.
[106] FO 371/31734 [F4519/2/61]: Clarke to Holmes, 1 July 1942.
[107] FO 371/31734 [F4651/2/61]: Clarke to Holmes, 1 July 1942; see also Monteiro to MFA, Telegram, 29 June 1942, 252, in DAPE:XI,131.

Australians another chance to surrender. He was given a signed undertaking, dated 17 June, promising they would be given proper treatment as prisoners-of-war (Callinan 1953:133–134). At the end of June, the military authorities in Darwin received a message from him. Since the occupation of Dili, he said, he had been 'close prisoner in house which has been looted by Japanese soldiers' and 'half starved' owing to the lack of food and the refusal of the Japanese to 'allow servants search for food in surrounding country'. The Japanese suggested that he might convey to the Australian Company a guarantee of proper treatment in the event of surrender, but

> I did not give any indication that I would return to Dili, but merely said that I would write and give the reply of the Australian Company. I do not intend returning for imprisonment in Dili and am writing to Japanese to give reply that Australians will not surrender.

Should he return to Australia, he asked, or become a fugitive in Timor in the hope that the Japanese might evacuate the capital?[108] The Australian Government gave him permission to return to Australia, 'which Army state can be arranged'.[109] He returned on 10 July (Gunn 1988:fn17).

Back in Australia Ross gave an account of the period following the Japanese landing on 19 February. The Dutch unit, 'mostly natives', had retreated into the mountains 'and gradually disintegrated'. The Australians' ambushes and raids were so successful that the Japanese were now 'practically confined' to Dili. Through Ross, they had asked the Australians to surrender, but as the force was substantially intact, 'had proved its superiority to the Japanese on each occasion when (contact) was made', and was well supplied with ammunition and food, surrender was not considered. Communication was established with Australia and supplies sent in by boat.

Before the Japanese arrived, the Australian troops made friends with the natives. 'Nothing was obtained from them without payment, they were not ill treated in any respect and to their greatest wonder were [treated?] as human beings and their salutations acknowledged and returned.' The troops could not have continued as a fighting unit 'without help of all Portuguese officers in interior and friendship and admiration of the natives'. The few young officials were Fascists, but the older ones 'not wholly in sympathy with the Salazar regime'. The bulk of the Portuguese population, consisting of political

---

[108] Shedden to Hodgson, 28 June 1942, in AFPD:V,857–858.
[109] FO 371/31734 [F4991/2/61]: Minister to Bruce, telegram, 8 July 1942.

deportees and retired officials, was 'friendly almost without exception'. The Japanese, by contrast, behaved like animals, stealing 'everything of value', molesting women. As a result, neither Portuguese officials in the interior nor natives 'could do enough for an Australian soldier'. The Australians were supplied with free food, transport and personal service, and with information of any Japanese movement outside Dili. The Japanese would be able to clear them out only with heavy reinforcement and at the cost of severe casualties. Dr Evatt, the Minister for External Affairs, thought Ross's report 'most heartening from the point of view of future offensives against Japanese-occupied islands north of Australia'.[110]

Salazar spoke to Campbell in September. The Japanese had accused the Governor of favouring the Australian forces and had finally taken over the radio station and prevented his sending more messages. In Lisbon they had made it known that they had had to send additional forces. Presumably, Salazar said, they must by now have requisitioned all stocks and trade must be at a standstill. 'Things could not go on like that; something must be done, but what? It was even impossible to send a ship to Timor without passing through several belligerent zones, nor could any ship make the double voyage without refuelling.' Salazar 'seemed at a complete loss' and 'made no concrete suggestion'. He did disclose that when Portugal suggested the withdrawal of the Allied remnants to Dutch Timor if the Japanese withdrew from Portuguese Timor, 'the Japanese as well as we had refused to consider it'.[111]

The Australian guerrillas were finally evacuated from the south coast in January 1943 (Jolliffe 1978:46). They were 'no longer serving any effective purpose' (Callinan 1953:214). Their endeavours were, however, to be utilised in their country's endeavours to assert a role in the area at the end of the war and to form something of a legendary background to its later involvement in the fate of Timor. The help they received also gave the East Timorese 'a special place in Australian affections' (Farram 2004:186), especially after the publication in 1953 of Bernard Callinan's book about the forces he led. But the cost to them was very great, and increased by Allied bombing and Japanese brutality, and their sacrifice was redeemed neither by the Australian Government in 1975, nor indeed by Callinan himself, who ruled out a mediation among the contending Timorese parties when it was suggested by some of the veterans of the 2/4th (Scott 2005:66–67).

---

[110] FO 371/31734 [F5780/2/61]: DEA to HC, 7 August 1942, S.L.47.
[111] FO 371/31734 [F6422/2/61]: Telegram, 7 September 1942, 346S.

Chapter Three

Wartime Negotiations

To deal with the threat of U-boats in the Atlantic, the Allies sought the use of bases, not by seizing them, but by negotiating with the Portuguese for them. Evoking the ancient alliance, Salazar agreed so far as Britain was concerned. He secured assurances over the future of Portugal's colonies and indicated that, when the time came, he wished to participate in operations to oust the Japanese from Timor, the only colony in enemy occupation. The Australians agreed, at the same time suggesting staff conversations on the common defence of the area and a trade and aviation agreement. In mind was the larger interest the Australian Government took in the future of the region, subsequently also manifest in the Australia–New Zealand agreement of 1944. The United States was slow to respond to Salazar's wish to take part in the military planning for operations against the Japanese in Timor. He himself indicated that he hoped to get the Japanese out by negotiation particularly because, if he went to war, they might take vengeance on Macau. The Americans wanted to build a large airport on Santa Maria in the Azores. Salazar proposed an exchange of notes under which the granting of facilities there would represent Portugal's indirect contribution to the war in Asia, just as participation would be its direct contribution. He thus hoped to establish his claim to the recovery of Timor, even if the Portuguese took no part in military operations. In 1945 he became apprehensive that they would not have the chance. And the Australians declined to train and maintain the 4,000 Portuguese troops required, just as they had withdrawn their agreement for Dutch troops and advisers to go to Australia to be on hand for the recovery of Netherlands India.

The Azores Agreement of 1943

As the Second World War continued, Timor's fate continued to be affected by events in the West as well as in the East, since the interests of the Allies and their opponents abutted on Portuguese dependencies in the Atlantic. Indeed the Allies' need for mid-Atlantic bases grew as time went on. In 1942 a major danger area for their shipping emerged north of Azores, where U-boats were out of reach of aircraft, and later in the year another developed in the South Atlantic. Based in Terceira in the central Azores, Allied bombers would be able to intersect the patrol area, permit convoys to route further south and facilitate attacks on submarines in the Bay of Biscay. The Trident Conference in Washington in May 1943 decided on occupation by a British force the following month. Cadogan advised Eden: 'we might ask Salazar for facilities, but must *not* seize them' (quoted in Wigg 2005:97). The British decided to approach the Portuguese Government and Roberts went to Lisbon.

On 23 June Salazar agreed in principle to provide Britain with bases and to allow all Allied war and merchant ships to refuel in the Azores. The agreement would be based on the ancient treaty and Allied nations other than Britain would not enjoy full facilities until Portugal entered the war. Churchill told President Roosevelt that the Portuguese might eventually waive that limitation. He suggested that he should be authorised to promise that the United States, like the United Kingdom, should give Salazar assurances over the future of the Portuguese colonies. Salazar was also promised fighter aircraft and anti-aircraft guns and told that the Allies would declare war on Spain if it attacked Portugal. The agreement was concluded on 17 August and took effect on 8 October. British forces landed in the Azores on 10 October 1943 (Toynbee 1956:336–337).

Salazar indicated that he did not want to be drawn into the war if it could be avoided, but he made an exception over Timor: 'Whenever the United Nations had a plan for liberating the Archipelago he would wish Portugal to participate in the operation to oust the Japanese from Portuguese Timor.'[1] Churchill declared that the agreement in no way affected Portugal's policy of preserving its neutrality on the mainland. The Portuguese declared that their neutrality had always been conditional on Britain's right to invoke the alliance and they had explained that to the Spaniards. Salazar's address to the Assembly on 26 November stressed the British guarantees, especially noting that some British dominions had associated themselves with the United Kingdom in promising respect for Portugal's sovereignty throughout its empire. A German spokesman protested, but no action ensued (Toynbee 1956:338–339).

Among those Commonwealth governments were South Africa and Australia. A British aide-memoire of July 1943 had pointed out to the latter

---

[1] CAB 121/772 [160]: Telegram to Washington, 12 October 1943, 6910.

that recent Allied successes, particularly in North Africa, had removed the threat that Germany would invade Spain and Portugal. The United Kingdom had therefore approached Portugal for permission to use the Azores as a base for Allied ships and planes operating against German U-boats. In return it had offered a guarantee of Portugal's sovereignty over its colonies post-war. Portugal agreed, on the understanding that it would take part in operations to drive the Japanese from Timor, and that Australia should, 'if it is considered requisite', give a guarantee of Portugal's eastern colonies.[2]

Churchill and Eden both expressed anxiety that Australia should co-operate and Evatt, as Minister for External Affairs, indicated 'our general willingness to do so. The military significance of the Azores is of course very great'. But the proposal might offer

> a good opportunity to discuss the future of Portuguese Timor. Our giving a guarantee of retention of sovereignty over Portuguese Timor means no more than we should be prepared or have to do in any case. It does not affect defence control or economic arrangements.

He had replied that Australia would participate in the guarantee of sovereignty if the Portuguese pressed for it. Portugal should denounce continued Japanese occupation 'as soon as reasonably possible', and agree to participate in operations to expel the Japanese from Timor. Evatt continued:

> We also think that the Portuguese Government should recognize Australia's fight to preserve the integrity of Timor against Japanese aggression and should indicate its readiness to enter into negotiations with Australia both in relation to the inclusion of Portuguese Timor into an Australian defence zone, and also with a view to closer transport, trade and economic relations with Australia.[3]

Curtin agreed there was a favourable opportunity to secure 'special rights'. Success or failure would depend on presentation:

> We must be careful not to treat it in a manner which would give the Portuguese an excuse for hesitation and delay, with consequent prejudice not only to the immediate question of the Azores, but to our ultimate

---

[2] Aide-memoire, 1 July 1943, summarised in AFPD:VI,443n.
[3] Evatt to Curtin, 1 July 1943, EC 27 in AFPD:VI,443–444.

plans. We should endeavour to obtain Portuguese agreement in principle now to common defence measures which may be later expanded.

Assurances to Portugal should be coupled with the suggestion of staff conversations on the common defence of the area, and the desirability of a general commercial agreement, covering air communications as well, borne in mind.[4]

In late June Roosevelt had told Churchill he was happy with the way things were going with Portugal:

> The thought has come to me that if any question arises in regard to Timor, Australia might be interested in purchasing it in the interest of the defense of the South West Pacific. I think it has never brought the Portuguese Government any interest on the investment.

But the question could be left till the war was over. 'The same thing applies to Macau.'[5]

The Prime Minister agreed. 'Meanwhile we have told the Portuguese that if they help us now we are ready to give them assurances regarding maintenance of Portuguese sovereignty over all Portuguese colonies', including Timor and Macau.

> The Portuguese would therefore probably resent any early suggestions concerning the disposal of Timor and we shall have to tread warily. They are particularly touchy about Timor in view of Allied military occupation without prior agreement in December 1941 which imposed a severe strain upon our relations with Portugal.[6]

Salazar had looked for an assurance from the Australians as well. That was forthcoming, as the British Chargé in Lisbon told him in September. ''They… added that the maintenance of such Portuguese sovereignty is of particular importance to Australia because of the proximity of Timor, where Australian troops have been giving their lives in the struggle against Japanese invaders.' They noted 'with great satisfaction' Portugal's wish that its troops should take part in the operations eventually undertaken to oust the Japanese. As

---

[4] Curtin to Evatt, 3 July 1943, L53 in AFPD:VI,445–446.
[5] CAB 121/772 [151]: Roosevelt to Churchill, 22 June 1943, T 867/3.
[6] CAB 121/772 [152]: Churchill to Roosevelt, 27 June 1943, 331.

for the future, they hoped for staff conversations on concerted measures for the defence of Timor and Australia against aggression. They also hoped for a general commercial agreement covering air communications.[7]

Salazar accepted the Australian ideas 'with pleasure'. Given the lack of progress in his negotiations with the Japanese Government and the consequent need to consider taking part in the eventual operations, he wanted to know how the question could be discussed and with whom.[8] As Roosevelt was informed, the question was referred in October to the COS.[9] The COS considered the matter very slowly. Only in December was the FO able to suggest to the United States a reply welcoming early staff conversations in order to draw up a plan of Portuguese co-operation in the war against Japan, to be held in London.[10]

An early declaration of war might be more difficult to secure than the COS thought, Campbell commented. 'When the Japanese overwhelmed the Allied force in Timor, the Portuguese submitted to *force majeure*. There was nothing else they could do.' A row with the Japanese would have led to the seizure of Macau and possibly submarine attacks off Moçambique. The Portuguese resolved to do what they could by negotiation to restrain Japanese interference with the local administration and 'mitigate the evils of the occupation until the tide turned'. They had little success. There were 'vague assurances' from Tokyo, but the Japanese forces made it impossible for the Governor to carry out his functions and 'perpetrated their usual barbarities on the population'. The Government at home sought to hide the truth, lest the situation should be aggravated by popular indignation.[11]

Campbell continued:

> When, recently, our military successes justified the belief that the war in Europe might be over before very long, after which our united efforts would be concentrated against Japan, Salazar thought the time had come to talk to us about Portugal joining in the recapture of Portuguese Timor and thus redeeming the national honour.

He had not yet had an answer. Meanwhile Japanese atrocities had become known 'and the Government allowed it to leak out that they were

---

[7] CAB 121/772 [153]: Hopkinson to Salazar, 14 September 1943.
[8] CAB 121/772 [155]: Telegram from Campbell, 5 October 1943, 2026.
[9] CAB 121/772 [160]: Telegram, 12 October 1943, 6910.
[10] FO 371/39586 [C1788/89/36]: Minute by MS Williams, 3 February 1944.
[11] FO 371/39586 [C281/89/36]: Campbell to Eden, 24 December 1943, Personal and Secret.

contemplating strong measures against Japan', confirmed by his recent speech in the National Assembly. His remarks in the Assembly, however,

> were so worded as not to give the impression that action of any kind was imminent. One reason for this was that the Germans had made clear to him at the time of the Azores operation that, whilst they might swallow this as something which the Portuguese could not help, they would be less lenient towards a Portuguese declaration of war on Japan.

An early declaration of war would risk losing Macau, but

> also bring Germany's wrath down on his head…Not only is Salazar more impressed than we by Germany's capacity to take it out on him in some way or another, but I believe it still to be his aim to maintain the best relations possible with Germany up to the end of the war if he can do so.

That would justify his policy of neutrality; 'There is no question of Salazar "climbing onto the band-wagon". The essence of his policy is independence and non-subservience to any other, including the Allied, Power. He is firmly determined not to become a pawn in anybody else's game'.

Events might be too much for him 'and no doubt we can apply a bit of pressure', telling him, for example, 'that it does not suit us that he should come in at the precise moment which suits *him*, and if he wants the eventual glory of sharing in the recapture of Timor he must come in when it suits *us*'. The operation to eject the Japanese might be nearer than Campbell thought likely. But unless that were so, Salazar would be found 'very reluctant to jump into war *prematurely*'.

MS Williams of the Central Department thought there was 'great force' in what Campbell wrote, but it was suggested to the COS (Colonel Price) that he might be 'overlooking the fact that we would actually be responding to an original proposal from Dr Salazar himself, when he asked last June for staff conversations with a view to participation in operations for the recovery of Timor'. No doubt he would be reluctant to come into the war if operations were not immediately in prospect. But 'our means of persuasion may be somewhat stronger than the Ambassador suggests' and pressure should be applied:

> The guarantee that we have given of Portuguese colonial possessions need not deter us from making it clear to the Portuguese that, so far as Timor is concerned, it clearly must be considered conditional upon the Portuguese

themselves doing everything possible to defend, protect and recover their own colonial territory. In short it seems to us that in this matter it is not we who are asking a favour of the Portuguese and we should therefore be able to lay down the conditions on which we will agree to help them.[12]

The Australian Government feared that it was being by-passed. Yet for it Timor was only part of a larger concept, in some ways echoing security notions of the 'Near North' held as far back as the 1880s (Dalziel 1975:98,114). Australians, Evatt had declared in October 1943, had to show 'a particular interest in the welfare and system of control of these islands that lie close to our shores. From the point of view of defence, most of them can be fairly described as coming within an extended Australian zone.' He alluded to New Caledonia and Timor. 'The island in enemy hands is a constant threat to Australia. If properly placed within a zone of Australian security, it would become bastion of our defence' (quoted in Hastings 1975:328).

In December 1942 Sir Ronald Cross, the British High Commissioner in Australia, had reported 'grandiose ideas', such as the future of the East Indies under an Australian-led condominium. In January 1943 Dr Evatt told him that 'he was anxious that we should not tie our hands much at this stage'. He had Netherlands India in mind: 'he was thinking of an economic and political participation in those territories'. In late 1943 and early 1944 he tried to prevent Hubertus van Mook coming out to Australia as Lieutenant Governor-General of the Indies—'most embarrassing' at a time when he had in mind a long lease of Dutch Timor and New Guinea (Thorne 1988:110). The Australians were concerned lest the United States pre-empted decision-making about the region and the Cairo conference in December 1943 did nothing to reduce their anxiety. As Thorne (1978:366) puts it, 'where the future of the South and Southwest Pacific was concerned...concern was all the greater as a result of Australia's own ambitions'.

The Australian Government thus expressed its regret that the United Kingdom had not consulted it before suggesting to the United States the proposed communication to Portugal over Timor. It recalled the arrangement made in July 1943 between Churchill, Eden, Attlee and Evatt in relation to the protection of Australian post-war interests in Timor, 'including defence, trade and communications. We cannot forget that no assistance whatever was received by us from Portugal at the crucial time and even if Portugal now proposes to engage in active combat with Japan the arrangement made

---

[12] FO 371/39586 [C281/89/36]: Roberts to Price, 25 January 1944.

is necessary to protect our interests.' A phrase in the communication that referred to 'the liberation of Timor' might suggest to the United States 'an absolute restoration of Portuguese sovereignty without any of the necessary qualifications or addenda. Presumably Australia's special interests, having already been made clear to the Portuguese, will be made equally clear to the United States Government.'[13] Cranborne thought the United States would be aware of Australia's interests, since the correspondence had been included in the documents attached to the Azores agreement. The 'brief phrase' on Timor could not lead to any misunderstanding.[14]

At this time Evatt was getting ready to welcome a New Zealand delegation, headed by Prime Minister Peter Fraser, though he had not revealed his agenda. Evatt was in fact seeking to limit the post-war role of the Americans in the Pacific: it would be well if they controlled the former Japanese mandates, the Caroline and Marshall islands, but Australia should establish a sphere of influence south of the Equator, 'taking over British colonies in the western Pacific and assuming undefined security responsibilities even over Portuguese Timor and the Netherlands East Indies', as Gerald Hensley (2009:282) puts it. The meeting was designed to win New Zealand's support. The approach did not help, but there was in any case a difference of emphasis. New Zealand had no wish to exclude the British or to rely only on the Australians, though it did agree to a clause in the agreement that was made, asserting, with an eye to the Americans, that, 'as a recognized principle of international practice', the construction or use of bases in territory held by another power 'does not, in itself, afford any basis for territorial claims or rights of sovereignty or control after the conclusion of hostilities' (quoted in McIntyre and Gardner 1971:371).

The two Dominions, moreover, announced that no change should be made to the control of any Pacific islands without their concurrence—'an unblushing Monroe Doctrine', as a State Department official put it (Hensley 2009:291). The State Department, said Cordell Hull, the Secretary of State, was 'almost flabbergasted' (McLean 2003:135). They also agreed that Australia should call a conference for 'a frank exchange of views' on the Pacific, including the United States, the United Kingdom, the Netherlands, the French National Committee (Free French) and Portugal. Evatt, moreover, insisted that the agreement should be published, even though the United Kingdom was not consulted. That was not vanity. He wanted to make sure the United States

---

[13] CAB 121/772 [173]: Telegram, 2 January 1944, 2; also in AFPD:VII,1.
[14] CAB 121/772 [173]: Telegram, 7 January 1944, 12; also in AFPD:VII,21–22.

did not ignore Australia's views (McLean 2003:294). It was a proclamation. The first news he had of the Cairo conference, he told the Americans, was in the press.[15]

The discussion between the United Kingdom and United States Chiefs of Staff on possible staff conversations with Portugal had meanwhile reached no conclusion. The American chiefs of staff did not agree with the British that a Portuguese declaration of war was necessarily an advantage. It might, Admiral Leahy believed, lead to a call to support Portugal against Germany. Admiral King thought that, if the Portuguese declared war on Japan, Japan would ask Germany to take some action against Portugal and 'embarrassing demands' for assistance would ensue.[16] The British Embassy in Washington expected a further delay before a decision was reached. Meanwhile there had been several reminders from the Portuguese, who, 'while not seeming very anxious to participate in the Far Eastern war in the immediate future', did want to know where they stood. 'They also held some abortive discussions with the Japanese in an endeavour to reach an agreement with them.' Perhaps, Williams suggested, they should have an interim reply. Since their request was made in October, moreover, the Australia–New Zealand agreement had been announced and it provided for co-operation with the Dutch and Portuguese in matters of defence, economic and political developments and civil aviation, and the calling of a conference. 'From the Portuguese point of view such co-operation, both during and after the war, would seem likely to be easier if Portugal became a full belligerent.' There was no point in giving Salazar a sense of grievance, Roberts added. The agreement, which had been published, would have 'stimulated his interest'.[17]

The Combined Staff Planners reached an impasse late in February. The Americans thought there was no military advantage in the Far East in a Portuguese declaration; that conversations would lead to a discussion of United States/United Kingdom Far Eastern strategy 'with great risk of compromise'; and that operations against Timor formed no part of any present plan and could be dealt with only 'when the strategical situation is ripe, which is not now'. Negotiations over extending facilities in the Azores to the United States should come first. The Americans were saying in effect: 'if you give us facilities in the Azores we will then consider the question of your Far Eastern Colonies'. The British argued that the best way to hasten

---

[15] Evatt to Johnson, 24 February 1944, in AFPD:VII,126.
[16] FO 371/39586 [C2063/89/36]: CCS (44) 143rd, 28 January 1944, 6.
[17] FO 371/39586 [C2063/89/36]: Minutes, 3 February 1944.

the Azores negotiations was 'to evince interest in Portugal's Far Eastern possessions by agreeing to Staff conversations'. That argument cut no ice with the Americans; they feared it would lead to demands for equipment and to 'interminable delays' over the Azores.

> The unfortunate fact is that the military arguments are not sufficiently strong to convince the Americans, or indeed, if truth be told, to convince us, that on military grounds…a declaration of war by Portugal on Japan would be of any value to them except in so far as it assists in the Azores.

Even if they secured their facilities in the Azores, they did not consider that they should press Portugal to declare war or even suggest it. 'They will go no further than non-committal Staff conversations on the occupation of Timor.' They would not object to a Portuguese declaration if it were 'spontaneous', since that would relieve the Allies of any obligations.[18]

'They must be mad', Eden wrote in the margin. 'This all seems to me completely crazy', he expostulated, 'I am not surprised that our military operations are so ill executed if these are the folk who plan them. It is clearly to our advantage that Portugal should be at war with Japan.' He asked the Department to look at it.[19] Williams pointed out that back in June 1943 Salazar had himself indicated a wish to take part and that the FO had passed on Australia's expression of satisfaction. The initiative was thus Portugal's. The offer of staff conversations would involve no obligation to supply equipment or any other aid. 'On the contrary we can hope for valuable additional help from the Portuguese Government such as bases in Portuguese East Africa and possibly in the Cape Verde Islands.' The United States apparently considered that any communication on Timor should follow satisfaction on the Azores, and the Portuguese, it seemed, the reverse. The solution was simple:

> we should immediately inform the Portuguese Government in very general terms that we welcome the prospect of eventual Portuguese entry into the war against Japan or if the Americans prefer it, in the operations for the recapture of Timor and that we will make practical proposals concerning staff talks as soon as practicable.[20]

---

[18] FO 371/39587 [C2794/89/36]: Telegram from JSM, 25 February 1944, 1537.
[19] FO 371/39587 [C2794/89/36]: Note, 27 February 1944.
[20] FO 371/39587 [C2794/89/36]: Minute, 29 February 1944.

Roberts thought that solution might meet the 'difficulties' the Far Eastern Department felt.[21] In fact, as Ashley Clarke put it, it agreed 'to a considerable extent' with the Combined Staff Planners. It had always deprecated pressing the Portuguese to declare war on Japan. The 'ostensible advantages'— the propaganda effect, the withdrawal of the Japanese Minister from Lisbon—were of little value and, from a military point of view, Portuguese participation would be 'a liability and not an asset'. Macau would go, 'and if we press Portugal to come in we should be involved in obligations to recover it eventually, perhaps from the Chinese'. Finally, the Department did not believe 'that any serious agreement could be reached between the Portuguese and the Japanese'. If, however, agreeing to the Portuguese request would secure important advantages in Europe, such as new bases in the Cape Verde islands or in Portugal itself, the Department had always agreed that its objections should be 'overridden'. It agreed with Williams' suggestion.[22]

The Americans changed their views during April, perhaps with the approach of D-Day, the invasion of Europe, and the Combined Chiefs of Staff (CCOS) decided to recommend welcoming 'any voluntary step taken by Portugal to become an active ally in the war against Japan and also in the war against the European Axis'. There was no military objection to Portuguese participation in 'any eventual operation to liberate Portuguese Timor', but a definite commitment on that question required preliminary staff conferences for the discussion of logistical and other problems in detail. Those might be held in Lisbon with the participation of military representatives under the direction of the British and American ambassadors. Portugal's most important immediate contribution to the war with Japan and the liberation of Timor would be granting additional facilities in the Azores.[23] The belated decision of the CCOS came at an inconvenient time, RL Speaight commented at the FO, which was planning to put strong pressure on Salazar over his failure to restrict the supplies of wolfram to Germany.[24] It was a 'most inopportune' moment for responding to 'Salazar's long outstanding request'.[25]

The British had been informed through MAGIC intercepts of Portuguese discussions with the Japanese Government, but the Portuguese themselves also relayed some information. In March 1944 Monteiro had told Cadogan

---

[21] FO 371/39587 [C2794/89/36]: Minute, 29 February 1944.
[22] FO 371/39587 [C2794/89/36]: Minute, 1 March 1944.
[23] FO 371/39587 [C5786/89/36]: Telegram from JSM, 29 April 1944, 26.
[24] FO 371/39587 [C5786/89/36]: Minute, 3 May 1944.
[25] FO 371/39587 [C7535/89/36]: Minute by Speaight, 20 May 1944.

that they had reached agreement on a visit of inspection by a Portuguese official from Macau. 'The Portuguese were resolved to state as their minimum demand to the Japanese that the latter should evacuate Timor and hand over full administration to Portuguese authorities'. Monteiro said he thought that his Government 'must be aware that this could not possibly lead to any agreement'. He was 'probably right', Cadogan reflected.[26]

The Portuguese Government, Campbell had reported early in April, was 'keenly anxious to uphold the national honour and dignity by participating, if only more or less symbolically, in any operations for the reconquest of Portuguese Timor'. Such participation, 'assuming that the Japanese wait to be ejected', would have no value except, perhaps, in respect of knowledge of the terrain. Satisfying the desire would be a favour that Britain and the United States 'would be more than justified in the present circumstances either in shattering altogether or in exploiting to their advantage'. The 'boldness' with which the Portuguese displayed in their initial approach had 'fizzled out' and there was evidence that they were 'wondering whether they could not achieve their aim without a declaration of war against Japan'. Probably, Campbell thought, the Germans had warned them that they would regard it as a hostile act against them, too, and unless that were 'merely bluff', it would involve a rupture or even a war with Germany. In any case, Campbell thought, Salazar would not contemplate a declaration of war on Japan at the present juncture. Even in his bolder moments, he probably did not think of doing it 'earlier than on the eve of operation against Timor'. A German warning, bluff or not, was enough to intimidate him. He would not commit himself without staff conversations and an agreement of some sort and the American Ambassador, Henry Norweb, had put it into his head that operations against Japan might by-pass Timor. So using Timor to secure the stoppage of wolfram was excluded for the time being.[27]

When the moment was ripe Salazar might be told that his proposal of participation was accepted, 'that we are ready to discuss ways and means', that his government could not be admitted into discussing secret Allied plans unless it promised to declare war on Japan at the moment the United States and United Kingdom deemed appropriate—presumably after the opening of the Second Front—and that he would have to sever relations at least with Germany at the same time. The time for such a communication might be after the commission sent to Timor had made its report. If that led to Japanese withdrawal, Salazar 'might jump at it and ground would be cut from under our feet'. But it was

---

[26] FO 371/39587 [C3347/89/36]: Minute, 10 March 1944.
[27] DO 35/1718 [37]: Telegram, 8 April 1944, 618.

more likely to 're-inflame' his indignation against the Japanese.[28] Indeed the report Captain Silva Costa, the chief secretary at Macau, made after his one-week visit in March was very critical of the Japanese, who, he said, disregarded Portuguese rights. Timor, he added, had no military value for them, since operations against Australia were impossible (Goto 2003:36–37).

The threat to Macau and the Santa Maria facilities

Britain's attitude to the economic blockade on 'adjacent neutrals' changed during 1943 and 1944. By May 1944 its patience over Salazar's refusal to implement an embargo on wolfram exports was exhausted: 'The Allies were by this date no longer prepared to tolerate delays, refusals or compromises, when these might have a direct bearing on the conduct of decisive military operations' (Toynbee 1956:278). Salazar agreed to the embargo on 5 June, one day before D-Day.

The conversations on the Portuguese contribution against the Japanese should now begin, Campbell suggested.[29] The State Department agreed but wanted to avoid any connection between the Anglo–Portuguese Azores agreement and its negotiations over the Azores island of Santa Maria, where it was seeking to build an airport.[30] The FO undertook to eschew any reference to Santa Maria. Salazar would probably want to connect the Anglo–Portuguese agreement with the negotiations over Santa Maria, 'but we need not anticipate this in the original approach'. There were other facilities that could be 'obtained from Portuguese association with the war in the Far East, either directly, eg in Portuguese India and Portuguese East Africa, or indirectly through a more forthcoming Portuguese attitude in regard to any further requirements in the Azores'.[31]

The ever-observant Campbell presumed that it was not intended that the conversations should cover matters connected with the common defence of Timor, the desire to discuss which Australia had expressed when indicating its readiness to associate itself with the guarantee of Portuguese sovereignty at the times of the Azores agreement. 'This and kindred matters arising out of the Australian–New Zealand agreement of last January would seem to belong more properly to sphere of a general post-war settlement regarding

---

[28] DO 35/1718 [38]: Telegram, 8 April 1944, 619.
[29] FO 371/39587 [C7842/89/36]: Telegram, 9 June 1944, 1040.
[30] DO 35/1718 [74]: Memorandum, 20 June 1944.
[31] DO 35/1718 [86]:.Telegram, 26 June 1944, 5768.

international and regional security.' World opinion might oblige Portugal 'certain partial derogations of Sovereignty' after the war, but raising such matters now would complicate, if not prejudice, the staff conversations. If there were to be an Australian representative, he should avoid raising them.[32]

The DO told the Australians that the scope of the conversations would not cover 'common defence of Timor against future aggression', lest it prejudice their success. Campbell thought that they were most likely to succeed if he approached Salazar in the first instance as offering a response to his own request that his forces might take part in eventual operations against Timor and the conversations focused on the contribution they might make. He doubted if Salazar could be induced voluntarily to declare war or even break off relations much in advance of operations, and so thought that point should be 'kept in abeyance'.[33] On 7 July Campbell and Norweb called on Salazar. If he had received no reply on the matter he had raised in June the previous year, 'it was because it had been impossible to foresee the course which the war in the Far East might take'. Now that 'a general picture' could be formed, the United Kingdom and the United States wished to open military conversations on 'ways and means'.[34]

Salazar replied that he was 'ready, indeed anxious' to open military conversations, but that 'he must say quite frankly that he was still trying and would continue to try to get the Japanese out by agreement. He could not shut his eyes to the fact that Macau was held in forfeit.' Its population had swollen to 400,000, the majority Europeans (including Americans). 'War was going none too well in China and these people might soon be surrounded by the Japanese as well as hostile Chinese. Their fate if the Japanese indulged in a vengeance reprisal might be something too awful to contemplate.' He felt it incumbent on him to continue to try to negotiate for the evacuation of Timor. He recognised that preparing plans and training would take some time, however, 'and it would be well to be ready for every eventuality'. He would appoint a small delegation.[35]

Returning from a visit to Lisbon, Monteiro had on 3 July spoken to Eden about the Azores and also offered an expression of Salazar's 'real feelings' about the Far East. The Portuguese had 'no illusions' about the Japanese, and expected conversations with them to lead nowhere. 'The one factor which

---

[32] DO 35/1718 [80]: Telegram, 22 June 1944, 1103.
[33] DO 35/1718 [91]: Telegram, 5 July 1944, 984.
[34] FO 371/39588 [C9038/89/36]: Telegram, 8 July 1944, 1191.
[35] FO 371/39588 [C9039/89/36]: Telegram, 8 July 1944, 1192; see also Conversation, 7 July 1944, in DAPE:XI,304–307, and Telegram to Commonwealth of Australia, 12 July 1944, D1006, in AFPD:VII,446–447.

held the Portuguese Government back from breaking with the Japanese was the position at Macau.' There were now 200,000 refugees there, 'British, American, Indian, Chinese, etc. If Portugal broke with Japan, Macau would be occupied and all these people murdered.' Eden responded: 'Up to the present we had not asked the Portuguese to break with Japan'.[36]

'The Macau point seems to me very important at the present time', Churchill wrote. 'In fact it outweighs any advantage we could get from Portugal declaring war on Japan at this particular time…Are you not worrying too much about a Portuguese declaration of war, and are not the refugees at Macao more important?' he asked Eden.[37] Eden reassured him.[38]

Late in June 1944 Salazar had told Moroshima Morito, the Japanese Minister, that there was no longer any reason for the Japanese to hold Timor since they were on the defensive and it was not needed as a base for attacking Australia. If Britain and the United States attacked the Japanese forces in Timor, he added, Portugal would face a 'difficult international situation'. Japan, Moroshima replied, reserved its right to attack Australia. Even if Japan withdrew its forces, he doubted if the United States and Britain would respect Timor's neutrality.[39] Salazar, the Japanese thought, would soon propose talks on the withdrawal of their forces. A refusal might lead to a break with Portugal, especially if the Allies pressed Portugal to join in despatching troops (Gunn 1999:9).

In August 1944 Salazar told Moroshima that, when it obtained Azores base rights, Britain had renewed its obligation to protect the Portuguese colonies. He thought that the United States would send troops to Timor if Japan declined to withdraw and Portugal would not be able to look on 'with folded arms'. It wished to forestall the eventuality by coming to a prior arrangement with Japan. Moroshima advised his superiors to assent to withdrawal in principle, but not in practice, staging a withdrawal only ahead of the arrival of a Portuguese force, which could not arrive for a long time, if at all. The Japanese government ruled a deal out, though telling its ambassador not to make it appear that it was refusing Salazar's request (Gunn 1999:9–10).[40]

The following month Campbell reported that the United States Embassy in Lisbon had information that the Japanese Government had offered to withdraw from Timor if the Portuguese Government undertook not to

---

[36] DO 35/1718 [94]: Telegram to Lisbon, 4 July 1944, 955.
[37] FO 371/39588 [C9040/89/36]: Minutes by PM, 8, 10 July 1944.
[38] FO 371/39588 [C9040/89/36]: Minute, 17 July 1944.
[39] Record of Conversation, 26 June 1944, in DAPE:XI,296–301.
[40] Conversation, 8 September 1944, in DAPE:XI,319–22.

embark on a campaign to publicise atrocities.[41] MAGIC did not confirm that. '[A] most secret and reliable source', Campbell was told, 'indicated that the Japanese had told the Portuguese that they could not withdraw their troops nor agree to the despatch of Portuguese troops.' The Japanese Minister had been instructed 'to play for time', to say that his government wanted friendly relations, and that withdrawal was 'not impossible'.[42]

The United States Ambassador 'taxed' Salazar 'outright' with the 'rumour' of renewed negotiations. Salazar replied that he had 'quite recently' sent for the Japanese Minister and told him 'that the time had come when he must know where he stood one way or other'. Moroshima had taken the line 'that it was all very difficult but that he could be given a little time, he was not un-hopeful of inducing the Japanese to order the withdrawal of their forces'. The German Minister told Salazar that he understood that the Japanese Government was 'ready to be reasonable'. Did Salazar still want the staff talks to go ahead? Norweb asked. The reply was 'affirmative'.[43]

The Portuguese told the United States/United Kingdom delegation to the conversations that their government was negotiating for a Japanese withdrawal from Timor, allowing the Portuguese to reoccupy it. If that failed, the plan was to participate in United Nations operations and that participation formed the subject of the conversations.[44] The papers the Portuguese put forward at once raised what Campbell called 'a cardinal point of principle'. A Portuguese–Japanese agreement might be concluded on the eve of the joint operation against Timor:

> In other words we might have gone to the trouble, expense and diversion of effort involved in helping to transport and convoy the Portuguese contingent there only to find at the eleventh hour that the Japanese had offered withdrawal from the colony on condition that it would in no circumstances thereafter be placed at the disposal of the United Nations.

It was doubtful that the Portuguese–Japanese negotiations would produce a result, but the possibility could not be excluded. Did the Joint Chiefs of Staff want to take the risk? Or did they want to know where they stood before entering a commitment? If the point was allowed to go by and the

---

41 FO 371/39588 [C11968/89/36]: Telegram, 9 September 1944, 1544.
42 FO 371/39588 [C11968/89/36]: Telegram, 12 September 1944, 1248.
43 FO 371/39589 [C12300/89/36]: Telegram, 14 September 1944, 1568.
44 FO 371/39589 [C12445/89/36]: Telegram, 19 September 1944, 1610.

Portuguese and Japanese did reach an agreement, Salazar 'would be able to claim that we had acquiesced in his heads-I-win-tails-you-lose policy'. But if 'we force the issue', he might break off the negotiations with the United States and the United Kingdom 'rather than commit himself at this stage to a course of action which would ensure the failure of his negotiations with the Japanese in any circumstances'.[45]

'Dr Salazar, with his usual thoroughness, is seeking to provide for every possible contingency', IP Garran commented at the FO. A last-minute Japanese withdrawal was 'most unlikely'. At present the Japanese government ruled it out. If, under threat of Allied operations, it changed its policy, it would mean 'a considerable loss of face', and shipping difficulties would probably make it impossible to do more than withdraw the troops into West Timor. The Portuguese proposal, Garran thought, was, however, 'inspired principally by national pride' and the desire that Portuguese troops should recover Portuguese soil. If it were a matter only of liberating Portuguese Timor, Garran thought there would be 'no difficulty' in meeting Salazar's wishes. The question was bound up with that of Dutch Timor. Presumably bases in the East would be needed for operations in the West. The matter, Garran thought, should be settled, not allowed to slide, even though the United States Ambassador was insisting on remaining 'aloof'.[46]

Perhaps it was natural, Roberts suggested, for the Americans to try to brush the matter aside. They no doubt saw the conversations 'as merely a device to facilitate their obtaining later on whatever facilities they required from Portugal'. They were, too, 'probably quite ready to force the hand of the Portuguese and operate in Timor regardless of Portuguese wishes, if and when this becomes operationally desirable'. Britain could not take the matter 'so lightheartedly', if only because it had already landed in Timor once without Portuguese consent and to do so again would impose 'an altogether unnecessary strain on Anglo–Portuguese relations'. The answer to the Portuguese point would be obvious if Britain was determined to bring Portugal into the war 'at any cost'. But the Prime Minister and the Foreign Secretary had both taken the view that it would be a mistake to force Portugal into the war if the result were to precipitate the Japanese occupation of Macau.

> Furthermore we in the Foreign Office have no idea whether it is in fact ever proposed to operate in Timor, or whether our present strategy is

---

[45] FO 371/39589 [C12671/89/36]: Telegram, 22 September 1944, 1636.
[46] FO 371/39589 [C12671/89/36]: Minute, 25 September 1944.

simply to outflank Timor, both Portuguese and Dutch, and leave it to fall into our hands in due course.

He agreed with Garran. A formula could be agreed on. If the British forced Portugal into the war, Bennett noted, '[w]e should of course be incurring a possibly embarrassing moral obligation to re-instate Portugal in Macau'.[47]

The conversations suffered from 'a certain malaise', Campbell wrote. Not only was it a question of personalities. He and Ashley Clarke, now in Lisbon, were 'in some embarrassment due to the fog created by the number of imponderables and hypothetical circumstances that are obscuring the prospect, and by our ignorance indeed as to what we are really aiming at'. Coupled with 'the microscopic importance of the affair in relation to other events', that enveloped the proceedings in 'an aura of unreality'.

There was evidence that the Japanese were not sincere in their negotiations with the Portuguese, but they might agree

> to clear out on the eve of the operation (if there is one) on the condition that allied forces are not allowed in. It would be the clever thing to do and, stupid as the Japanese are, one cannot be sure that they will not occasionally do the clever thing, if only by accident. By doing so, they would both stand a good chance of creating another Timor incident and be able to concentrate all their forces in the Dutch end of the Island, which might be of some military advantage to them.

No Allied commander was likely to consent 'at the eleventh hour to hold his forces back and send in the Portuguese contingent alone with his love and good wishes'. But Campbell did not want his mission to end, as it began, with a Timor incident, and for the sake of Anglo–Portuguese relations it should be avoided, 'especially as the Americans…would shed no tears at the sight of Salazar's wrath descending once again on our heads'.

To ensure the avoidance of such an incident, Salazar might undertake not to accept

> a Japanese condition that, if they go out, we must not be allowed in. He could, I suppose, tell the Japanese bluntly that, if by a certain date they have not undertaken to go, he will consider himself free to take whatever measures he may consider necessary. But would he do so?

---

[47] FO 371/39589 [C12671/89/36]: Minute, 26 September 1944, and marginal note.

Campbell was not sure. He might prefer to break off the conversations, which 'would be a foolish attitude, but I am not certain that the lure of preserving his neutrality, which possesses him like a disease, would not weigh heavier with him than the advantage on the other side'.

The Ambassador was not certain what to advise 'without having some idea whether the Chiefs of Staff are prepared to face a certain diversion of effort in the knowledge that it might be thrown down the drain, and whether the Foreign Office are prepared to take the consequences in the event of a second Timor incident'. Perhaps it would be best to carry through the technical discussions 'so that at the proper time a single complete picture can be presented to the Chiefs of Staff who cannot be expected to give much attention to so unimportant a matter'.[48]

Formulae were found. Should they have taken over, the Portuguese would offer any base the Allies needed; they would assist against the Japanese if they were still in West Timor; and they would not maintain their neutrality after their forces had left Moçambique.[49] The assurances were satisfactory, Garran commented, and that solved the problem the Ambassador had raised.

The question remained, however, 'whether it would on balance be an advantage to get Portugal into the war with Japan on a voluntary basis', Garran pointed out. The conversations were undertaken on that assumption, but the world situation had changed. There would no longer any military advantage in it and the political advantages were 'somewhat intangible'. There was something to be said, as Campbell had suggested, 'for having as many colonial powers at the Far Eastern conference table as possible'. A Portuguese declaration of war would involve 'a considerable loss of face for the Japanese' and it might be followed by a rupture between them and the Spaniards, through which they would lose the rest of the observation posts on the Iberian Peninsula to which they attached 'inordinate importance'. A negative advantage would be that a declaration would avoid a second Timor incident. The Americans, Garran pointed out in conclusion, might try to precipitate a declaration if it would facilitate the attainment of their requirements regarding the aerodrome on Santa Maria in the Azores.[50]

During the Azores negotiations, Roberts recalled, the FO thought it would ease American–Portuguese relations and help the United States

---

[48] FO 371/39589 [C13151/89/36]: Campbell to Roberts, 23 September 1944, personal and secret.
[49] FO 371/39589 [C12897/89/36]: Telegram, 26 September 1944, 1665.
[50] FO 371/39589 [C 13151/89/56]: Minute, 3 October 1944.

obtain its requirements in the Azores if it responded to Salazar's wish to discuss ways and means of recovering Timor.

> At that time we thought on balance that it might even be advantageous for Portugal to come into the war, and that it would at least prevent the Americans from resorting to force to obtain their needs in the Azores. We always, however, insisted that a Portuguese entry into the war must be voluntary so that we could not be blamed for any resulting troubles in Macau.

The Service Departments also hoped for some facilities in Portuguese colonies in Africa and India.

The Service Departments in the United States and in the United Kingdom were slow in dealing with the matter. By the time they were ready to do so, 'the Americans had, thanks to us, obtained substantially all their requirements in the Azores. One of the main reasons for holding staff talks had therefore gone.' For 'some obscure reason', the Americans still wanted staff talks, and there was no reason for the British to oppose, especially as they were 'morally committed' to give Salazar an answer. Talks began as a result 'in an atmosphere of unreality, more particularly as by that time we had decided that there would be no advantage in bringing Portugal into the war if as a result she lost Macau, where there are several hundred thousand Chinese and European refugees', and it was also 'becoming unlikely that the early recovery of Timor would be a major factor in our Far Eastern strategy'.

The reply to Campbell, Roberts thought, should 'bring out this back history', and he should be told

> that we have no very strong views now as to whether Portugal comes into the war or not. We certainly do not wish to provoke the loss of Macau and we should ourselves much prefer any Portuguese decision to be reached entirely independently and not as a result of pressure from us. If, however, the Portuguese wish to declare war on Japan and do not call upon us to pay too heavy a price in the form of assistance, etc., then we should not wish to dissuade them. We shall, of course, know better where we stand when the staff talks are concluded and we can see what the Portuguese want from us and also what the Americans think.

The argument that it would be useful to have Portugal's voice at the conference had little weight, Roberts thought. Colonial questions, as distinct from military ones, would have to be settled in consultation with all the colonial powers, 'and that…is the point at which the Portuguese voice will be useful to us'.[51]

Bennett did not think the presence of Portugal at a Far Eastern conference would be advantageous:

> She may, of course, have to come in, so that she may be fitted into her place in any international security or economic arrangements. But it seems to me much better that she should not come in with the prestige [?] of a last-minute belligerent. I presume we do not want to get involved as between Portugal and China in the question of Macau. No doubt we may be brought into that question anyhow, but if Portugal became a belligerent we could hardly avoid it.[52]

The British COS had not gone back on their earlier decision to welcome any voluntary step the Portuguese took to become an active ally against Japan, observed Roger Allen, but he was 'pretty sure they would not be prepared to pay anything more for such participation than they may be prepared to pay for the ultimate recapture of Timor. And that will not be very much.' The American COS might have different ideas, perhaps thinking 'that Portuguese entry would help them to get what they want at Santa Maria'. If that situation developed, Allen wrote

> we must be on the lookout to see that the Portuguese do *not* try an appeal to use for protection against the Americans. If they do, a possible get-out might be for us to say that Timor is in an American theatre of operations, and it is not therefore primarily our concern whether Portugal comes into the war or not.

Nobody cared very much whether Portugal entered the war against Japan or not, he concluded, but it was in Britain's interest

> to ensure that the present discussions do not (a) land us in a military commitment which we are not prepared to undertake and (b) embroil us politically with either the Americans or the Portuguese owing to possible differences of view between ourselves and the Americans.[53]

---

[51] FO 371/39589 [C 13151/89/56]: Minute, 7 October 1944.
[52] FO 371/39589 [C 13151/89/56]: Minute, 9 October 1944.
[53] FO 371/39589 [C 13151/89/56]: Minute, 10 October 1944.

The United Kingdom did not get embroiled, but it did get involved. Late in July Salazar had allowed the Americans to land building materials for the airfield at Santa Maria, but not given permission to build (Toynbee 1956:340). They wanted him to agree, he said, that a larger airport should be constructed at Santa Maria than had originally been planned and that operational facilities should be granted direct to them. He resisted, even hinting that operational facilities would be under the Anglo–Portuguese agreement on the Azores. Learning that it was Britain's wish, however, he gave way. But he wanted to find a juridical basis for his action. That he found 'in the principle that the grant of operational facilities is to represent Portugal's *indirect* contribution to the Far Eastern war, as participation in the reconquest of Portuguese Timor would represent her *direct* contribution'. To obtain and put on record British and American acceptance of the principle, he put up a formula to be embodied in an exchange of notes. There would also be a United States–Portugal agreement over the construction and utilisation of the Santa Maria airfield.[54] According to his draft the United States would welcome Portugal's participation in operations 'to expel the Japanese from their territory with a view to its return to full Portuguese sovereignty', and recognised that it could be effected directly and indirectly. Indirect participation would be through conceding facilities in Santa Maria designed to facilitate the transit of American forces to and from the Pacific under a United States–United Kingdom–Portugal agreement.[55]

The Americans, Salazar told Campbell, had seemed

> incapable of grasping that it was not enough that he was bringing off a good 'deal' in getting an airfield on easy terms and that his sovereignty and neutrality were not for sale for all the dollars in the world. With more difficulty than he had known in teaching his most refractory pupils at Coimbra University he had at last convinced Mr Norweb and had thereafter succeeded with much trouble (for he was deficient in imaginative powers) in devising a formula which would enable him to meet the American requirements and would at the same time provide juridical basis which for him was a *sine qua non*.

He had also agreed to Norweb's request to allow work to start on bringing the airfield up to American requirements.

---

[54] FO 371/39590 [C13933/89/36]: Garran for Roberts to Hollis, 14 October 1944.
[55] FO 371/39589 [C13862/89/36]: Telegram, 11 October 1944, 1747.

Salazar wanted the United Kingdom to be associated in the arrangements for Portugal's indirect as well as direct participation in the war against Japan. It must have the right to share the Santa Maria facilities, just as the Americans were sharing the facilities in Terceira. 'He would not give in on this point and he looked to His Majesty's Government to back him up if the Americans made difficulties.' Campbell told Salazar that the formula seemed to meet the case and thought Britain would be able to accept it. Norweb had already told him he foresaw no difficulty in Britain's sharing the Santa Maria facilities.[56]

The exchange of notes, as Garran put it, would connect the questions of Timor and Santa Maria as parts of a single question, Portugal's participation in the Far Eastern war. Salazar would thus establish his claim to the recovery of Timor even if no operation for its liberation took place and also a claim to a seat at a Pacific peace conference. He recommended approving the proposal. Whether or not Portugal took part in the recovery of Portuguese Timor was 'presumably of little or no account from a military point of view', but United States use of Santa Maria was of urgent importance. Agreeing, Roberts added, would solve 'these ridiculous American–Portuguese quarrels'.[57]

The FO pointed out to the War Cabinet Offices that the solution would give the United States all it wanted on Santa Maria. 'As against this it involves accepting…Portuguese participation in any eventual operation which may take place against Portuguese Timor.' That had been envisaged in May, though the CCOS had not finally committed themselves pending the staff conversations, 'now…practically completed'. Could Britain now agree to the solution? Campbell recommended it and Norweb had recommended it to his government. The FO considered it 'entirely satisfactory'. The Chiefs of Staff agreed that Campbell should support it, but the Joint Staff Mission should point out to the CCOS that under the agreement Salazar would secure participation in some way or other in the Timor operation and that it might involve equipping his forces.[58]

Salazar had attempted to secure some additional 'economic and political assurances', including economic assistance over and above the current supply program, a promise that Portugal would have a place at the Pacific peace conference, the release of merchant shipping tonnage, arms and ammunition for the Portuguese army, and military and civil planes. The State Department

---

[56] FO 371/39589 [C13932/89/36]: Telegram, 12 October 1944, 1756.
[57] FO 371/39589 [C13865/89/36]: Minutes, 12 October 1944.
[58] FO 371/39590 [C14315/89/36]: Telegram to JSM, 16 October 1944, COS (W) 381.

was said to be 'astounded': the demands were 'little more than plain blackmail' and had to be resisted on principle, quite apart from the obvious absurdity of a neutral demanding a place with the victorious Allies at the future peace table.[59]

If the State Department was astounded, Salazar was 'at a loss'. He could not understand the 'explosion', he told Campbell. Surely the request that the United States would view Portuguese participation at the peace conference was 'reasonable'? Norweb had constantly said it would be an advantage Portugal would gain as a result of participation in the war. The request for shipping assistance involved no definite US commitment and, as for war material and aircraft, the Portuguese only wanted 50 more jeeps and some training machines. 'What, I ask you, can be so dreadful in any of this?' Campbell replied that the Americans, chafing over delay, had not unnaturally seen the requests as a further source of delay. But, he reported, Salazar seemed no longer to be making them a pre-requisite.[60] The FO was puzzled. 'The truth probably lies somewhere between Dr Salazar and the Americans.'[61]

The staff conversations concluded soon after. Salazar's attempts to 'safeguard his...liberty of action and...have the best of all possible worlds' had been met by the Anglo–American delegation with 'searching questions', Campbell commented, and they had produced 'unexpectedly straightforward' replies. From the moment the Portuguese contingent left Moçambique in a partly Allied convoy, Portugal would be 'in co-operation with the Allies' and bases available in Timor. 'If the Japanese withdraw voluntarily from the whole island Portuguese troops would make the first landing alone; but it is the understanding of our delegation that there would be no objection to Allied forces following close upon their heels.' If the Japanese simply withdrew into Dutch Timor, the Portuguese would take part in operations to turn them out. Bases in Portuguese Timor would still be available to the Allies. One further contingency was not covered. 'No doubt Dr Salazar purposely left this loop-hole open'. That was that the Japanese might withdraw before the convoy had left Moçambique. But the British delegation, headed by Major-General HJ Hayman Joyce, thought it 'most improbable that a Portuguese expedition of adequate size could proceed to Timor and maintain itself there without Allied assistance'.

---

[59] FO 115/4016: Telegram from Halifax, 10 October 1944, 5475.
[60] FO 371/39590 [C14045/89/36]: Telegram, 13 October 1944, 1765.
[61] FO 371/39590 [C14045/89/36]: Minute by Roberts, 16 October 1944.

Salazar had given 'no definite indication of the manner in which he would make an open break with the Japanese', Campbell noted, but thought he had made up his mind that a reoccupation of Timor by or with the aid of Portuguese arms had to be undertaken while the war with Japan was still in progress. Failing a voluntary withdrawal by the Japanese, the moment for a break would depend on the date of departure from Lourenço Marques. A member of the Portuguese delegation remarked that, since the Japanese had not declared war on entering Timor but theoretically had maintained their neutrality, it might be that Portugal would not declare war. 'The shadowy distinction between being at war with Japan as a result of formal declaration to that effect and being in a state of "co-operation with the Allies" in the war against Japan is one which need cause us no concern', Campbell commented. He did not in any case expect Salazar to come out into the open until the contingent was on the point of sailing or had sailed from Moçambique.[62]

Hayman Joyce confirmed Roberts' impression that the Portuguese were anxious not to be involved in war with Japan unless it was the inevitable preliminary to reoccupying Timor. They were very worried about Timor and hoped the Japanese would leave voluntarily. But they were also fearful that, if they were not on the spot, the Americans, the Australians or the Dutch might profit from their absence—hence their readiness to agree on facilities. And they had begun sending troops to Moçambique.[63] Eden was 'much puzzled' by the papers. 'I thought that we were agreed that it was more important that Macao and its refugees should not fall into Japanese hands than that Portugal should become involved in hostilities with Japan over Timor.'[64] The notes were exchanged on 28 November (DAPE:XI,331–334).

The Australians, the Dutch and the Portuguese

The Dutch were apprehensive over Australia's ambitions as expressed by Evatt and evident in the published Australia–New Zealand agreement. In April Evatt had told the Dutch Minister in Canberra (van Aerssen) that he was keen on 'close co-operation…in regard to the future security and welfare of the peoples of the region'. In June van Mook warned Prime Minister Gerbrandy that 'in Australia there undoubtedly exists an annexationist group'. General MacArthur privately warned a Dutch official (van der Plas)

---

[62] FO 371/39590 [C14734/89/36]: Campbell to Eden, 23 October 1944, 325.
[63] FO 371/39590 [C14734/89/36]: Minute, 1 November 1944.
[64] FO 371/39590 [C14734/89/36]: Note on minute.

in August that General Blamey and others wanted to split the NEI from his command as a step towards annexing them (Thorne 1978:481).

In September 1944 the FO informed the Dutch government in London of the decision to start staff conversations with the Portuguese. They were, Oliver Harvey told Michiels, of 'a very preliminary nature' and not concerned with strategy or politics. The Ambassador suggested that, 'in view of the proximity of the Netherlands East Indies and the dependence of Timor on Dutch resources there', Salazar might be well advised to suggest that the Dutch join the conversations. The relations between the Netherlands and his government had not been 'very favourable' and it might find itself 'at some disadvantage at a later date in respect of Timor' if it had not taken 'some steps to elicit Netherlands interest'. Participation was impractical, Garran minuted.[65]

In the New Year Teixeira de Mattos, the Counsellor at the Netherlands Embassy in London, enquired at the FO about the negotiations. Oliver Harvey said the agreement was now with the Combined Chiefs of Staff. Teixeira asked if he could be given an idea of the contents. The Dutch were 'much interested as the other half of Timor belonged to them', and they had 'a reversionary interest' in Portuguese Timor, 'as they had an agreement by which, if the Portuguese ever wished to relinquish it, it might be acquired by the Dutch'. The agreement dealt only with military questions, Harvey responded. Teixeira asked if he could at least glance at it, as 'it would help him in dispelling suspicions among his people'.[66]

Ten days later Teixeira called again. Harvey assured him 'that nothing in the agreement contemplated any alteration in the existing political status of the island, divided as it was between the Portuguese and the Dutch'. The Portuguese wanted to take part in the reoccupation of their part as a result either of fighting or of Japanese evacuation. Teixeira asked if their contingent would be confined to operations in Portuguese Timor. The agreement provided that it could be required to operate against the Japanese in the rest of the island, Harvey responded, but that was 'permissive' and would be at the military commanders' discretion. 'It would be clearly too one sided an arrangement if the Portuguese, having been brought at great labour and expense to help in the recovery of their own part of Timor, were not required if necessary to help us in the recovery of the remainder.'[67]

---

[65] FO 371/39589 [F12400/89/36]: Minutes, 12, 19 September 1944.
[66] FO 371/49492 [Z974/50/36]: Minute, 9 January 1945.
[67] FO 371/49492 [Z975/50/36]: Minute, 18 January 1945.

The British Ambassador to the Netherlands, Sir Nevile Bland, was formally told of the agreement on 24 January.[68] At the end of the month the persistent Counsellor sought a copy. Frederick Hoyer Millar suggested that, to allay their suspicions, the Dutch might be given part of it,[69] but the War Cabinet Office was not in favour of asking the Combined Chiefs of Staff.[70]

In the meantime the Portuguese had been seeking information on the military planning they expected to follow the staff talks. Their Ambassador, the Duke of Palmela, put the question to the FO: it was important to know what was being done and if possible the time of the year operations might take place, 'particularly in view of the long distance separating them from the base in Moçambique where the Portuguese troops are to concentrate'. Cadogan replied that it would depend on operations in the Philippines.[71]

Early in February the Portuguese Ambassador expressed his government's 'growing concern' at the absence of any reply to the various démarches it had made. It wanted to complete its plans through a continuation of the staff talks. The reasons were 'juridical'; there were also political considerations. The operations in the Philippines were reaching a successful conclusion, making United States forces available for operations in Formosa, on the China coast, or the Japanese mainland; British and Australian forces were substituting for American troops in certain Pacific theatres and a large British fleet was gathering; and the rainy season was coming to an end. An Anglo–Australian–American offensive against the Japanese-occupied islands in the South West Pacific became possible as a result, 'in conjunction with the American operations…which might well ease the position in Macau'. The Portuguese could not be absent from any operations for the reoccupation of Timor. The government did not need to know the probable time for the start of the operations, but it was necessary to define 'the essentials of Portuguese co-operation' and to ensure 'the concentration of the Portuguese forces at a base near the theatre of operations'. It had not been possible even to send the nucleus of officers and non-commissioned officers to Australia for training as instructors, as had been intended.[72]

---

[68] FO 371/49492 [Z264/50/36]: Eden to Bland, 24 January 1945, 24.
[69] FO 371/49492 [Z1653/50/36]: Minute by Harvey, 31 January 1945; Millar to LL Carver, 20 February 1945.
[70] FO 371/49492 [Z2643/50/36]: Hollis to Millar, 23 February 1945.
[71] Conversation, 21 December 1944, in DAPE:XI,341–342.
[72] FO 371/49492 [Z1674/50/36]: Memorandum, 3 February 1945.

The Portuguese were nervous, Hoyer Millar commented, lest the Allies invaded Timor before they were ready. The CCOS wanted the question held over till the end of the German war. Shipping stringency seemed an inadequate response, as the United States was sending Brazilians to Italy.[73] The FO suggested a more encouraging answer.[74] The result was a telegram to the Australian Government. It was proposed to suggest to the CCOS that the Portuguese Government should be invited to concentrate in Australia an expeditionary force of 4,000 and to despatch a training cadre of 100 officers and non-commissioned officers, 'on the understanding that, because of requirements of German and Japanese war, we shall be unable to provide ships or to give compensation in tonnage for Portuguese shipping used', though once it was in Australia, ships might be found to take the force to Timor 'when need arises'. Would the Commonwealth Government accept cadre and force and provide them accommodation and training? 'It should be added that Portuguese are very short of shipping and might on this account feel unable to take advantage of proposed offer.'[75]

The proviso over shipping, the embassy in Lisbon commented, would 'come as a serious shock; and we shall probably once again be accused by Salazar of pocketing the advantages accruing to us from a bargain and then fading out when it comes to fulfilling our commitments'. It had been clear in the staff talks that the Portuguese could contribute practically no shipping, while it had not been made clear that the United States and the United Kingdom might not be able to either. It was, however, on the strength of their undertaking not indeed 'to do certain definite things' but to work out a plan on the basis of the conversations that Salazar had allowed the Americans belligerent facilities on Santa Maria. He might well claim that, if he had known he would have to provide all the shipping—'an impossibility'—he would have broken off the conversations and the Americans would not have got their aerodrome in Santa Maria. The United Kingdom was brought in, the Ambassador believed, as a guarantee of execution. He thought 'that we should go as far as we *can* to facilitate Portuguese participation in the operation without prejudicing our own plans, and should take no more than our share of the odium of disappointing the Portuguese'. He suggested getting the staff talks going again 'on quite a small scale'. That would show Salazar 'that we are not trying to run out altogether and make it easier for

---

[73] FO 371/49492 [Z1674/50/36]: Minute, 11 February 1945.
[74] FO 371/49492 [Z1674/50/36]: Millar/Carver, 13 February 1945.
[75] FO 371/49492 [Z3605/50/36]; Telegram, 13 March 1945, 72; also in AFPD:VIII,83–84.

him to grasp that the shipping difficulty is an honest military one'. In the end the participation of the Portuguese might be only token. That would disappoint them, but not 'cause either us or the Americans to shed any tears'.[76]

The shipping shortage was acute, Garran minuted. Perhaps Salazar could be offered a small standing committee in Lisbon?[77] Monteiro had spoken to Eden on 8 March and to Cadogan on 29 March, and, after a visit to Lisbon, he called on Sargent and Harvey in early May. The answer was delayed by the lack of any reply from the Australian Government over accommodating and training Portuguese forces. The FO suggested to the War Cabinet Offices on 9 May—one day after VE Day—that the CCOS might proceed with the final examination of the question, on the understanding that it would be 'subject to the concurrence and approval of the Australian Government'. The Portuguese had 'blotted their copy book' by half-masting their flags for Hitler's death,

> and we need not be too much concerned over their feelings at the moment. All the same we and the Americans have entered into certain commitments concerning Portuguese participation in the eventual liberation of Timor and have for our part already benefited from the Azores half of the bargain. So we ought really to try and get on with this business, tiresome though it is.[78]

But the idea of by-passing the Australian Government was not pursued.

It had received more than one reminder from the DO and also some prompting from its High Commissioner in London, Bruce. Initially it had replied on 14 April saying the matter had been referred to the Service advisers. Bruce tried yet again after Eden spoke to him early in June. The failure to reply was causing the United Kingdom 'considerable embarrassment'. The United States and the United Kingdom, he pointed out, could go ahead, leaving the question open, 'but in view of the fact that Australia has played so prominent a part in the discussions from the beginning, this would be unfortunate'. Bruce had sensed an 'atmosphere of suspicion' when he had seen the Duke of Palmela the previous week. 'Our agreement in principle over the Cadre will probably not impose any heavy burden on us but it may well prove to be a useful gesture, particularly with a view to Portuguese

---

[76] FO 371/49492 [Z4542/50/36]: Clarke for Ambassador to Millar, 2 April 1945.
[77] FO 371/49492 [Z4542/50/36]: Minute, 15 April 1945.
[78] FO 371/49492 [Z5555/50/36]: Millar to A Earle, 9 May 1945.

about the future of Timor.'[79] At the previous week's interview, Bruce had told Palmela that his government could not agree to the appointment of a Portuguese chargé in Canberra. The reason he gave was that it would not be able to reciprocate, as it was 'heavily committed with regard to new missions abroad'.[80] One of the reasons it had given Bruce was that the matter was better deferred pending 'some clarification of the military and political position of Portuguese Timor'.[81] So there was ground for some Portuguese concern.

Bruce now received an answer from Canberra, which retailed the observations of the Service advisers: 'The war effort is still in a state of disequilibrium and this disequilibrium would be further increased by the acceptance of additional commitments'. It was very difficult to maintain the strengths of the Australian forces and meet the needs of the Australian services and those of the Royal Navy, and no commitment to the Portuguese could be allowed to prejudice the fulfilment of those tasks. The cablegram also retailed comments the Acting Prime Minister had made in Parliament: the government, he had insisted, should not make commitments it could not fulfil. The government, it concluded, had fully considered the proposal to train and maintain 4,000 Portuguese troops to participate in the liberation of Timor, 'but it is averse to undertaking a further commitment to provide requirements for this force, having regard to existing commitments on Australian resources'.[82]

The delay and the handling of the chargé question suggest that the strain on Australian resources was not the complete answer. The Commonwealth Government also procrastinated over implementing an agreement in principle for Dutch troops and administrators to come to Australia to be on hand and finally withdrew it (Thorne 1988:110; Henry 2010:74–75).[83] It seems clear that it wished to limit the role of the returning colonial powers and boost its role with a view to attaining the objectives it had set out, somewhat vaguely, in 1943 and 1944. Procrastination and delay were part of the scheme. As the defeat of the Japanese drew closer, delay turned to denial. Then, of course, the war was ended with unexpected suddenness by the dropping of the atomic bombs on 6 and 9 August 1945 and the Japanese surrender on 15 August.

---

[79] Bruce to Curtin, 11 June 1945, Telegram 72A, in AFPD:VIII,209–210.
[80] Bruce to Curtin, 7 June 1945, Telegram 71A, in AFPD:VIII,206–207.
[81] Bruce to Curtin, 7 June 1945, Telegram 71A, in AFPD:VIII,206n.
[82] Telegrams from Commonwealth of Australia, 16 June 1945, 158, 159, in AFPD:VIII, 215–216.
[83] Chifley to van Aerssen, 11 September 1945, in AFPD:VIII,410–412.

Chapter Four

The Re-establishment of Portuguese Rule

The mutual distrust the military intervention of December 1941 had engendered was renewed in 1945. The Portuguese wanted to take the Japanese surrender in Timor. The Australians argued that the surrender should be made to their forces and wanted to keep them there, with a view to ensuring the objectives they had set out in 1943. Britain, of course, wanted to avoid a row between their European ally and their Commonwealth partner and tried to distinguish between the surrender of the Japanese and the restoration of Portuguese authority. It consulted Australia, which then had no representative in Lisbon. In the event the cabinet in Canberra accepted that the Japanese surrender in Kupang covered the point, while a small Australian party went to Dili to congratulate the Governor on the restoration of his authority. Post-war the Australians did not pursue the agreement they had envisaged in 1943; they were content with good informal relations with the Governor. The Menzies government withdrew the Consul in 1950. It was, however, concerned that newly independent Indonesia would claim West New Guinea, which the Dutch had declined to transfer. Would it also claim Portuguese Timor? Not at least until it had secured West New Guinea, the British believed. It was Indonesian rebels who were connected with the disturbances in Timor in 1959. Even when Indian troops marched into Goa in 1961, Sukarno did not follow suit in Timor. But by now the African empire of the Portuguese was in question.

The Japanese surrender

When, following the dropping of the atomic bombs, Japan surrendered on 15 August 1945, Timor was still in Japanese hands, though theoretically under Portuguese sovereignty. The Japanese had continued to stonewall (Gunn 1999:231). Salazar had received Moroshima on 11 August. He had asked for a clear statement of Japan's attitude, Salazar's adviser Mathias told Ashley Clarke. The envoy had frequently said that his country continued to recognise Portuguese sovereignty and that its troops would hand back the territory when the strategic situation permitted. Would that still stand? Moroshima agreed, even at that late stage, to enquire of his government. Clarke commented that Portugal would be 'very ill advised to enter some last moment agreement with the Japanese Minister'. A secret source gave Sir Owen O'Malley, Campbell's successor as ambassador, a rather different slant on the interview: the Portuguese Government wanted the troops withdrawn after a diplomatic settlement between Portugal and the Japanese Government, the reason being fear of an Australian occupation. Possibly Salazar would prefer that Portuguese troops took over from the Japanese, O'Malley thought, but the report had 'a distinctly Japanese flavour' and had to be taken with reserve.[1] According to Palmela, Salazar had requested that the Japanese authorities should immediately restore full powers to the Governor. He and his staff, the Portuguese Ambassador believed, were in a position to resume authority.[2]

On 17 August, two days after the surrender, Moroshima told the Portuguese Ministry of Foreign Affairs that Japan was ready to return Portuguese Timor to full Portuguese control and instructions had been sent to Dili. Actual withdrawal, he added, could be effected only on the instructions of the Allied High Command. The Portuguese did not regard that as satisfactory. Could the Allies regard the two sloops they were sending to Colombo and the troops from East Africa that were to follow as instalments of the contribution contemplated in the Santa Maria agreement? If the Japanese handed over, no problem would arise. If there were indications they would resist, the Portuguese would wait till the Allied High Command decided that it was opportune to occupy Timor and then join the expedition as foreseen. The Portuguese, as O'Malley put it, wanted to re-establish their sovereignty by surrender to themselves or by forceful measures in which they took part. That was their motive in the Santa Maria agreement and it was more than ever so now that Japan had surrendered without their having the opportunity to show the flag.[3] Moroshima's statement was announced in the Lisbon press on the 18 August.[4]

---

[1] FO 371/49493 [Z9489/50/36]: Telegram, 13 August 1945, 860.
[2] FO 371/49493 [Z9610/50/36]: Telegram, 14 August 1945, 591.
[3] FO 371/49493 [Z9647/50/36]: Telegram, 17 August 1945, 887.
[4] FO 371/49494 [Z10090/50/36]: Clarke to Bevin, 20 August 1945, 232.

At Cadogan's suggestion Palmela visited Bruce to invoke his help in ensuring surrender would be to Portugal and to no-one else. The Australian High Commissioner told him he had nothing to worry about. 'I took advantage of my close personal relations with him to ask him privately how he thought his Government would react to the suggestion for a lease of Portuguese Timor to Australia for a hundred years...his reply was that such a suggestion would touch Portugal in her most sensitive spot, namely her prestige' (quoted in Hastings 1975:part 3,331). His Roosevelt-type suggestion rejected, Bruce said he presumed the Portuguese would give Australia all it required over defence and communications, provided its sovereignty was respected. Palmela said yes.

Bruce related the conversation to Frederick Hoyer Millar at the FO. The suggestion of a lease had been made more or less tongue-in-cheek and had not gone down very well with the Ambassador, 'who had launched into a long speech about Portuguese honour and prestige'. Earlier the conversation had dealt with the surrender: it should, Palmela had argued, be made 'ostensibly to the Portuguese Government'. Bruce asked what Britain's view was. Hoyer Millar told him that the British were anxious to help the Portuguese Government and facilitate the rapid re-establishment of their authority in Timor. They understood that the Japanese had arranged direct with the Portuguese in Lisbon for surrender to the Portuguese in Timor, as they had hoped would happen. Bruce was at first inclined to think that the Australian authorities would be concerned, since the whole of Timor lay within the Australian Command and said he was thinking of suggesting to Canberra that any surrender should be made to the local Portuguese Government, 'and that any Australians should only be there, so to speak as witnesses'. After consultation with the Cabinet offices,

> it was possible to convince Mr Bruce that neither the Allied Governments in general nor the Australian Government in particular had any concern with Portuguese Timor, which was technically still neutral territory, or any interest in the surrender of the Japanese forces there...All we had to do was to make it easier for the Portuguese to get their own forces on the spot as soon as practicable.[5]

Bruce thought he would not need to telegraph to Canberra.

---

5   FO 371/49494 [Z10047/50/36]: Minute by Hoyer Millar, 25 August 1945.

In fact the authorities in Canberra were taking a different line. Bruce, as Hoyer Millar noted, might be in 'rather an embarrassing position'.[6] Two Portuguese ships, the Australian Government had learned, were on their way. It called the DO's attention to the position likely to arise. It recalled the air attacks on Northern Australia that had used Timor in 1942; the tentative agreement for post-war relations reached in 1943 among Churchill, Eden and Evatt and approved by the Portuguese, giving Australia 'important priorities in relation to defence, trade and communications'; and the fact that Portugal 'failed us completely in arrangement made for defence of Timor with their concurrence', leaving Australian forces to sustain 'an epic guerrilla warfare which had an important effect on operations in the area'.

Now the Portuguese were trying to 'capitalise on Allied successes'. The surrender of Timor should be 'made to Australian forces, who alone defended it'. If possible, the sloops should 'not be allowed to go forward', and the Australian forces should be maintained until an arrangement had been made with the Portuguese Government for fulfilling the 1943 objectives. An important point was the welfare of the Timorese, 'notoriously neglected' by the Portuguese. In this territory, as in others in the Southwest Pacific, 'surrender arrangements should not prejudice readjustments found desirable in interests of security and welfare, always subject naturally to consent of powers concerned'. The surrender being made to Australian forces, no facilities should meanwhile be given for the despatch of Portuguese forces; interim arrangements for 'the restoration of administration communications etc.' should be made between the Australian forces and whatever local Portuguese administration was still in existence; and those arrangements should be made 'with a view to the conclusion of a long term arrangement… including as a minimum the objectives of the 1943 understanding'.[7]

The Canberra telegram was discussed on 29 August at a meeting of FO, DO and Admiralty representatives in Oliver Harvey's office. It was agreed to tell the Australian Government that the FO was ready to propose surrender to an Australian force, 'with which, however, the local Portuguese authorities should be associated (though it was recognised that such a proposal would be extremely unpalatable to the Portuguese government)'. But it was also agreed that a temporary Australian occupation would be 'wholly unacceptable to the Portuguese' and prejudice any chance of a satisfactory negotiation. Such an occupation would, moreover, be at odds with Australia's 1943 undertaking

---

[6] FO 371/49494 [Z10157/50/36]: Minute by Hoyer Millar, 31 August 1945.
[7] DO 35/1720 [2]: Telegram, 28 August 1945, 256; also in AFPD:VIII,374–376.

to respect Portuguese sovereignty after the war. There was no justification, it was also agreed, for holding up the sloops and troops.[8]

The Australian Government, Harvey believed, wanted to get Australian forces into Portuguese Timor quickly and keep them there until it could 'extort' the facilities it wanted, while Portuguese forces were held off. In view of the 1943 undertaking that was 'quite inadmissible'. Moreover the Portuguese were 'able and anxious to reoccupy' the territory. The line in the proposed reply to Canberra was 'the furthest we can properly go to meet the Australian government without violating the undertakings we have given'.[9]

One sloop, the *Bartolomeu Dias*, had been despatched, the DO's telegram ran, and would shortly reach Colombo. The *Angola*, carrying troops, would shortly leave Lourenço Marques. The Portuguese Government also claimed to be informed that the Japanese Government was now ready to restore Timor to full Portuguese control, 'though whether this arrangement can in fact be effected must be open to doubt'. The Portuguese were anxious to re-establish their authority without delay, if possible by their own efforts. But the DO understood the Australian wish to take the surrender of the Japanese and was prepared to approach the Portuguese accordingly. They were likely, however, to want to associate their local authorities and probably the first of their ships with the surrender. They would also insist on an undertaking that Australian troops would leave once the Japanese had surrendered and been rounded up and Portuguese authority re-established, and in any case not later than the arrival of the *Angola*.

The DO saw the surrender as a military act. The restoration of civil administration should by contrast be left to the Portuguese. Any suggestion that Australian troops should temporarily occupy Timor, or that there should be interim arrangements for its administration, would be rejected, 'would arouse great suspicion' and would prejudice any future negotiations Australia might have in mind. The Portuguese would recall the undertaking of September 1943 but maintain that the discussions on defence and commercial relations then contemplated could not take place till their sovereignty was fully re-established. Any dispute between Portugal and Australia would react on Portugal–United Kingdom relations and also interfere with the smooth working of the Azores agreement between Portugal and the United States. Whatever happened in 1941, Portugal had

---

[8] FO 371/49494 [Z 10157/50/36]: Minute by Garran, 30 August 1945.
[9] FO 371/49494 [Z 10157/50/36]: Minute, 30 August 1945.

served the Allied cause in Europe and the Far East in respect of the Azores and it had been 'ready and eager to take part in any operation to recover Timor'.

The focus should be on the surrender. The British Ambassador should ask the Government to agree that Australian forces should take the surrender on the understanding that they should withdraw when the surrender arrangements had been completed, and that the Governor and the *Bartolomeu Dias* be associated with it. Australian troops should not be sent in the meantime.[10] Canberra's response to the DO was slow in coming. Hoyer Millar feared that the matter might develop into 'a serious crisis in which we might find ourselves in the awkward position of having to side more with the Portuguese than the Australians'. Australia should take no precipitate action, such as sending troops in: confronting the Portuguese with a *fait accompli* would 'create great difficulties'.[11]

The reply arrived on 3 September.[12] The suggestion of interim arrangements, it explained, arose from a wish 'to anticipate difficulties of a confused situation'. The Portuguese would need some help in re-establishing effective control, and the Australians' operations in 1942 had given them 'special knowledge and experience of local conditions…Surrender and handing over should be regarded as logical sequel of Australian military activities in Timor'. The Australians should also be in a position to investigate war crimes. 'We would therefore propose that the withdrawal of our force should not take place immediately after the surrender, but when Portuguese authority has been effectively established.' Portugal had not been at war with Japan and had no claim to participate in the surrender. The Governor could, however, be present at the ceremony. The role of the Portuguese forces should be confined to taking over at a time to be agreed. 'It would be highly incongruous if Portugal, which has been an acquiescent spectator in the Pacific war, were to be more than a spectator at the surrender to a victor State.' The prestige of the victorious states must be re-established by overt acts and the arrangements made in other areas by Mountbatten, the Supreme Allied Commander Southeast Asia, were designed with that in view.

'We originally sent forces into Portuguese Timor at your request and when the Portuguese protested we allowed the objection to be directed against

---

[10] DO 35/1720 [6]: Telegram, 30 August 1945, 344; also in AFPD:VIII,377–380.
[11] FO 371/49494 [Z 10157/50/36]: Minute, 1 September 1945.
[12] DO 35/1720 [28]: Telegram, 3 September 1945, 269; also in AFPD:VIII,391–393.

Australia in order to help you in Europe', the Australians noted. In order to assist over the Azores, 'we acquiesced in the recognition of Portuguese sovereignty, but this was on the distinct understanding that there should be conversations between Portugal and Australia with a view to definite [defence] and economic arrangements'. The conversations should be 'taken up immediately', not 'postponed indefinitely'. The 'vacillation and timidity' of the Portuguese in face of Japanese aggression showed them 'unfit to be entrusted with defence of territory so important to the security of this area'. There was much to be said for putting it under the United Nations trusteeship system, with an emphasis on its security clauses. The necessary consent of the Portuguese should be obtainable 'since there would be no derogation from the sovereignty o[f] the parent State'. Evatt could discuss the matter in England.

Britain should help Australia resist any move towards the precipitate restoration of the status quo 'without regard to our bitter experiences in the Pacific war'. Australian forces could be delayed if the Portuguese were.

> The Representative of the victorious powers should not be embarrassed by the untimely arrival of these forces which we recollect left Lourenço Marques in 1942 to assert Portuguese sovereignty but retreated as soon as they ascertained that the operation would be difficult. Nor should any delay on our part permit Japanese, by handing over to the Portuguese, to save face and support their pretence that they occupied Timor only to protect the Portuguese.[13]

'If Portuguese amour propre is sacrificed to Australian amour propre in matter of Japanese surrender', O'Malley commented, 'it will be a great shock to Portugal and will make our path more difficult than otherwise in negotiations about other matters'.[14] Canberra's reply was, as Hoyer Millar put it, 'not very helpful'. FO and DO officials discussed it as soon as it came. They agreed that Britain should resist the suggestion that the Portuguese should not be allowed to re-establish their authority until they had satisfied Australian demands about future arrangements, but it should help the Australians over the surrender of Japanese troops, a 'separate issue'. Telegrams to Lisbon and Canberra were drafted accordingly, but next day it was learned that Evatt would shortly reach London, well before any

---

[13] DO 35/1720 [28]: Telegram, 3 September 1945, 269; also in AFPD:VIII,391–393.
[14] FO 371/49494 [Z10160/50/36]: Telegram, 1 September 1945, 938.

Portuguese ships could reach Timor. It seemed better to postpone any action on either issue:

> The Dominions Office seemed to think that if they could only speak to him instead of having to telegraph to him that they might be able to make him realise that by being too rough with the Portuguese over the immediate question of the surrender of the Japanese troops he might prejudice the chances of reaching agreement with them over the much more important long term issues.[15]

This line of action was in agreement with various suggestions Bruce had put forward. Anything he could do to 'urge moderation' when Evatt arrived would be 'very useful'.

The instructions for O'Malley were sent to Australia for approval, though action was postponed. Australian forces, whose local knowledge and experience made them especially suitable, were to take the surrender, he was to say, a procedure analogous to that being followed in Netherlands India, where South East Asia Command (SEAC) troops were to act. That would not derogate from Portuguese sovereignty, but help in fully restoring it. The Governor could represent the Portuguese Government at the surrender ceremony. If it wanted a separate civil ceremony, it would no doubt wish to make the arrangements itself. The Australian forces would withdraw when the surrender had been completed and Portuguese authority 'effectively re-established'. Nothing in the proposal modified either the assurance conveyed on Australia's behalf in September 1943 or Australia's desire, in which the Portuguese note of 4 October concurred, to hold conversations on defence, commercial relations and communications.[16]

'From our knowledge of Portuguese mentality', the DO telegraphed to Canberra,

> we fear that even though they might be induced to concur, albeit with reluctance, in proposed surrender arrangements, the making of such representations in this manner would arouse their suspicions and so poison the atmosphere as to make it much harder subsequently to obtain Australian Government's long-term desiderata.

---

[15] FO 371/49494 [Z10421/50/36]: Minute by Hoyer Millar, 4 September 1945.
[16] DO 35/1720 [31]: Telegram, 4 September 1945, 353.

Australian action should not be taken without Portuguese concurrence, and nothing should be done to delay the restoration of their authority. The United Kingdom would not feel justified in seeking to delay the Portuguese ships, even if it had the power.

In fact they would not arrive for some time, as the telegram pointed out. The sloop *Bartolomeu Dias* was at Colombo but dry docking would delay it some days and, even if it sailed at once, it would not reach Dili till 19 September. The next sloops would not reach Colombo till 12 September or Timor before 25 September. The transport *Angola* left Lourenço Marques on 1 September. If she went to Colombo as advised, she would not get to Timor till 26 September.[17] Hoyer Millar suggested to the Cabinet Office, moreover, that the *Bartolomeu Dias* could be held up in Colombo.[18] Britain could not officially detain the ships. But spinning out the docking process would 'give us a few days more…to fix things up with Dr Evatt'.[19]

If he were eventually instructed to speak to Salazar along the lines suggested to the Australians, O'Malley thought he would argue that Portugal had not entered the Pacific area because the COS did not make it possible and the use of Australian territory for training was refused; that the United States and the United Kingdom, 'in return for value received', undertook to allow for Portuguese participation; and that the Japanese collapse having rendered an expedition of the kind originally contemplated unnecessary, the despatch of the ships nevertheless flowed from that agreement. In this context Salazar would be 'liable to ask me how we can escape from an obligation of honour to arrange for the Japanese military surrender in Timor to be made to the Portuguese and Australian forces jointly'.[20]

The Political Director at the Portuguese Foreign Ministry, Dr Mathias, sent for Britain's Minister in Lisbon, Ashley Clarke, on the evening of 7 September. The *Bartolomeu Dias* had arrived at Colombo on 2 September. The *Gonçalves Zarco* was due on 10 September and the *Angola* on 13 September. The *Afonso de Albuquerque* was in dry dock at Durban and the *Sofala* at Lourenço Marques. The British Commander-in-Chief East Indies had indicated that the *Bartolomeu Dias* should wait for the others and in any case not leave till 16 September. Dry docking was not available till 10 September, but the government was anxious that it should leave at once

---

[17] DO 35/1720 [30]: Telegram, 4 September 1945, 352; also in AFPD:VIII,395–397
[18] DO 35/1720 [47]: Millar to Stapleton, 6 September 1945.
[19] FO 371/49494 [Z10423/50/36]: Minute, 5 September 1945.
[20] FO 371/49494 [Z10425/50/36]: Telegram, 6 September 1945, 967.

without cleaning. It also wished the *Afonso de Albuquerque* and the *Sofala* to proceed direct to Timor. It wanted representatives of the Portuguese forces to reach the island as soon as possible. The Japanese Minister said that formal surrender had been made to the Governor, but Japanese troops had not yet handed in their arms. A Reuter message said that Australian planes were flying over Timor and reporting on the movement of Japanese troops. When Portuguese forces who could accept the surrender arrived, they would provide full information about them and dispose of them as the Allied High Command directed. Meanwhile they trusted there would be no 'unheralded [group undecipherable] intervention elsewhere'.[21]

The Japanese Minister, Mathias added, had pointed out that MacArthur's instructions were that Japanese troops were to surrender to the Allied forces and had asked if he should telegraph his government to seek his permission for those in Timor to surrender to Portuguese forces. Did Clarke think that would be a good move? He himself thought it superfluous, given that the United Kingdom and the United States had no objection in principle to the movement of Portuguese forces to Timor. Clarke said it did not matter what the Japanese Minister did, but if MacArthur had made an order, it was 'a military matter which it would be necessary to clarify'. Later Mathias phoned to say that he had requested the Japanese Minister to take no action. He also asked that the British Embassy should not raise with the FO 'the question of whether it was necessary to refer to General MacArthur'.[22]

The Australian Government accepted the idea that the matter should be discussed with Evatt. He arrived on the night of 6 September. Garran summarised the objectives of the Australians:

> Their short term aim is that the surrender of the Japanese forces in Portuguese Timor should be to Australian forces, partly for reasons of prestige and partly to ensure that the Japanese forces in the colony are effectively rounded up and any Japanese wanted for war crimes apprehended.

The long-term aim was an arrangement 'regarding the defence of the area, (presumably including the cession of some kind of a base in Portuguese Timor) commercial and aviation matters'. The Australians certainly had 'some moral claim' to take part in the surrender of Japanese forces in Timor

---

[21] FO 371/49494 [Z10426/50/36]: Telegram, 7 September 1945, 972.
[22] FO 371/49494 [Z10427/50/36]: Telegram, 8 September 1945, 973.

as elsewhere, but, if they insisted on an arrangement objectionable to the Portuguese, they would prejudice the chances of a long-term arrangement. In their first telegram, they expressed the intention of occupying and holding Timor till they had secured the long-term arrangement. In later telegrams they appeared to recede from that point of view, but still insisted that the Japanese forces should surrender to the Australians alone. The FO had drafted instructions in that sense, but believed it was an unwise course.

Garran advocated an attempt to induce Evatt to agree to a surrender to Portuguese and Australians jointly and to give 'all necessary guarantees about the respect of Portuguese sovereignty'. If Evatt accepted that, the best course might be for him, possibly accompanied by High Commissioner Bruce, to discuss the position frankly with the Portuguese Ambassador. 'We should not then have to come into the picture.' If Evatt were adamant, there would be no advantage in his seeing Palmela, and O'Malley should carry out his dormant instructions. As for the long-term aims, Britain would be prepared to use its good offices with Portugal.[23]

Hoyer Millar endorsed the idea. The Portuguese Government appeared to be ready to grant Australia 'any reasonable post-war facilities', provided the immediate question of restoring its authority in Timor was settled satisfactorily:

> All that the Portuguese really want is to be quite sure that their Governor's authority will be re-established and the Portuguese flag run up at once over the island. If this can happen they will then be able to reassure their own public opinion at home. Anything, however, suggesting that the Portuguese were only being allowed to return to the island on sufferance would be bitterly resented by the Portuguese Government and would put them in a very difficult position in Lisbon.[24]

Lord Addison, now Secretary of State for the Dominions, wanted Ernest Bevin, now Foreign Secretary, to broach the matter when they met Evatt. He could, of course, point out that the United Kingdom would be 'put in a very embarrassing position' if there were a serious dispute between Portugal and Australia'. The allegations Evatt made in 'his recent telegrams' were 'far from accurate'. Garran prepared a note[25] in case he raised them again.

---

[23] FO 371/49495 [Z10505/50/36]: Minute, 7 September 1945.
[24] FO 371/49495 [Z10505/50/36]: Minute, 7 September 1945.
[25] FO 371/49495 [Z10505/50/36]: Memorandum, Portuguese Timor, 7 September 1945.

It was 'not correct', Garran's note suggested, to state that the Portuguese Government 'failed us completely' in December 1941; it had agreed to conversations. Nor was it fair to allude to 'Portuguese vacillation and timidity': Macau was in danger and the fate of 250,000 refugees in question. The Portuguese Government was anxious to take part in the recovery of Timor in 1944, as shown by the conversations in Lisbon, at which an Australian staff officer, Brigadier AW Wardell, was present. The exchange of notes that followed accepted that granting facilities on Santa Maria was an indirect contribution to the war, 'which in fact it was'.

Bevin and Addison met Evatt on the evening of 7 September and it was agreed that Hoyer Millar should talk to him about Timor the following day. He was ill, so Garran and Hoyer Millar saw his secretary, John Hood, Assistant Secretary at the Department of External Affairs. He was 'pretty tough and…evidently the author of some of the recent telegrams from Canberra', but he seemed to realise 'the importance of [from?] the UK point of view of not starting a first class row with the Portuguese', and to agree that, if the surrender were 'tactfully handled', the Portuguese would probably be 'quite forthcoming' over Australia's other desiderata. Australian troops should accept the surrender, but the consent of the Portuguese Government should be obtained and the 1943 assurance renewed. Garran and Hoyer Millar tried to persuade Hood to agree that the Australian forces should arrive simultaneously with the Portuguese. He was sure Evatt would not agree 'and we therefore fell back on the second alternative of promising to withdraw the Australian forces as soon as the Portuguese forces got there'. Hood was certain that the Australians would want the Portuguese Governor associated with any surrender ceremonies. He was 'rather cagey' when asked how soon the Australian force would withdraw. It was agreed that Evatt should see Palmela. Meanwhile O'Malley would be told to inform the Portuguese Government of the position. The telegram to him was agreed upon with Hood.[26]

No doubt, it ran, the Portuguese Government would await the outcome of the Evatt/Palmela conversations before deciding whether to make any alterations in the sailing arrangements of the various Portuguese vessels. Evatt would explain why it was felt that, despite the apparent re-establishment of the Governor's authority, the formal surrender of Japanese troops must be made to Allied forces, given MacArthur's orders and the need to round up them up with minimum delay. He would therefore seek Portuguese

---

[26] FO 371/49495 [Z10506/50/36]: Minute by Hoyer Millar, 8 September 1945.

concurrence in the immediate despatch of Australian forces to the island. That, he would make it plain, involved neither a derogation of Portuguese sovereignty nor a departure from the assurances of 1943. The Australian forces would be withdrawn as soon as the surrender was completed and Portuguese authority effectively established. Evatt would probably also emphasise Australia's desire to start conversations on the matters of common interest referred to in the 1943 correspondence.[27]

The discussions with the Portuguese, O'Malley was told, should probably now focus on London rather than Lisbon. But, if they raised with him the questions he had suggested Salazar might raise, 'the short answer… is that a distinction must be drawn between the restoration of Portuguese authority…and the surrender of Japanese forces'. The two questions were 'quite separate', one political, one military, the FO again asserted. 'There is not and never has been any suggestion of putting any obstacle in the way of the re-establishment as early as possible of Portuguese sovereignty and authority.' But, quite apart from the practical difficulties in making the surrender effective, it was 'difficult to see how Japanese forces can properly surrender to representatives of a country with which they have not been at war', particularly in view of MacArthur's orders. The argument seemed to amount to saying that, neutral during the war, Portugal now wished to claim the rights of a victorious belligerent:

> Portugal may be justified in claiming to be given certain degree of special treatment and not to be regarded in the same category as the other neutrals, but she clearly cannot claim to be treated on a par with the Allied belligerents.[28]

The conversation was in fact conducted by John Hood, as Evatt was still indisposed. Afterwards Palmela called on Cadogan 'in a state of some perturbation'. The Australian communication, which had come in the form of a note, was 'a complete surprise', contrary to what he had been led to believe over the surrender procedure and likely to come as 'a considerable shock' in Lisbon. Palmela went on to say that, according to the Japanese Minister in Lisbon, the surrender had been made to the Portuguese Governor on 5 September and he had retained 100 Japanese police to keep order. Cadogan put the points made in the telegram to O'Malley, adding, as he had said to

---

[27] DO 35/1720 [56]: Telegram, 9 September 1945, 675.
[28] DO 35/1720 [58]: Telegram, 10 September 1945, 677.

Palmela, that in Hong Kong Admiral Harcourt had received the political surrender in the name of the British Government and the military in the name of Chiang Kai-shek.[29]

Hood had told the FO that, according to an Australian telegram, the Portuguese Government planned to issue a statement that the Japanese troops had surrendered to the Governor. Evatt wanted O'Malley to support a request to postpone that.[30] The Ambassador relayed the request to Mathias and said none would be issued for the moment. He then made 'a full and very vigorously expressed statement of the Portuguese case'. That was a matter for London, said O'Malley, but he summarised it for the FO:

> that the disembarkation in face of Portuguese objections on territory already fully under Portuguese sovereignty of foreign troops for the purpose of receiving surrender of Japanese troops which had already surrendered to Portugal and were consequently no longer a belligerent army would be (a) illegal (b) inconsistent with Anglo–Portuguese Alliance and friendship and (c) a violation of an understanding that surrender of Japanese troops in Timor should be to Portugal rather than to Britain or Australia. This understanding, though not embodied in 'expressis verbis' was the obvious and only construction which could in his view be put on all relevant correspondence and conversations which had taken place since the Azores agreement.[31]

Salazar was going to be difficult, Garran noted.[32] The FO concluded that the Portuguese might return a 'flat refusal' to the Australian note and that in turn Evatt might advise his government to send the Australian forces in without Portuguese approval. That had to be avoided, if possible, as 'it would provoke a tiresome crisis with the Portuguese Government, in which the Australian Government would have put themselves in the wrong by taking unilateral action and in which we should inevitably be involved', and it would prejudice Australia's own chances of negotiating a satisfactory agreement on future defence. Perhaps Bevin could see Evatt at his meeting with the High Commissioners? He might say that Britain was 'in full sympathy'

---

[29] FO 371/49495 [Z10507/50/36]: Minute by Cadogan, 10 September 1945, and Telegram, 11 September 1945, 681; note in Palmela to MFA, 11 September 1945, and Telegram 564, in DAPE:XI,470–471; Telegram, 11 September 1945, 566, in DAPE:XI,472–474.
[30] FO 371/49495 [Z10508/50/36]: Telegram, 10 September 1945, 680.
[31] FO 371/49495 [Z10526/50/36]: Telegram, 11 September 1945, 984.
[32] FO 371/49495 [Z10526/50/36]: Minute, 11 September 1945.

with Australia's wish to take the surrender, 'which we agree is necessary (as otherwise there will be a small body of Japanese forces who will have avoided surrendering to any Allied force)', but that if the Portuguese initially returned a negative reply, it was very much hoped that Australia would consult Britain over further action. 'What we want to do is to persuade Dr Evatt to be gentle to the Portuguese and to give them a chance of salving their national pride.'[33]

The Portuguese reply was not, however, a flat refusal. The Portuguese Government, it said, would have no objection to a formal surrender carried out by the Australian Command on board a warship in Portuguese waters—rather as had been done at Kupang—or to a surrender in Australia or to a small Australian mission in Dili in the presence of the Governor. It could not, however, assent to the landing of Australian forces in Timor. It would be useless, since there was no possibility of fighting and the Japanese forces had placed themselves under the orders of the Governor on 5 September, and it would be 'contrary to the orientation agreed upon with the Combined Chiefs of Staff in regard to the retaking of Timor'. Occupation by Australian troops, at a time when Portuguese ships and troops had been ordered to proceed to or remain at Colombo, 'could not receive a satisfactory interpretation in the eyes of the Portuguese nation'.[34]

Palmela told Cadogan that the reply met 75% of Australia's wishes.[35] 'From the political angle' Evatt deemed the reply adequate.[36] In Canberra the Cabinet decided that, as the surrender on HMAS *Moresby* off Kupang on 11 September had included all the Japanese on the island, another surrender would be inappropriate and unnecessary. The Australian Commander should arrange with the Governor for a small party to visit Dili to check that the terms of the surrender were effective, to arrange for the transport of Allied prisoners-of-war, civilian internees, Japanese troops and war material, and to collect information of Allied war graves and of war crimes.[37]

Evatt informed Palmela, who asked his government to agree.[38] The Ambassador reported back that the solution was welcomed by his government

---

[33] DO 35/1720 [67]: Memorandum, 13 September 1945.
[34] Telegram from Evatt, 14 September 1945, EC 8, in AFPD:VIII,415–416; note in Salazar to Ambassador, 12 September 1945, telegram 560, in DAPE:XI,479–481.
[35] FO 371/49495 [Z10984/50/36]: Telegram, 16 September 1945, 690.
[36] Telegram, 14 September 1945, EC 6, in AFPD:VIII,414.
[37] Minute 4448, 19 September 1945, summarised in AFPD:VIII,416–417n.
[38] FO 371/49495 [Z10986/50/36]: Telegram, 21 September 1945, 712.

and that appropriate instructions had been sent to the Governor.[39] Hood told an official at the Dominions Office that Australia never intended a military occupation: 'I can't refrain from saying that if so the earlier telegrams had been misleading!' The 'private war', he noted, appeared to have terminated 'without expenditure of any ammunition more dangerous than paper'. 'The Australians could have obtained all this with much less trouble and fuss if they had not opened their mouths too wide in the first place', Sir J Stephenson of the DO commented. 'But Dr Evatt has secured one of his points'.[40]

WD Forsyth of the Australian Department of External Affairs arrived in Kupang on 21 September and then, with a member of Brigadier Dyke's staff, flew to Timor for an informal talk with the Governor. He agreed to meet Dyke on 23 September. Arriving with five corvettes that day, Dyke informed the Governor of the surrender of Japanese forces in Timor, congratulated the Governor on the restoration of his authority and requested authority for a public announcement. 'In order to mark publicly the association of Australia with the liberation of Portuguese Timor', a ceremony was held on shore in Dili on 24 September at which the Australian Commander and the Governor made speeches 'and laid wreaths in honour respectively of the victims of Japanese aggression and of the Australians who fell in Portuguese Timor'.[41]

The Portuguese Government had turned to the United States for support.[42] The State Department expressed its views, indicating that it might be obliged to make them public. As alternatives to the Australian proposal to land troops in Portuguese Timor, the Portuguese Government, its ambassador related, was proposing a surrender ceremony on a cruiser in Dili Bay or on Australian territory. That was a matter for the appropriate British Commonwealth Commander, but the State Department had to express its concern, and trusted that the United Kingdom would concur in its views and place them before the Australian Government 'in such a manner that the latter will agree to respect the spirit of the commitments which were entered into by necessity as part of our common war effort'. The commitments called for Portuguese participation 'in expelling the Japanese and in surrender and occupation arrangements'. Given 'the very definite

---

[39] DO 35/1720 [79]: Palmela to Evatt, 22 September 1945; Telegram from Salazar, 21 September 1945, in DAPE:XI,502–503.
[40] DO 35/1720: Minutes 14 and 24, 24 September 1945.
[41] Report by Forsyth, 1 October 1945, in AFPD:VIII,470–471; Agreement between Governor and Dyke, 24 September 1945, in DAPE:XI,509–510.
[42] Salazar to Bianchi, 12 September 1945, 439, in DAPE:XI,476–478.

language' of the agreements, in exchange for which the United States and the British Commonwealth obtained valuable facilities on the Azores, it would be 'unfortunate…if there were any untoward delay in the arrival of Portuguese forces in Timor'.

The Santa Maria–Timor agreements of 28 November would not be violated by landing more Australian troops than were needed for accepting the Japanese surrender and maintaining security, but it would not be justified. There was no question of expelling the Japanese by force. The presence of excessive numbers of Australian troops would not be compatible with full restoration of Portuguese sovereignty. The Japanese commander seemed, moreover, already to have surrendered, Portuguese forces were en route, and the Portuguese Government had offered full co-operation in evacuating the surrendered Japanese.[43]

It was 'rather amusing', Hoyer Millar thought, that the Portuguese, who frequently looked to Britain to protect them from the Americans' activities in the Azores and elsewhere, had turned on this occasion to them. They had intervened without going into the matter very thoroughly and without any considering whether they had any *locus standi*. The conditions obtaining were quite different from those the 1944 agreement contemplated. The only questions were the surrender and round-up of the Japanese and that had been delegated to Supreme Allied Commander South East Asia (SACSEA) and by him to the Australians. Talking to Gallman, the Counsellor at the United States Embassy, Harvey, Hoyer Millar suggested, might express his surprise that the Americans had taken the matter up and could also make it plain that the suggestion that the State Department might make their views public sounded 'unpleasantly like blackmail'. If it was still not satisfied, it could communicate to Canberra direct.

What was really behind the State Department's representations, Hoyer Millar thought, was 'their suspicion that the Australians are up to no good in Timor, and want to extract some concessions out of the Portuguese'. Probably the Portuguese Ambassador in Washington had been speaking along those lines, and Hoyer Millar 'would not like to say that such suspicions are altogether unfounded'. If Gallman alluded to them, it might be possible to 'remind him tactfully that the Australians…are almost equally suspicious of the United States' intentions in regard to some of the islands in the Pacific under Australian mandate'.[44] At the United States Embassy, however, an

---

[43] FO 371/49495 [Z10863/50/36]: WJ Gallman to OC Harvey, 18 September 1945.
[44] FO 371/49495 [Z10863/50/36]: Minute, 21 September 1945.

official more or less laughed the matter off. The State Department's action was 'rather lighthearted and unpremeditated'. He thought the Portuguese Ambassador in Washington, João de Bianchi, had acted without instructions from Lisbon.[45]

The emergence of an independent Indonesia

At the end of October 1945 Norman Makin argued in the Australian Cabinet that recent events in Southeast Asia, especially the Netherlands Indies and French Indochina, made it necessary for Australia to acquire adequate information, as both its security and its economic interests were involved.[46] The Cabinet approved the immediate appointment of consular representatives in Portuguese Timor, New Caledonia, Singapore and Manila.[47]

Australia took a close interest in the developments in Netherlands India from the end of the war and came to play a substantial role in the attempts to reach a settlement between the Dutch and the nationalists after the first police action in 1947. The emergence of an independent Indonesia altered Australia's somewhat inchoate concepts of security in the near north. The idea of an Australian Naval Station, as Peter Hastings (1975:pt 3,333n) puts it, 'disappeared with the collapse of British imperial power and the emergence of an independent Indonesia'.

Portuguese Timor was also seen in a different light. In March 1946, responding to a gracious message from Salazar on Australia's role in Timor, Evatt said Australia looked forward to agreements on defence and aviation. The Opposition spokesman, Percy Spender, was not satisfied (Hastings 1975:pt 3,331,333), and another member of the Opposition, Abbott, pointed out that Evatt showed 'little desire to explore under the terms of the treaty [of 1373] the right to construct and operate under Australian control aerodromes in Portuguese Timor or to fortify the island in the interests of the defence of this country'.[48] Evatt gave full details of the 1943 agreements and, in 1947, when the Governor of Timor visited Australia between 10 June and 5 July, he expressed the hope that it would facilitate preparations for formal discussion of them (Hastings 1975:pt 3,334).

---

[45] FO 371/49495 [Z11185/50/36]: Minute by Hoyer Millar, 28 September 1945.
[46] Submission, 29 October 1945, in AFPD:VIII,544–545.
[47] Submission, 29 October 1945, in AFPD:VIII,545n.
[48] DO 35/1720[110]: Extract, Australian House of Representatives proceedings, 26 March 1946, in Western Dept to Chancery Lisbon, 6 May 1946.

In April 1947, John Burton, the newly appointed Secretary of External Affairs, had suggested to the Dutch Chargé that the Netherlands could alleviate its war debt by allowing Australia to administer West Timor. It would be amusing to see what the Indonesians would think of the idea, de Ranitz reflected (Farram 2004:223). Burton was certainly content with much less in respect of East Timor. In November 1947 he said that Australia's objective since the end of the war had been 'to bring about close relations' with the Timor Government. 'By establishing a Consulate there and later by inviting the Governor…to Australia for informal talks we have, I think, largely succeeded in attaining our objective. The important thing now is to maintain those relations.'[49]

The Governor had been concerned in April that the 'nationalist agitation' in Dutch Timor might spread to his territory. 'Special steps were taken to strengthen the frontier province guard which in its zeal evidently crossed into Dutch territory and clashed with Dutch guards.' An exchange of strongly worded notes followed. The Dutch were reportedly concerned that the nationalists might launch an anti-Dutch 'campaign of incitement' from the Portuguese side and had approached the Portuguese with a view to collaboration between intelligence services.[50]

Approached by the Australian Consul in Dili, HD White, on the matter, the Governor, OF de Vasconcelos Ruas, seemed to know nothing about the Dutch request. As for the possibility of nationalist aspirations in Portuguese Timor, he had 'no doubt whatsoever of the loyalty of the Timorese to the Portuguese'. All taxes had been collected even in Oé-kussi and the Fronteira circumscription. The Dutch were indeed 'experiencing real difficulties since their natives have become imbued with the spirit of "democracy", which means no work and hostility towards Europeans', but that attitude, the Governor insisted, had not affected the Portuguese Timorese. They were in fact hostile to the 'Dutch natives' and welcomed the presence of African troops in the Fronteira circumscription. In the Portuguese Military Department, Captain JN de Costa Branco even professed ignorance of any troubles in Dutch Timor.[51]

In 1947 India became independent; in 1949 the Chinese People's Republic was proclaimed and the independence of Indonesia recognised by

---

[49] Burton to Officer, 7 November 1947, in Dorling (1994:386–387).
[50] Office to Evatt, 8 October 1947, 26, in Dorling (1994:348).
[51] White to Burton, 26 November 1947, in Dorling (1994:421–422).

the Dutch. The changes, as Salazar noted in a speech on 20 October 1949, posed problems for the Portuguese, possessors of Goa, Macau and Timor.

> The people of Timor, immersed as they were in the task of repairing, with the help and direction of the Portuguese, the havoc wrought by the 'liberating' Japanese, had shown no inclination to respond to the advances made to them in the name of nationalism. But when conditions in Timor become normal again, it must be expected that its people would feel the full impact of the forces which had destroyed the Dutch empire.[52]

If the Portuguese were aware that the context was changing, so were the Australians. At the same time, their government changed, following the Australian Labor Party's loss in the 1949 general election, and Spender replaced Evatt as Foreign Minister. In a landmark speech on 7 March 1950 he unveiled the Colombo Plan and placed a regional security pact on the agenda (Meaney 1985: 557–566). There was also a shift of emphasis in respect of Indonesia. The Australian Government now affirmed that West New Guinea was a vital interest and that its transfer to Indonesia would be viewed with 'profound misgivings',[53] even though the Indonesians claimed it as having been part of Netherlands India.

Coincidentally, on the day of Spender's speech a note was addressed to the Portuguese Government, indicating that the Consul in Timor might be withdrawn. The Australian Government, it said, had hoped that a considerable commerce might be developed, but the hope had been vain. Before it decided on the withdrawal, however, it would be grateful, it declared, if the Portuguese Government would 'indicate its general policy on the development of the territory by foreign capital'. Australia also had 'a very direct interest in the security of Portuguese Timor'. The last war proved that, and developments in Southeast Asia since had tended to increase that interest. 'It is considered, therefore, that the time has arrived when our two Governments should consult together on matters of mutual security interest, as well as mutual commercial interests.' If Australia were 'encouraged to pursue this thought it would be a relevant consideration in deciding the future of the Australian Consulate'. The government would welcome

---

[52] FO 371/76083 [F15924/1513/61]: Colville for Grey/Bevin, 21 October 1949, 239.
[53] FO 371/83703 [FH 1022/2]: Telegram from the Australian High Commission, 11 February 1950, 103.

comment and discussion.⁵⁴ On 29 March 1950 the Portuguese Consul in Sydney offered 'an evasive reply' to this curious note and the Consulate in Timor was withdrawn on 23 June.

British officials watched for any sign of the long-deferred negotiations between Australia and Portugal. They were anxious as ever to avoid damage to their relations with the Portuguese. At the same time they had now become aware of a new issue. Would newly independent Indonesia claim Portuguese Timor? Along with Malaya and Borneo, it had been included in the pre-surrender concept of a Greater Indonesia advanced by Mohammed Yamin and supported by Sukarno (Mackie 1974:21). The fact that Indonesia claimed West New Guinea seemed to argue that it might; but the fact that it claimed that territory on the basis that it had been part of Netherlands India suggested that it might not. If, indeed, it claimed Portuguese Timor, it might damage its claim to West New Guinea, both in practice through alarming other states and in principle by undermining its own case.

The FO briefed the Foreign Secretary on Timor in case Spender raised it on his visit to London in August 1950. The Australians were interested in it because of its strategic position and were therefore 'anxious to see an efficient and co-operative administration there'. If Spender remonstrated too strongly about the 'laxity' of Portuguese administration in Timor when he visited Lisbon, it might adversely affect Portuguese co-operation on other points; he might better approach the matter 'from the angle of the common defence of the area and of the development of economic relations between Portuguese Timor and Australia which both Governments agreed during 1943 to discuss at a convenient opportunity'.

As for the Indonesians, the FO did not expect them to make any formal claim to Portuguese Timor and, if they did, the Portuguese should be able to refute it. 'Its status is in some ways similar to that of the British territories in Borneo in that it is a colonial possession adjoining Indonesian territory. The Indonesians might, on these grounds, make a specious ethnological claim to it, but could not make any convincing claim on legal grounds.' An attempt to take it by force would constitute a casus foederis under the treaty of 1373. 'We might, however, find ourselves in the same position as we are in with regard to Macau…we have already told the Portuguese that in the event of an attack on the latter colony it is unlikely that we should be able to send forces to its assistance.'⁵⁵

---

⁵⁴ Note, 7 March 1950, in AIPT:21.
⁵⁵ FO 371/83588 [FE 1022/1]: Brief, 24 August 1950.

On 12 September the Portuguese Ambassador asked Sir William Strang, now Permanent Under-Secretary, if the FO had information on the Indonesian attitude. He recalled a recent statement by the Indonesian Government that its claim to Dutch New Guinea was 'not based on racial considerations'. Its attitude to Portuguese Timor was not based on racial considerations either, 'since, although the population…was of Indonesian stock, Indonesia laid no claim to that part of Timor'. The Ambassador found that 'reassuring, so far as it went. But it could not be foreseen how long this attitude would be maintained.'[56]

There was nothing in any Indonesian pronouncements about a claim to Timor, JO Lloyd commented. A recent press release on West New Guinea, dated 2 September, stated:

> We do not base our claim on ethnological or racial aspects of the position as put forward by Mr Spender. There are other territories which are racially and ethnologically identical with Indonesia, but no claim has ever been made to these territories by Indonesia.

The claim, as Lloyd put it, was on the basis that Dutch New Guinea was 'part of the old N.E.I.' administered from Batavia. 'This consideration does not apply to Malaya, Borneo, Timor or any other country in the area', and Robert Scott of the FO, whom the Ambassador was now going to see, could set his mind at rest. 'A new situation would obviously arise if the Indonesian Govt. ever laid any official claim to foreign territories in the area other than Dutch New Guinea.'[57]

Scott told the Ambassador that he thought

> that there was no particular immediate cause for anxiety on the part of the Portuguese Government as regards Portuguese Timor. Obviously, it would depend on relations between Portugal and Indonesia and on developments inside the Colony, but the grounds on which the Indonesians were claiming Dutch New Guinea did not apply to Portuguese Timor.

The Ambassador was sure the population was 'extremely loyal'. That had been demonstrated during the occupation. He also mentioned that Spender

---

[56] FO 371/83588 [FE 1022/2/]: Minute, 14 September 1950.
[57] FO 371/83588 [FE 1022/2]: Minute, 14 September 1950.

had told him of Australia's desire to promote trade.[58] The Indonesians were pushed into a mention of Timor and Borneo in order to make their point of view clear, as the British Ambassador in Jakarta, Dermot Kermode, pointed out. 'There are no indications that Indonesia has any designs on Portuguese Timor.'[59]

In 1951 the British Embassy in Jakarta sent its third secretary, Robert Brash, to report on Portuguese Timor. The embassy in Lisbon suggested he should bear in mind the possibility of trouble involving Britain under the alliance should Indonesia contemplate annexing Timor when it had secured West New Guinea. The suggestion that it might be lost produced hysteria in Portugal; look what happened when Australian troops occupied it.[60] The Army was too busy internally, the Jakarta embassy commented. 'Ultimately' the Indonesians might 'turn their eyes' on Portuguese Timor: 'as it is they probably regard it as a ripe plum which can be plucked when the time suits them'.[61]

'The Portuguese', wrote Brash, who went to West Timor too, 'give the impression of having learned little from the last ten years in South East Asia and of having little intention now of making any alteration in their habits.' Indeed their administration had been 'largely undisturbed by the problems of the world around them'. The war had done 'little or nothing to inculcate into the Timorese any feeling of nationalism or of anti-colonialism'. They witnessed 'no organized humiliation of the White. There were no prison camps on Timor.' The respect for the 'white face' was indeed increased by the 'courage and determination' of the Australian troops. The Japanese brought 'a weak administrative unity to the whole of Timor', but developed no sympathy in the people. Indonesian nationalism had 'almost no effect'. Indonesian authorities were 'prone to emphasise' that they had no territorial ambitions, they directed no propaganda towards Dili and their attitude to Portuguese authorities was co-operative. 'Privately they can be critical of Portuguese administration.' Only one official, the Chief Immigration Officer at Kupang, Arsil, remarked 'that though non-intervention was their present policy they could change it as they wished and that it lay within their power to acquire Portuguese Timor at any time'.

---

[58] FO 371/83588 [FE 1022/3]: Minute, 14 September 1950.
[59] FO 371/83588 [FE 1022/3]: Minute by RF Stretton, 19 September 1950.
[60] FO 371/92399 [FE 10362/1]: Chancery Lisbon to South East Asia Dept, 17 August 1951.
[61] FO 371/92399 [FE 10362/2]: Chancery Jakarta to South East Asia Dept, 10 September 1951.

The difficulties between the two halves of Timor were minor. The Indonesian administration was 'inefficient' and kept the frontier less controlled than in the past, so that there was 'a steady flow of wrongdoers and settlers moving over into the easier and more uncontrolled existence on the Indonesian side'. The Portuguese condoned the smuggling of copra from the Lesser Sundas, but, despite the loss to the Central Indonesian Copra Control, the Indonesians did not complain. The smuggling was no doubt 'a fruitful source of foreign currency for some interests, probably Chinese, within Indonesia'.

The old autocratic administrative structure had been reintroduced:

> The Roman Catholic church is in great power. The police, certainly in Dili, are efficient, if prone to summary, harsh methods. The Army looks poorly equipped, but its 250 African troops would probably fight well in the hilly Timorese country; the Timorese troops, being trained by some 200 Portuguese officers are of more doubtful value.

The Timorese themselves were 'backward', Brash wrote. 'They may well be happy. They are certainly very submissive to the regimen forced upon them.' If they could not meet the head tax, they had to work for the government without pay and food for an allotted period, 'and several hundreds of these debtors can be seen every day on the water-front at Dili waiting with infinite passivity for the work which the authorities presumably through incompetence are usually unable to give them'.

'There is much talk of economic reconstruction and development.' The colony, Brash was told, had received substantial financial support from the home government since the war. In Dili the results were not apparent; it was 'small, dingy and very dusty'. There were no metalled roads, no electric light,

> no trustworthy transport (certainly outside the Australian consulate) and little social life. Dili's graces are its natural setting, its supply of cheap and excellent vegetables and its abundance of wine, perfume and American cigarettes. (And, be it noted, all but two of the shops are Chinese).

Something, it was said, had been done in respect of irrigation and housing for officials outside Dili.

Perhaps, Brash concluded, the Portuguese doubted if it were 'worth attempting to do much more'. After spending 12 million patacas, they could still not make Timor pay for itself, and it is questionable if increased endeavour will ever produce any suitable return. Although relations with Indonesia are at present amicable they may well have fears also for the future independence of their territory. I may add that I heard no word of optimism about the future of Timor and no suggestions from the Portuguese that they could ever regard it as a satisfactory home'.[62]

No further reports were made, but the British High Commission in Canberra received some of the reports Francis Whittaker made from the Australian Consulate. In 1955 he wrote that the native chief at Baucau had been thrashed because road repairs had not been up to standard. The local administration was fortunate that the Timorese were patient, but if such methods persisted they could have serious political results 'in the event of an emergency in South East Asia'.[63] The FO sent the report to the embassy in Lisbon. If such methods were characteristic, 'it would appear that the Portuguese are running the risk of having another Goa on their hands, whenever Indonesian preoccupation with West New Guinea allows them to turn their attention to Portuguese Timor'.[64]

In 1959 Whittaker reported on political disturbances in Portuguese Timor. A plot to attack the Benfica Club in Dili on 29 May had been foiled. The aim had been to kill or immobilise the Portuguese military officers and senior officials during a festival, then win over the Timorese troops and massacre Portuguese male civilians. Another party, assuming the Dili plan had been carried out, cut telephone wires and established roadblocks, but an attempt to murder the administrators in Viqueque and Baucau failed. A few days later a sub-post near Baucau was raided and the Assistant District Officer at Baguia was obliged to fire on hostile demonstrators. Some 120 arrests had been made, which

> included a locally engaged member of the Indonesian Consulate and several native chiefs who had been reasonably well educated by the Portuguese. The perpetrators were[,] however, apparently half-castes and assimilated Timorese fanatics, helped by some Indonesian political refugees, who had been granted asylum in Timor in 1958.

---

[62] FO 371/92398 [FE 1015/1]: Report, enclosed in AC Stewart to Eden, 22 November 1951, 233.
[63] DO 35/6124 [16]: Report, 5 December 1955, in Fingland to Cosh, 16 February 1956.
[64] DO 35/6124 [18]: South East Asian Dept to Chancery, Lisbon, 2 March 1956.

Nazwar Jacub, the Indonesian Consul, was 'fully implicated', it seemed, and probably largely responsible. The Portuguese, however, did not think that he was acting under instructions from Jakarta, but that that he was working for the Indonesian rebels, as well as having a personal grievance. He had been replaced. The ringleaders expressed many grievances during the interrogation, including inadequate wages for Portuguese-speaking Timorese officials and lack of agricultural development. 'Only a very small fraction of native Timorese seem to have been actively involved.'[65]

The 1959 uprising was later seen as 'a landmark in the growth of opposition in East Timor and the first time modern anti-colonialist perspectives were introduced to the people of the territory' (Hill 1978:62). Various accounts have been given of it, but it seems clear that the Indonesian element derived not from Sukarno's government but from its Permesta opponents in Sulawesi. The later Apodeti party, which sought integration with Indonesia, claimed that it was founded by participants in the 'movimento de 1959'. But Francisco Xavier do Amaral, a leading Fretilin figure, also traced his opposition to this period. After the harsh suppression of the uprising, 58 Timorese were exiled to Moçambique, Angola and Portugal (Hill 1978:60–63; Dunn 1983:33). The political police, Polícia Internacional e da Defesa do Estado (PIDE), was set up in Dili (Gunn 1999:260–261).

The matter had come to the notice of the British Embassy in Lisbon when a number of prisoners were brought there. All the Ambassador could gather from the Minister of Ultramar was that the conspiracy had involved 'some minor government functionaries' and been 'started up by agitators from Indonesia concerned…to promote Portuguese Timor's Independence and presumably eventual absorption into Indonesia'.[66] The official line of the Indonesians was that they had no claims on Portuguese Timor, RP Heppel noted at the FO, 'even though it would not be surprising if they cast envious glances at it, as indeed at British North Borneo, Brunei and Sarawak'. On his visit to Australia earlier in the year, Foreign Minister Subandrio had said that success in the claim for West Irian would not be followed by claims for East New Guinea.

> He said it would not be [the] first time islands would be divided between Indonesia and a foreign country. There were Borneo and Timor. These

---

[65] FO 371/143955 [DE 1015/5]: JA Molyneux, British High Commission in Canberra to HA Twist Commonwealth Relations Office, 20 August 1959.
[66] FO 371/143955 [DE 1015/3]: JD Murray to Fry, 29 July 1959.

countries had been occupied rightly and historically by another power. It would be impossible for Indonesia to make any claim.

Heppel hoped that the Indonesians were not going to start an agitation

> designed to prove that there is a movement in Timor for voluntary attachment to Indonesia. If this goes on we should find ourselves faced with a New Guinea situation in miniature, which might necessitate some pretty stiff talking to the Indonesians on our part.[67]

Subandrio's comment had been designed to win the Australian Government's assent to the peaceful transfer of West New Guinea (Edwards and Pemberton 1992:202). Before he went to Canberra, Subandrio had told the British his country had no claim to North Borneo, Timor or Australian New Guinea.[68] The British Government, anxious to sell arms to Indonesia, was pressed by the Dutch to secure assurances over their use. A communiqué of 8 June 1959, issued following a conversation between John Profumo and Subandrio (Tarling 2008:195–196), might be regarded as the kind of 'stiff talking' to which Heppel referred.

Indonesia's 'confrontation' of the Netherlands was stepped up in the following months. It continued to raise apprehension over Timor, though also to moderate it. West New Guinea was on a different basis; it was the prime focus. That view Nasution repeated when he visited London in 1961. 'We have never claimed Portuguese Timor and as President Sukarno said when he was in Portugal a few years ago, we have no claim to it.' Indonesian claims, he said, were restricted to Netherlands Indies territory.[69] 'This is the official Indonesian line. Md Yamin's ideas for "Greater Indonesia" are officially disowned.'[70]

The British Ambassador in Jakarta, Sir Leslie Fry, reported that there was no evidence to support Portuguese suspicions:

> Indeed, for Indonesia to take forcible action against Portuguese Timor would be contrary to their many protestations that they will not resort to force even in pursuit of their claim to West New Guinea. That is

---

[67] FO 371/143955 [DE 1015/3]: Heppel to Murray, 10 August 1959.
[68] *Times*, 20 November 1958.
[69] FO 371/159809 [DE 1015/4]: Minute by M Geoghegan, 13 July 1961.
[70] FO 371/159809 [DE 1015/4]: Minute by Staples, 13 July 1961.

their major objective, and they are not likely to do anything calculated to reduce their chances of getting it.

Demonstrations might be engineered from West Timor and the President might break off relations in his speech on 17 August, but that would be the most that would happen.[71] In September 1961 the Portuguese Chargé, Garrido, left some papers at the FO covering reports on training, aircraft and troops in Kupang.[72] Probably, Justin Staples remarked, the Portuguese were 'alarmist about the immediate future. But there can be little doubt that the Indonesian Govt. look forward to acquiring Portuguese Timor eventually.'[73]

Nehru had in vain tried to negotiate the end of Portuguese rule in Goa. He met Salazar's intransigence and the United States, concerned over the Azores, declined to take sides. The revolt against Portuguese rule in Angola in 1961 prompted African criticism of Nehru's nonviolent approach: how would that end colonialism? A press campaign in India and anti-Portuguese demonstrations in the territory prompted him to move Indian troops to the border at the end of November 1961. Salazar called for British mediation and complained to the Security Council, and the United States tried to intercede. But at midnight on 17 December 30,000 Indian troops entered the colony and 'put a quick end to it' (Rotter 2000:181–185).

India's violence, thought Tunku Abdul Rahman, the Malayan Prime Minister, might provide Indonesia with moral courage over West New Guinea. In fact, Sukarno's speech on 19 December was milder than expected (Tarling 2008:424). A report in the *Djakarta Daily* of 28 December denied that Indonesia planned to move on Timor following India's move on Goa. A Foreign Affairs spokesman was quoted: 'We have no intention of taking over any territory which is not ours.' But the British Embassy thought it was not

> without significance that the Indonesians, despite their strong anti-colonial sentiments in general and their pro-Indian sentiments over Goa in particular, and despite the opportunities which the Goa incident would have afforded to them to broach the matter of Timor, have in fact been even quieter about Timor than they have been about North

---

[71] FO 371/159809 [DE 1015/5]: Telegram, 15 July 1961, 467.
[72] FO 371/159810 [DE 103162/2]: Minute by EE Tomkins, 18 September 1961.
[73] FO 371/159810 [DE 103162/2]: Minute, 25 September 1961.

Borneo, Sarawak or East New Guinea, where their protestations that they harbour no imperialist designs are probably, for the time being at least, reasonably sincerely meant.

Though their colleagues at the United States Embassy were 'more sanguine', the British had

> scarcely…any doubt that, if and when the West New Guinea issue is finally out of the way, the comparative Indonesian reticence about Timor will, after an interval which may or may not be decent, give place to demands for the liquidation of Portuguese at least and possibly other colonialist relics in other areas of this part of the world; and it is certainly difficult to imagine what future the Indonesians can visualize for an independent Timor except within the framework of their own Republic.[74]

The Indonesians must 'look forward' to incorporating Timor, Staples commented; the question was when. It gave fresh emphasis, James Cable observed, to the examination of Britain's treaty obligations the Central Department was undertaking.[75]

In March Lopes Vieira of the Portuguese Embassy in London relayed a report from Timor. The Indonesian Consul said that if his country attacked New Guinea it would at the same time attack Portuguese Timor with a 'liberation army'. The reason given was the fear 'that if Indonesia moved into Dutch New Guinea, Australia would occupy Timor'.[76] Cable doubted if Indonesia would attack Timor yet. After New Guinea, added Fred Warner, head of the South East Asia Department (SEAD) at the FO.[77] That view he confirmed after a talk with Governor Harriman and Sullivan of the State Department in July 1962. Did the Americans expect the Indonesians to seize Timor as soon as they secured West New Guinea? Sullivan thought they would wait till the planned United Nations handover was complete, 'as otherwise they might run into trouble in that organization. With luck therefore we should not hear much about Timor for the next two years.'[78]

---

[74] FO 371/166422 [DE 103162/1]: Chancery to South East Asia Dept, 3 January 1962.
[75] FO 371/166422 [DE 103162/1]: Minutes, 10, 13 January 1962.
[76] FO 371/166422 [DE 103162/2]: Minute by KD Jamieson, 20 March 1962.
[77] FO 371/166422 [DE 103162/2]: Minutes, 21 and 23 March 1962.
[78] FO 371/166354 [D 1015/25]: Record of Discussion on South East Asia, 22 July 1962.

There was now yet a larger context for discussing the future of Portuguese Timor than Salazar had envisaged in 1949. That was provided by the winds of change in Africa, in particular by the debate over the decolonisation of the Portuguese Empire in Africa that was taking place at the United Nations, where the General Assembly had in 1960 approved a declaration on granting independence to colonial countries and peoples. Australia had spoken in favour of self-determination and on 18 October 1961 Menzies wrote to Salazar about Angola (AIPT: 24n).

Self-determination had been brought into the West New Guinea dispute in the 1950s. The Dutch had adopted it as one of their rationales. The Australians had planned to bring it into their discussion with Subandrio, but in the event emphasised it only *ex post facto* (Tarling 2008:185, 188). It was bound to arise in the case of Timor. In January 1962 the Portuguese Chargé asked for a definition of Australia's attitude in the event of Indonesian aggression against Portuguese Timor. Sir Arthur Tange, permanent head of External Affairs, approved an oral reply. It would depend on circumstances, but include support in the United Nations for a ceasefire and withdrawal of forces. The Australian Government would like to know what objectives the Portuguese Government had for the status of the territory and the present state of its advance towards that objective.[79] In fact the Australian Government believed that the future of Portuguese Timor lay with Indonesia, but did not want it absorbed by aggression.

---

[79] Submission to Barwick, 16 January 1962, in AIPT:22–23.

Chapter Five

Confrontation

August 1962 saw the conclusion of an agreement under which West New Guinea would be transferred to the United Nations and then to Indonesia, 'an act of free choice' following in 1969. Would Indonesia now turn its attention to Timor? The Australians did not think the Indonesians should be left to seize it: it would encourage the pursuit of an aggressive policy that would imperil Papua New Guinea, then still a dependency. The Portuguese could perhaps be eased out, maybe via the United Nations. The British were clear that they could not give their old ally active military assistance, but, given their continued need for facilities in the Azores and elsewhere, they could not go as far as the Australians in a project to ease the Portuguese out. Their policy was affected by the Brunei revolt of December 1962. Would Sukarno, thwarted there, turn on Timor as an alternative? In fact he decided to 'confront' the federation of Malaysia that was being set up to attach Singapore and the Borneo protectorates to Malaya, which had become independent in 1957. Timor was on the agenda of two sets of quadripartite talks on Indonesia held by the United Kingdom, the United States, Australia and New Zealand during 1963. Again it was thought that Sukarno's frustration might lead him to turn on Timor. Britain re-examined its policy. If there were Indonesian guerrilla attacks, it might try to persuade the United Nations Security Council to interest itself and if possible assume responsibility. In the event Sukarno was overthrown in 1965 and confrontation was brought to an end over the following months. His successor, Suharto, was anxious to improve Indonesia's relations with the West and to shed the reputation it had acquired for mixing diplomacy and force.

Indonesian expansion

The agreement for the transfer of West New Guinea was signed on 15 August 1962 and went through the United Nations in September. It provided for transfer for a short period to a United Nations Temporary Executive Authority and then to Indonesian administration. In 1968 a representative of the Secretary-General would be invited to the territory to advise and assist Indonesia in making arrangements for the 'act of free choice' to be held the following year. Dahomey's representative at the United Nations looked in vain for the word 'referendum' (quoted in Saltford 2003:26). Leopold Senghor of Senegal said the settlement handed over 'Negro Papuans' to Indonesia, while Indonesian control of the act of free choice jettisoned self-determination.[1]

At the British Embassy in Jakarta RW Selby noted that the Indonesians had denied other territorial ambitions and he believed 'that as far as the Malaysia territories and East New Guinea are concerned this can probably be taken at its face value, anyhow for some little while to come'. He had 'some misgiving' over Timor. 'Portuguese colonialism is particularly obnoxious in Indonesian eyes' and, though there was no current indication of 'any aggressive intent', he feared 'that an incident along the border…might produce an Indonesian determination to invade the place based on the assumption that the rest of the world would react as little as they did over Goa'.[2]

The South East Asia Department at the FO, headed by Fred Warner, was against taking the initiative of speaking to the Indonesians on Britain's obligations to Portugal and assumed that the Indonesians were unlikely to raise the topic in the next few weeks. Fry agreed:

> It would almost certainly do more harm than good to say anything to the Indonesians about our ancient obligations to Portugal, particularly as we seem to be none too clear about them anyway, and we may safely assume, I think, that the Indonesians are not going to raise the subject with us or indeed with anyone else for the time being.

The Indonesian representative told the United Nations General Assembly on 18 October that Indonesia had no further claim, but the Indonesian news agency, Antara, reported border incidents. Fry's assessment continued:

> Indonesia will probably continue to profess to have no claim to Portuguese Timor; but it is not difficult to conceive of circumstances, real or imaginary, provoked or unprovoked, in which the Indonesians

---

[1] FO 371/166534 [DJ 1015/93]: Telegram from Palliser, 19 September 1962, 331.
[2] FO 371/166551 [DJ 1016/343]: Selby to Home, 5 September 1962.

would be disposed to take action against Portuguese Timor on the pretext of protecting Indonesian interests and nationals or restoring law and order in the island. The Indian 'police action' against Hyderabad State in 1948 would form a closer precedent, I think, than the action against Goa, but in any event I do not suppose that the Indonesians would bother about precedents if they decided to move.[3]

The Australian Government was anxious that the Indonesians should not be left to take the initiative. Mike Shann, about to take up his post as Ambassador in Jakarta, told Gordon Etherington-Smith at the United Kingdom's Commissioner-General's office in Singapore that departments in Canberra had been instructed to study the matter and

> said that it was becoming increasingly important to find a way in which the Portuguese could be eased out of this territory in an orderly and uncontroversial manner. If nothing was done it was odds on that the Indonesians would eventually grab the place and this would not be a good thing at all. The Indonesians had hitherto taken the line that their territorial claims were confined to those areas which belonged to the former Dutch East Indies. If a situation was allowed to develop in which the Indonesians deliberately departed from this position and violated what was tantamount to an international undertaking, the result would be not only to weaken the principle which they had themselves enunciated but if, as was most probable, they had little difficulty in achieving their objective, it would encourage them to try the same sort of thing elsewhere.[4]

Were there ways in which such a development could be avoided? Shann wondered.

> One possibility might be to try to have the territory placed under the United Nations or some other form of international authority, until such time as its final political status could be determined. It would not matter so much if, as seemed most likely, it eventually went to Indonesia provided the Indonesians did not seize it.

---

[3] FO 371/166551 [DJ 1016/349]: Fry to Warner, 23 October 1962.
[4] FO 371/166422 [DE 103162/4]: Etherington-Smith to Warner, 16 November 1962.

The Portuguese were, however, neither helpful nor, indeed, 'fully alive to the implications of their present position'. Etherington-Smith suggested to Warner that the British should think about the situation, too.

It was unlikely that Indonesia would try to take Timor before May 1963, the date of handover in West New Guinea, the FO considered. Indonesian leaders had recently proclaimed that they had no further territorial ambitions, but there had been indications of increased interest. Minor border incidents had been played up by the government news agency. An additional regiment was being sent to West Timor, an order of battle was being drawn up and closer interest was being displayed in activities within Portuguese Timor. Such indications were causing the Portuguese some concern. They had earlier increased their garrison and had now asked the North Atlantic Treaty Organization (NATO) to continue the exchange of information on significant arms supplies to Indonesia.

Under its treaty obligations Britain could be called upon to assist Portugal. Declining a request could damage relations and might lead the Portuguese to refuse strategic facilities the British could need, such as overflying their African possessions, staging facilities in the Cape Verde Islands and the Azores and, '[u]nder certain circumstances, the use of a land route through Moçambique, if military intervention in Rhodesia became necessary'. Any assistance the British gave, however, would antagonise Indonesia and put Britain's investments there (£100 million) at risk. Afro–Asian countries would consider it 'a firm indication that, irrespective of the merits, our sympathies in such situations would always be with the Colonialist power'. Nor was it likely to receive support from the United States or the majority of NATO allies or command general support at home.

The FO memorandum[5] listed the forms of assistance for which the Portuguese might ask. The first was 'active military assistance'. Britain could not provide it. At the NATO meeting in Athens in May 1962 the Foreign Secretary, Lord Home, had already told his Portuguese counterpart 'that our power to fulfil our commitments all over the world is limited and the Portuguese have probably taken the hint on this as regards Portuguese Timor'. Other types of assistance would have to be considered 'more carefully'. How far they would be sought would depend on how the Indonesians went about the takeover. That could not be predicted, but the most likely course of events would begin with a press campaign 'based on frontier incidents, real or imaginary, probably coupled with reports that the majority of the

---

[5] FO 371/166422 [DE 103162/5]: Memorandum, Portuguese Timor, undated.

native population in the territory wanted an end to the Colonialist régime and for the territory to become part of Indonesia', followed by '"evidence" that the Portuguese were victimising the pro-Indonesian elements in the Colony'. Then there would be a call for the Portuguese to have 'a plebiscite or general vote on the part of the native population to decide their future' and, '[o]n the rejection of this Plebiscite, a short sharp military campaign by the Indonesians to obtain control'.

In face of such events, the Portuguese might ask the British to use their influence with the Indonesians to stop them interfering in the internal affairs of Timor, although this 'would be futile since the only Western country who has the power to sway Indonesian policies is the United States'. The Portuguese might ask for transit rights for troops and supplies at Aden and Mauritius. That could be 'turned round by the Indonesians into evidence that we were prepared to support the Portuguese in their aggressive intentions against Indonesia'. They could create disturbances in Aden, since Sentral Organisasi Buruh Seluruh Indonesia (SOBSI), the communist-controlled trade union federation, closely followed the fortunes of the 'progressive elements' there. But the request would resemble a request Britain might have to make to the Portuguese one day and a rejection might lead to a loss of its rights in the Azores.

Another step the Portuguese might seek before the colony was taken over would be to draw United Nations attention to Indonesian efforts to subvert the government of East Timor. Britain could, 'without causing too much harm for ourselves', support a resolution that called, for instance, for the provision of United Nations observers. The Portuguese were likely to seek an arms embargo at NATO. Their delegate had already asked that members should continue to exchange information on significant deliveries of arms, even after all Dutch forces had left New Guinea. Such a request could be followed by a request that some particularly substantial order should not be licensed and then by a request for a full embargo. NATO was unlikely to accept a full embargo and, in any case, the Indonesian takeover might have been completed before the discussions. But there was no reason not to agree to an exchange of information and, as to the possibility of asking a NATO country to stop a significant military order, 'we might very well feel the same way for reasons other than Timor'. Internal security was now a weak justification: 'we must think of possible future Indonesian aggressive intentions against other territories in the area, for which we are either responsible or in which we have a direct interest'. A final step the Portuguese might seek was the lifting of the embargo on military supplies to Portuguese colonies. That 'would cause us trouble in direct proportion to the amount of publicity' it received.

On 15 November 1962 a meeting of representatives of relevant FO departments considered what assistance, if any, the United Kingdom would be prepared to give the Portuguese in the event of 'Indonesian action against Portuguese Timor' and, in particular, what response to make to the Portuguese request at NATO that members should continue to exchange information on supplies of significant quantities of arms to Indonesia. The meeting agreed to announce the end of the embargo applied in the West New Guinea crisis through parliamentary questions. Britain would be ready to continue the exchange of information on arms supplies, but would be unwilling to reintroduce the embargo. No definite decisions on 'diplomatic support' could be taken at the current stage, but 'if the Portuguese were to raise the question of Indonesian aggression at the UN we should give them our support and make efforts to ensure that the issue did not become obscured by the Indonesians identifying it as one of self-determination'.

The Foreign Secretary had already informed his Portuguese counterpart 'that our power to fulfil our commitments all over the world is now limited'. If Salazar raised the question of military assistance with the Ambassador in Lisbon, 'he should be given, in general terms, the same indication of our incapacity to act'. The Indonesians were unlikely to raise the question with the British Ambassador in Jakarta, but 'if they did so our representatives should merely condemn aggression in general terms and should not become involved in any discussion of possible action under the Anglo–Portuguese Treaty'. At present 'there was no clear indication of how the Indonesians would go about taking Portuguese Timor, nor the precise way in which the Portuguese would react to any such Indonesian action'. It was thus 'impossible to go much further in considering possible courses of action'.[6]

'We can only guess at this stage what the timing of the Indonesians will be', as Warner put it, 'and the method which they will adopt in taking over Timor', and both would affect 'what the Portuguese may ask of us'. The interdepartmental FO discussion was thus 'mainly exploratory', though establishing a measure of agreement. 'On speaking to the Portuguese or the Indonesians, we intend to say as little as possible to either of them and to avoid substantive discussion'. The Australians had agreed to provide copies of the reports their consul at Dili sent to Canberra.[7]

---

[6] FO 371/166422 [DE 103162/5]: Record of Meeting, 15 November 1962.
[7] FO 371/166422 [DE 103162/5]: Minute, 20 November 1962.

Fry was apprehensive about Portugal's request for continued exchange of information at NATO. Britain's relations with Indonesia had been handicapped by its support, 'quite ineffective', for the Dutch, 'and it was mainly by the grace of God that the outcome was not disastrous', he wrote. It would be 'foolish' to allow the Portuguese, 'with no more justification', to impose another handicap. 'I need hardly remind you how, in the Dutch case, one thing led to another: agreement to Staff talks ended up in the assumption by the Dutch that we were somehow going to give them logistic support if it came to a fight.' Fry thought that the Portuguese request was 'the first move in an attempt to start us down the same slippery slope'. He urged 'that we take advantage of it to make clear to the Portuguese forthwith that, even though we do not mind disclosing information about arms deliveries, we are in no position to help them over Timor, now or later'.

The pattern of events leading to a takeover might be as swift as or swifter than the takeover of Goa:

> Certainly the final phase of the operation would be swift; and it seems likely that the Indonesians would not be prepared to wait as long as the Indians waited during the preliminary phase of unsettled conditions in Timor and increasing Indonesian clamour against the Portuguese.

The phase might, however, go on for some time and, meanwhile, the Portuguese turn 'with increasing importunity' to their old ally for diplomatic and other support.

> What are we to say in reply? In the case of Goa, we were able to say that India was a Commonwealth country. What shall we say in the case of Indonesia? And should we not say something to the Portuguese now?

The British should 'start thinking' about their attitude 'and meanwhile give no encouragement at all to the Portuguese to suppose that we can do anything for them if it comes to a show-down'. Shann agreed: he had expressed the same opinion when he arrived.[8]

Lord Home asked how Britain would be placed if Indonesia attacked Timor. Britain had a treaty obligation to defend and protect its colonies, Warner responded, but could not provide military assistance. Home

---

[8] FO 371/166422 [DE 103162/6]: Fry to Peck, 12 December 1962; for an account of relations with the Dutch, see Tarling (2008:chapter 3).

had himself warned his Portuguese colleague at the NATO meeting in Athens in May 1962 'in general terms that our power to fulfil our treaty commitments all over the world was limited'. Warner summarised the conclusions of the interdepartmental meeting of November: if the Portuguese raised the question, the general warning should be repeated; if the Indonesians raised it, 'we should condemn aggression in general terms but not mention the Anglo–Portuguese alliance'. The embassies in Lisbon and Jakarta would prefer 'a more clear-cut policy. We ought not however to throw in our lot with the Portuguese;'—'Not against external aggression?' Home queried—

> we have our own troubles in Borneo and association with the Portuguese would be more of a hindrance than a help. On the other hand, we cannot go as far as the Australians who want the Portuguese out and are studying the idea of some form of UN trusteeship for Timor. So long as we need Portuguese help elsewhere, it seems impossible for us to take any initiative of the kind the Australians, and probably the Americans, would like to see.

Intelligence showed that the Indonesians were 'undoubtedly plotting some action against Portuguese Timor, though we still cannot predict how or when they might act'.[9]

The British had just been facing the Brunei rebellion of December 1962 (Hussainmiya 1995:chapter 10). 'If Sukarno feels thwarted over Brunei, he may well turn to Timor as an alternative adventure, which could provide a cheap and rapid return', Edward Peck, Assistant Under-Secretary, commented on 7 January 1963. 'As was the case with West New Guinea, a peaceful solution, diplomatically arrived at, would suit us best. The Australians see this too and are better placed than we are to pursue it.' The 'wait-and-see' policy was the best Britain could follow in the meantime. 'What we should *not* do…is to brandish the Anglo–Portuguese Alliance as a "deterrent" to the Indonesians.'[10]

Sir Harold Caccia, the Permanent Under-Secretary, thought that might be right and he entirely agreed 'that we must give prior importance to dealing with our own direct interests over Brunei and Malaysia'. But he doubted if waiting and seeing should go on too long:

---

[9] FO 371/169801 [DE 101362/1]: Minute, 4 January 1963.
[10] FO 371/169801 [DE 101362/1]: Minute, 7 January 1963.

The Americans as well as we have a special as well as a general interest where Timor is concerned. We both want staging facilities from the Portuguese Government. What is more, the Americans have a lever if they want to use it. They give considerable aid to Indonesia and a threat to stop that would be serious for the Indonesian economy, unless they could be quite sure that the gap could be filled by someone in the Communist bloc.

The Joint Intelligence Committee (JIC) was preparing a paper on evidence of Indonesian involvement in Brunei. That would be communicated to the Americans and it would be advantageous to suggest some joint discussion in the near future. Timor might be an 'anomaly', Caccia added. But he thought 'the sort of charade' Shann suggested, 'ie of arranging a play as a result of which the Indonesians ended up with Timor in their possession', was 'full of danger'. If there were talks with the Americans, there should be talks with the Australians too.[11]

Lord Home, 'not happy', asked for an office meeting. That was held on 9 January 1963. It was agreed that Caccia should write to Sir David Ormsby Gore, the Ambassador in Washington, asking him to discuss with the Americans 'the threat of Indonesian expansion' and to propose tripartite talks, including the Australians, 'with a view to containing it'. The JIC should prepare a paper on the military threat to the Borneo territories and the COS consider plans for meeting it. Lord Home would mention the matter at Cabinet on 10 January and later circulate a paper.[12]

The confrontation of Malaysia and its implications

The FO officials were, of course, now considering Timor not in the context only of the recent experience of West New Guinea but also of the current experience of the Brunei revolt. Since 1961 negotiations for setting up the federation of Malaysia—to comprise Malaya, Singapore, the protected sultanate of Brunei, and the colonies of North Borneo and Sarawak—had been under way. For Britain it was an exercise in decolonisation: the northern Borneo states and Singapore, it was believed, could not survive on their own and the new federation might provide security for the base in Singapore, likely to be undermined in the next elections in the city state. For Malaya,

---

[11] FO 371/169801 [DE 101362/1]: Minute, 7 January 1963.
[12] FO 371/169801 [DE 101362/1]: Minute, 9 January 1963.

too, there were security considerations, one of which was, again, the future of Singapore politics. Less frequently remarked, there was also the question of Indonesia: the northern Borneo states must not fall into its hands.

In August Foreign Minister Subandrio had assured Lord Selkirk, the Commissioner-General in Southeast Asia, that Malaysia was a matter for the territories concerned (Easter 2004:28) and in October he had wished it well (Jones 2002:109). Lord Home suspected that Indonesia had designs on the Borneo territories, 'though they have been careful never to put them forward' (quoted in Jones 2002:109). Indonesia had indeed not so far openly objected to a scheme that, if it placed obstacles in the way of realising the Greater Indonesia of nationalists like Yamin, was also something of a challenge to its existing status: could even a more conventional state readily accept so substantial an alteration in the status quo of its neighbours? The incorporation of West New Guinea perhaps absorbed its attention during 1962. Observers had thought it might then turn its attention to Timor. David Easter (2004:28–29) has shown that British and American intelligence had evidence, however, of Indonesia's complicity in the Brunei revolt.

Whatever the extent of that complicity, the revolt ensured that Indonesia turned its attention to Borneo and to Malaysia. In a speech of 19 December Sukarno expressed sympathy for 'the just struggle of the people of North Borneo' who were 'fighting for their independence' (quoted in Easter 2004:28). On 20 January Subandrio announced that Indonesia would have to adopt a policy of confrontation since the Malayans were acting as 'the henchmen of neo-imperialism and neo-colonialism pursuing a policy hostile to Indonesia' (quoted in Easter 2004:36).

In mid-1962 the Laos agreement had been signed, the West New Guinea agreement finalised and the London talks on Greater Malaysia concluded. But now Britain's plans were threatened because 'Indonesia's attitude placed in doubt many of the strategic benefits Britain had expected to receive from the establishment of Malaysia'. Indonesia's hostility threatened the security of the Singapore base and thus the future defence of Australia and New Zealand. The Brunei revolt suggested that a prolonged military commitment would be required and that, as a result, it would be impossible to cut Britain's defence spending. Lord Home was anxious for talks with the United States and Australia. He hoped for pledges of support lest Britain found itself in the same position as the Dutch over West New Guinea (Easter 2004:33–36,38). The Indonesians had to be told, as Warner put it on 29 January, 'that if they continue their present course the Western world would be united against them. We do not want this to develop like the West Irian dispute with Sukarno knowing perfectly well that the West will not stand together' (quoted in Jones 2002:132). The British were, however, to be disappointed with the response of Americans who retained the attitude they had adopted in the West Irian negotiations—Sukarno must not be encouraged to turn to the Communist bloc.

Nor were the Australians persuaded by Britain's argument that Sukarno was bent on incorporating Borneo, wished to take over Malaya and had designs on the other half of Timor and Eastern New Guinea. Shann thought that the Indonesians wanted to acquire Portuguese Timor and thwart Malaysia but that their ambitions did not go beyond that. For the quadripartite talks involving the United Kingdom, United States, Australia and New Zealand in Washington in February, Tange and Sir Howard Beale, the Australian Ambassador, were briefed to support the concept of Malaysia, but to advise the United Kingdom to obtain the acquiescence of Indonesia and the Philippines (Lee 1997:78–79).

Timor was on the agenda of the talks as well as Malaysia. It was, said the JIC in London, 'such an anomaly in modern Asia' and, with Portugal so unpopular in the United Nations, the Indonesians 'need not expect much opposition to its annexation'. There was no ethnic issue, as with West New Guinea. 'Militarily, it should be an easy operation' and annexation would not add much to Indonesia's burdens. 'Almost any Indonesian Government could be expected eventually to initiate a political campaign against Portuguese Timor, and if necessary to follow this fairly soon with military measures.'[13] There were preliminary exchanges about it before the talks.

External Affairs in Canberra agreed with the assumption made at the United States' State Department that Indonesia had

> at least a long term intention to acquire Portuguese Timor. If Indonesia were to seek to realise its objective by genuinely peaceful means and provided that a change was in accordance with the freely expressed wishes of the indigenous inhabitants we would have little alternative but to acquiesce. Indeed such an arrangement might have advantages over other possibilities.

But Australia 'should not take any action without very careful consideration and planning'. Indonesia might take military action to help 'liberate' Portuguese Timor, possibly in association with action in Africa, but that

---

[13] CAB 158/46: JIC (62) 58 (Final), 28 January 1963.

seemed unlikely before the end of 1963, given its preoccupation with West New Guinea, its disclaimers and its doubt about American reaction. It was likely, however, to build up its forces in West Timor, increase propaganda about border incidents and 'encourage any dissident movement which may emerge or even inspire one'.

Beale should emphasise to the State Department that public opinion in Australia would be 'roused by any Indonesian attempt to take over Portuguese Timor by military action' and its relations with Indonesia would deteriorate. It was 'essential' that the Indonesians should not be given the impression that the United States and Australia 'would be indifferent to the means by which they acquired the territory'. Australia recognised the problem of 'Portuguese intransigence'. There had been no reply to the question put in February 1962 on Portuguese aims for the territory. Australia wanted to keep in close touch with the United States on a question in which, because of its geographical position, it took a deep interest. But its studies were at an early stage and it could not provide the State Department with 'any considered views for some time. We would be glad to have any ideas on tactics'.[14]

Beale saw the Portuguese Ambassador in Washington on 17 January. Having just had talks with the State Department, he told Pereira, he felt that Portugal's attitude 'would make it difficult for her friends to give her the full diplomatic and political support they would wish in the event of an attempted take-over by Sukarno'. The United States, with its tradition of opposing colonial rule, would feel 'greatly inhibited in giving support to Portugal if the latter's present stand remains unchanged'. Could the government 'take some steps or come out with some announcement indicating the Government's intention to introduce welfare or education measures and generally to indicate their intention to give the natives an opportunity for self-determination'? Portugal, as Pereira said, had refused to do so as it regarded Timor as part of metropolitan Portugal. But if it made no adjustment to its position, it would make it impossible for others to give more support.[15]

At Tange's suggestion, Sir Garfield Barwick, the Australian Minister for External Affairs, told Beale he should not give Pereira 'any reason to hope that we can support Portugal's position in Timor'. The Prime Minister had already indicated that Australia believed that the principle of self-determination

---

[14] FO 371/169801 [DE 103162/4]: Telegram from the Dept of External Affairs to the Australian Ambassador in Washington, communicated to FO, 14 January 1963.
[15] Cable, 21 January 1963, in AIPT:24–25.

should apply to Portuguese colonies. Beale should express his personal opinion that neither Australia nor the United States would be likely to send a man to defend Timor against Indonesian attempts to take it by force. 'You could then suggest that Portugal would do well to approach some international body to recommend future for the Timorese.' It could not remain in Portugal's control much longer. Other colonial powers had recognised that colonies must be given the right to determine their future.[16] Pereira was 'not very responsive to the idea of approaching any international body'.[17]

The United States believed that Portugal should be induced to bring in a ten-year development plan with an act of self-determination at the end of the period. But, due to NATO's need for the Azores bases, the United Kingdom and the United States were in no position to influence the Portuguese, and it was felt that Australia should 'take the lead in persuading [them] to make reforms' (Singh 2002:47). Averell Harriman, the Deputy Secretary of State, told Ormsby Gore that he had asked Beale why Menzies had not tackled Salazar 'on the problem of constitutional change and economic and social development in Timor'. The Americans and Australians were agreed that if Indonesia tried to take over,

> the arguments in defence of the Portuguese would be considerably weaker than in the case of Goa. Timor ran at a deficit whereas Goa was a running concern. The Portuguese were doing nothing to advance the well being of the inhabitants. If however those of us who had to defend the Portuguese had previously put to Dr Salazar the difficulty of the position in which we were placed, we would be in a better position when the time came.

Beale said Menzies had spoken to Salazar; Harriman urged that he should do so again. He asked Ormsby Gore whether Britain could take the matter up with Salazar. He replied that Britain had incurred 'ill-will in Lisbon' over Goa and that Australia should be in a better position, given its proximity. The Ambassador asked whether the FO had considered the question.[18]

Sir Archibald Ross, the British Ambassador in Lisbon, commented. He did not know what action the Australian Government, or indeed the British, might be prepared to take in the event of a serious Indonesian threat,

---

[16] Cable, 28 January 1963, in AIPT:25–26.
[17] Cable, 28 January 1963, in AIPT:26n.
[18] FO 371/169801 [DE103162/5]: Telegram, 30 January 1963, 52S.

apart from employing the usual arguments against the interference, subversion and aggression, which are valid in any case. Can it honestly be said that we would be more active or more outspoken if the Portuguese were 'doing something to advance the well-being of the inhabitants'? If not, I fail to see how we would be in a better position just because we had told the Portuguese Government that there was little we could do to help them.

At least so far as the United Kingdom was concerned, they could indeed be under no illusions in that respect.

Any approach along the lines Harriman contemplated

> would mean either that we were excusing ourselves in advance for doing nothing effective or that we were, by implication, taking on a further commitment over and above that enshrined in the Treaties, which, in the event, we should equally be incapable of fulfilling. It could of course be argued that the Portuguese Government could make Timor so prosperous that the Indonesians would leave it alone.

That would be 'a complete delusion and we should no more be thanked by the Portuguese for suggesting it than we should thereby escape from the dilemma in which our Treaty obligations place us'. Arguments about the wellbeing of the inhabitants should be reserved for the African territories, where they were relevant and spoke for supporting the Portuguese. The Ambassador would see 'no harm and some advantage' in Australia's telling Portugal it could not help. Britain had given sufficient warning at Athens, '[b]ut for either of us to speak of the "well-being of the inhabitants" would do more harm than good'.[19]

Malaysia was the main topic in the forthcoming talks, as an Australian Cabinet meeting recognised. The problem of Timor, said Barwick in a preliminary note, was different.

> It is difficult to see a practicable alternative to the Timorese people joining Indonesia. Vague talk of raising standards of living will not achieve a permanent solution. We must be at pains to impress on Indonesia our disapproval of a military attack on Timor. We must show that such action could only have a most detrimental effect on our

---

[19] FO 371/169801 [DE103162/5]: Telegram, 13 February 1963, 1S.

relations with her and that a patient approach to the problem in the United Nations would in the long term be to her real advantage (quoted in AIPT: 26n).

In relation to Portuguese Timor, the Cabinet accepted the view that in the current state of world opinion, no practicable alternative to eventual Indonesian sovereignty...presented itself. It would not be acceptable to Australia or the West for Indonesia to proceed against Portuguese Timor with arms, and this must be brought home to Indonesia. But otherwise the course which it seemed best to follow is for Australia to bring such quiet pressure as it can upon Portugal to cede peacefully and in addition to explore ways by which the international community might bring pressure on Portugal (quoted in AIPT: 26).

Menzies wrote to Salazar on 8 February. He alluded to his letter of 18 October 1961, dealing with the United Nation's consideration of Angola. The present letter was to indicate that Australia would continue to support the principle of self-determination in the United Nations General Assembly Committee of 24, which dealt with the implementation of the declaration on colonialism. The Committee might discuss Timor and Australia would have to take part in the debate. Menzies explained:

Portuguese Timor is geographically close to Australia and has a land frontier with the people of Indonesian Timor. My Government is concerned that, in the absence of any intention of allowing the Timorese people to express a choice as to the international relationships and status which they desire, there will arise a serious threat to the peace of the territory (AIPT:27).

The FO briefs for the quadripartite talks also covered Timor as well as Malaysia. There was, under the 1899 declaration, an obligation to defend and protect all Portuguese colonies, although the Foreign Minister had been warned in general terms that Britain's power to fulfil its commitments was limited. Britain had commercial interests in Indonesia, but also commercial and financial interests in Portugal. It needed strategic facilities in the Azores and the Cape Verde Islands. over-flying facilities in Africa and, under certain circumstances, the use of a land route through Moçambique, but '[a]s a result of Goa and Angola our relations with the Portuguese Government are in a poor state'.

Timor had 'no close neighbour other than Indonesia', nor was it 'either large enough or sufficiently viable to have an independent existence'. There were no racial differences between Portuguese and Indonesian Timor, but it had never been part of the Netherlands Indies, nor had there been any indication that its inhabitants wished to become part of Indonesia. 'There was no evidence of any serious resistance within the territory to Portuguese rule.' But there were indications that Indonesia would 'at some stage, and possibly in the not too long-term', try to take it over. 'It is unlikely that the Indonesians would encounter any serious opposition.'

After the West New Guinea settlement Indonesia had increased its garrison in West Timor and subsequent secret reports suggested that it would refurbish its airstrip and establish a naval base and that the Communist Party (PKI) was penetrating the colony. 'Now it is clear that President Sukarno is determined to seek other territorial gains Portuguese Timor seems too good an opportunity to miss.' There was unlikely to be serious military resistance, and the Portuguese colonial record was 'so unpopular' at the United Nations; it would seem 'a good opportunity for a quick victory'.

Shann had put forward the idea 'that if the Indonesians show further interest in Portuguese Timor they should be encouraged to put the question before the United Nations', and 'eventually' the United Nations would make 'some face-saving arrangement whereby the territory would eventually pass to the Indonesians by means of a United Nations plebiscite or hand-over'. The Australians thought Timor would go to Indonesia, but it should be in such a way that it could not be 'shown as another territorial victory' for Sukarno. Given that change was inevitable,

> the ideal from our point of view would be for the Portuguese to give in with a good grace and in such a way that the transfer to Indonesia is not the result of aggression or a cynical placatory move to appease President Sukarno's expansionist aims. In view of our interests and the state of our relations with Portugal we cannot ourselves press the Portuguese to do so; even if we did we would certainly not succeed; the Portuguese are at present determined not to give up an inch of their territory.

The matter should be raised in the Fourth (Trusteeship) Committee of the United Nations or in the Committee of 24—not necessarily by the Indonesians, as Shann suggested—where they would be certain of support 'and where U Thant would probably be prepared to accept the responsibility of pressing the Portuguese to accept a solution such as the one which was found for West New Guinea'. It was unlikely that Portugal would accede to that pressure, '[b]ut these tactics might possibly inhibit Indonesian aggression, which is our main concern, by placing the future of the territory in the hands of the United Nations'.

Besides considering the threat to Timor and what to do about it, the brief also considered 'the question of bringing the Portuguese in on any multilateral consultation or action' on which the Washington talks might decide. Bringing the Portuguese in on a warning or other action might be regarded as a commitment on the part of the other powers to defend Timor. Not bringing them in, however, would deal 'a serious blow' at already bad relations with Portugal. 'It would give the Indonesians the impression that we are not interested in what happens to Timor; and the whole point of the exercise is to stop Indonesian aggression.' Bringing the Portuguese in could enable Britain to plead that it was fulfilling its treaty obligations. 'Whatever we do we shall be faced with Portuguese requests for help if the Indonesians should attack Timor.' The conclusion was that it was advisable to associate Portugal with any multilateral action.

> If the Indonesians should attack Timor at any stage it is clear that we cannot give the Portuguese any effective help. In these circumstances our best tactics would be, if there were signs of an impending Indonesian attack, to urge the Portuguese to raise the matter in the Security Council where, notwithstanding any action which might simultaneously be going on in the 4th Committee or the Committee of 24 we could support Portugal, eg in a request for the despatch of observers.[20]

Timor was discussed at a lunch Harriman gave the four delegations on 11 February. 'All delegations accepted that the territory would inevitably go to Indonesia in the end', Ormsby Gore reported. 'There was little hope of persuading the Portuguese to make progress towards self-government.' The letter Menzies had sent to Salazar was 'unlikely to make any impression'. Britain and the United States 'would consider whether they could say anything to the Portuguese, but were unlikely to do so in view of the problem of our military staging rights in Portuguese territories'. Western interests would best be protected if the United Nations took charge of the problem

---

[20] FO371/166908 [DH1071/15]: Quadripartite Talks – Washington February 1963, Brief No15.

'at an appropriate stage'. When that would be was disputed. Australia and New Zealand would like to get a United Nations rapporteur to visit the territory as soon as possible. 'We argued that United Nations discussions will inevitably embarrass us both with the Portuguese and Indonesians, and it may therefore be better to avoid them until the situation is serious.' It was agreed to recommend that the four governments should set up a quadripartite committee of officials in Washington 'to keep the matter under review, and particularly to make recommendations about the timing and nature of action in the United Nations'.[21]

Ormsby Gore had put the point Ambassador Ross had made and, he thought, it could again be made at the standing committee:

> The most sensible suggestion made by the American United Nations experts was that the Portuguese might be encouraged to accept that the United Nations rapporteur, whom they have accepted for [their] African territories, might extend his responsibilities to include Timor. The object of this would be the establishment of some sort of a United Nations presence, which would give the Secretary General an opening, if it were found desirable to internationalise the issue.

The Australian representative said that Menzies had described the situation as 'a threat to the peace'. That did not go far as the suggestion Ross had made, but 'it might well be interpreted by the Portuguese Government as fair warning that the Australians for their part can do nothing more under present circumstances'.[22]

The FO generally agreed with the line the Washington embassy had taken. It did not think that Indonesian action against Timor would necessarily encourage China to take Macau: 'In our view, Chinese tolerance of Macao stems from their belief that its existence (like that of Hong Kong) has certain advantages for them and is not due to concern for sentiment in United Nations.' But, 'in the interests of our relations with Portugal as well as on general principles', the United Kingdom and the United States 'ought to be prepared in the event of an actual or imminent Indonesian attack against Timor, to encourage the Portuguese to appeal to the Security Council, where we would give diplomatic support'. The FO endorsed the view that United Nations discussions should be put off as long as possible for two

---

[21] FO 371/169801 [DE103162/4]: Telegram, 12 February 1963, 483.
[22] FO 371/169801 [DE103162/5]: Telegram, 16 February 1963, 77S.

reasons. First, it wanted to avoid simultaneous discussion of Malaysia and Timor, which 'might have the effect of appearing to put the Malayans and ourselves on the same footing as the Portuguese'. Second, the Portuguese were unlikely to make any concessions, and so United Nations action of the kind could only be 'a very temporary brake on Indonesian direct action. This is therefore a card which we should not play too soon.'[23]

No direct Indonesian action followed. *The Economist* reported a statement of 14 April from Jakarta by the Liberation Movement of Timor, proclaiming the United Republic of Timor Dili.[24] In Jakarta Ambassador Gilchrist suggested that Sukarno was not keen to publicise the movement at that point: 'Indonesians are trying hard to avoid being branded as expansionists and aggressive, thereby crystallising Philippine doubts and Western solidarity on Malaysia'.[25]

Though there were reports of Indonesian plans to extend guerrilla activity in Borneo, a diplomatic process was under way. The Indonesian, Filipino and Malayan foreign ministers reached an accord in Manila in June, based on setting up consultative machinery in a regional association, Maphilindo, and on an 'ascertainment' by the United Nations Secretary-General of Bornean opinion on joining Malaysia (Easter 2004:46,49,50). Subsequently, however, the accord disintegrated. Malaysia was proclaimed on 16 September, but the Philippines and Indonesia refused to recognise it. On 18 September a mob, 'unhindered by the police', set fire to the British Embassy in Jakarta. Trade unions seized control of British businesses and Sukarno declared that he would 'crush' Malaysia.

Keen not to drive Sukarno into the communist camp, the Americans were still not ready to believe that he wished to destroy Malaysia. The British sought to influence them through another sequence of quadripartite talks (Easter 2004:68). Again the FO's briefing covered the question of Timor. It recalled the previous talks, noting that no quadripartite committee had been set up, as they had recommended, and then put the question in the new context. Indonesia consistently maintained it had no territorial ambitions in Timor. But secret reports indicated that its interest was now quite active, and that it might soon 'embark on an extensive campaign of infiltration and subversion', and in July a report from Jakarta alluded to a Military Council for the Liberation of Timor.

---

[23] FO 371/169801 [DE103162/4]:.Telegram to UK Mission, 13 February 1963, 688.
[24] FO 371/169801 [DE103162/8]: Telegram, 29 April 1963, 642.
[25] FO 371/169801 [DE103162/8]: Telegram, 3 May 1963, 395.

> President Sukarno's failure to prevent the formation of Malaysia and the set-backs suffered by Indonesian-based guerrillas infiltrated into Sarawak might, if these are not soon offset by greater triumph than the destruction of the British Embassy, persuade him to seek a more successful diversion in Timor. He knows that there is unlikely to be any serious military resistance and the Portuguese colonial record being so unpopular in the United Nations, it offers obvious attractions for a quick victory and will probably be treated as such.

Portuguese forces could put up no more than 'a symbolic resistance'. Their build-up had been token.

Australia and New Zealand were anxious to arouse United Nations interest in the hope that Portugal might be persuaded to accept United Nations mediation or trusteeship in connection with the transfer of sovereignty to Indonesia. The Indonesians might be less disposed to accept United Nations mediation after their experiences with the Secretary-General's Malaysia mission,

> but a face-saving arrangement through the United Nations is probably the only way to arrange an Indonesian take-over with the least danger of the transfer being shown to be another territorial victory for President Sukarno. Any arrangements to change the status of the territory should be of a kind which we could accept for one of our own territories. This consideration would be met if the right of the inhabitants to self-determination were preserved in implementing any settlement.

The briefing, however, repeated the view of the earlier briefing that the United Kingdom should take no initiative in bringing the matter before the United Nations. It should also try to discourage Australia and New Zealand from doing so 'at present'. Should, however, a serious situation arise in Timor, as it might well do so during the following months, an Australian or New Zealand initiative might inhibit Indonesian aggression. If a United Nations initiative failed to inhibit aggression, 'a Portuguese approach might at least elicit some reference (be it only a Russian veto) which we might employ to excuse our own inaction'.

There was little to be gained from 'further probings' of the position of the Portuguese. They were 'not going to tell anyone if they do not intend to put up much of a fight' and any attempt to bring them into discussions might be regarded as a commitment to defend Timor. The United Kingdom did not, however, wish to create the impression either that it was not seriously concerned about Timor, since that might encourage Indonesian aggression, or that it was not prepared to fulfil its treaty obligations. Whatever happened, the Portuguese would seek Britain's help if attacked, but it could offer nothing effective. The best tactics would be to urge the Portuguese to go to the Security Council if there were signs of 'an impending attack', and there the United Kingdom could support Portugal in seeking, for example, the despatch of observers. [26]

At Washington Australian diplomat, Sir Keith Waller, said that the Australian Government had sent a further note to Salazar, suggesting forestalling Indonesian support for revolutionary movements by radical political reformation in Timor and asking the United Nations to interest itself in its economic development. Salazar was not expected to take any notice, but when trouble came, the Australian Government would be able to take the line with the public and at the United Nations that it had urged reasonable courses on him and he had rejected its views.[27]

After the quadripartite talks in February 1963, Tange had set up a working group on Timor. Three things were clear, he said: the Portuguese would do nothing for the Timorese; the United States would not support Portuguese colonialism; and the Indonesians would move against the territory. If they achieved their objective by force, it would be 'a most serious encouragement to irresponsible and expansionist elements in Indonesia' and 'do the greatest harm to Australia's long-term interests'. The United States and the United Kingdom were looking to Australia to take some initiative. The working group was to 'explore all possible measures'.[28]

Portugal, the working group concluded early in April, was 'primarily interested in Angola and Moçambique', and it would not take any action over Timor that would compromise its position on those territories. Self-determination, it conceived, would lead rapidly to the collapse of its colonial system. Its interests, and those of Australia, thus diverged. Australia wanted 'to find peaceful and legitimate processes to end Portuguese rule in Portuguese Timor'. It was also concerned that Indonesia should not forcibly annex it. 'Portugal, on the other hand, would probably prefer Portuguese Timor to be speedily and forcibly annexed rather than enter into agreements.' The Australian Cabinet wanted Portugal to 'cede peacefully', the working group noted, but would certainly want 'some expression of self-determination'.

---

[26] FO 371/169909 [DH1071/24]: Brief No10, October 1963.
[27] FO 371/169909 [DH1071/27B]: Telegram from Ormsby Gore, 17 October 1963, 3212; Menzies' letter was sent only on 15 October, in AIPT:35–36.
[28] Memorandum, 25 February 1963, in AIPT:28.

Perhaps the problem could be overcome by 'a West New Guinea type of arrangement'. But, even if it were, Portugal was quite unlikely to cede.

The working group thought that Australia should discuss the future of Timor with Indonesia, perhaps as a first step. It could be told that Australia would not oppose Timor's eventually becoming part of Indonesia 'through satisfactory processes of self-determination', but that there were other possibilities that stopped short of full incorporation, such as autonomy under Indonesian protection. 'We should make continued reference to the argument of self-determination.'

The group was inclined to think—unlike the FO—that the sooner the matter was brought before the United Nations the better. 'What we have most to fear is a movement of resistance which will either be aided by Indonesia or will be so regarded by the Portuguese.' Indonesia could not stand idly by and nor could Australia.

> Under these circumstances, if the United Nations was already seized of the matter and Australia and Indonesia were on record there, it might be good practical diplomacy in the interests of both countries to have speedy recourse to the United Nations. We believe this would add a valuable element to present policy.

At present the Ambassador in Jakarta was instructed to 'speak in sharp terms if there were clear indications of an Indonesia threat'; then Indonesia would be arraigned at the United Nations and that would be followed by 'the sterile process of urging a cease-fire and withdrawal of forces'. What was needed were

> courses of action which would dispose the Indonesians to co-operate with orderly and constructive United Nations processes rather than taking unilateral action and relying on its appeal to Afro–Asian and communist countries as anti-Portuguese, anti-colonial liberating force. Given the importance which Indonesia places upon its standing in the United Nations this is a not unrealistic objective.[29]

The Cabinet, however, rejected the proposal to engage the attention of the United Nations.[30]

---

[29] Report by Working Group, 4 April 1963, in AIPT:29–32.
[30] Minute, 23 May 1963, in AIPT:35.

The working group also recommended that Menzies reply to Salazar, who had responded to the note of 8 February by arguing that Timor could not be independent, that it must be part of Portugal or Indonesia and that 'a Portuguese Timor seems incomparably safer and more attentive to the interests of Australia than the same Timor integrated in that Republic'. He referred to the statements Australia made in the Second World War. A note of the British Embassy of 14 September 1943 said that Australia hoped that Portugal would agree to concert measures for a common defence of Timor and Australia. 'This was the line of thought of the Australian Government of those days, and it does not appear that the world situation enables it now to think differently.'

Menzies wrote of a threat to peace. 'By whom and why?', asked Salazar. Sukarno and his representatives had declared that they did not wish to possess Timor 'and we cannot doubt their word'. That seemed to exclude a direct attack. But he might be able to accept the territory if offered and agents were 'preparing manifestations of popular will to that end'. That had 'nothing to do with any promises of self-determination', but would be 'a pretext to unleash movements and hold out threats to the territory'. What could Australia do to maintain the status quo? Its presence in the Committee of 24 would be useful if it dropped the view

> that the people of Timor were in a position to express their choice as regards international relations and to define their internal statute, and that recognition of such a position would result in altering the situation in the territory in a manner that would be favourable to Australia.

For many years India voted for self-determination. Then it annexed Goa.[31]

Menzies' reply to this, the note to which Waller referred in October, suggested that the Committee of 24 could not be brought to accept the status quo. Could Portugal indicate prospects for Timor that would attract support in the United Nations and create 'a positive sentiment...that Portuguese Timor should be protected from outside pressures'? Indonesia had indicated it had no claim on Timor, but it might feel bound to declare its support for an 'independence' movement. Portugal might be 'wise to secure the interests [sic] of the United Nations in Portuguese Timor before such an "independence" movement develops rather than after it is claimed to exist'. Menzies concluded by sending Salazar a text of the broadcast he made in Papua New Guinea on 6 September, indicating his government's 'continuing

---

[31] Salazar to Menzies, 1 March 1963, in AIPT:28–30.

effort to bring about conditions under which the peoples of the territories [sic] can freely choose a future separate from Australia'.[32]

As Waller had told Ormsby Gore, the Australians did not expect Salazar to take any notice. Nor did he. In reply he indeed dismissed Menzies' proposal. The suggestion that a United Nations interest would help to protect the territory was somewhat naïve. The United Nations 'took a profound interest in Dutch New Guinea: but that did not secure self-determination for the people of West Irian'.[33]

In Jakarta, JC Petersen reported from the British Embassy in February 1964 that José de Mello Gouveia, the Portuguese Chargé, was focusing on Timor. 'It will fall, as he says, like a ripe fruit into Indonesian hands on the day they decide to go to the trouble of taking it over.' He saw the Malaysia dispute as a godsend. 'By keeping Indonesian eyes turned firmly to the north, and by inhibiting the Indonesians from alarming the Australians and shocking world opinion with yet another external venture, the dispute has kept the question of Timor in cold storage.' But he had noticed an 'East Timor' flag at a rally and he had found 'some colonels' anxious that Indonesia should cut its losses in Borneo and take over Timor instead, giving the President another triumph. He also found a unit at the University of Bandung training Timorese and others in administration and teaching Indonesians Portuguese.[34]

'We have hitherto been working on the assumption that the Indonesian programme was first, West Irian; second, Malaysia; third, Portuguese Timor; and fourth, Australian New Guinea', JE Cable of the FO wrote to AL Mayall in Lisbon. Timor might, however, bear watching.

> The Indonesians might see an attack on Portuguese Timor as one way to gain a cheap victory (and much face), thus offsetting a tactical withdrawal on Malaysia. Or perhaps they would move against Portuguese Timor if they foresaw a period of military stalemate in Borneo.

A move on Timor would not need to draw down the forces engaged in the Malaysia campaign, but Indonesian leaders appeared to see 'a causal relationship between the two problems, and would not make a decision on Portuguese Timor without pondering deeply on their Malaysian campaign'.[35]

---

[32] Menzies to Salazar, 15 October 1963, AIPT:35–36.
[33] Salazar to Menzies, 5 March 1964, in AIPT:37–38.
[34] FO 371/175162 [DE1015/1]: Petersen to Cable, 11 February 1964.
[35] FO 371/175162 [DE1015/1]: Cable to Mayall, 11 May 1964.

Through Canberra the Commonwealth Relations Office secured comments from the Australian Consul in Dili, James Dunn. Two incidents, he said, had undermined 'the complacent attitude held by many officials that Timor has no need to worry while the Malaysia dispute continues'. Late in May 1964 a small party of armed Indonesians landed on the north coast near Lautem, but was soon captured. Their aim, the Intendant (Head of Administration) said, was to carry out subversive activities. In June a meeting of Timorese from both sides of the border reportedly took place at Batu Gade. According to the Indonesian Consul, an independence movement, Gerakan Timor Merdeka, was formed. Other reports said that when Portuguese troops and police arrived, 'the malcontents retreated over the border into the Indonesian sector'.[36]

The meeting was presumably related to the 'liberation movement' mentioned in *The Economist* in 1963. According to an appeal for support it sent to U Thant in December 1964, a Union of Timor Republic was set up at Batu Gade in April 1961.[37] It was, the FO told its mission at New York, an Indonesia-supported, perhaps Indonesia-sponsored, venture, its headquarters just on the Indonesian side of the border.[38]

At the end of 1964, though having 'nothing more than the merest indication that something could be brewing over Timor', the FO decided, 'in view of the continuing pace of Indonesian confrontation', to consider afresh Britain's attitude to Timor and possibly to exchange views with Australia on the policy to adopt in the event of an Indonesian attack. There were indications that the Indonesians might 'embark on an extensive campaign of infiltration and subversion to win over the Timorese'. Indonesia had always denied territorial ambitions, but its interest, as the FO had 'always been aware', was 'quite active'. A Union of Timor Dili had been reported, also a Military Council for the Liberation of Timor. Failure against Malaysia might lead Sukarno or his successor 'to seek a more promising diversion in Timor'. No serious military resistance was likely, and Portugal's colonial record was unpopular in the UN. 'Timor offers obvious attractions for a quick victory.'

Sukarno might indeed aim at a swift military victory Goa-style. But it was more likely that Indonesia would follow its West Irian/Malaysia pattern

---

[36] FO 371/175162 [DE1015/1]: Report by Dunn, 5 July 1964.
[37] FO 371/180256 [DE1015/2]: Abbay R Maly, Minister of Foreign Affairs to U Thant, 9 December 1964.
[38] FO 371/180256 [DE1015/2]: South East Asia Dept to Chancery, United Kingdom mission, 17 February 1965.

of political subversion, resorting to guerrilla attacks or armed intervention 'only in the unlikely event of Portuguese ability to contain this subversion'. If the campaign was limited to political subversion and terrorism, it would be 'exceedingly difficult' to assist the Portuguese, and, as they would surely not accept any recommendations on internal reforms, 'a British presence in an advisory capacity would be a waste of time'. Nor could Britain help in the event of overt military intervention. Oè-kussi could be occupied within hours. In dry weather key points could be taken in two or three days. The Portuguese forces were unlikely to resist a serious attack or even take to the hills.

In respect of guerrilla attacks, however, Britain would need to decide on a policy. It might be faced with a request for assistance and it could not argue, as over Goa, that there was no time. Even more likely, Portugal might 'seek our good offices to press the Australian Government to intervene'. From a strategic point of view, the problem was indeed of more importance to Australia than to Britain.

Britain was not inhibited, as over Goa, by 'divided loyalties to a NATO ally and a member of the Commonwealth', and there were arguments in favour of providing military assistance to defend Timor, outlined in earlier briefings. Britain had considerable commercial and financial interests in Portugal and some need of strategic facilities. Relations were, as a result of Goa and Angola, 'no longer very close', and would be improved. The 1899 Declaration, it could be argued, imposed a treaty obligation, though Lord Home had told the Foreign Minister 'that our power to fulfil our treaty commitments all over the world was limited'. Even if intended as 'a smokescreen to cover a retreat elsewhere', a further success might encourage Indonesia 'to persist in foreign adventures'. Aggression against Australian New Guinea, probable under Sukarno 'or some of his possible successors', would be brought nearer.

There were also arguments against providing military assistance. It would prejudice the United Kingdom's standing in the United Nations if it were linked with Portuguese colonialism, of which Timor was scarcely an enlightened example. Indonesia should not be given 'an excuse to blur her dispute with Malaysia...Sukarno's propaganda theme of the New Emerging Forces battling with and continually threatened by the Old Established Forces, would be "proved" by a British–Malaysian–Portuguese alliance'. Britain accepted that Timor would go to Indonesia sooner or later. An Indonesian attack on Timor would not affect its capability against Malaysia, but defending Timor would be at the expense of the forces Britain and Australia needed to defend it. 'The precedent might be cited by the Portuguese at a later date in the event of Chinese action against Macao.' The Indonesians would present their attacks as 'liberation' and the Afro–Asian bloc would share that view. Malaysia would side with the Afro–Asians, despite its quarrel with Sukarno, and might challenge Britain's use of bases in Malaysia.

In view of such arguments Britain should consider whether, in the event of guerrilla attacks, it could avoid a Portuguese request by taking an immediate initiative of its own. The best course would be to try to persuade the Security Council to interest itself and if possible assume responsibility. Indeed United Nations interest seemed to be 'the only means of neutralising the issue'. But it was 'extremely unlikely' that Portugal would accept United Nations intervention or acquiesce in a hand-over to Indonesia under United Nations auspices, 'whether the wishes of the inhabitants were consulted or not'. That line would have to be reconsidered in any case if the Australian Government considered 'that Australia's safety would be endangered by a further Indonesian encroachment near her mainland and decided to warn Indonesia off an aggressive course'. If it did not so decide, however, it would be 'unwise' for the United Kingdom alone to offer support.[39]

Early in January 1965 the DO sent the FO memorandum to Canberra so that the High Commission could sound out Australian officials.[40] Sir William Oliver discussed it with the Acting Secretary at the Department of External Affairs (DEA). 'Considered Australian views are not available and in absence of Ministers may be slow in coming', especially as the DEA and the Prime Minister's Department differed. The main comment from the DEA was

> that Australia would not regard Portuguese Timor as being of strategic concern to her and, from this point of view, would acquiesce in it passing to Indonesia. They consider the main threat to Timor is not overt aggression but Indonesian subversion.

The matter should be handed over to the United Nations trusteeship for settlement. These views, Oliver commented, were a 'reversion' to the ideas put forward after the tripartite talks of 1963. The Prime Minister's Department had

---

[39] FO 371/180256 [DE1015/1]: Memorandum, 1 January 1965.
[40] FO 371/180256 [DE1015/1]: Pritchard to Oliver, 7 January 1965.

then refused to take the matter far with Sir Robert Menzies on that basis, as it was politically impracticable in their view for any Australian Government with Indonesia behaving as she has in the last two years [to advocate] taking any move which could be presented as encouraging Indonesia to expand further.[41]

Ambassador Ross in Lisbon commented on the FO memorandum. He was not sure 'that we can count on being able to take an immediate initiative in order to anticipate a Portuguese request for help'. Remembering Goa, he thought the Portuguese Government might 'tease us by (a) asking us in general terms what we were prepared to do to frustrate Indonesian aggression and (b) requesting permission for special flights of aircraft, including military aircraft, through Gan and Singapore'. Either of those steps could be taken before Britain had decided that the matter required recourse to the United Nations. 'The answer to (a) would', Ross thought, 'be precisely to go to the United Nations either with or without the Portuguese (who have no illusions about the impartiality, let alone the efficacy of that body)'. As to (b), he wondered if Gan could still only be used by the RAF and if Singapore could be used only if Malaysia agreed. If so, Britain would need to have a constructive answer ready, to back the request with the Malaysians, perhaps, or to propose a flight via the United States and Australia. The Portuguese might only want help in withdrawing key personnel, Ross added; he thought there were only 120 Europeans in Timor. The Australians could do worse than invite them to immigrate.[42]

The Portuguese might well make embarrassing requests in the event of an Indonesian move against Timor, Peck responded. 'We certainly have no love for the Indonesians and it is all the more important that we should have our line well thought out before the perhaps inevitable event.' If the Portuguese Government asked in advance what Britain was prepared to do to frustrate Indonesian aggression, 'there would really be no alternative for us but to avoid rising to any such Portuguese bait'. The Australians, it seemed, would probably acquiesce in Timor's passing to Indonesia and they would be those most directly affected. Peck continued:

[A] *fortiori* we for our part would not be prepared to intervene on Portugal's behalf in spite of the ancient Treaty. The Portuguese know

---

[41] FO 371/180256 [DE1015/1]: Telegram from Kimber, 25 January 1965, 105.
[42] FO 371/180256 [DE1015/1]: Ross to Pritchard, 1 February 1965.

this as much as we do and that is why our only response to such a move on their part would seem to be to advise them to neutralise the issue by going to the United Nations.

The use of Gan would require the consent of the Government of the Maldives, 'which they would be unlikely to give'. That of Singapore would require Malaysia's consent. Its answer was 'not predictable', but in any case Portuguese military aircraft could probably not reach Singapore without using Gan. They could cross the Pacific. Over the use of Fiji the CO would have to consult the Governor. His answer might be conditioned on his assessment of the attitude of the Indian community. 'We think it more probable…that the Portuguese will be more interested in getting people out of Timor than in.' The Europeans would probably go to Australia in the first instance, which 'leaves out of the question the Timorese proper but it is impossible to estimate how many of these could or would leave the island'.[43]

After Confrontation: its legacy

Though the stepping-up of confrontation had produced new anxieties, in the event Indonesia did not take on Portuguese Timor. The destruction of Sukarno's power after the 30 September 'coup' and the takeover by Suharto led in 1966 to the abandonment of confrontation and to the creation of the Association of Southeast Asian Nations (ASEAN) in 1967. External Affairs in Australia felt confident enough to recommend again withdrawing the Consul from Dili in 1970. There was 'no likelihood that internal developments in Timor will become significant from Australia's point of view'. Its political interest was limited to the question of the territory's disposal 'in the event (not now in prospect) that the Portuguese voluntarily withdraw their administration' or 'an external "takeover bid"'. There was 'no early prospect' that Indonesia would seek to take over and there was no threat from other sources, which in any case Indonesia would strongly resist. 'In the long term the sensible disposal of the colony would be by incorporation in Indonesia.'[44] The consulate was closed in 1971 and Dunn (1983:136) later suggested that the reason was Australia's desire to distance itself from Portugal's colonial position. It expected Timor to go to Indonesia and removal would avoid

---

[43] FO 371/180256 [DE1015/1]: Peck to Ross, 9 April 1965.
[44] Submission, 1 December 1970, in AIPT:42–43.

embarrassment. The rationale was obscure, as it had been over the Consul's withdrawal in 1950.

The withdrawal certainly deprived the Australians of first-hand reporting on the increasing unrest among the small educated elite in Timor. Many of its members came from the Jesuit seminary at Dare, 'an eagle's nest perched high above the city of Dili' (Cardoso 2002:28). *Seara*, a Catholic newspaper, was a focus for the unrest, since it was outside normal censorship laws, and among its contributors were Nicolau Lobato, José Ramos Horta, Xavier do Amaral, Mari Alkatiri, a Muslim, and others. It was closed down at the instance of the Portuguese secret police, PIDE, on 24 March 1973, but some of its contributors subsequently met regularly. A few of them had been to Africa—in the course of their studies or as a result of exile—and observed nationalist movements in operation. Ramos Horta saw Frelimo in action, and Mari Alkatiri studied in Angola and met an MPLA representative (Jolliffe 1978: 55–57; cf Hill 1978:66n).

Coming to power in an orgy of attacks on the PKI and its sympathisers, the Suharto regime enjoyed far better relations with the West than its predecessor, but it had not abandoned Indonesia's claims to leadership in the region. With the post-confrontation withdrawal of British forces and the creation of ASEAN, its ambitions were substantially achieved, albeit in a more acceptable way. The Act of Free Choice, 'popularly called the Act of No Choice', had secured West New Guinea in 1969 (Crocombe 2007:284). The Sukarno regime had no doubt aspired to take over Timor, though it had failed to do so. That did not mean that Indonesia would drop the idea. It would wait for the right moment. After all, the Dutch colonial regime, of which it was the successor, had no claim to the territory other than a reversionary one, but clearly found it an administrative inconvenience and a possible source of insecurity, and had been quick to move in 1941.

In a press release of 5 April 1972 that was not without ambiguity, Indonesian Foreign Minister Adam Malik said that the independence movement in Timor would be supported only if the indigenous people sincerely wanted independence. 'Indonesia cannot push them towards independence if the people themselves remain passive about it. It is most important that the issue is not to be rushed.'[45]

There had been border incidents, the British Embassy in Jakarta reported in May, but they were apparently associated with 'local frictions', and not with subversion or Indonesian–Portuguese confrontation. 'Memories of

---

[45] FCO 24/1480 [3]: PR, Canberra, 5 April 1972; cf Dunn 1983:106.

Confrontation and of the Indonesian claim to what is now West Irian appear to have no similarity to border frictions between Indonesian and Portuguese Timor.' The Portuguese Consul in Jakarta was reported as saying in April 'that the trouble sprang from the smuggling of cattle and electrical equipment between the two territories'. Both countries, Richard Field wrote, seemed to be 'trying to prevent the border from becoming an issue between them'.

Indonesia Raya had printed an April Fools' Day article about 'Russia's support for subversive movements in Timor and the use of the island as a base for Russian ambitions in Asia'. On 8 May an editorial referred to the attacks Moscow Radio had launched against the paper: 'It seems', the editorial ran, 'the mop [joke] really reached its target so that the Soviet Government feels it necessary to instruct Radio Moscow to make a counter-attack'. Moscow had been made to drop its mask, the article declared, concluding:

> We believe that every Indonesian will sympathise with the people's struggle in Portuguese Timor for independence and drive (out) the Portuguese colonialists. But Indonesia will not allow Portuguese colonialism to be replaced by Moscow's or Peking's colonialism in Portuguese Timor.

Those strong words, Field commented, 'should not be seen as the official attitude of the Indonesian Government'. Malik's comments had 'given no indication of an Indonesian hard line against Portuguese Timor'. It was likely that the Indonesians had 'mixed feelings about the continuing existence of Portuguese Timor but they are unlikely to change their policy in the foreseeable future. Any form of confrontation with the Portuguese would be out of line with current Indonesian policies'. But, 'should there be a resurrection of Soekarnoist ideas, Portuguese Timor might prove a tempting target as a focus of diversion from domestic frustrations'.[46]

The Military Attaché had reported an earlier article in a Jakarta paper *Minggu Chas* on the alleged interest of the Russians in Timor. A senior diplomat was trying to buy a map; the Russians wanted to communicate with the political prisoners on Buru; they wanted to build a base. *Minggu Chas* was supported by the Army. 'Why they flew this kite is difficult to analyse. Are they trying to provoke the Portuguese or the Russians?'

---

[46] FCO 24/1460 [4]: RJ Field to JS Chick, 24 May 1972.

The German Attaché thought that the Chinese were 'carrying on some subversive activity. I have spoken to some Indonesian officers I know and they give it little credence. They shrug their shoulders and rather laugh the whole thing off.'[47]

Perhaps the April Fools' Day joke was in fact more kite-flying. Malik dismissed it, it was reported. The editor said it was published in good faith, but conceded that the broadcasts from Radio Timor on which the article was based could have been a hoax.[48] The purpose of the kite-flying is in both cases obscure. But it seems likely that it was domestic rather than international and that it related to the contest between the Army leaders and civilians like Malik. One focus of that was Timor.

The Australian Department of Foreign Affairs seemed to share the view that Field offered. In 1973 Richard Woolcott of the South Asia Division told the Labor Prime Minister, Gough Whitlam, that two of Indonesia's prime policy objectives were

> to secure international recognition for its own borders and to project an image of a country which does not threaten its neighbours but which on the contrary co-operates peacefully with them. Both these considerations impel Indonesia not to question its common border with Portuguese Timor and not to give the impression that it has designs on the Territory (which in any case is no prize to excite covetousness).

Indonesia, Woolcott said, did not foster a 'liberation' movement: it co-operated with Portugal. 'Occasional border incidents, arising out of cross border cattle rustling or tribal disputes, are settled amicably and without publicity.' Last year, he continued, *Sinar Harapan* published an April Fools' story that rebels had proclaimed independence in Portuguese Timor. That led to Malik's press comment 'that, if there were a nationalist movement... Indonesia would support it. He was obviously speaking in a purely hypothetical context'. He often spoke off the cuff.

> In this case we interpret his remarks as meaning that Indonesia—or at least its Foreign Minister—feels compelled to take an anti-colonial stance if circumstances force it into having to take an attitude. But

---

[47] FCO 24/1460 [2]: RE Blenkinsop to WO, 8 February 1972.
[48] *New Zealand Herald*, 4 April 1972.

Indonesia would much prefer such questions not to arise in relation to Portuguese Timor.

If a nationalist movement were to develop in Timor, 'Indonesia would be principally concerned with the potential effect on [its] own security. Clearly the prospect of prolonged instability or of a weak government open to Chinese or other influences hostile to Indonesia would be unwelcome to Jakarta.' The people of Timor would probably be 'marginally better off' under Indonesia. But 'Indonesia would be very reluctant to take over, lest this led to fears of Indonesian expansionism being revived in Malaysia and Papua New Guinea'. The status quo suited Indonesian interests.[49]

Jan Arriens, First Secretary at the Australian Embassy in Jakarta, qualified that view:

> [I]t would probably be more correct to say that the *status quo*…is acceptable to Indonesia, rather than describing it as suiting Indonesian interests…[I]f there were a well-established liberation movement that had attracted international attention, Indonesia would lend support. Even so, Indonesia would be extremely careful about lending material support, either overt or clandestine, until they judged that international opinion had reached the point where Indonesia's motives could no longer be impugned.[50]

Instead of abstaining on an United Nations General Assembly resolution attacking Portugal's colonial policies, Australia had supported it, Brian Toohey of the *Australian Financial Review* had reported on 15 May 1973. As a result, he said, talks between Australia and Portugal over offshore oil rights had 'got nowhere'. On the other hand, the activities of BHP, which had mineral exploration rights in Timor, were being condemned by the Australian Government. There were also 'signs that various church and other overseas aid groups will put increasing pressure on the Government to take what they see as more positive action against Portugal's colonial policies, than simply voting in favour of condemnatory UN resolutions'.[51] A similar story appeared in the *Canberra Times*: 'Africa has been remote enough from

---

[49] Submission to Whitlam, 30 May, 1973, in AIPT:44–45.
[50] Memorandum, 6 August 1973, in AIPT:45n.
[51] *Australian Financial Review*, 15 May 1973.

Australian interests to allow symbolic support for liberation movements but Timor may prove to be rather too close to home.'[52]

Indonesia, however, seemed to the reporter Michael Richardson to be content to let sleeping dogs lie. It had, he said, 'quietly suggested to the Portuguese authorities that it would be wise to actively prepare the ground for independence', but stressed that Indonesia 'did not intend to become embroiled in any kind of anti-colonial confrontation with Lisbon'. It would prefer the Labor government in Canberra 'to proceed cautiously when tilting at this particular windmill'. The Suharto government had a herculean task of national development and it would arouse suspicion if it started to stir up a hornet's nest. A full-fledged nationalist movement could be captured by communists linked through the PKI with China or Russia. But there was a tradition of anti-colonialism and the government had to consider the credibility of its non-aligned image. If the Timorese said they wanted independence, it could not remain silent.[53]

In August 1973 the Portuguese Foreign Minister told the British Ambassador in Lisbon of his concern over statements in Jakarta and Canberra about Timor, presumably prompted by the recent furore over Portugal's policy towards its colonial possessions,[54] which resulted from reports of massacres in Moçambique (Sobel 1976:44–47).[55] The Indonesians' policy, Field commented, was to co-exist with Portuguese Timor; they managed to 'harmonise this with their declared anti-colonial status'. Malik had touched on the question more than once:

> The substance of his remark[s] boils down to the view that there is no liberation movement in Portuguese Timor, so it is not proper for Indonesia to consider the question. Indonesia had some unhappy experiences with the revolts which troubled the years between 1950 and 1965 and she is not likely to try and stir a movement up which might endanger the stability of her own part of Timor.

A contact at the Jakarta-based think tank Centre for Strategic and International Studies (CSIS) told Field 'that nothing was happening between Indonesia and Portuguese Timor and that the policy was one of co-existence'.

---

[52] *Canberra Times*, 15 May 1973.
[53] *Australian Financial Review*, 21 May 1973.
[54] FCO 24/1773[1]: RJS Edis to Field, 14 August 1973.
[55] See also *Times*, 10 July 1973.

Elsewhere Field had heard that the Indonesians were 'worried by the possibility that Timor may be used as a base for subversive operations against Indonesia'. They speculated 'that some of the Sino–Indonesians who are now trickling back from the mainland may enter Indonesia via Portuguese Timor'. That was indeed possible, but there was no evidence to suggest that there was subversion in Timor.

Field had visited West Timor in August. The Deputy Governor of East Nusatenggara told him that Dili imposed 'a tough colonial rule'. Economic development was centred there, but the standard of living near the frontier was higher than elsewhere, probably in order to discourage the movement of people into Indonesian Timor. 'The population on both portions of Timor had many family connections and did not feel particularly "Portuguese" or "Indonesian" and families were allowed to cross the frontier pretty freely. Border incidents in 1972 had been concerned with cattle rustling.' Telephone communications between Dili and Kupang were opened in June and the Indonesian Government had agreed that the Portuguese airline TAT might fly between the two Timors. Dili made 'a sad impression', Field concluded, 'with no future and little present'.[56]

On reading of the Portuguese Foreign Minister's concern, the British High Commission in Canberra forwarded copies of some of the articles in the Australian press. The only official statement it could find were the answers to two questions in the Senate about TAA flights to Timor. On 23 May 1973 Senator Lawrie asked if the report that the Australian airline was carrying Portuguese troops were true. Senator Willesee, Special Minister of State, replied that it had not knowingly carried groups of military men or equipment. He pointed out that the operational parts of United Nations General Assembly resolution 2918, which reaffirmed the right of Portuguese territories to self-determination, were specifically directed to the African territories. Asked the same question in August, he pointed out that TAA was not the sole airline operating into Timor.

'Were it not for the cautious attitude taken by Indonesia', British diplomat Richard Sands suggested, 'the Australian Government might well prefer to be seen to ostracise the Portuguese over Timor (as well as the African territories) and, if the opportunity offers, join with others—eg in the Committee of 24—actively to seek Portugal's withdrawal.' In protest in particular against the alleged atrocities in Moçambique, Dr Cairns, Minister of Overseas Trade, had declared he would not meet a Portuguese

---

[56] FCO 24/1773 [2]: Field to Edis, 4 September 1973.

trade mission and his stance appeared to have the government's backing, '[b]ut the priority accorded by the Australian Government to this aim is probably dictated by considerations of neighbours' attitudes, in particular that of Indonesia'. The Indonesian diplomats in Canberra, Sands added, were

> quite relaxed about Portuguese Timor. They say that they have no conflict with the Portuguese, whose administration of the territory they describe as not at all oppressive. They add that, of course, if a viable independence movement were to emerge, the Indonesians would be bound to support it; but see little likelihood of this in the short term.[57]

'Timor was effectively taken off the international agenda when Indonesian foreign policy shifted to give priority to the "Crush Malaysia" campaign in early 1963', Farram (2004:340) writes. That was clearly not the case. Timor was considered by the powers concerned over Confrontation, who feared lest it might be taken up as an easier option for the Sukarno regime. Only the collapse of the regime removed Britain's anxiety. Subsequently it was to try to bring its 'East of Suez' responsibilities to an end and 200 years of strategic interest in the region came to a conclusion. More surprisingly Australia withdrew its Consul from Portuguese Timor. The Government seemed satisfied that the Indonesians were pursuing a policy of co-existence.

---

[57] FCO 24/1773 [3]: Sands to AR Clark, 13 September 1973.

Chapter Six

The Carnation Revolution

The situation in Timor was transformed by the Carnation Revolution in Portugal, but not at once. In 1974 the Armed Forces Movement in Portugal overthrew Caetano, who had taken over as Prime Minister on Salazar's death in 1968, and pledged to bring democracy to Portugal and peace to Africa. The Movement's leader, General Spínola, wanted a federation that included the African colonies. What might be intended for Timor was unclear. Australian planners did not think East Timor was viable as an independent state and believed that 'integration' with Indonesia was the logical outcome. There were arguments against it, however, and in any case there should be an acceptable act of self-determination before Timor's status was changed. Nor was it clear that takeover would be as easy as the Indonesians and others seemed to think. Political parties emerged in Timor more quickly than expected. The Indonesians thought in terms of a clandestine operation to ensure that the Timorese opted for incorporation and hoped that the Australians would help to neutralise unfavourable opinion in other countries. That was going too far for the Canberra officials, as the Australian Government could not be associated with a covert operation. Two officials were sent to report on the situation in Portuguese Timor. Their report led the DEA to talk in terms of preparation for self-determination rather than hasty Indonesian action. Prime Minister Whitlam, however, told Suharto he believed Timor should become part of Indonesia, but in accordance with the properly expressed wishes of the people. That prioritisation may have encouraged the Indonesians to press ahead. Britain's diplomats reported on the exchanges among other governments. No longer possessing a strategic interest in Southeast Asia, the British Government sought to stand aside.

Regime change in Portugal and the African liberation movements

After the aged Salazar suffered a brain haemorrhage on 16 September 1968, his long-time associate, Marcelo Caetano, was appointed prime minister on 27 September. There was no need, Caetano said, for 'stubborn adherence to formulas that he at some time may have adopted...Life is a constant adaptation', but he pledged to continue to maintain the African colonies (Sobel 1976:13). In the election of October 1969 the opposition to the long-established Estado Novo government failed to win a single seat. The previously exiled Socialist leader Mário Soares was exiled again in August 1970.

In December 1970 Caetano proposed that a new constitution should provide for greater local autonomy to the African territories: they would become 'autonomous regions within the Portuguese unitary state'. The legislation of 1972 in fact designated Portugal's overseas territories as states. Elections were held in Angola, Moçambique, Portuguese Guinea, Cape Verde, and São Tomé and Príncipe in March 1973. In Timor a new Legislative Assembly replaced the Legislative Council, but its role was advisory, only half of its members were elected, and the franchise allowed only 2.07% to vote. Most of the candidates belonged to the Timor branch of the corporatist party, Acção Nacional Popular (Hill 1978:36). In Portugal the Acção won all 150 seats in the National Assembly elections in October 1973. Opposition candidates had withdrawn, charging harassment and suppression of all discussion of independence for the colonies (Sobel 1976:52).

In Africa the African Party for the Independence of Guinea and Cape Verde (PAIGC) had declared an independent Republic of Guinea-Bissau in September, which was recognised by 50 countries. The guerrillas, with ground-to-surface missiles, were better armed than the Portuguese forces. Some right-wing generals wanted the African wars pursued more vigorously, but middle-level officers sought a negotiated conclusion and General António Sebastião Ribeiro de Spínola, who had been Military Governor of Guinea, saw no military solution, seeking an answer in some form of federation. Unlike the regime in Spain, which underwent slow change, the Estado Novo found its strength in intransigence under Caetano as it had under Salazar. Caetano preferred defeat to compromise: 'If the Portuguese Army is defeated in Guinea after having fought to the limit of its possibilities, this defeat would leave intact the legal–political possibilities of defending the rest of the Overseas' (quoted in Bruneau 1984:34).

Spínola was dismissed as Deputy Chief of General Staff on 14 March 1974 after writing a book severely critical of government policies, especially in the colonies, arguing that it could not win victory in Africa. He is said to have met Amílcar Cabral, the PAIGC leader, before he was assassinated in January 1973 and offered him leadership of Portuguese Guinea if it became part of a 'commonwealth' (Sobel 1976:52). The book, *Portugal e o futuro* (Portugal and the future), which had been published on 22 February, became a bestseller. Right-wing military officers and officials were infuriated, as was President Américo Thomaz, who forced Caetano to fire Spínola and his immediate superior Francisco da Costa Gomes, who also called for changed policies. In addition the Naval Secretary of the Armed Forces Defence Staff was dismissed for opposing colonial policies. Caetano asserted that African policy would not change. On 17 April the outlawed Socialist party called for negotiations with liberation movements in Moçambique, Angola and Guinea. The Armed Forces Movement seized control of the government on 25 April and its tanks were greeted in the streets of Lisbon with carnations. Caetano and Thomaz were arrested and a junta of national salvation was set up, led by Spínola and including Majors Melo Antunes and Vítor Alves in its political section. It pledged to bring democracy to Portugal and peace to its African colonies.

Back again from exile, Soares called for independence for the African colonies as soon as possible. Spínola preferred to see the territories in a federation with Portugal. The 'self-determination' promised by the junta should not, he said, be confused with independence. He told representatives of the Portuguese Democratic Movement on 29 April that the colonies were not ready for self-determination. Once it was possible, his government would press them to vote to remain in the Portuguese orbit (Sobel 1976:58). But what kind of government would it be? Spínola was, according to Birmingham (1993:178), 'the improbable mascot of his Marxist juniors'. But the communists themselves were unreconstructed hardliners (Birmingham 1993:180).

'In one sense it was in Africa that the MFA [Armed Forces Movement] was born', Rona Fields writes. Some of the senior officers there met leaders of the liberation movements, 'and these contacts, however brief, had probably engendered some respect for the fascist regime's African enemies'. Military personnel were aware of their rhetoric.

> The influence of the insurgent groups in stimulating the evolution of a leftist military organization among officers of the colonial army is not

directly traceable. Perhaps it is more accurate to say that the economic exploitation of the African colonies and of metropolitan Portugal itself had produced the necessary conditions for revolution in both places at the same time. The revolutions were thus mutually dependent, or symbiotic.

The military had been 'fighting and losing a colonial war for thirteen years'. History could provide a precedent for an army coup in such circumstances, but the nature and direction of the Portuguese revolution, as of the African revolutions, 'resulted from reaction to a political system that was equally repressive to the homeland and the colonies' (Fields 1975:5–6).

'The armed forces had not unanimously nor consistently supported the Salazarist regime or its African policies', Fields continues. General Humberto Delgado had led an opposition party in the late 1950s, only to be assassinated at the government's instance in 1965. By 1973 '[s]oldiers in Mozambique, called upon to massacre whole villages, were alienated from the colonials; they had stopped fighting in Guinea months before the revolution, and Angola, they knew, would present the most difficult problem of extraction'. Military officers differed politically, 'but they shared a commitment to end the colonial wars and see their country through to elections'. Caetano ignored calls for better salaries, pensions and promotions, or offered only token answers. Officers 'began to organize in secret cells in each service in the fall of 1973'. The MFA was composed of a representative congress of some 200 officers and a co-ordinating executive commission of 20 elected officers (Fields 1975:6–7).

As Fields puts it, '[o]ngoing contact with the African liberation movements provided both the future members of the MFA and opposition political forces in metropolitan Portugal a revolutionary model that was contemporary and appealing—that of a liberation movement'. Like them, it was pragmatic. 'It would be misleading to suggest that the MFA was or is an imitation of the African liberation movements', and it did not emulate France or Cuba. 'It would be fair to say that the MFA drew inspiration from all of revolutionary history and thinking, appraised its own circumstances and did their planning in the context of the reality of Portugal of 1974' (Fields 1975:11–12).

Bruneau (1984:36–39,44) stresses that the coup was mainly the work of middle-level officers—most of the higher-level officers had been bought off by the regime—and that they had concrete professional grievances.

In particular, they resented a law of July 1973, which, in order to expand recruitment, had given officers who had gone through a shorter course of training the same benefits as those who had gone through the full course. The publication of Spínola's book brought the discussion of war and the colonies into the open. His removal was the signal for the coup. But his program was not the same as that of the middle-level officers.

The colonies had been an integral part of the Estado Novo and they had begun to make an economic contribution to the metropolis. 'Africa stimulated the Portuguese economy', as Birmingham (1993:176) puts it. It was not surprising that regime and empire disintegrated together. The most important colonies were, of course, in Africa. Timor was indirectly affected by what was initiated there and in Portugal itself and the international reaction to it. But there were also some direct links between the leadership that was emerging in Timor and the liberation movements in Africa, which were indeed more significant than the links with the Soviet Union and the People's Republic of China that Indonesia seemed to fear.

In Canberra Department of Foreign Affairs (DFA) officials prepared a press statement for Senator Willesee, their Minister, who agreed to it. Australia, they suggested, could wait for West European governments before extending recognition to the junta. The statement would refer specifically only to the African territories.

> There is also, of course, Portuguese Timor…we would propose that any press enquiries on this point should be answered along the lines that while Australia is interested in these developments from the point of view of Portugal's overseas territories generally, we would regard any initiative in respect of Timor as a matter primarily for the Indonesian Government. For the time being the Australian Government would adopt a 'business as usual' approach to its relations with Portuguese Timor.[1]

The Indonesian Embassy enquired about Australia's position on the change of regime. It was referred to the press release and told that the Minister's emphasis on Africa was deliberate, 'but that we should nevertheless also welcome political evolution in Portuguese Timor'. In response to press enquiries, the Department proposed to say

---

[1] Submission, 29 April 1974, in AIPT:49.

that while Australia is interested in the developments from the point of view of Portugal's overseas territories generally, in the absence of an armed liberation struggle in Portuguese Timor, we would see the situation as different to that obtaining in the African territories.

The Ambassador in Jakarta was asked to report on Indonesian views but not to raise the matter formally.[2] The Indonesians, the embassy replied, would be glad to see Timor liberated 'under conditions favourable to Indonesia', but would not want a small neighbour that could be a base for subversion (AIPT:50n).

Australia's policy had indeed not been settled. There were new elements in the situation. In a policy planning paper[3] DFA officials in Canberra recognised the need to clarify Australian policies, given the change of government in Lisbon and the differences with Portugal over the definition of the seabed boundary between Australia and Timor; Indonesia had conceded the 'Timor Trough' principle, which benefited Australia, but Portugal had not (Jolliffe 1978:58). The Spínola government looked towards 'progressive self-determination within the Portuguese Federation'. More radical groups were likely to seek 'further liberalisation', especially in Africa. If Guinea Bissau, Moçambique and Angola became independent, 'Portuguese Timor could assume greater significance in the eyes of the Portuguese Government and a change in its status could then become less likely'. The prospects for tourism and the possible discovery of oil and gas might make the Portuguese more reluctant to leave. Timor had always been useful 'as a "safe" territory for soldiers on national service, as an assignment for recalcitrant government officials, and as a prison'. Such a rationale would be more valid if Portugal left Africa.

The administrations in Portuguese Timor and Indonesia had generally been on good terms, the paper continued. 'In the absence of any significant political agitation in Portuguese Timor or an active liberation movement in Indonesian Timor the Indonesian Government has shown no inclination to interfere with the status quo.' Timor could be an economic liability and the Indonesians did not want to fuel suspicions of expansionism among its neighbours, especially Papua New Guinea. Nevertheless, '[i]f a national liberation movement developed that attracted international attention, Indonesia would probably lend material and moral support'.

---

[2] Cable, 2 May 1974, in AIPT:49–50.
[3] Policy Planning Paper, May 1974, in AIPT:50–52.

Portuguese Timor 'would have no capability in the short-term to handle a self-governing or independent status', and the 'logical long-term development is that it should become part of Indonesia'. Australia's attitude should continue to be 'governed by that of Indonesia'. It should press ahead with negotiations on the seabed, but bear in mind that Indonesia would probably be more prepared to accept a compromise. 'For precisely this reason...we should not be seen as pushing for self-government or independence for Portuguese Timor or for it to become part of Indonesia', as that would be interpreted as self-interest.

An ad hoc departmental task force on Portugal considered that for Australia 'the real interest of the coup would be in its effects on Portugal's colonial policy'. Among other items it considered the policy planning paper on Timor.

> It was thought that the logical long term prospect for the economically non-viable territory was integration with Indonesia, under United Nations auspices in the first instance. The need to take Indonesia's attitudes to Timor into account was noted. The meeting also considered the possibility of UN Trusteeship for the Territory but this was not regarded as a viable solution in this day and age.

The economic situation in Timor might improve if oil were found, 'but there appeared at present to be no indigenous movement capable of providing an alternative to the Portuguese'. Australia should 'beware' of criticism that it might be favouring union with Indonesia because of its dispute with Portugal over the seabed and oil rights.[4]

Alan Renouf, the DFA permanent head, had questioned the policy planners' Barwickian view that Indonesia's attitude should guide Australia's. 'There is no I. *claim* to Timor: hence, there is no rationale for such a claim. "Give it to I." is the easy way out but not necessarily the right one.'[5] There was indeed no claim and transfer could 'create procedural problems in the United Nations context', GC Evans, a member of the task force, commented: unlike West New Guinea, it had not been part of Netherlands India. If, however, it became independent it would need substantial outside assistance, 'and, except in the unlikely event of a drawn-out armed struggle, would have little effective indigenous capacity for government except at the village level...[A] politically unstable state' might 'emerge on one of Indonesia's land borders'.

---

4   Notes of Meeting, 3 May 1974, in AIPT:52–53.
5   Note, 7 May 1974, in AIPT:51n.

Such a state could become a focus of Great Power rivalries and a rallying point for Indonesian irredentist movements. This would be obviously unacceptable to Indonesia, and for domestic political reasons probably to either party in Australia. For this reason, and because of its geographic proximity and its ethnic and cultural links with Indonesian Timor, the most logical long-term development is that it should become part of Indonesia.

The most likely way in which the issue would arise for Australia would be in the United Nations General Assembly Committee of 24, which was dedicated to implementing the 1960 resolution on terminating colonialism. In the absence of a liberation movement, that was unlikely in the short-term and it would be 'foolish' to press the matter in the United Nations without 'thorough consultations' with the Indonesians.

The outcome of an act of self-determination under United Nations auspices, in which continued membership of the Portuguese federation would not be an option, is unpredictable, and presumably Indonesia would wish to bring about a situation in which they were reasonably certain that the Timorese would wish to join Indonesia.

An additional reason for Australia not to be too active would be an implication of self-interest in the seabed dispute. But it must also be careful about a criticism that it was adopting a double standard over Africa and Timor. As a step towards formulating a position, it was necessary to consult the Indonesians and develop 'a clearer picture of their thinking'.[6]

From Lisbon the Australian Ambassador, Kevin Kelly, reported the plans to establish constituent assemblies in each of the colonies, all of which could be exploited by international power politics. Timor might survive as a colony longer than most, but was included in the plans. If the Portuguese Government could be overthrown by a handful of men, so could the government of Portuguese Timor. 'If the Junta and the AFM fail, one may have to contemplate the coming into existence of a possible Soviet or Chinese base within three or four hundred miles of Darwin.'[7]

Renouf talked to members of the British High Commission in Canberra, indicating that he wanted closer relations with them. Kelly, he said, was

---

[6] Evans to Curtis, 10 May 1974, in AIPT:53–54.
[7] Cable, 10 May 1974, summarised in AIPT:58n.

sending highly coloured reports on the possibility of a communist counter-revolution in Portugal. In his own department he was trying to counter the assumption that the best future for Timor would obviously lie with Indonesia: 'he saw no reason why the principle of respect for the wishes of the inhabitants should be over-ridden in order to "hand over" Timor to the Indonesians, who would only make a mess of it.'[8]

At the end of May, Sir Morrice James, the High Commissioner, talked to Renouf, who said

> that he thought that Australia might find itself in an embarrassing position. They know that the Indonesians might wish eventually to have Timor incorporated into Indonesia and that they were in no hurry. From Australia's own point of view they would prefer to see the status of Timor remain unchanged in the immediate future, and hoped that some generalised expression of an intention to move towards self-government might hold off the United Nations. If it did not, events might move at a pace which was by no means ideal. The territory was tiny and desperately poor.[9]

More information was needed, the ad hoc task force in Canberra considered, on the thinking of the Timorese and the attitudes of the Indonesians.[10] The Department decided to send two officers to Timor to make a first-hand assessment of the situation. The Consulate had been closed down in 1971 as an economy measure, though Australia had made arrangements for visits to the territory. The officers would be sent from Canberra rather than Jakarta. One would be AD McLennan, head of the Indonesia section, the other James Dunn, the former Consul now working in the Parliamentary Library.[11]

Information from Jakarta included an account of a conversation between Arriens and Satari, a member of the Indonesian intelligence agency Badan Koordinasi Intelijen Negara (BAKIN). The Indonesians did not consider that there was any evidence of an indigenous liberation movement in Portuguese Timor. Their concern was rather that post-coup developments in Macau might 'spill over', and that, 'having dealt with China by the front door, they might

---

[8] FCO 15/1956 [4]: BL Barder to JK Hickman, 10 April 1974.
[9] FCO 15/1956 [5]: Extract, Record of Conversation, 27 May 1974.
[10] Second meeting, 17 May 1974, in AIPT:54–55.
[11] Submission, Feakes to Willesee, 24 May 1974, in AIPT:56–57.

now have to deal with a backdoor threat'. They did not appear to favour an independent Timor, 'as this too they see as a potential source of instability'. They did not wish to give the appearance of expansionism, but their first preference would be for 'eventual incorporation'. One possibility would be to make informal soundings of international and United Nations opinion.[12]

'We are at the beginning of an eternity of relations with the Indonesians in the Indian Ocean', JD McCredie reported. Australia's attitude to Timor could be 'very important' for the future relationship. Incorporation made 'geopolitical sense'. Any other solution would be 'potentially disruptive of both Indonesia and the region'. It would help to confirm the seabed agreement and perhaps encourage Indonesia to discuss its Indian Ocean strategy more generally. The problem with the alternative of waiting and seeing was that 'time may turn against us'. The argument for a third possibility, 'staying at arm's length', was partly based 'on a hope that things would work out as they may well do without Australia's support'. The Government might 'attract some flak' if it appeared to encourage a military regime to take over 'a possibly reluctant population close to our doorstep. It might also be argued that, in the long run, this would not do us any good as it would lead Indonesia to regard us as over-anxious to please'. A fourth possibility was 'to take up a legalistic stance seeking genuine self-determination'. That did not seem 'a very practicable option', but it could arise 'if there were a communist-backed effort in the UN to set up an independent state'.[13]

GB Feakes of the Southeast Asia section felt, like most of his colleagues in the Department in Canberra, 'that there will have to be an internationally acceptable act of self-determination in Portuguese Timor before any change in its international status takes place'. The best result of that would be for the Timorese to choose union or association with Indonesia. 'The diplomatic problem for us is how to bring that about.' The Timorese might choose independence. Radical opinion in Australia might not be 'at all happy' to see transfer.

> But another point is that Timorese resistance to absorption…may come as a shock to the Indonesians; and we may have a role in suggesting to the Indonesians that they take into account the possibility of such resistance and start to think seriously about how Indonesia might live with an independent Portuguese Timor. We should not assume that it

---

[12] Telegram from Jakarta, 22 May 1974, in AIPT:56.
[13] McCredie to Feakes, 29 May 1974, in AIPT:57–59.

would be beyond the Indonesians' capacity to do so and fairly quickly to gain a dominant influence there.[14]

At the governing council of the United Nations Development Programme in Manila early in June, the Portuguese observer insisted that the new government's policy was based on self-determination. He talked, however, only of negotiations in London between Soares and the representatives of Guinea-Bissau and Cape Verde and in Lisbon between the Foreign Ministry and Frelimo and made no specific reference to Timor. The FO in London understood that the government had 'not yet considered seriously the future of their territories in the Far East: they have been fully preoccupied with the more urgent and complex problems of the future of their possessions in Africa'.[15] But two representatives of the Lisbon government, Major Francesco Rebelo Gonçalves and Major José Eduardo Garcia Leandro, had arrived in Timor late in May. They announced that the Portuguese planned to hold a referendum on the political future within a year (Hill 1978:71).

With the Carnation Revolution in Portugal and the collapse of the Acção Nacional Popular political parties emerged in Timor more quickly than had been expected, though 'no one wanted to take the first step' (Cardoso 2002:95). One was UDT União Democrática Timorense (UDT), the Timorese Democratic Union. Its leaders included Mario Carrascalão, a forestry engineer who had been a member of the Acção. The party and its program of 'progressive autonomy' were supported by higher civil servants, landowners, some chiefs, some Chinese and the Portuguese. A second party was the social democratic association, Associação Social-Democrata Timorense (ASDT), which in September 1974 assumed the name Frente Revolucionária de Timor-Leste Independente (Fretilin). Its manifesto advocated the 'right to independence' and rejected colonialism, and, unlike other parties, it had a social and economic program. Unlike the others, too, it sought to internationalise its activities, aiming to identify with PAIGC and with Frelimo in Moçambique, but not confining itself to Portuguese Africa. It was supported by lower civil servants, teachers, students, workers and immigrants to the north coast towns. Its leaders included some of the *Seara* group and the fiery speeches of men like Ramos Horta and Xavier do Amaral gave the party a radical reputation. A third main party, much smaller than the other two, emerged at the end of May, Associação Popular Democrática

---

[14] Feakes to McCredie, 6 June 1974, in AIPT:59–60.
[15] FCO 24/1905 [9,10]: Telegrams, 12 June 1974, 450, 451.

Timorense (Apodeti), which advocated unification with Indonesia and won support from some Catholics, from villagers near the border with West Timor and from the small Arab minority (Hiorth 1985:21; Hill 1978:71,104).

In Jakarta *Suara Karya*, the Golkar newspaper, said that on 28 May Governor Fernando Alves Aldeia had told their reporter that a plebiscite would be held in March 1975. On 25 May a correspondent in Dili, John Syukur, met José Fernando Osório Soares, a leader of the pro-Indonesia group in Timor and secretary of the Apodeti party. Ramos Horta, ASDT secretary, had met Malik in Jakarta and told *Sinar Harapan* early in June that it was 'too soon' to talk about integration. *Kompas* reported on 15 June that, after seeing Ramos Horta, Malik had said 'that Indonesia would not interfere in the internal affairs of Portuguese Timor but would support the Timorese desire for independence'.[16] Indeed the Foreign Minister wrote to Ramos Horta on 17 June, saying that Indonesia would strive to maintain good relations with an independent East Timor.[17]

First Secretary Arriens had a rather different conversation with Colonel Sunarso of BAKIN on 27 June. Tribal chiefs, it seemed, favoured incorporation, but BAKIN thought that if a referendum were held at that point the result would favour independence. By March the elite might have come 'to see the difficulties of going it alone', but the intervening period could also 'see a strengthening of separatist sentiment'. The scope and the temptation for 'manipulative guidance' he agreed were 'very obvious'. One of the difficulties about incorporating Timor, Sunarso said, would be its status: Would it be a province in its own right? Would it then receive exceptional financial treatment? It would in any case be a financial burden. Prompted by Arriens, he said that would be a small price to pay for the potential political problems a takeover would avoid. The conversation suggested, as Arriens reported, that Indonesian thinking on a takeover was 'well advanced'.[18] Indeed, as he put it in a letter to McLennan, he thought the Indonesians were going to find interference 'irresistible…Portuguese Timor is simply too important to them to take a chance.' But they would act 'very discreetly', and might wish to build up 'a close degree of co-operation' with Australia.[19]

Harry Tjan of the CSIS think tank told Arriens that he intended to submit a paper to the President recommending a clandestine operation in Portuguese

---

[16] FCO 15/1956 [11]: Field to RE Palmer, 20 June 1974.
[17] The letter, dated 17 June 1974, is printed in Jolliffe (1978:66).
[18] Memorandum, 28 June 1974, in AIPT:60–61.
[19] Summarised in AIPT:61n.

Timor to ensure that it would opt for incorporation. The recently established party favouring incorporation would be a starting point. Australia's role, he thought, 'could be to "neutralise" unfavourable opinion in other countries towards an Indonesian takeover; to prevent untoward repercussions in Papua New Guinea; and to take initiatives (or persuade others to) in the United Nations for the international formalisation of a transfer'.

'Tjan's extreme frankness indicated that the Indonesians are confident that we would favour an independent Portuguese Timor as little as they do.' He seemed, Australian Ambassador to Indonesia, Bob Furlonger commented, to have gained that impression from a conversation with Whitlam's secretary, Peter Wilenski. The information about the clandestine operation was

> elicited by some leading questioning in which Arriens stressed that in his personal view Timor would scarcely be a viable state, that he was aware of marked concern in Indonesian circles about the potential dangers of an independent Portuguese Timor, and that it seemed to him a relatively simple matter to do something about it. Tjan then revealed his intentions, but at no stage sought Australian co-operation. Nor was there any suggestion that we should be privy to Indonesia's activities in exchange for diplomatic co-operation.

The discussions with the Indonesians were all initiated by the Australians, Furlonger admitted, 'but the Indonesians clearly decided to take the opportunity offered by them to try to take us along on a *realpolitik* approach to the problem; and they are speaking surprisingly frankly. We are, in effect, being consulted.' They expected a response and failure to offer one soon would be taken as 'tacit agreement'. The situation was not one in which policy was 'best left grey and obscure'. In some respects and in some quarters the Portuguese Government was now regarded as 'more respectable' than the Suharto Government. 'It seems to me that, whilst we would doubtless prefer Indonesia to control the whole island, independence cannot be ruled out in all circumstances, and that the nature and extent of our support for Indonesia would need careful consideration.' So, no doubt, would 'domestic problems'. The Indonesians would expect Prime Minister Whitlam to discuss the whole question when he visited their country.[20]

---

[20] Furlonger to Feakes, 3 July 1974, in AIPT:62–63.

'I think our policy should be one of discouraging a weak non-viable independent state', Deputy Secretary Woolcott commented, 'and of encouraging (or at least simply favouring) association with Indonesia. But we shall need to go along with the freely (and fairly) expressed will of the people—and put this to the Minister'.[21] The dilemma—the relationship with Indonesia versus the support for self-determination, 'realism' versus 'idealism'—was not new; it had been experienced over West New Guinea. But the unsubtle approach the Australian Embassy adopted clearly encouraged the CSIS to think that Indonesia could secure positive support.

John Beaven of the British Embassy in Jakarta, travelling to Irian Jaya with the Air Attaché, spent a day in Dili on 8 July. He paid a courtesy call on the Governor's chef de cabinet, Captain Silva Duarte and reported him as saying 'that Timor presented a special problem for the Portuguese government since it depended heavily upon grants in aid and there seemed very little prospect of its becoming economically self-sufficient'. The main hope was tourism. The new government was therefore fulfilling the promise of the old to improve air transport facilities.

The Governor had wanted to leave Timor after the coup, but he had been 'asked by the people on Timor to stay', and he had agreed to do so for the time being. Three political parties had emerged since the coup and Governor Alves Aldeia had 'encouraged their development'. He had announced that a referendum would be held in 1975, but all the parties had asked for its postponement 'on the grounds that the Timorese people were not yet ready to decide their future'. Beaven asked Duarte what he thought the result of the referendum might be, to which he replied

> that if one was held soon, the majority would probably vote for a continuation of the *status quo*, if only because the economy depended so much on Portuguese support. In the longer term there would probably be increased support for the party seeking independence, but he thought that those wanting association with Indonesia would continue to remain very much in the minority.

Beaven had a longer discussion with Alfredo Naronha, the airport manager and the secretary of ASDT, a Goanese who had lived in Timor for about ten years. He confirmed that the Governor was a popular figure, but that he had determined to leave shortly, 'for the main reason that as

---

[21] Note, 11 July 1974, in AIPT:63n.

an old guard representative it would be more difficult for him than for a newcomer to carry out the policies of the new regime'. Naronha said it would be in the interests of his party if the referendum were deferred for three or four years. He agreed with Duarte that an early referendum would decide 'overwhelmingly' for continued ties with Portugal. 'The two main parties did not rate highly the chances of the APDT [Apodeti] who wanted to join Indonesia', but thought it was receiving some help from the Indonesian consulate in Dili. The Timorese, Naronha thought

> had a very long way to go before they could govern and administer themselves…His party hoped that their political development would not be force-fed. He did not anticipate substantial support from the Timorese for joining Indonesia, but his party, which wanted independence, fully recognised that Indonesia might not look favourably on a fully independent Timor which they could well see as a centre for dissidence too close to home for comfort.[22]

In Canberra BL Barder of the British High Commission had a conversation with James Dunn after he had returned from his visit to Timor with McLennan. Dunn later told Gavin Hewett of the High Commission he dissociated himself from two points in an article that subsequently appeared in the *Canberra Times* of 10 July. ASDT did not aim at independence in a year, but in the year after a plebiscite held within five years. The number of educated elite was not 20,000, but possibly between 4,000 and 5,000. Dunn said he was 'greatly struck by how run down' Timor had become since he was there as Consul. He dissociated himself from the suggestion that Australians were 'hoping that nothing more than a takeover by Indonesia would happen in the end'.[23]

The Dunn/McLennan report led the DFA in Canberra to prepare a new assessment of the political situation and prospects in Timor.[24] 'In the absence of a nationalist movement, political evolution in Timor has awaited the stimulus of change in Portugal itself.' The Timorese were ill prepared for genuine self-determination, but elections to Portugal's constituent assembly were promised for March or April, as well as a plebiscite, the date of which was less certain. The Governor fell in with the coup, reputedly

---

[22] FCO 15/1956[16]: JL Beaven to Palmer, 16 July 1974.
[23] FCO 15/1596[14]: Barder to CW Squire, 12 July 1974.
[24] Savingram 26, 3 July 1974, in AIPT:63–68.

under the pressure of younger army officers. Much of the drive for political progress seemed to come from Major Metello, the official delegate of the junta.

The new assessment noted the emergence of the three parties. UDT put its faith in Spínola's promise that Portugal would not forget the overseas provinces that wished to stay with it. ASDT represented itself as the party of native 'intellectuals' who favoured independence. Generally they talked of thorough preparation for it over five to 50 years, although it was noted that Ramos Horta had recently returned from a visit to Jakarta advocating independence within a year. 'His radical attitude stemmed from the guarantee of Indonesian non-interference which he believed that he secured from Adam Malik.' Apodeti, advocating integration, was 'the weakest of the three parties', but none of them had a mass base and there were tribal and regional divisions.

'Because of their fear of Indonesian attack during the Sukarno era, the Portuguese have educated many Timorese to a deep suspicion of Indonesia.' The Portuguese now had good relations with the authorities in West Timor, but

> the old attitude persists among Timorese. At the same time, it is said that many Timorese might be sympathetic to the idea of association with Indonesia if they felt free to express their opinion. But they are fearful that the Portuguese might return to Timor after decolonisation as they did after the Pacific War.

Opinion could change with 'increasing maturity'. The Indonesian Consul in Dili emphasised non-interference, but it was suspected that a subordinate at the consulate engaged in interventionist activity.

'Timorese who fear Indonesia are apt to assume that Australia would support Timor against Indonesia...A sentimental association with Australia lingers from the Pacific War, as do memories of the destruction caused by Australian operations.' Some, notably ASDT, claimed that Australia had 'an unsettled debt'. The politically educated assumed that Australia would offer protection and aid. There was a 'uniform demand' for renewed Australian representation. The Timorese, and indeed the Portuguese, were ignorant of their other regional neighbours. 'They are unfamiliar with regional co-operation—which in the long run might provide a means of drawing Portuguese Timor into the regional community and of harmonising its relations with Indonesia.'

The lack of preparedness for self-determination was widely recognised, and there was, the DFA assessment concluded, much to be said for

> a gradualist approach, provided that in the meantime a serious effort is made to develop the political consciousness of the Timorese people and their power of choice…Slow and careful political development will probably suit Indonesia's interests by increasing its chances of winning the confidence of the Timorese and perhaps of fostering the idea of integration. For Australia, an opportunity is emerging to develop stronger bilateral relations with Timor if it wishes to do so.

Perhaps in the hope of influencing them, the Australian Embassy in Jakarta was asked to discuss this assessment with the MFA and 'other interested Indonesian agencies. Those parts of the assessment that relate to the role and interests of Australia and Indonesia obviously require sensitive handling'. Time was clearly required 'to develop the political consciousness of the people to a point where genuine self-determination is possible. The lapse of time should suit both Australian and Indonesian interests.' Australia wished to 'avoid any possibility of differences' with Indonesia. 'At the same time we consider that the Timorese should not be denied the chance to exercise self-determination.' The embassy should convey the impression 'that there seems no cause for immediate anxiety about Portuguese Timor. The situation there is orderly and is developing in a favourable direction.'[25]

Feakes cautioned Furlonger over his earlier report. The information Tjan gave Arriens was most valuable, but 'we should not encourage the Indonesians to talk in any way along these lines'. Australia could not afford to be associated with a covert operation; even acquiescence would damage its reputation overseas. At home there were problems enough in maintaining the present policy towards Indonesia without associating with 'a doubtful operation'. It was thought that the Indonesians themselves might be underestimating the difficulties of such a venture and might find themselves with very little international support. 'The suggestion that Australia might help by "conditioning" opinion in countries such as PNG makes me nervous.' The Indonesian Army's special operations unit, OPSUS, had demonstrated its skills in West Irian, but the Indonesians might 'overreach themselves'.

At this stage, Feakes maintained,

---

[25] Memorandum to Jakarta, 5 July 1974, in AIPT:68–69.

we cannot endorse the bare proposition that the absorption of Portuguese Timor into Indonesia would probably best suit Australia's interests. It might not, for example, if the means used to bring about such a result seriously damaged Indonesia's regional standing and aroused fears of Indonesian expansionism.

An independent Timor was 'at least conceivable'. Australia and Indonesia could surely 'contain the problems' that it might present. 'There is much to be said for patience all round…The lapse of time that careful preparation for self-determination would entail should increase the chances of the Timorese agreeing to association with Indonesia.'

Policy towards Timor was still being considered, but the Prime Minister would be briefed for his meeting with Suharto. 'Our preliminary view is that Australia should not adopt firm and binding positions at this stage. We should prefer to see how the situation develops.' Furlonger could put these views to the Indonesians.[26] Feakes enclosed an account of a conversation between Renouf and Wilenski on 23 July. Tjan had 'pleaded' that Australia and Indonesia should work together for early incorporation. Wilenski had agreed to have the proposition studied, but stressed that it had to satisfy the principle of self-determination. Tjan told Arriens that his paper on the clandestine operation had been submitted to Suharto on 18 July. The President appeared to conclude that incorporation was the only option, though it had to be done in a 'discreet' and honourable manner that did not implicate him (AIPT:72n).

Furlonger thought Feakes' thinking had changed: he seemed more neutral than before over the outcome of the plebiscite, 'whereas formerly we saw the best result of an act of self-determination as union…if it could be decently arranged'. Australia needed to adopt a definite policy. Suharto would raise the matter with Whitlam and would expect the Australians to share the view that it would be in the interests of the region for Timor to become part of Indonesia. Furlonger himself had no difficulty with the proposition: a weak independent East Timor, open to exploitation by other powers, was not in Australia's interest. 'Let us not be too swayed by possible criticism from radical academics.' Whitlam could indicate that he shared the view and then qualify it by adding that self-determination could not be ignored. That could 'open up the question of independence and other options'.

---

[26] Feakes to Furlonger, 26 July 1974, in AIPT:70–72.

The Ambassador was concerned lest the President should tell the Prime Minister that Indonesia was considering covert activities. He would have to say no, 'as he could never be on record as having even tacitly acquiesced to such a proposal'. Arriens had told Tjan that, if such a decision were taken, 'he doubted that we would wish to hear about it officially'. Tjan should be reminded of the point before the visit, 'so that the Indonesians would not be under any possible illusion that we might take a diplomatic initiative as our part of a deal in which they did the dirty work in Portuguese Timor'. An additional reason for developing a position promptly was that there might not be as much time as Feakes suggested. The Indonesians did not foresee a rapid development and McLennan found the Timorese emphasising the need for time. Nevertheless, it appeared at one stage that a plebiscite might be held in 1975, and decolonisation in the African territories might accelerate events in Timor. Furlonger said that he 'would be surprised if we had as much as five years grace'.[27]

On 13 August Tjan put another paper to Suharto in preparation for Whitlam's visit. As discussed, it advised him not to raise the question of a clandestine operation and it suggested that he might discuss 'the scope for international initiatives to pave the way for the integration of Portuguese Timor into Indonesia', for example a United Nations trusteeship. The President said he would only be prepared to talk on the matter if he was certain that Australia's attitude were favourable. He wanted Tjan to find out, if necessary by visiting Australia. Arriens told him that 'the mood at present in the Department appeared to be one of keeping our options open'. Time, said Tjan, might be running out. The Portuguese might dispense with a plebiscite and simply grant independence as in Africa.[28]

Officials briefed the Prime Minister on 2 September. Australia appreciated Indonesia's strategic concern over Timor and was itself concerned that hostile external influences should be excluded. It was committed to decolonisation on the basis of a valid act of self-determination. Any future disposition contrary to the wishes of the people would by contrast have a destabilising effect in the region. It was necessary to proceed slowly and prepare the people. Australia and Indonesia could join to put that to the Portuguese. Whitlam

> could conclude by saying that, underlying Australia's attitude, is the wish that Portuguese Timor should not become an obstacle to good

---

[27] Furlonger to Feakes, 30 July 1974, in AIPT:72–74.
[28] Arriens to Furlonger, 14 August 1974, in AIPT:79–80.

relations...You would be worried if Australian public opinion became agitated about developments in Portuguese Timor or if they gave PNG grounds for concern.

Such an approach should head the Indonesians off 'over-hasty action that could disturb public opinion in Australia or confidence in PNG'.[29]

The Whitlam visit to Java

Whitlam put a different emphasis on the officials' advice when he met Suharto in Yogyakarta on 6 September. 'What he might say to the President about his own views on Portuguese Timor was most likely...to become the attitude of the Australian Government', he said. Two things were basic to his thinking. 'First, he believed that Portuguese Timor should become part of Indonesia. Second, this should happen in accordance with the properly expressed wishes of the people.' Indonesia, Suharto responded, was 'committed to the principle that the people of Portuguese Timor had a right to self-determination', but if it proved they wished to be independent, that would 'give rise to problems'. It was not viable and there was a danger that the Soviet Union or People's Republic of China might be able to intervene.[30] In a second conversation that evening Whitlam said 'that the successful incorporation of the province in Indonesia would, from the Australian point of view, depend on whether the public was satisfied that the people of the province had joined Indonesia happily and willingly'.[31]

Whitlam thus restated the Australian dilemma, but he went beyond that: his words would encourage the Indonesians to go ahead. He concurred, however, in a background paper the DFA produced which stressed Australia's concern with two questions—self-determination and the long-term stability of the region. An act of self-determination would need to be prepared over 'a period of time', lest the people made a decision that was not 'based on a full and informed appreciation of the best future interests of the territory and could therefore prejudice regional stability. At the present stage Australia doubted whether Timor would achieve real independence if the people chose completely separate status', given its weak economy and limited defence capability. It thus shared Indonesia's belief that 'voluntary

---

[29] Brief for Whitlam, 2 September 1974, in AIPT:90–93.
[30] Record of conversation, 6 September 1974, in AIPT:95–98.
[31] Record of second meeting, 6 September 1974, in AIPT:99–100.

union' with Indonesia, based on 'an internationally acceptable act of self-determination', would serve the objective of decolonisation and the interests of stability. A dialogue with the Portuguese Government would be in the interests of all parties. Australia was consulting the authorities in Lisbon and had suggested that Indonesia should reopen its embassy there.[32]

In his memoir Alan Renouf argues that Whitlam had no time for ministates and believed that a non-viable Timor would be a legitimate concern on Indonesia's part. He produced 'a policy marrying his two principles—integration through self-determination. By stipulating integration first, he indicated that this was more important than self-determination'. The DFA did not favour his approach, 'at least not as formulated'. Integration made good sense, but the Department 'rated the means of integration as at least equally important to integration'. Indonesia had used force over West New Guinea and Malaysia and if it did again, 'there could be sinister future implications, notably, for Papua New Guinea', then on the verge of independence. The DFA succeeded in rephrasing the policy, though it could not refuse to follow it. Approved by Whitlam and by Willesee, it came to be 'that Australia's primary concern was self-determination in East Timor but that voluntary union through an internationally acceptable act of self-determination would best serve the objectives of decolonisation and regional stability' (Renouf 1979:443–444).

Other issues were also in mind. One was public opinion in Australia. Indonesia was already criticised, as Whitlam indeed reminded Suharto, for its handling of the post-1965 detainees. Public opinion would be alienated if it became clear that Australia sanctioned Indonesia's clandestine operation. That, it had been agreed, could not be mentioned when President and Prime Minister met, but it was surely assumed. The DFA sought to bring Portugal into the picture. But the Portuguese, as Dunn says, noted the reference to 'an internationally acceptable act of self-determination', and its contrast with Australia's prompt recognition of the PAIGC in Guinea-Bissau (Dunn 1982:81). No doubt, too, it had the overtone of a West Irian 'act of free choice'.

Liem Bian Kie (Jusuf Wanandi), private secretary to Ali Murtopo, deputy chief of BAKIN, had talked to Richard Field at the British Embassy late in July. Of the three alternatives, he said Indonesia would prefer Timor to remain linked with Portugal. It wanted 'a secure Timor and was worried

---

[32] The Future of Portuguese Timor, in AIPT:101–102.

about the links between Chinese in Macau and Portuguese Timor—links which were enabling them to pass into Portuguese Timor'. Independence 'could mean an unstable Timor with the chances of outside interference'. Joining Indonesia, the third alternative, was causing the Indonesians some concern. 'Indonesia knew Timor was not economically viable and had no wish to take on any more problems.' Other countries might think it had 'done a "Goa"' or was set on 'some sort of expansionistic swing', though Indonesia had no wish to be the beacon of the 'new emerging forces' as under Sukarno. The Embassy report continued:

> Liem added that he would be interested in the British view of the problem and that it might be possible at some future time that Indonesia would ask for Britain's good offices in the problem of Portuguese Timor. It is not clear what he meant by this.[33]

'I cannot see how we can possibly help in its solution', RE Palmer wrote at the FCO, 'but I suppose we could tell the Indonesians that we, like they, hope for an arrangement which will contribute to stability in S.E. Asia, but that the decision must rest with the Timorese'.[34]

Alison Brimelow of the FCO South West European Department asked the Lisbon Embassy what the views of the Portuguese on Timor were. The FCO, she added, would not relish being involved.[35] They had said little publicly, Richard Ralph replied. 'For obvious reasons they are probably keen to keep it on the back burner for as long as they can.' Almeida Santos, the Minister for Interterritorial Co-ordination, had touched on it in the press, however. He pointed to the three political groupings and seemed to think continued association with Portugal inevitable. 'Frankly', he had added, 'I do not much like the idea that the only remnant of our ex-colonial empire should turn out to be a foothold in Indonesia…However, that is what it may come to.'

Ralph had asked his Australian colleagues if they had been able to get any more out of the Portuguese. Dr Magalhães Cruz, a senior official in the Armed Forces Movement, had been 'vague', he gathered. He said that the Portuguese had now shifted away from a referendum, but were still attached to a 'popular consultation…which could mean almost anything'.

---

[33] FCO 15/1956[18]: JL Beaven to Palmer, 30 July 1974.
[34] FCO 15/1956[18]: Minute, 7 August 1974.
[35] FCO 15/1956[19]: Brimelow to Ralph, 9 August 1974.

The Australians thought that, at the current stage, the Portuguese were not prepared to take any initiatives:

> Instead, they seemed to be content to sit back and allow the political movements in Timor to make the running. If the result of this was the emergence sooner or later of a strong tide of opinion in favour of independence, they would not stand in the way.[36]

A fortnight later Furlonger informed the British Ambassador in Jakarta, Willis Combs, that during his visit Whitlam had told Suharto

> that Australia would prefer Timor to be incorporated into Indonesia provided this could be done in a way which would satisfy international opinion. Mr Whitlam said that he regarded Timor as belonging to the Indonesian area. This had seemed to correspond with President Suharto's views.

There were, however, indications that Malik was 'not entirely happy with the way things appear to be going', according to the telegram. He had said he was glad to note that the people would be given an opportunity to express their opinion and that Indonesia would welcome the decision they took. Officials had expressed some concern that incorporation would be seen as a reversion to expansionism.[37]

Gavin Hewitt called on McLennan in Canberra to discuss the Whitlam visit. An Australian briefing after the Yogyakarta talks indicated that the Prime Minister had expressed the view that an independent Timor would be 'unviable' and 'a potential threat to the stability of the area'. McLennan said Suharto was concerned lest Indonesia should be accused of meddling or aggrandisement. Self-determination should be the guiding principle, McLennan concluded. The press had suggested that there might be a joint Indonesian–Australian approach to Portugal at the United Nations. McLennan said that was not the case, though the matter might be raised in the corridors.

The FCO observed that Whitlam had somewhat departed from his brief. In reporting his discussion with McLennan, Hewitt noted that the line Whitlam was now apparently taking was not in accord with that taken by Renouf in talking to the High Commissioner back in May. He had said

---

[36] FCO 15/1956[20]: Ralph to Brimelow, 26 August 1974.
[37] FCO 15/1956[22]: Telegram, 16 September 1974, 557.

he was trying to counteract a tendency in the DFA to assume that the best future for Timor was with Indonesia. A lot had indeed happened since May. Hewitt asked if Renouf had changed his view.[38]

Renouf had just had talks with the Permanent Under-Secretary in London. He had then said that officials sent to Timor about a month ago had concluded that, so far as majority opinion could be ascertained, it seemed to be against incorporation with Indonesia and in favour of self-determination

> leading most probably to staying with Portugal…Renouf then went on to say (his comment has not been included in the agreed record at the Australians' request) that the DFA had put forward the view that Australia should support the principle of self-determination, but Mr Whitlam had, somewhat surprisingly, come out in favour of incorporation into Indonesia, subject to an internationally accepted act of ascertainment of the people's wishes.

Renouf's own views, it was clear, had not changed.[39]

The Indonesian Ambassador to Belgium, Frans Seda, a mate of Murtopo, and a special representative of Murtopo visited Portugal secretly and met the Deputy Foreign Minister, Jorge Campinos, on 13 September, Tjan told Furlonger. He agreed that Timor should become part of Indonesia. It was arranged that Seda and Murtopo himself would visit Lisbon in October. The two parties would work towards forming a joint Portuguese–Indonesian administration, thus avoiding action in the United Nations. Campinos, taking an anti-communist line, said China had interests in Timor as well as Macau, and Joseph Luns, the NATO Secretary-General, had told Seda that it wanted the matter handled at the United Nations where it could use its Security Council veto. Tjan seemed 'a little apprehensive' lest Australia initiated action at the United Nations, which Willesee was to attend. Malik was not being kept fully informed, Furlonger added, and not too much would emerge from the talks Willesee would have with him. The Australian delegation should keep in touch with Liem Bian Kie who would be loosely attached to Malik's delegation.[40]

---

[38] FCO 15/1956[30]: Hewitt/ to Palmer, 19 Septemer 1974; another copy, FCO 24/1905[12], has the FCO annotation.
[39] FCO 15/1956['20'] [misnumbered]: PG de Courcy Ireland to Hewitt, 26 September 1974.
[40] Cable, 19 September 1974, in AIPT:106–107.

This and other reports seemed to Feakes to play down the need for an act of self-determination. The Indonesians appeared to ignore Whitlam's comments to Suharto and also to think the Portuguese were content for Timor to become part of Indonesia, whereas their public statements stressed self-determination. There were also reports that political activity was picking up. Ramos Horta had held a public demonstration. The United Nations Secretariat had received a telegram from 'what it regards as a very small Maoist group'—Fretilin. Feakes thought that Whitlam, who was acting Foreign Minister while Willesee was away, should give Willesee and Furlonger guidance about his reactions to these developments in the light of his conversations with Suharto.[41] The resulting cable stressed Australia's concern for self-determination. A joint administration would seem to prejudge or preclude it and the proposal was likely to bring the matter promptly to the United Nations.[42] When he approved the cable, Whitlam wrote:

> I am in favour of incorporation but obeisance has to be made to self-determination. I want it incorporated but I do not want this done in a way which will create argument in Australia which would make people more critical of Indonesia.[43]

Willesee met Foreign Minister Soares and then Malik, who had also talked to each other beforehand. Soares said that no referendum would be held in Timor before the Portuguese elections in March 1975, that he wanted the three countries to stay in contact 'over the coming months of preparation', and that Malik had declared that Indonesia intended not to 'intervene'. Willesee said he found Soares' statement 'reassuring', since it avoided any suggestion that 'outside powers' were doing a deal to hand the territory to Indonesia over the head of the inhabitants, and added that it would require 'some form of UN blessing'. Malik discounted the possibility of Chinese interference. Willesee said it was essential to prepare Australian opinion—'already critical of Indonesia for its treatment of political prisoners'—for the course Australia and Indonesia agreed would have 'least problems in the long run, that of eventual incorporation'. But if it were 'handled in a precipitate and hole-in-corner fashion', there would be 'mounting domestic criticism

---

[41] Submission, 23 September 1974, in AIPT:108–109.
[42] Cable to New York, 24 September 1974, in AIPT:110–111.
[43] Minute, Woolcott to Renouf, 24 September 1974, in AIPT:111.

of what would be taken to be Australian connivance with Indonesia, with obvious effects on Indonesian/Australian relations'.[44]

Ali Murtopo and Almeida Santos

The British Embassy in Jakarta had reported that Murtopo had spoken to the press on 18 September. Soares, according to Murtopo, had 'made a statement in favour of Portuguese Timor becoming part of Indonesia'. The government 'harboured no desire for territorial expansion, but if the Timorese people themselves decided to integrate into Indonesia, "the government will not rule out the possibility"'. Timorese representatives had appealed several times for its help 'in bringing back [sic] the island into Indonesia', but it 'maintained an attitude of non-interference'. Murtopo quoted Whitlam as saying the previous week 'that Australia was certain to support Portuguese Timor becoming part of Indonesia if the people there voted for this through an internationally accepted election'. Malik and Soares would discuss the future of Timor on 22 September when both would be in New York for the United Nations General Assembly.[45] They reached a tacit agreement that Portugal would not discourage support for integration (Dunn 1983:84).

Murtopo, who had run clandestine operations in Irian, was clearly playing a major role, the embassy commented. He also ran CSIS and Liem Bian Kie, a leading member, would be in New York too. The British Embassy's view was

> that Liem's main brief will probably be to try to steer opinion, particularly that of Portuguese delegation, away from full independence and towards a continuation, in the short term, of *status quo* in Portugal/Timor relations. This would give the breathing space needed by those in the Indonesian government (whose view at present appears to be prevailing) who favour eventual assimilation of Timor into Indonesia.

Liem might be seen in New York as pursuing a different line from Malik and he might have difficulty in persuading some delegations to support the colonial status quo. CSIS had indicated he might wish to call on the British delegation, although the Embassy did not think that, 'at least at this stage, he would seek to secure active British support'. If he made an approach,

---

[44] Cable, 26 September 1974, in AIPT:113.
[45] FCO 15/1956[24]: Telegram, 19 September 1974, 564.

the delegation should bear in mind that relations with DFA were more important than those with CSIS. He should be 'given a friendly even if non committal reception but as a member of Indonesian delegation, even if he is in fact operating independently of delegation'.[46]

Liem saw members of the United Kingdom delegation in New York on 25 September. Clearly the Indonesians had been 'scarred' by their defeat in the Security Council in 1964 over confrontation and Liem also recalled that the claim to West Irian had met 'unexpected opposition' from some African countries in United Nations discussions in 1969 (Saltford 2003:172ff). Liem 'implied that the Indonesians intended to play their hand more carefully this time, and assured us that Indonesia had no intention of trying to take Timor by force'. He was nevertheless worried at what might happen when the territory is discussed in the United Nations. His remarks indicated that the Indonesians wanted Timor 'not so much because of its intrinsic value but because they fear that an independent Timor would encourage the already existing separatist tendencies within Indonesia'.

The British Mission discussed the question further with the Indonesians, the Portuguese and the Australians. A member of the Indonesian mission said that Indonesia would like Portugal 'to hold on for another 2 years or so'. His remarks about 'the need for a free exchange of ideas between the two halves of the island' suggested that the Indonesians thought that delay would benefit the unionist group among the Timorese. 'Indonesia would, however, accept the decision of Timor's inhabitants on their future status.' That might involve a United Nations-supervised referendum or a mission.

The Indonesians were afraid that United Nations General Assembly's Fourth Committee might pass a standard resolution about Timor's right to self-determination and independence 'and would like no reference to Timor at all'. The Portuguese representative on the Committee told the British Mission Portugal would be happy for union to be a referendum option. His speech did, however, refer to the right to self-determination. The Australians had not intended to mention Timor in the debate on Portuguese territories, although they been instructed to say that union should be one option '(and by implication the preferred one)'. The British Mission found that 'mildly embarrassing given Australia's commitment to the right to self-determination elsewhere'.[47]

---

[46] FCO 15/1956[25]: Telegram, 19 September 1974, 565.
[47] FCO 15/1956[29]: Telegram, 4 October 1974, 1277.

Early in October the Australian Ambassador in Lisbon, Cooper, called on Campinos, who stressed that Timor was 'a Portuguese problem'. Portugal's chief objective was the Timorese should have 'the opportunity for a genuine act of free choice'. The Government 'would not welcome interference by Indonesia or anyone else'. Cooper said Australia was 'on common ground on the self-determination issue'. But it thought incorporation in Indonesia would be the best outcome. The views Campinos expressed were very different, he noted, from those Indonesian officials had reported to Furlonger.[48]

His standing with the President damaged by the Malari riots earlier in the year, Murtopo, with his allies Liem and Tjan, was anxious to demonstrate that he was effective and trustworthy (Anderson 1995: 140–141). Authorised by the President to handle negotiations with Portugal, he now visited Lisbon where he was welcomed by Campinos, also a friend of Frans Seda. Murtopo had been concerned at the implications of Spínola's resignation at the end of September. But, according to the Indonesian account, President Costa Gomes described full independence as 'unrealistic' and Prime Minister Gonçalves allegedly said it was 'nonsense'. Almeida Santos had set off for the Far East, but the Prime Minister apparently told him to abstain from public references to independence as if that were on the same plane as the other options (Hill 1978:36; Dunn 1983:84–85).

Whatever weight should be accorded these reports, Cooper was clear at the time that there was no meeting of minds. Murtopo seemed to think his talks with the Portuguese had gone well, but based that on the fact that they had said that, if the Timorese voted for incorporation, they would accept that. They had 'given nothing away in regard to their own wishes or attitudes…although Ali [Murtopo] does not seem to realise this'. Until Whitlam's visit, Murtopo told Cooper, the Indonesians had been 'undecided about Timor. However the Prime Minister's support for the idea of incorporation into Indonesia had helped them to crystallise their own thinking and they were now firmly convinced of the wisdom of this course'. Malik, Cooper observed, seemed to favour independence for Timor: did he now favour incorporation? 'Ali avoided a direct answer but implied that Malik was not yet fully on side with presidential thinking.' Murtopo seemed to think, Cooper reported, that already a majority of Timorese favoured joining Indonesia. The Portuguese were 'equally convinced of exactly the opposite'.[49]

---

[48] Cable, 7 October 1974, in AIPT:117–118.
[49] Cable, 14 October 1974, in AIPT:119.

Gerald Clark of the British Embassy in Lisbon discussed the Murtopo visit with Ian Cousins of the Australian Embassy, who pointed to the misunderstanding between the two parties;

> When I pressed him on the point Cousins was inclined to think that Ali Murtopo's visit and the more positive interest expressed by Indonesia in Timor's future were the direct result of Mr Whitlam's remarks in September. Mr Whitlam had, of course, not gone as far as the subsequent interpretation of his remarks suggested, but nevertheless he had put the idea into the Indonesians' head that Australia at any rate would not object if they absorbed Timor.

Cousins thought the 'driving force' came from the President's office—hence the apparent contradiction with the Foreign Minister's 'earlier stated reluctance to show an interest…for fear of reviving suspicions of Indonesian imperial ambition'. But the President's office would have the dominant say and Murtopo more influence than Malik. Returning from his tour, Clark noted, Almeida Santos told a press conference in Lisbon on 22 October that he had been 'astonished by the great attachment the inhabitants of Timor had towards Portugal', that they could choose their future, and that Timor might 'remain integrated within the Portuguese Community'.[50]

Clark's conversation with Cousins interested him in a letter Barder had sent from Canberra the previous week. Dunn had given him on a strictly personal basis a copy of a further report he had made. It contained

> a barely disguised plea that Australia should not countenance or encourage the integration of Timor with Indonesia, but that if, as Dunn evidently expects, the majority view in the territory eventually favours independence, Australia should 'seek Indonesia's co-operation in helping to bring about the birth of the new state'.

The report was prepared at the request of a number of MPs on both sides, including some Ministers, concerned over the reports of Whitlam's support for the eventual association of Timor with Indonesia if it were internationally acceptable. '[T]his piece of *realpolitik* is proving difficult to swallow for some in the DFA—including Renouf…—and indeed other sections of opinion both political and official.' The report would have some

---

[50] FCO 15/1956[35]: Clark to de Courcy Ireland, 23 October 1974.

effect on MPs, and the fact that he had sent the British High Commission a copy suggested that he might be seeking to influence opinion outside Parliament. McLennan himself stressed self-determination. The joint report stated: 'it is said that many Timorese might be sympathetic to the idea of association with Indonesia, if they felt free to express their opinion'. Dunn's new report said the integration had attracted very little support and that it seemed 'inconceivable' that Timorese would freely choose that option.[51] 'It may seem tempting to pander to those influential elements within Indonesia, who may wish to incorporate Portuguese Timor, in order to avoid the risk of endangering our present good relations with Indonesia', Dunn had written.

> In the long run, however, this policy seems unlikely to serve Australian interests in the region. We could well lose respect in other South East Asian capitals, particularly in Port Moresby, and, further, we might find ourselves encouraging a dangerous trend in Indonesian politics, with implications inimical to regional security. A more positive course...would be for Australia to seek Indonesia's co-operation in helping bring about the birth of the new state, if it becomes clear that complete independence is what the Timorese want.

The consulate should be restored. A mission, including Australia and Indonesia and perhaps others, should assess the situation and make recommendations on its development and political status. That would present, Dunn continued,

> a unique opportunity to co-operate in helping the Timorese emerge from their long isolation and colonial bondage, and, to our mutual advantage, extend to the Portuguese some positive and timely assistance. A circumspect Australian participation in such a joint venture would also serve to weaken the influence of those Indonesians who might seek to subvert the independence movement and incorporate Portuguese Timor into Indonesia against the will of the Timorese.[52]

Hewitt called on Tony Vincent, Head of the West Europe section in the DFA, after Almeida Santos' visit to Canberra. He had seen Whitlam,

---

[51] FCO 15/1956[33]: Barder to de Courcy Ireland, 16 October 1974.
[52] FCO 15/1956[33]: Portuguese Timor before and after the Coup, Options for the Future, prepared by JS Dunn, 27 August 1974; also partly in Dunn (1983:140–141).

Willesee and others, and explained that his main reason for visiting the area was to ensure that the Indonesians understood Portugal's intentions. The Portuguese

> did not really have much interest in Portuguese Timor; but at all costs they wished to avoid creating tension in the area. Portugal would do nothing to alter the status of Portuguese Timor without close consultation with both the Indonesians and Australians.

It was not now its intention to hold a referendum: it intended to hold elections for a constituent assembly possibly in 12–18 months' time; and that body would canvas options among the Timorese. Santos 'thought it likely that the Timorese would opt for association with Portugal. Portugal would accept this decision at least for the next few years.' He believed it was 'unrealistic to think of independence … since Timor was not economically viable'. The most likely long-term solution was 'absorption…by Indonesia but he had the impression that the Indonesians did not yet favour this course'. Portugal would welcome a joint Indonesian–Australian–Portuguese aid program with the aim of helping Timor to 'become self-sufficient'.

Whitlam said that Australia welcomed the suggestion of aid programs, but made no firm commitment. When he explained what he understood to be the Indonesian position 'and the Australian view that the best long term solution for Portuguese Timor would be integration into Indonesia in four or five years time, Almeida Santos had not demurred'. Willesee stressed that 'undue haste' had to be avoided: 'a hasty decision to integrate…could leave an unnecessary bad atmosphere'. The Ministers, Vincent said, 'had stressed that Australia's interest was limited to ensuring stability in the area. They had no wish to interfere or to affect the choice of the Timorese about their own future.'[53]

Almeida Santos had next gone to Jakarta, storms having altered his plan to go first to Dili. Beaven discussed his visit with Akosah of the Asia and Pacific Directorate at the Indonesian Ministry of Foreign Affairs. At the meeting with the President, both sides, he said, had 'formally restated their main concern that the political future of Timor should be decided by the people of the country, who should be given the opportunity freely to express their wishes'. But the Ambassador, Beaven noted, was told that Suharto mentioned the Sabang to Merauke concept, which presumably meant that

---

[53] FCO 15/1956[37]: Hewitt to Palmer, 24 October 1974.

Timor lay in the Indonesian area, and stated that Indonesia could not afford to see instability there.

Malik, too, emphasised the formal position, but then, according to Akosah, the conversation 'took a more practical turn'. Santos said that Portugal felt 'a special sense of responsibility' arising from its '400-year presence in Timor'. But though it was anxious that the Timorese should express their views, they were 'politically unsophisticated', and 'the prospect of independence had probably come as something of a shock to them and he thought it was the less desirable choice. For these reasons they did not think it wise to try to proceed to a referendum too quickly.' A constituent assembly for Portugal and territories like Timor would come first, then a law on political parties and another on elections. Only then would there be 'a consultation with the people of Timor on their future'. Like Suharto, Malik was anxious that any action Portugal took should not harm the stability of the area. Santos said his government would consult the Indonesians fully. Santos also saw Maraden Panggabean, the Army leader, who, 'speaking as a simple military man…thought it would be better for all concerned if Portuguese Timor were to become part of Indonesia'.

Beaven concluded that, judging by Akosah's account, Santos' meetings in Jakarta 'marked a further step towards the eventual assimilation of Portuguese Timor into Indonesia'. Akosah said that Indonesian security authorities were 'increasingly concerned over the potential dangers of an independent Timor which would be economically non-viable and politically exposed to undesirable foreign influences'. BAKIN had evidence that Chinese were entering Indonesia via Portuguese Timor. General Yoga Sugama, head of BAKIN, told the Ambassador that Chinese were moving out of Macau, some to Timor, and that five Communist Chinese from Paris had gone to Timor, by which it seemed he meant five Timorese who had been in Lisbon. Santos had said there were only a few Communists in Timor, but the Indonesians thought he would get a surprise when he went there.[54]

Tjan gave Furlonger an account of Murtopo's visit to Lisbon and of Santos' visit to Jakarta. The Indonesians recognised, the Ambassador reported, that they did not receive

> any outright assurance from the Portuguese that the latter themselves favour the incorporation of Portuguese Timor into Indonesia. This

---

[54] FCO 15/1956[38]: Beaven to Palmer, 22 October 1974.

emerged only by implication from the fact that Portugal was not anxious to continue its administration of the territory and they regarded independence as unrealistic.

During Santos' visit the Indonesians, Tjan said, all played down Indonesia's interests and concentrated on listening, apparently concerned over the possibility that Spínola's resignation might have changed Portuguese thinking. But neither Ali Murtopo's talks nor these talks, Furlonger thought, bore out the suggestion that the Portuguese had changed their minds or that they were never in agreement with the Indonesians in the first place. The Portuguese, as the Indonesians now saw it, regarded incorporation as 'the most sensible solution', provided it expressed the will of the people, which 'falls short of collusion in assuring the outcome, as at one stage appeared to be the case'.[55]

In Canberra, the DFA pointed out, Santos had made more of the question of timing than the Jakarta reports did. He envisaged association with Indonesia as a long-term outcome and continued association with Portugal in the meantime. If the Indonesians misunderstood the pace of Portugal's program, that might encourage the sort of precipitate action on their part which Australia wished to avoid. There was indeed a risk that the longer the delay, the stronger the political forces in favour of independence would become. But 'delays give the Indonesians time to influence opinion within Timor in their own favour and the Portuguese seem ready to help them'. It was important that Indonesia should not feel committed to early incorporation since delay would then mean 'some loss of self-respect'.[56]

Probably, Furlonger replied, Murtopo avoided discussing timing lest the discussion exposed differences. He and his advisers thought timing critical. Liem Bian Kie favoured a resolution within 18 months.[57] Tjan told Arriens on 26 October that Indonesian policy had hardened. Benny Murdani of the Indonesian Defence and Security Ministry, HANKAM, had talked of a takeover. Tjan said nothing would be done before the Portuguese elections. A swing to the left was expected, in which case 'pre-emptive action by Indonesia should not worry Australia unduly'. A real threat of Moscow or Peking penetration would 'dampen down' Australian public opinion:

---

[55] Cable, 21 October 1974, in AIPT:124–125.
[56] Cable, 22 October 1974, in AIPT:126–127.
[57] Cable, 24 October 1974, in AIPT:127.

'we need not worry that there would be adequate evidence of communist subversion…"we will look after that"'.[58]

In Timor Almeida Santos spoke in Dili and Maubisse. Whatever his Prime Minister had told him, he told his audience in the capital that there were three options: continued association with Portugal; incorporation in Indonesia; or ultimate independence. Whatever the choice, the Portuguese would not leave till it was made. Back in Lisbon, he gave a press conference on 23 October. He said he understood the Australians' anxiety that Timor 'should not become a reason for instability in that part of the world. I gave them a guarantee that…as far as we can we will avoid that happening'. Indonesia's 'only fear, which coincides with that of Australia, is that Timor should not become a source of instability in the area…the Government of Indonesia only fears premature independence'. He had unexpectedly found 'a mythology of love of Portugal' (Hastings 1975:30). He had been moved by UDT's display of ancient flags (Hill 1978:84).

Gerald Clark of the British Embassy in Lisbon decided to make enquiries of officials who had accompanied Almeida Santos to the Far East and was put in touch with Major Hugo dos Santos, who was a member of the 5th Division of the General Staff and therefore of the Co-ordinating Committee of the Armed Forces Movement and had special responsibility for decolonisation. He said that, like Almeida Santos, he had been struck by the attachment of the Timorese population to the Portuguese flag, but that otherwise 'there was virtually no political consciousness…whatever'. The three main parties that had sprung up since April 1974 had hardly any support outside Dili. About 70% supported UDT, which favoured continued association with Portugal, 25% ASDT, which favoured independence, and about 3% Apodeti, which favoured integration with Indonesia. ASDT and UDT had most of their support among the young, especially students or former students returned from abroad. They would mature, Clark suggested. But Dos Santos was inclined to dismiss their ideas 'as a passing intellectual craze'.

The territory was underdeveloped, and 'even with a crash development programme it would not be easy to organise the political education of the population, any more than their physical well being'. As a result, though the authorities had originally envisaged a referendum more or less simultaneous with the Constituent Assembly elections, they now accepted the view of the two larger parties that it would be inappropriate. Instead it was planned

---

[58] Minute, Arriens to Furlonger, 26 October 1974, in AIPT:128–129.

that, in response to local wishes, elections would be held in March 1975 for a local assembly 'which would itself, in due course, decide on the best method of local participation in the administration of the territory, and on the ultimate future of the territory'. A referendum might be appropriate in a year or two, but it would be up to the assembly to decide. It was significant, Dos Santos said, that the party favouring independence—ASDT—favoured a referendum, but not for at least five years.

Clark questioned whether Portugal would be willing to continue an association with Timor when its other dependencies were rushing to independence. Dos Santos said the MFA did not seek to impose uniform solutions. He also said that Timor was fertile, that oil might be found and that development money could be better spent. Clark thought there was 'a certain naivety' in the idea that Timor, 'backward for so long', could pull itself up 'without the injection of large additional resources from Portugal'.

The delegation, Dos Santos said, had found Malik 'evasive', but received assurances from Suharto that Indonesia had 'no predatory designs', which they accepted 'as being in good faith'. The outcome that would most alarm the Indonesians, Dos Santos agreed, would be complete independence, 'partly because it would give other powers an opportunity for meddling, and partly because it would give a bad example to other Indonesian islands which wished to be independent from Jakarta'. If continued association with Portugal was demonstrated to be the preference of the Timorese, he thought that would be acceptable to the Indonesians 'as it had the merit of preserving the present situation'. He thought it 'inconceivable' that the Timorese would ever favour integration, as 'the traditions of the two countries were quite different' and the standard of living lower in West Timor.[59]

The British Embassy in Jakarta by contrast commented on the 'apparently increasing pace' of Indonesia's campaign for the 'assimilation' of Timor. Ali Murtopo was 'being given considerable rope' and was 'using it'. The Americans had read his report on his discussions in Lisbon and found it 'a thoroughly bad piece of work, full of special pleading and of over-enthusiastic accounts of the responsiveness of all the Portuguese he met...to all his arguments'. Compare Almeida Santos' statement that the Timorese still had a great attachment to Portugal and that it was possible that Timor would remain integrated in the Portuguese community.

Beaven wondered why Ali Murtopo apparently thought that

---

[59] FCO 15/1956[45]: Clark to Palmer, 7 November 1974.

whatever has to be done…must be done with the greatest possible speed. It would seem to be more in the Indonesian interest to work for a continuation for the time being of Timor's association with Portugal, thus giving themselves time to try to organise a pro-Indonesia movement.

That seemed to be the aim at the time of Liem Bian Kie's visit to New York. Probably the Indonesians were 'worried about left-wing influences which may lead the Portuguese government to decide that Timor should be made independent, and which will disincline them to check communist infiltration into Timor in the meantime'. They had enquired about Portugal's relations with NATO.

There was 'some wishful thinking' in Jakarta about the Portuguese attitude, it seemed. Beaven found it

> difficult to see how an Indonesian campaign to take over Timor could succeed without active Portuguese support and equally difficult to understand what the Portuguese government would stand to gain from associating themselves with such a campaign, especially if the Indonesians handled it in a ham-fisted manner.

The United States Embassy had heard that a 'long-dormant' plan for a military occupation had been 'dusted over'. But Murtopo told the United States Ambassador that his government was well aware of international interest in its actions and, in particular, that any military action over Timor 'would not be well regarded internationally'.[60]

Australian and British Policies

At a party Barder gave at the British High Commission in Canberra on 28 November the Indonesian Minister, Sabir, made 'a very deliberate and emphatic pitch' at Dunn. He said 'that Indonesia was quite prepared to see Timor independent if the Timorese were to choose independence, although they (the Indonesians) would prefer that Timor should join with Indonesia since it could not be economically viable as an independent unit'. But 'if the present tendency to ever closer association with the Communists were to continue in respect of an independent Timor, Indonesia would take military

---

[60] FCO 15/1956[46]: Beaven to Palmer, 9 November 1974.

action to annex it', relying on the precedent of Goa. Sabir said that his remarks reflected the thinking of Malik. He also expressed concern over the 'unduly close links between Ramos Horta and the Communists. Dunn replied

> that although it was difficult to imagine Australia intervening militarily to prevent an Indonesian takeover of Timor, such an act by Indonesia would do grave damage to its relations with Australia: if these were taken seriously in Jakarta, they should think twice before embarking on it.

Dunn told Barder afterwards that Ramos Horta had made contacts with Australian Communists. He had reported the conversation to the DFA, noting that he interpreted Sabir as wishing him 'to stimulate a warning by the Australian Government to the emerging Timorese political leaders, including Mr Horta, not to go too far to the left'.[61]

Ramos Horta visited Australia again in early December. The Minister of Foreign Affairs had not received him when he had visited in July and Feakes again advised Willesee not to receive him, as it would arouse Indonesian suspicions, particularly as Whitlam had told Suharto the previous decision was deliberate.[62] Willesee, however, took the view that refusing to see him would be seen as a lack of support for self-determination (AIPT:135n). In Singapore for a Colombo Plan conference, Willesee reiterated to the press on 5 December that Australia was committed to self-determination and refused to rule out the possibility of an independent Portuguese Timor, which, given that Malik had reportedly said there were only two choices, was seen by Michael Richardson in *The Age* as the first sign of a rift with Indonesia (AIPTL137n; Hastings1975:31). In a resolution adopted in anticipation of Ramos Horta's visit, a Labor Caucus Committee had advocated a parliamentary visit to Timor. The DFA favoured a policy of 'non-involvement' and Willesee hoped a parliamentary delegation could be avoided.[63]

Working out that policy was not done without doubts and differences. Warwick Mayne-Wilson, Head of Public Information, did not agree with the approach. He thought that Australia was

---

[61] FCO 15/1956[54]: Minute for Hewitt, 29 November 1974.
[62] Submission, 25 November 1974, in AIPT:134–135.
[63] Willesee to Whitlam, 10 December 1974, in AIPT:142–143.

already on a path that is (a) driving FRETILIN into the arms of the extreme left, and perhaps the Chinese (b) giving the Indonesians the very excuses they need to intervene in P. Timor to prevent a 'communist takeover' (c) and thus leading to an unpleasant period in our relations with Indonesia, with calls for suspension of aid, etc.

He did not believe that 'we should detach ourselves and do nothing—or wait to be asked to join some Indonesian/Portuguese arrangement that may never materialise'. The Australians had to 'get the idea across [to the Indonesians] that they *can* live with an independent P. Timor, if we and they take measures to integrate it *economically* into our region and help make it viable. Its political co-operation would automatically follow.'[64]

Officials, however, affirmed the recommendation. Australia should follow a policy of 'non-involvement', implying 'caution in the frequency and wording of public statements' and 'a discreet distance from Indonesia's own public pronouncements', as well as 'regarding the association of Portuguese Timor with Indonesia as only one of several acceptable results of an act of self-determination'. At the same time Australia should maintain a dialogue with the Indonesians, trying 'to divert them from too forward a policy', and to bring them to recognise that, if the Timorese were 'clearly intent on independence', they could live with it. It should also try to influence Ramos Horta and other leaders from courses of action that might play into Indonesian hands. The policy, officials recognised, might have to be revised if developments moved more rapidly than currently expected.[65]

In the discussion that preceded the finalisation of the policy paper, two officials had warned against treating Timor like West New Guinea. There was more likely to be a resistance movement and it would become more of an international issue. The people of Portuguese Timor were 'not malleable'. At the end of the discussion Woolcott observed that the Prime Minister thought incorporation was best, 'but he had escape clauses if necessary'. Feakes said the paper was 'in part designed to invite the Prime Minister to take the escape route'. If he did, 'we of course had a problem with Indonesia'.[66] DFA was thus shaping its policy to back down from Whitlam's line, with which

---

[64] Minute, Mayne-Wilson to Feakes, 27 November 1974, in AIPT:135.
[65] Submission, 13 December 1974, in AIPT:148–153.
[66] Record of policy discussion, 11 December 1974, in AIPT:145–148.

Willesee did not in any case agree. But it depended on developments in the interim period not getting out of hand.

During his visit to Australia in December Ramos Horta addressed a number of sympathetic groups, called at the Indonesian and other embassies, lobbied MPs and met Willesee and DFA officers. He was told that the Australian Labor Government 'stood firmly by self-determination'. He wanted it to come out firmly against Indonesian 'interference'. He was reminded that Indonesian leaders had said on a number of occasions that, though they thought incorporation the best solution, they would respect the outcome of an act of self-determination, and that Malik had now clarified a statement in which he appeared to rule out independence.[67] Indonesia would be aware that Australian public opinion would 'react adversely to any move aimed at forestalling or pre-empting an act of self-determination'. No public statements were needed. Horta's fears were exaggerated. He should be doing more to allay Indonesia's fears and consider the possible disadvantages of some of the associations he appeared to be developing. In response he strongly denied that Fretilin was a communist movement.[68]

The Ambassador in Jakarta was told he could convey this account of the Ramos Horta visit to the Indonesians. Mayne-Wilson gave it to Hewitt. He explained that Willesee had been ready to see Ramos Horta because he felt he should keep in contact with leading personalities in Timor following his discussion with Portuguese and Indonesians in New York and elsewhere. 'There was, however, some concern about the motives of Horta's sponsors [the Campaign for the Independence of East Timor] who seemed to wish to use the visit to promote their anti-Suharto campaign.' Ministers were concerned about the parliamentary visit he had suggested, Mayne-Wilson added, and the DFA advised caution over reopening the consulate. 'The Australians did not want to find themselves in a position of being seen or being used as a counterpoise to Indonesian interests and influence in the territory.'

A submission to Willesee, Mayne-Wilson said, argued that the interests of the Australians would best be served by

> distancing themselves somewhat from the Indonesian line and using their influence with the Indonesians to impress on them the need for

---

[67] Malik had said – hardly a clarification—that he had meant that there were three alternatives, but only two choices (*Kompas*, 7 December 1974, quoted Hoadley (1975:19)).
[68] Memorandum to Jakarta, 13 December 1974, in AIPT:154–156.

a genuine and internationally acceptable act of self-determination... The Australian Government should seek to calm what in their view were exaggerated Indonesian fears about the future of the territory, and to persuade the Indonesians of the need to live with an independent Portuguese Timor, if that was the choice of the inhabitants.

Privately the Australians had made it plain to the Indonesians that they would not 'countenance Indonesian interference' in Timor. The press briefing given after Whitlam's discussions with Suharto 'had given the wrong flavour to Australian sentiments', Mayne-Wilson acknowledged.

Not enough emphasis had been put at the time on the need for an act of self-determination by the Timorese. This had led to a misunderstanding of the Australian position: the DFA now hoped that the early impression created by the press briefing had been corrected.[69]

Late in October the FCO in London had drafted a policy document on the future of Portuguese Timor. By contrast to Australia's, Britain's interest in its future was 'minimal', but the question had 'some relevance in the regional context'. It was likely to be discussed in the United Nations General Assembly, before which Britain might be lobbied by Portugal and Indonesia, 'and we may need a line to take in Parliament and with the public'. The line would need to recognise that 'while we support the principle of self-determination..., the possible existence in the Indonesian archipelago of a mini-state of doubtful economic viability could become a minor irritant in the region, particularly if a country hostile to us were to try to meddle in its internal affairs'.

The document analysed the attitude of the political movements in Timor and of the other powers involved. The Portuguese would probably prefer to be rid of it, but recognised the feeling in favour of continuing association. Indonesia wanted integration but, with the Irian experience in mind, saw that it had to result from 'at least some kind of expression of the will of the people of Portuguese Timor', the United Nations perhaps playing something like the 'figleaf' role it played over Irian. Whitlam appeared to favour integration, if it could be done in a way that satisfied international opinion. 'However, the Australians will probably wish to maintain a fairly

---

[69] FCO 15/1956[54]: Hewitt to Palmer, 20 December 1974.

flexible attitude in case this policy proves impractical.' China had not expressed a view, though it had supported liberation movements in Africa.

The conclusions the draft reached were that integration, if done in a way that satisfied international opinion,

> would suit us best. Continued association with Portugal would be acceptable provided that this was the demonstrated wish of the majority of Timorese. Although the least satisfactory outcome, we could live with an independent Timor. If asked to comment on association we could say that we wonder whether there might not be some merit in the continued *status quo* for a time to enable the Timorese to consider the implications of each possible solution to their future.

The Portuguese and the Indonesians would have to work out a solution. 'We should keep in touch with both parties and with the Australians at the UN. We shall not wish to initiate any action ourselves.' The Portuguese could be told that Britain supported their aim 'to consult the wishes of the inhabitants of Timor about their future', but that it had 'no strong feelings about the eventual outcome', though sharing their doubts about the viability of independence. Indonesia could be told that Britain would support integration if it were acceptable to the Timorese and to international opinion. 'The timing should be left to the Portuguese.' If asked in public, the British should say that they believed 'that any solution…should conform to the wishes and interests of the people'.[70]

The FCO had earlier decided that it wished to avoid involvement. Britain had indeed now no strategic interests in Southeast Asia. But it had connections with Portugal and with Australia, and, still with a remnant of empire, it had an interest in self-determination. Commenting on the draft from Canberra in early November, Hewitt suggested that since Whitlam's talks Australia's stance had been 'somewhat modified in the face of the generally hostile reaction from the Australian press and public to what was widely suspected of being a rather cynical act of *Realpolitik*'. Whitlam still seemed to favour incorporation, but the Government seemed to be stressing self-determination 'rather more loudly…The line seems therefore to be swinging back more to the DFA's position.'[71]

---

[70] FCO 15/1956[36]: Draft, The Future of Portuguese Timor, sent by Palmer to Clark for comment, 28 October 1974.
[71] FCO 15/1956[43]: Hewitt to Palmer, 5 November 1974.

GA Duggan of the British Embassy to Indonesia asked the new Australian Counsellor in Jakarta, Alan Taylor, whether Whitlam had not made his country's attitude 'absolutely clear…namely integration'. He 'hastily' replied

> that their view had always been two-pronged, ie integration with proper regard to the principle of self-determination; he went on to underline that the self-determination aspect was an important one for Australia. Clearly, no options are being publicly closed.[72]

But it might be argued that Whitlam had in fact reduced the options Australia possessed, narrow as they perhaps were. And it was also clear that the British were now even less prepared to offer options than they were over West Irian, when Australia turned them down. Nor did there prove to be as much time as DFA thought or hoped. The development of the nationalist movements and the strife among them cut it down.

---

[72] FCO 15/1956[55]: Duggan to Palmer, 31 December 1974.

Chapter Seven

Timorese Conflicts

In Portugal the Armed Forces Movement (MFA) became rather more radical during 1974. Spínola attempted a coup in September and fled Portugal in March 1975. His concept of a Lusitanian federation was already being overtaken by moves towards independence in Africa. The leftward trend in Portugal did not mean Communist domination but, together with the Communist victories in Indochina in April 1975, it aroused apprehension in the United States. It also gave the Indonesians a rationale for intervening among the parties that had emerged in Timor and helped to lead to civil war among them, from which Fretilin, the most left-wing, emerged victorious. The events presented Australia with dilemmas: its government preferred the incorporation of Portuguese Timor into Indonesia, but wanted to acknowledge self-determination. In particular it wished to avoid Indonesian action that might alarm newly independent Papua New Guinea and involve Australia in a commitment against Indonesia. Suharto was cautious and perhaps missed an opportunity to intervene. British diplomats continued to report; if questioned, the FO told the Ambassador in Jakarta, he should support the principle of self-determination, but it hoped that Britain could stand aside.

Portugal and its colonies

Spínola, the first President of Portugal after the Carnation Revolution, had originally set up a holding action kind of provisional government, designed to get a constitution in order in preparation for elections. The first cabinet had fallen apart early in July 1974 and a 'behind-the-scenes revolutionary struggle' commenced. Spínola was seen to be out of step with the MFA Assembly. A new Prime Minister, Vasco dos Santos Gonçalves, brought together a more responsive cabinet, including seven MFA leaders, and ministers selected from the Popular Democrats (PPD), Portuguese Socialist Party (PSP) and Portuguese Communist Party (PCP) (Fields 1975:89), including Mário Soares as Foreign Minister, António de Almeida Santos as overseas territories minister, and Vítor Alves and Ernesto de Melo Antunes as ministers without portfolio. After a failed attempt to call on the 'silent majority' to oppose the prospect of 'anarchy' and union rule, Spínola resigned on 30 September (Birmingham 1993:183) and was replaced by Francisco da Costa Gomes, chief of the joint military staff, who reappointed Gonçalves as Prime Minister.

Spínola had demanded changes in the MFA Program, chiefly in respect of the empire. It was indeed the colonial issue that was the main source of his conflict with the Movement. He still believed in some kind of Lusitanian federation. As his political support evaporated, decolonisation was expedited, with independence as the focus. So far as the African colonies were concerned, the only questions came to be timing and the recognition of liberation movements (Bruneau 1984:64).

Portugal announced the *de facto* recognition of the independence of Guinea-Bissau in September 1974 and, under an agreement with the PAIGC, a transitional government was set up with a view to the proclamation of independence by an assembly elected by universal suffrage in July 1975. Talks between Frelimo and Portugal led to the Lusaka Agreement, after which a provisional government took control, and Moçambique's independence was to be proclaimed in June 1975. A meeting with the leaders of São Tomé and Príncipe in Algiers led to the setting-up of a transitional government and envisaged independence in July 1975. Angola was the most problematic of the African colonies, because it was wealthier than the others and its liberation movement was divided. An agreement concluded in January 1975 between Portugal, the Frente Nacional de Libertação de Angola (FNLA), Movimento Popular de Libertação de Angola (MPLA) and União Nacional para Independência Total de Angola (UNITA) provided for a transitional government, with the proclamation of independence to follow in November 1975. In the event, however, civil war broke out in March 1975 and no elections were held. Outside powers intervened and, anxious to leave, Portugal turned over sovereignty to 'the people of Angola' (Bruneau 1984:65).

Bruneau argues that the MFA was radicalised not because of individuals like Vasco Gonçalves, who may have been a Communist sympathiser, but because the PCP provided organisation and ideology. In their conflict Spínola increasingly relied on old regime elements, while the PCP had a glorious history of opposition to the Estado Novo and a cadre of political workers. It took part in the Vasco Gonçalves governments, in which its leader, Álvaro Cunhal, was a minister. It was, however, too old-fashioned to win wide popular support (Birmingham 1993:180). After the resignation of Spínola, Costa Gomes visited Washington in October 1974 in order to reassure a worried Henry Kissinger (Sobel 1976:86).

On 11 March 1975 a coup against the regime proved abortive and Spínola fled, though he denied involvement. The PCP took advantage of the coup to ingratiate itself with the MFA. At the same time, however, the MFA both institutionalised itself and allowed other parties to organise. Under the Party Pact of 2 April 1975 it was agreed that elections for the Constituent Assembly would be held on 25 April, but that the MFA Revolutionary Council would retain a supervisory role for 3–5 years (Bruneau 1984:46). Vasco Gonçalves reaffirmed Portugal's commitment to NATO and said that the United States could still use the Azores air bases, though not, as in 1973, for anti-Arab shipments. The United States, which had denied involvement in the coup, remained concerned over Communist influence in the government, though the party had secured only 13% of the votes in the Constituent Assembly elections and the Socialists nearly 38%. President Gerald Ford said on 23 May 1975 that he intended to enquire when in Brussels whether Portugal ought still to be a member of NATO, given the Communist influence in its government. He met Vasco Gonçalves on 29 May, but reiterated his concern the following day (Sobel 1976:91,96,99,102). In the meantime, Communism scored a major victory in Southeast Asia with the collapse of the Republic of Vietnam. The Democratic Republic of Vietnam's troops entered Saigon on 30 April.

Perhaps these events at least superficially lent some validity to the concerns the Indonesians allegedly felt over Communist influence in Portuguese Timor. At a British Embassy party in Jakarta on 16 June, General Hatmojo suggested it might come either through Maoists in the Chinese community or through Russia's relations with the MFA in Portugal.[1] Neither were likely sources, but the fear of Communism, genuine or not, could certainly be utilised.

The Coalition of the Timor parties

In Canberra in January Senator Willesee formally approved the recommendations his Department had made in December. He had earlier

---

[1] FO 810/29[64]: Minute by Duggan, 17 June 1975.

given Whitlam the gist of them, apparently securing his general approval (AIPT:143n), and now sent the document itself. Two main elements, he said, had emerged in Australia's policy towards Timor since the coup in Portugal the previous April:

> first, an appreciation that the association of Portuguese Timor with Indonesia would best suit our national interests; and second, our commitment to the right of the people of Portuguese Timor to decide their own political future by means of an internationally acceptable act of self-determination.

The evolving situation in Timor pointed to their incompatibility. The paper sought to place more emphasis on the commitment. At the same time it suggested 'that we should take a step backwards from involvement in the problem of Portuguese Timor in order to avoid becoming any more enmeshed in it than we need be'. Australia should try to maintain a dialogue with the Indonesians 'in order to try to divert them from too forward a policy' and ensure that developments there did not become 'an obstacle to good relations'. It should take 'suitable opportunities' to advise Timorese leaders that it would respect the wishes expressed in 'a genuine act of self-determination', and that they should of course beware of 'action which would risk playing into Indonesian hands'. No consulate should be opened in Dili. If aid were to be provided, it should be under a joint Portuguese–Indonesian–Australian umbrella.[2]

Willesee also sent the paper to the Minister of Defence, Lance Barnard. Arguments for Indonesian control were perhaps stronger, he replied, but the establishment of an independent state, 'if this were acceptably and securely achieved', would also be 'acceptable to Australia from a military-security point of view'. In either case it was important that the final settlement should not develop into a 'running sore' that would complicate Indonesia–Australia relations and attract unwelcome attention from other powers. What was therefore of central concern was the manner in which either solution was reached. He was deeply concerned at the indications that Indonesia was planning to take 'immoderate action'. That would undo the constructive relationship it had taken years to build and it would be hard to restore, particularly if the public reaction in Australia prompted adjustments in its defence program. Differences would become

---

[2] Willesee to Whitlam, 14 January 1975, in AIPT:160–161.

more difficult to resolve and it might be necessary to assume a definite commitment to an independent Papua New Guinea.

If Indonesia moved against Timor militarily despite Australian representations, 'we would have to assess very closely whether we had to deal with a neighbouring state in which dominant elements were disposed to deal with neighbourhood problems by use of military force'. That assessment would have implications for Australia's strategic outlook and defence expenditure. 'In addition, we have to consider our credibility in the neighbourhood and the region at large as a power concerned with stability and security and able and ready to exercise worthwhile influence in these respects.'

The Indonesians had heard only what they wanted to hear, 'namely our acceptance of their interest in the future of Portuguese Timor and of its eventual absorption into the Indonesian state'. They did not have 'a clear understanding of our opposition to the use of military force and the dangers of this for our relationship, or of our emphasis on the importance of an act of free choice by the people of Portuguese Timor'. Australia should try to moderate their fears of an independent Timor and encourage them to build relations with the political forces that were gaining support there.[3]

In the DFA Lance Joseph thought Indonesia had a better chance of getting away with it than the Department of Defence suggested. His Department would also 'err on the cautious side in regard to the imminence of any Indonesian military intervention'. Otherwise, however, it largely agreed with the main thrust of the Defence Department's views. Perhaps Australia should take up the proposal for a tripartite aid program? Feakes thought that the Defence Department had 'overlooked the possibility that a radical, Marxist, regime could emerge in Portuguese Timor that did indeed evince a compulsion to meddle, not only in Indonesia, but perhaps among the aboriginal population in Northern Australia'.[4]

Talking points for the new Ambassador to Indonesia, Richard Woolcott, were discussed between the DFA and the Department of Defence. Bill Pritchett of the latter thought that oral presentation would not suffice and that there should be a letter from the Prime Minister to the President. He offered an additional suggestion for inclusion—encouraging the Indonesians, Portuguese and Timorese 'to arrange that at independence the Timorese should enter a basic treaty relationship with Indonesia', the treaty containing 'a key article whereby the parties would agree to consult together about

---

[3] Barnard to Willesee, 11 February 1975, in AIPT:176–180.
[4] Minute, 14 February 1975, in AIPT:184–186.

developments affecting their common interest in the security and stability of the region'. With that Australia might become associated.[5]

Whitlam decided that Woolcott should deliver a letter to Suharto. At the very time it was being drafted reports suggested Indonesia was planning an invasion. This was denied in Jakarta, though Antara claimed that hundreds of refugees were crossing into West Timor and that East Timor was moving towards a Communist takeover.[6] In fact the military exercise Indonesia carried out was part of Murtopo's 'Komodo' operation, designed to show Portugal and the Timorese that Indonesia was serious about invading if things did not go as it wished (Taylor 1999:40). It had a contrary effect. It strengthened the Portuguese administration's resolve to extend the Timorese right to choose and encouraged a coalition of the two main Timorese parties (Dunn 1983:88–89).

The Prime Minister's letter to Suharto recalled the discussions of September 1974. Developments in Timor had been more rapid than then expected, it suggested. But the 'drift' in Portugal had been arrested, the elections there were to proceed, the Armed Forces Movement 'apparently overruling the opposition of the Communist Party', and there was no evidence that other powers were likely to intervene. Thus the dangers discussed in September 'need not now be seen as immediately pressing'. In that connection the Prime Minister referred to the public debate in Australia precipitated by newspaper reports of possible military action by Indonesia. He was glad to have denials from the Indonesian Defence and Foreign Ministries and from the Ambassador, but the debate did 'indicate the delicacy of the question, the widespread support here for an internationally acceptable act of self-determination…and the great sensitivity of Australian Parliamentary and public opinion to any suggestion of a possible resort to unilateral action'. No Australian Government could allow it to be thought that it supported such action. Any damage to the close relationship of Indonesia and Australia 'or any action that could disturb it or evoke public controversy and criticism', would be very distressing. Whitlam looked for a political solution and thought there was scope for one. UDT and Fretilin were not seeking immediate independence, but had proposed an eight-year program of transition, and also a policy of non-alignment and a pact of non-aggression and co-operation with Indonesia. That seemed to call for 'active efforts' on Indonesia's part to establish co-operation with Portugal and friendly relations with the Timorese leaders.[7]

---

[5] Pritchett to Feakes, 21 February 1975, in AIPT:190–192.
[6] *Financial Times*, 27 February 1975.
[7] Whitlam to Soeharto, 28 February 1975, in AIPT:200–202.

The letter, as Renouf later wrote, was a warning against the use of force. It was also a proposal that Australia, Portugal and Indonesia should co-operate to see that East Timor became independent through self-determination, but 'would, in effect, be a client state of Indonesia; the proposal would be implemented by a joint aid package, by Portugal's good offices and by UN approval'. It seemed to have 'a reasonable chance', but, as he puts it, 'Indonesia rejected the proposal' (Renouf 1979:444–445).

The Australians had decided to tell only the United States and New Zealand about its moves,[8] but the British High Commission in Canberra was quite well informed. The parliamentary and press comment that week had been sparked off by an article by Peter Hastings, now at the Australian National University, in the *Sydney Morning Herald*, quite probably, Hewitt thought, based on unattributable briefing from the DFA. The press argued that an independent Timor was not a prospect either Indonesia or Australia would relish, but that armed intervention by Indonesia would be 'precipitous [sic] and foolish'. The Shadow Foreign Affairs Minister, Andrew Peacock, accused the Government of encouraging a takeover and said it should seek a firm Indonesian statement on self-determination. The Government spokesman, Bill Morrison, Minister assisting the Foreign Minister on Papua New Guinea, said that Indonesia well understood Australia's view, that it would be 'seriously concerned if there was any unilateral action by Indonesia which would prevent an act of self-determination'.

In spite of such 'soothing words' and Indonesian denials, the DFA was 'concerned about the latest noises coming out of Jakarta', Hewitt wrote. Whitlam might favour incorporation, but officials did not widely share his views. They recognised that an act of self-determination would probably result in an independent Timor, 'if not immediately, at least after a period of association with Portugal'. That was what Indonesia most feared and could push it into a takeover bid. 'Australia would then be caught in the dilemma of choosing between her close relationship with Indonesia and the often stated ALP principle on decolonisation and opposition to armed aggression.'

The Australian Government could be expected 'to continue to warn Indonesia of the dangers of military intervention and to try to persuade Indonesia of the need to live alongside an independent Timor, if that is the option chosen by the Timorese', and might or might not be successful. Whatever the future held, it would place more emphasis on the relationship

---

[8]   Submission, 22 February 1975, in AIPT:194–195.

with Indonesia than the principles of non-aggression and decolonisation. 'If armed aggression took place', the Australian Government

> would no doubt condemn Indonesian aggression for the sake of their international standing; but at the same time they would hope that a take-over would be little more than a nine-day wonder, just as in the case of Goa, and that once the dust had settled their relations with Indonesia would generally be unaffected, as though nothing had happened.[9]

'This may be over-optimistic', Richard Palmer presciently commented at the FCO.[10]

Visiting Portuguese Timor in December 1974, Steve Hoadley, a University of Auckland academic, found the political stance of Fretilin and UDT had become almost identical. Fretilin's call for independence had become a call for independence in five to ten years and UDT now looked for total independence at the end of such a period. A coalition was formed on 22 January 1975, claiming the exclusive right to negotiate with Portugal on self-government and independence, thus evoking the examples of Guinea-Bissau and Moçambique. Hoadley wondered if the Portuguese 'engineered the coalition from behind the scenes' (Hoadley 1975:14).

A new Governor, Mário Lemos Pires, had arrived on 18 November 1974. He had served under Spínola in Guinea-Bissau and was himself a supporter of independence within a federation, Spínola-style. Without clear instructions from Costa Gomes, he was, however, accompanied by 15 majors whose brief was to manage decolonisation and some of them were quite radical, such as Francisco Mota, who became chief of the Political Affairs Bureau, and Costa Jónatas, who became chief of the Social Communications Bureau. The initial plan was to set up a three-party advisory council as a step towards a transitional government. It would work with the Portuguese administration for two years. Then for another three years three secretaries of state would consult with a High Commissioner. A third phase would add an elected assembly to decide on the constitution to be adopted after independence or an alternative had been decided upon. But the advisory council never eventuated, since the three parties would not serve together. The focus came to be on a decolonisation commission, a series of committees dealing with a range of subjects. On these Fretilin and UDT collaborated (Hill 1978:114–119).

---

[9] FCO 15/1704[11]: Hewitt to Palmer, 28 February 1975.
[10] FCO 15/1704[11]: Marginal comment on Hewitt to Palmer, 28 February 1975

Their coalition, organised by Ramos Horta and Domingos Oliveira, was promoted by fear of Indonesian invasion. It looked for a transitional government leading to total independence; repudiated Apodeti and rejected integration, and called for the United Nations to assist Portugal in decolonisation. It despatched a letter to Suharto, stressing its wish for friendship with Indonesia. Mota and Jónatas supported the coalition, but wanted Apodeti in it (Hill 1978:143–144,146). Conflicts among parties would impede the emergence of an elite to oversee the creation of a new state. A coalition, Lemos Pires thought, would be 'the best buffer to Indonesia' (Taylor 1999:38).

In Jakarta Duggan had discussed the coalition of Fretilin and the UDT with Akosah of the Asia and Pacific Directorate at Ministry of Foreign Affairs. Fretilin, he thought, was trying to establish itself, in the manner the pre-independence groups had in Moçambique and Guinea, as the main representative of opinion 'to whom full authority would be granted on independence'. He went on to outline Indonesia's attitude: 'the people should be given the right of self-government', but that must not 'present any threat to the security of Indonesia'. It already faced to the north 'an area of considerable insecurity, and had no wish for similar conditions to develop to its south, whether in Portuguese Timor or in Papua New Guinea'. The Australian Counsellor told Duggan that, in setting out the same attitude, Akosah had told him 'that if such a situation did develop, Indonesia would have to take other steps'.[11]

In February, no doubt as another part of Operasi Komodo, the Indonesian press carried articles suggesting that the new Governor and officials were communists, carrying out forced 'communisation'. One of Ali Murtopo's papers carried the headline 'Coup d'État in Portuguese Timor'. State Secretary Sudharmono repeated that Indonesia had no territorial ambitions, however, and Malik that the military option was one Indonesia had never dreamed of. Editorial comment had generally reflected the official line, 'denying that Indonesia has any territorial ambitions, but expressing concern about the officially inspired move towards Communism'. Akosah took a similar stance. Normal troop movements might have accounted for the story in the *Sydney Morning Herald*. 'He went on, however, to state quite firmly that there had been intimidation in Portuguese Timor of pro-Indonesian elements, that this had been going on for months, and that there were refugees in Indonesian Timor.'

---

[11] FCO 15/1704[3]: Duggan to Palmer, 27 January 1975.

Duggan also reported the version offered by the Portuguese Chargé:

> He was of the view that the only factor that stopped the Indonesians invading was their inability to carry out a quick and successful military action. The invasion, whether amphibious or airborne, would have to be completed within 24 hours to present everyone with a *fait accompli* and avoid the international odium which a messy and long drawn out campaign would provoke.

The Portuguese garrison would not put up much of a fight: 'the resistance would come up country'. The Chargé dismissed the statements that the Indonesians had no territorial ambitions: 'the Germans had said that up to the last minute about the Sudetenland'.

He claimed that all was calm in Portuguese Timor and dismissed stories about refugees, though also expressing concern that Indonesia was training them and sending them back. UDT-Fretilin, he said, were recommending the establishment of de facto self-government on the lines of that in Moçambique under a Portuguese High Commissioner. That would prepare the way for de jure independence in ten years' time, perhaps preceded by a referendum at some stage. That was the sort of development, Duggan commented, that the Indonesians said they feared.

It was difficult to say what all this meant, Duggan concluded. The present campaign was clearly orchestrated. 'No-one really believes that there is terror in Portuguese Timor', but the Governor and his staff were probably too left-wing for the Indonesians. It was even more difficult to say whether Indonesia would in fact invade.

> The final decision will rest with the President and he is probably receiving conflicting advice. But he is a cautious man and Indonesians, who are ever ready to quote the lessons of their own history, recall that it was diplomacy spiced with sabre rattling that won West Irian while confrontation was a failure. Invasion cannot be ruled out and Indonesia could probably live with whatever international odium she incurred thereby, on the assumption that it would be short-lived. For the moment, the propaganda effort commits Indonesia to nothing, and Indonesia may consider it worth her while to wait on events in Lisbon.[12]

---

[12] FCO 15/1704[16]: Duggan to Palmer, 3 March 1975.

British attitudes and assessments

In London the South East Asia Department had been consulting other departments at the FCO, the South West Europe, South West Pacific and United Nations departments in particular, over Britain's attitude, since the issue was likely to come to a head and ministers needed to be alerted. One official remarked that 'no line we take is likely to be easy to square with Indonesian hopes, Portugal's cavalier attitude to self-determination (on past form) and traditional policies on decolonisation'.[13] He did not mention Australia's viewpoint, though the paper, drafted by CW Squire, did, of course, cover it. 'Our interest is minimal', the final version observed, 'but the question may impinge on our bilateral relations with both Portugal and Indonesia. It is bound to be discussed at the United Nations and is already the subject of articles in the press. What should our attitude be?'

The main political groupings seemed to want a greater degree of autonomy and eventual independence. They and the Portuguese understood that independence, given the 'rudimentary' economy, would present 'considerable difficulties'. The Portuguese recognised that integration with Indonesia was also an option and a small party favoured it. The Indonesians wanted integration, but, with their West Irian experience in mind, they knew it had to take place 'as a result of at least some kind of expression of the will of the people of Portuguese Timor'. They might accept continued association with Portugal for a time, which they would use to win support for integration. There were, however, signs that they might be forcing the pace, perhaps fearing that left-wing influences in Portugal might lead to the grant of independence and in the meantime expose Timor to Communism. Whitlam had told them that Australia would favour integration if done in a way that satisfied international opinion.

> But public reaction to this attitude...has driven the [Australian] Government further towards recognition of the need to respect the principle of self-determination, and the Government's line in public is now that integration has to be the express wish of the Timorese.

Recent developments had prompted a concern 'that they might be forced to condemn a rash move by Indonesia which would have unfortunate repercussions for their relations with an important neighbour'.

---

[13] FCO 15/1704[13]: Minute, 3 March 1975, on draft.

It was not an issue, the memorandum continued, in which Britain wanted 'to play a prominent part'. If Portugal and Indonesia could sort the matter out 'amicably, it need not impinge on our relations with either country. We agree with Mr Whitlam that Timor's eventual integration with Indonesia is probably the right answer in terms of regional stability.' But Britain might have to take a position, for example in the United Nations, 'favouring one side or the other to the detriment to our relations with the other party'. If pressed to express views by either side,

> we should restate our support for the principle of self-determination. In addition we might tell the Portuguese that we support their aim to consult the wishes of the Timorese about their future, that we have no strong feelings about the eventual outcome, but that we understand their doubts about the present viability of an independent Timor. To the Indonesians we might say that in accordance with our support for the principle of self-determination we could support integration into Indonesia only if this is acceptable to them and is the choice of the inhabitants of Timor. We could make to both the Portuguese and the Indonesians the standard point that in our opinion the timing and method of implementing the principle of self-determination is a matter for the administering power.

Britain should keep in close touch with Australia, both at the United Nations and in Canberra. In public, if asked, the FCO should say it had repeatedly welcomed Portuguese moves towards decolonisation and 'should avoid being drawn into commenting substantively on the merits of the various options and stand pat on the statement of principle that we support self-determination'.[14] At ministerial level, Lord Goronwy-Roberts endorsed the recommendations.[15]

The Political Counsellor at the Australian Embassy in Jakarta, Alan Taylor, visited Timor for two weeks in late February and early March 1975. He was 'highly impressed', he told Duggan, with Governor Lemos Pires. He had been rather left on his own in recent months, 'trying without any great success to get the political parties to reach agreement on the fate of the colony', but had now gone to Lisbon and might come back with some sort of constitutional formula. Apodeti had cabled an appeal to the United Nations

---

[14] FCO 15/1704[22]: CW Squire, The Future of Portuguese Timor, 5 March 1975.
[15] FCO 15/1704[22]: Minute, 17 March 1975.

about intimidation. In fact, Taylor said, 'all really is quiet in Portuguese Timor'. A report in *Sinar Harapan* suggested that a new political party had been set up called ADITLA with a program of independence and integration with Australia. On his arrival on 3 March, Woolcott

> turned aside questions on this development and on Portuguese Timor in general by saying that Australia 'has no special interest in Portuguese Timor', while expressing the hope that sufficient time would be allowed to permit a political solution which would accommodate both the wishes of the people of the territory and the natural interests of Indonesia in its future.[16]

Duggan secured a fuller account from Taylor on 12 March. He found the main Army officials, probably hand-picked by Lemos Pires, 'intelligent, well-educated, shrewd, dedicated and altruistic', and 'had the impression that they genuinely wanted to help the people fulfil their political wishes, whatever they might be, and they were working hard to prepare the people for this decision'. He did not think their views could be described as communist. They were, he thought, 'great believers in democracy, genuinely wishing to educate the people in democratic processes and firm believers in the individual's right to choose his own future'. But his main impression was 'that these ideas had not really been thought through in the sense of how they would be implemented to give Portuguese Timor a viable political and economic future'.

Major Mota had probably been closely involved with the politicians in preparing the UDT–Fretilin program of political advance, which envisaged immediate *de jure* independence, followed by a staged process towards *de facto* independence. In 1975 and 1976 the colony would be ruled by a Governor assisted by a council containing three representatives of each of the two parties. In 1977 to 1979 there would be a transitional government under a High Commissioner—the Governor with a new title—with three secretaries of state, one each from Fretilin and UDT and one appointed by the Governor. In the final period from 1980 to 1982, a Prime Minister would be appointed within the transitional government, which, representing Fretilin, UDT and the Portuguese Government, would prepare a constitution. There was no mention of Apodeti. The Governor told Taylor he aimed to get it involved in the program.

---

[16] FCO 15/1704[21]: Duggan to Palmer, 10 March 1975.

Taylor mentioned Indonesia's opinion that Portugal had failed to offer the regular consultation Almeida Santos had allegedly promised. He had the impression that Lisbon had not yet focused on Timor and that the Governor had been left to sort things out and that the undertaking 'had been lost in the wash'. The Governor insisted, however, that no decisions would be taken without full consultation, and Taylor found that all the Portuguese officials recognised that Indonesia had security interests and understood its fears, but that they also thought 'that the people of Portuguese Timor wanted independence and that the Act of Self-Determination would not produce a majority in favour of integration with Indonesia'. Taylor did not know how such a decision could fit in with Indonesia's known views. Again, the future had not been thought through. The Governor said there would be talks with Indonesia, but where, when and how had not been decided.

The Portuguese were serious about decolonisation: the number of troops was being reduced; native officials were working alongside Portuguese; local elections had been held in Lauten. Ramos, the Head of Military Intelligence, claimed that the Indonesian Army was undertaking training in Java that could fit it to invade. There was evidence of Indonesian support for Apodeti. Two officers from the Indonesian Army's paracommando unit (RPKAD) had visited Dili recently on false passports. There seemed, however, to be no great fear of an invasion. Taylor's impression was that, if there were a military action, Portuguese troops would 'stand aside'. He found 'nothing that might be interpreted as in any way constituting foreign communist infiltration'. The long-established Chinese community focused on commerce and some people were sending their families out.[17]

At a British Embassy lunch attended by Liem Bian Kie and Harry Tjan, Ambassador Combs reported, the former

> made it clear that Indonesia regards itself as having the right to intervene. When I said that all experience since the war suggested that intervention was a risky policy, he said people would forget about it after three months. I then said I was not thinking about the attitude of the outside world so much as the continuing problem which those who intervened would face.

Liem said that Ali Murtopo was going to meet Soares in Paris after an Organization of the Petroleum Exporting Countries (OPEC) meeting and, if

---

[17] FCO 15/1704 [24]: Memorandum by Duggan, 12 March 1975, enclosed in Duggan to Palmer, 17 March 1975; also in FO 810/29[25].

that meeting was satisfactory, go on to Lisbon. The main purpose, he implied, would be to represent that the Portuguese had not fulfilled the promises they had given. Liem claimed that the visit to Lisbon was at Portuguese invitation. But Combs thought Ali Murtopo might see it as 'useful cover for any further plans the Indonesians might have. If they decided to intervene they would be in a position to bring home to the Portuguese the dangers of the present situation in Portuguese Timor.'[18] The understanding Ali Murtopo had reached in Lisbon the previous autumn, Liem said, had been 'thrown out of the window' as a result of the replacement of Major Manthelo by Major Mota, 'whose views are too leftish (*anglice*; liberal?) for Liem's taste'.[19]

Duggan sought Akosah's views on recent developments and reported him as stating 'quite categorically that independence was not a possibility for Portuguese Timor'. It had to have help. Duggan asked him 'whether any form of association would be acceptable; he said that for security reasons Indonesia could not allow a situation to arise where, for example, China could offer Portuguese Timor massive amounts of aid'. Duggan pointed out that a number of African countries were dependent on foreign aid. The difference, Akosah said, was 'the security aspect'. The only choice was integration and the population had to be prepared for it. Duggan asked whether the Indonesians would be 'willing to see Portuguese authority continue for some period of, say, ten years until the population was prepared for integration'. Akosah said they were thinking of only two or three years. The joint program of the two parties was 'quite unacceptable, in particular the first requirement of de jure independence'.

Duggan asked about consultations with the Portuguese. He said Ali Murtopo had gone on from the OPEC summit in Algeria to London—not Paris—for discussions with the Portuguese, and implied that they were 'substantive and significant'. He confirmed that the Australians would not be involved in any tripartite talks and that they had 'intimated that they were content to let Indonesia and Portugal work it out together'. Apparently Whitlam had issued an invitation to Suharto, but Duggan noted that the Australian Embassy in Jakarta 'has been unwilling to say anything about the instructions which the new Australian Ambassador brought with him'.[20] Perhaps they included something 'very personal' from the Prime Minister, he speculated; it would be 'interesting to know exactly what terms the

---

[18] FO 810/29[15]: Minute by Combs, 5 March 1975.
[19] FO 810/29[25]: Minute.
[20] FCO 15/1704[24]: Duggan to Palmer, 17 March 1975.

Australians are currently using to the Indonesians'. Hewitt's letter suggested that the DFA was '"hoping" that the issue will not go wrong rather than themselves having any clear idea what to do about it'.[21]

Meetings in London and Townsville

Whitlam's letter was delivered on 4 March. Woolcott presented his credentials on 8 March and then had 25 minutes' private conversation with the President, during which 'Suharto said categorically that Indonesia had "no intention" of attempting to integrate Portuguese Timor by military force'. He asked Woolcott to pass the assurance to Whitlam. Indonesia wanted to see an 'orderly and proper decolonisation process in Portuguese Timor'. It wanted neither to 'impair its improved international standing' nor to see the situation in Southeast Asia and the Pacific 'disturbed'. He invited Woolcott to send an officer to the border to see refugees and to witness the lack of military preparations. But 'pro-Indonesian elements in Timor were being persecuted and this created difficulties for Indonesian Government'.

As his letter showed, Woolcott said, the Prime Minister

> had not moved away from the position he had adopted in Yogyakarta and Wonosobo in September, at which he said that the future of Portuguese Timor, including the possibility that it become part of Indonesia, would need to be the outcome of the properly expressed wishes of its people and that there should be an act of self-determination.

Australia appreciated Indonesia's legitimate interest in Timor, but was concerned about the effect on their relationship of parliamentary and public reaction to any military action. The Portuguese needed to allow time for a political solution to be worked out 'in cooler circumstances', taking account of Indonesia's interest and Timorese wishes. The President told Woolcott that there was really no difference in the Australian and the Indonesian positions. He had instructed Ali Murtopo to meet a Portuguese minister in London. The Prime Minister, Woolcott said, had told him before he left that 'the long term importance of the Australian/Indonesian relationship was [the] overriding issue and any possible complications in our relationship should be seen in that context'. The President agreed.

---

[21] FO 810/29[22]: Minute by Duggan, 14 March 1975.

Some hardliners in HANKAM and at CSIS looked for a military solution, Woolcott added at the end of his report, but his preliminary impression was that 'this should be seen, at present, *not* as Indonesian policy, but as one option which might be reluctantly adopted in certain future circumstances'. Indonesian defence planners 'probably feel a need to have the capacity on the ground to exercise the military option in case the situation in Portuguese Timor deteriorates to a point at which they consider their national interest is threatened'. But Suharto and 'other influential groups' seemed to be 'strongly opposed to military intervention', and the President would, Woolcott thought, 'be most unwilling to authorise it unless he considered the situation in Portugal had become hopeless and that there was real danger of chaos, a leftwing takeover in Timor, and the killing of pro-Indonesian elements there'. No early action was likely and Australia should use what influence it had with Indonesia and Portugal to work towards 'an acceptable political solution and a cooling of the developing animosities between Dili and Kupang and along the border'.[22]

The existence of Whitlam's letter was 'still not widely known', Duggan reported to the FCO on 24 March, when it was announced that Suharto would pay an unofficial visit to Australia. The fact and the contents, the Australian Embassy said, were 'being held very close'. Duggan gathered from the Indonesian DFA that 90% of it was devoted to Timor. Akosah commented 'that it read a bit like an internal ALP statement of position; the implication was that Mr Whitlam might find it useful to have on record the views expressed in the letter for use with sections of his own Party'. What sort of a reply was to be sent? Duggan asked. Much of what Whitlam said, Akosah responded, had been overtaken by the exchanges with the Portuguese, in particular Ali Murtopo's talks in London. In fact the letter 'could now be put away in a drawer'.

Governor Lemos Pires arrived in Jakarta unheralded on 17 March on his way back from Lisbon, as Duggan also reported. The Indonesians had some difficulty in fixing up a program and he did not stay on to meet Malik on his return from overseas. According to Antara, he told the press that Portugal was determined to grant 'rights for self-determination' and that there would be no problem if the majority wanted merger with Indonesia. Events in Portugal would have no effect on the situation in Timor. He ruled out a referendum and said that the future would be determined by a council of people's representatives set up through general elections.

---

[22] Cablegram, 8 March 1975, in AIPT:218–220.

The Portuguese Chargé said the Governor was to hold discussions with all three political parties and propose a conference in Macau, which 'might make it easier for Apodeti to take part'. The Governor gave no date for the elections or for the whole process, though he apparently mentioned to Woolcott 'a period of not more than eight years'. It was not clear, Duggan added, how much Lemos Pires knew about the discussions in London and the Chargé had no report. The Indonesian Foreign Ministry was awaiting Ali Murtopo's return, but they were concerned about the situation in Lisbon. The talks had taken place before the attempted coup of 11 March and Murtopo's interlocutors might have 'an uncertain future in Portuguese counsels'.[23]

The brief prepared for Whitlam before Suharto's visit suggested that he summarise the main points of his letter of 28 February and welcome the President's message that there was no intention to integrate Timor by force. At the time of the letter 'the drift to the left in Portugal seemed to have been arrested, at least temporarily'. Now there had been 'a fresh shift to the left', but there was no evidence of 'a spread of extreme left-wing influence to Timor'. Possibly recent developments could add to the risk that Portugal would drop self-determination and transfer power to pro-independence groups, Moçambique-style, but that was not inevitable. The arrangements being discussed envisaged a gradual approach and it was in the interests of both Indonesia and Australia that Portugal should maintain its responsibilities. UDT–Fretilin had proposed an agreement of non-aggression and co-operation. Indonesia regarded their coalition communiqué as provocative, but the criticisms of Australia and Indonesia were partly a response to their attitudes:

> the more strongly the idea of independence is thought to be rejected or under attack, the more extreme the supporters of independence may become. We need to avoid arousing radical and irrational attitudes among the present Timorese leaders…which could colour their outlook for years to come, whatever the final constitutional status of the territory may turn out to be.

Australia, Whitlam might recall, had welcomed Indonesia's constructive policies for establishing stability in its border regions, in relations with Malaysia, for example, and in the situation in Sabah and the southern Philippines:

---

[23] FCO 15/1704[27]: Duggan to Palmer, 24 March 1975.

(The same concern to help maintain stability in Southeast Asia is reflected in Indonesian policies in ASEAN and its membership of the ICSS in Viet-Nam and its efforts to bring about negotiations in Cambodia.) Do not these processes and institutions point the way for handling the question of Timor?

Australia would be willing to work with Indonesia in 'cultivating good and influential relations with the Timorese'. They could jointly offer aid, 'represented as assisting the Timorese to emerge from their isolation, making it unnecessary for them to look beyond Indonesia and Australia (and Portugal) for support'.[24]

Woolcott also offered his comments, which were very different in emphasis, in a letter to the Prime Minister. His context was

> the over-riding long-term importance of the Australian/Indonesian relationship...Whatever Government is in power in Indonesia and, indeed, whatever Government might be in power in Australia, the price of a hostile or unstable Indonesia for Australia would be very high, not only for us but for the Indonesian people themselves.

The President wanted to treat Australia as an 'honorary member of a sort of South East Asian Club', unique among Western countries, as Furlonger used to say, in its understanding of Indonesia's problems. 'This attitude is of great value to us and it would be a pity if we were to lose it.' Australia was 'committed to such principles as human rights and self-determination', but it should 'avoid a meddlesome attitude' and not 'seek to become the conscience of Asia'.

Over Timor Woolcott remained 'somewhat worried. We could be working ourselves into a position where we are impaling ourselves on the hook of self-determination'. There had been few proper acts of self-determination in recent times and none in Portugal's former colonies.

> To demand it too stridently in Timor at present can be equated with a demand for independence. Do we actually want to encourage an independent East Timor? I would doubt it. It is not wanted by Indonesia; nor, I believe, by any of the other countries in the region.

---

[24] Brief, 31 March 1975, in AIPT:236–238.

They were silent in February and March. The Australians thus 'appeared to become front-runners in support of Timorese independence'. Woolcott believed 'that we should seek to disengage ourselves as much as possible from the Timor situation which could well become pretty messy'. Indonesia was 'very unlikely' to invade unless it saw the situation 'as hopeless and as a real threat to its security'. But it had not abandoned the objective of integration and would pursue 'both covert and overt activity to influence Portuguese Timor to decide in favour of integration at the eventual act of self-determination'. It would be 'unfortunate' if Australia came to be regarded as 'a party principal' and then regarded as the only or main country 'obstructing what Indonesia and its other neighbours would see as Indonesia's legitimate national interest'.[25]

Before the meeting the Australian Ambassador in Lisbon, Frank Cooper, had secured from Almeida Santos an account of his talks with Ali Murtopo in London. The Portuguese scenario was similar to the UDT–Fretilin proposal: acceptance in principle of *de jure* independence and a transitional period of eight years before it could be implemented, divided into three stages, concluding with the election of a constituent assembly. A first step would be the meeting in Macau. 'There must be an act of free choice. But the proposed transitional period gave Indonesia and Apodeti plenty of time to work for integration into Indonesia if that is what the Timorese wanted.' Almeida Santos said Murtopo accepted the scenario, including the proposal that Apodeti should attend at Macau. In fact, Cooper noted, the record of the talks that Santos gave him showed that Murtopo 'in substance did not go beyond saying that he would convey the Portuguese views to President Suharto'.[26]

With Murtopo at the meeting at a detached house at 11 Mulgrave Street in London were the Indonesian ambassadors to the United Kingdom and France; with Almeida Santos were Campinos, Alves, and Mota. Subsequent accounts suggest that, as Cooper's report implied, the Indonesians got less than they expected. They looked for the withdrawal of radical Portuguese officers and the creation of a joint Indonesian-Portuguese consultative body in Dili, but the Portuguese threatened to internationalise the issue and rejected Indonesian participation. They would, however, set up a consultative council representing the three parties, which would give Indonesia time to demonstrate to the Timorese the advantages of integration, and the

---

[25] Woolcott to Whitlam, 2 April 1975, in AIPT:240–242.
[26] Cablegram, 3 April 1975, in AIPT:243–244.

Portuguese promised not to obstruct Apodeti activities (Taylor 1999:40–41; Dunn 1983:90–91).

In his conversation with Suharto in Townsville, Whitlam referred to the discussions of the previous December, saying 'that he still hoped that Portuguese Timor would be associated with or integrated into Indonesia; but this result should be achieved in a way which would not upset the Australian people'. He noted that Anwar Sani, the Indonesian representative at the United Nations, would become Chairman of its Committee of 24 and suggested that that presented opportunities for Australia–Indonesia co-operation in formulating measures for ascertaining the wishes of the Timorese. He also said that Australia would be pleased to give Portuguese Timor economic assistance. Australia did not, however, want to be 'seen as having a primary responsibility for the outcome in Portuguese Timor, an issue…essentially the responsibility of the people of Portuguese Timor, Portugal and Indonesia'. The Prime Minister devoted most of his remarks to public opinion in Australia, identifying issues that, as he put it, 'could be used by those…opposed to good relations with Indonesia'. One of them was Timor, but he 'would ensure that our actions in Timor would always be guided by the principle that good relations with Indonesia were of paramount importance to Australia'.

President Suharto said that, 'as a country which endorsed the principles of freedom and democracy', Indonesia would never contemplate an invasion of Timor. 'Like Australia', he continued, 'Indonesia sought to resist those tendencies which would divide Indonesia from Australia and prejudice the good relations existing between them.' In passing, he mentioned that the issue of Timor 'was, in fact, much less significant than the much more momentous and serious problems posed by recent developments elsewhere in the region'. Indonesia had 'no territorial ambitions', but had concluded that integration was 'the best solution'. Recent discussions with the Portuguese Government showed that it supported integration, 'provided the people of the territory desired it'. Some desired integration, but some did not and oppressed those who did, many of whom sought asylum in West Timor. Portugal did not propose to adopt the procedures adopted in Africa, since Timor did not have so many 'mature politicians'. Instead it had proposed a three-party provisional government to control Timor for three, five or possibly eight years. Alternatively, the President said, it proposed that Portugal would retain sovereignty and the Governor control of the government, assisted by a three-party consultative body, noting that 'Indonesia had firmly rejected the former and had accepted the latter'.

The Portuguese had agreed that there should be no 'international interference' in Portuguese policy and that it 'would be for Indonesia to achieve the integration of the territory'. It had the Portuguese Government's 'approval...to assist and to develop the pro-Indonesia APODETI party, and to make approaches to, and influence the line of policy of, the UDT and FRETILIN parties'. The President mentioned the Macau meeting of Fretilin, UDT and Apodeti, 'which Indonesia had expressly asked to attend. Indonesian delegates would be available for consultation. The purpose of the meeting would be to begin the process of assisting and developing APODETI and to come to terms with UDT and FRETILIN.' The meeting was secret because Indonesia did not want to be charged with interference.[27]

Murtopo and Murdani met Feakes and Curtin in Townsville on 4 April, discussing Indochina and then Timor. Ali commented on his talks with the Portuguese which had produced 'areas of agreement'. The Portuguese, he said, had agreed not to set up a provisional or transitional government and to defer the constituent assembly for five to eight years. Indonesia would be consulted on the appointment of Apodeti members to an advisory assembly or council. Apodeti officials would be trained in Indonesia and Indonesian 'economic affairs' and tourist offices established in Dili. The main thing, he said, was 'time'; it was a battle for votes and time would be needed for Apodeti to be sure of getting sufficient. He was not 'greatly worried' by Fretilin's call for immediate *de jure* independence: the final decision would be taken at the end of the process.

Murdani referred to the Australian reaction to press stories about invasion. He

> had hoped that we would have seen the difference between preparations and actual intent to act. He said that Indonesia was 'hoping for the best but preparing for the worst'...; the worst, he suggested, being hasty Portuguese withdrawal and a reneging on the understandings reached with Ali.

He was told that the Australian Government 'understood the distinction he was making'.[28]

As to the talks, Hewitt reported from the British High Commission in Canberra on 10 April, 'we have only the press reports to go on'. He could

---

[27] Record of Second Discussion, 4 April 1975, in AIPT:244–248.
[28] Record, 4 April 1975, in AIPT:248–250.

not get much from DFA: 'indeed the DFA doubt whether they will ever see a record of what was actually said'. The press reports indicated that Suharto gave Whitlam 'a fresh assurance that Indonesia was not planning to invade Portuguese Timor. He was reported to have said that Indonesia had no intention of military expansion and no territorial ambitions.' Whitlam again said 'that as far as Australia was concerned the people of the territory should be allowed to determine their own future, and that their wishes must not be presumed by Indonesia'. There was no doubt in Hewitt's view that Australians remained 'genuinely concerned' about Indonesia's intentions and 'not mollified to any great degree by assurances of Indonesia's peaceful intentions'. They were also carefully watching the political situation in Portugal and the effect it might have. The Australian Government was likely, he thought, 'to emphasise wherever and whenever possible Australia's insistence that the future of the territory can only be determined by its inhabitants without outside interference'.[29]

After the London meeting, the Indonesians adopted a new approach, 'the main expression of which', Duggan reported from Jakarta on 21 April, 'was not to antagonize the inhabitants'. A delegation from the Indonesian departments of Defence and Foreign Affairs and BAKIN had visited Dili in early April and invited representatives of the parties to visit Jakarta. UDT representatives, in Jakarta from 11 to 18 April, were given 'high-level treatment' and fairly wide press coverage. 'The Indonesians clearly went to some lengths to sell themselves and the virtues of association with Indonesia' and considered that they needed 'something like two years to make the new policy work.' Ramos Horta, chief of Fretilin's political and foreign affairs bureau, arrived for a week's visit on 17 April and forecast that a large delegation would follow.

Both he and the UDT leaders, Francisco Xavier Lopes da Cruz and Augusto César da Costa da Mousinho, stated that they believed Suharto's assurances that Indonesia would not use force. Ramos Horta went on: 'we have no doubt that the Government will respect the wishes of the people of Portguese Timor'. Lopes told a news conference on 18 April that the UDT wanted gradual independence and that his party respected Apodeti's program, but 'the majority wanted independence'. Ramos Horta said that it was 'not a question of being for or against joining Indonesia, but that the central issue involved the fate of a people that had known colonial rule for centuries and now wished to be free'.

---

[29] FCO 15/1704[35]: Hewitt to Palmer, 10 April 1975.

An election would be held the following year, Lopes said. Taylor, who had the UDT representatives and their Indonesian minders to lunch, found them 'confused' about the next constitutional steps. They appeared to have abandoned their demand for immediate *de jure* independence and it was not clear where the elections fitted in, and they 'apparently also indulged in some criticisms of their Fretilin colleagues to the Indonesians'.

The Australian Embassy was 'relieved and pleased about the new situation', Duggan concluded.

> The pressure does seem to be off and it is of course welcome that Indonesia should adopt peaceful methods in pursuit of her aims. But it is clear that the ultimate aim, integration, remains the same; the incalculable element now seems to be what happens in Lisbon.[30]

Ramos Horta spent most of his time with Ali Murtopo, Duggan added a week later. He was, Taylor said, 'extremely depressed'. In March he had said that they would take to the hills if necessary. Now he seemed to think integration was inevitable.[31] The Indonesians indeed hoped to break up the UDT–Fretilin coalition. Some of the UDT leaders were restive over it, especially in view of Fretilin's political activities in the countryside, which undermined their influence. They thought the government in Lisbon would favour Fretilin and were suspicious of Mota and Jónatas. Komodo officers encouraged their disillusionment (Taylor 1999:41; Dunn 1983:95; Hiorth 1985:25), and the UDT announced the end of the coalition on 27 May (Hill 1978:157).

On 21 May Vítor Alves had called on 'his old friend', Ali Murtopo. He had been in Timor, apparently to prepare for the Macau meeting. According to the Ministry of Foreign Affairs in Jakarta, he also went there 'to undo some mischief' Mota had been making among the political parties on the question of independence. He appeared to be 'something of a *bête noire*' for the Indonesians, Duggan commented. After a recent speech of his, the Ministry of Foreign Affairs said it asked its Embassy in Lisbon for reassurance from Santos that the understanding reached in London still held. He gave it.

The Macau conference—to be attended by officials from Lisbon and Dili as well as representatives of the three parties and possibly Indonesian observers—was to discuss the constitutional future. According to the

---

[30] FCO 15/1704[38]: Duggan to Palmer, 21 April 1975.
[31] FCO 15/1704[46]: Duggan to Palmer, 28 April 1975.

Indonesian press, Alves said on his return to Lisbon 'that Portuguese Timor would not be given independence but that elections would be held there; he claimed that the idea of a referendum had been dropped'. The Ministry of Foreign Affairs in Jakarta claimed to be 'totally confused' on the point. 'The Indonesian position continues to be that they would dislike independence to precede integration; this is described as not an "elegant" way of proceeding.'

The end of the UDT–Fretilin coalition provided 'a further complication'. There was talk as a result of Fretilin's not attending the Macau meeting. The Portuguese Chargé said that, if they refused to attend, it would not be held. Explanations for the break-up varied from 'seeing this as a first success in the Indonesian attempt to get alongside the political parties, to the view that the programmes of the two parties were basically incompatible and therefore the split was inevitable'.[32]

Items in the Jakarta press led JA Ford, the British Ambassador, to conclude on 11 June that the situation was 'boiling up again'.[33] A 'warning' telegram was sent to the FCO next day. Reports on atrocities and refugees looked like 'an orchestrated build-up', while it was also claimed that a 'large majority' was in favour of integration. Perhaps the Indonesian Government feared that it was 'losing control of the situation'. The parties seemed to be 'fragmenting, nullifying the persuasive work done on them in the past months by the Indonesian authorities'. The Portuguese ministers might be bringing to Macau proposals couched in terms of self-determination and independence. The Committee of 24, which apparently had a mission in Lisbon, was said to be talking in similar terms.

> If the Macau talks were to produce a result unpalatable to the Indonesian Government, and particularly if this were followed by unrest in the colony, however fomented, President Suharto could find himself under pressure here to force the issue, despite his past assurances, particularly to…Whitlam, that Indonesia would not invade Portuguese Timor.[34]

Perhaps collateral to the reports, Duggan wrote on 16 June, was the view the Ministry of Foreign Affairs expressed that the Portuguese were going back on the agreement reached between Murtopo and Almeida Santos in

---

[32] FCO 15/1704[41]: Duggan to DPR Mackilligen, 2 June 1975.
[33] FO 810/29[51]: Minute, 11 June 1975.
[34] FCO 15/1704[42]: Telegram, 12 June 1975, 215.

London. The Indonesian Chargé in Lisbon was informed on 5 June of the line the Portuguese Government proposed to adopt in Macau:

> It envisages elections in the autumn, probably October, to a constitutional assembly which would in turn prepare the ground for a provisional government; the latter would have extensive powers of self-government internally, though the link with Portugal would be maintained for some time, unspecified. The Indonesians choose to see this as a step on the road to independence and hence against their understanding with the Portuguese.

A marginal note in the FCO observed: 'The Portuguese similarly think the Indonesians are reneging on the agreement'.[35]

On 19 June Akosah gave Duggan more details of the Portuguese proposals, which the Chargé had received from Alves. Ninety days after the Macau meeting 'transitional organs of representation' were to be appointed: a High Commissioner, nominated by the President of Portugal; a transitional government made up of the High Commissioner and five Deputy Commissioners, nationality unspecified; and a consultative Council of Government made up of two members of each party and two members chosen by each of the regional councils. A mixed Portuguese Government/transitional Government committee would 'regulate agreements of active co-operation in all fields'. The next step would be the preparation of direct elections in October 1976 to an assembly, to which would be submitted 'a definition of the political future'. It would formulate statutes so that administration under Portugal would cease in October 1978 'without alteration in the co-operation between Portugal and Portuguese Timor'.

The Indonesians had sought clarifications. To what extent, they wanted to know, did the transitional organs represent self-government? Would the post-1978 co-operation represent 'a continuing close link (beyond aid and economic assistance) on the lines of a Greater Portugal'? Where did the proposals leave the London agreement? The main points of that, Akosah said, were that 'Indonesia gave up its proposal of a joint Portuguese Indonesian consultative body to prepare the future of Portuguese Timor', while Portugal dropped its proposal of a provisional government, 'which was to be replaced by a consultative body, made up of representatives of the three

---

[35] FCO 15/1704[44]: Duggan to JL Jones, 16 June 1975.

parties', working with the Governor. Establishing a provisional government seemed to mean reneging on that agreement.[36]

The Macau conference was delayed, the Indonesian Ministry of Foreign Affairs said, because a mission from the United Nations Decolonisation Committee was visiting Lisbon. Akosah told Duggan that the Portuguese were taking 'an increasingly less accommodating line'; if the Macau conference did not produce a result because the parties could not agree, then Portugal would have to do what it thought fit. Akosah took that to mean that Apodeti 'must not make too many difficulties about what the Portuguese are proposing'. If that meant that things went so badly that Indonesia felt Timor threatened its security, Duggan asked, would the possibility of using force be 'resuscitated'? No-one would use it without the President's assent, Akosah replied. His guess was that the President 'would still wish to find other means'.[37]

The Macau talks

Apodeti had refused to take part in talks the Portuguese had held in Timor early in May (Hill 1978:155). Fretilin refused to take part in the talks in Macau, which Apodeti agreed to attend. Its argument was that in the May talks the Portuguese had already accepted Timor's right to independence, and it could not join in talks with a party that sought integration. Ramos Horta in fact had argued that Fretilin should take part, but the social-democratic element in the party had been weakened by the break-up of the coalition and the nationalist–Marxist element strengthened by the rural program and attracted by the liberation front approach of the Africans. The majority prevailed (Hill 1978:164–165; Taylor 1999:48–49). An Indonesian delegation was present, though not formally involved in the talks.

The communiqué at the end of the conference affirmed the right to self-determination, rather than independence. Apodeti opposed the inclusion of that word and it appeared only once. The text was subsequently approved by the Council of the Revolution in Lisbon. It provided for the termination of Portugal's sovereignty over a period of three years. In the meantime the Governor would be replaced by a High Commissioner, who would have a Council including three Timorese and two Portuguese 'joint secretaries'. There would also be a consultative council, including two representatives

---

[36] FCO 15/170[47]: Minute, 19 June 1975.
[37] FCO 15/170[47]: Minute, 19 June 1975.

from each of 13 regional councils, and four members nominated by each political association. A popular assembly would be elected in October 1976. Portuguese sovereignty would end in 1978, though there would be provision for altering the date in line with 'the genuine wishes' of the people (Hill 1978:165).

The authorities in London sought information; if the Portuguese timetable had been shortened, the Indonesians might be alarmed and more inclined to intervene. Andrew Stuart, Counsellor at Jakarta, thought that the Embassy could say 'categorically' that an early invasion had not become more likely. The Australian Chargé's view, Stuart added, was 'that intervention was now probable at some stage; but the Indonesians will want to prepare the ground carefully and there is no immediate reason for them to be panicked into an invasion'.[38]

No comment could be secured from the United States Embassy—it was Independence Day—but RH Gozney of the British Embassy in Jakarta called on Van den Berg, the second secretary at the Dutch Embassy. He thought the Portuguese timetable for decolonisation was 'still very loose in the sense that it left open the question of how and to whom responsibility for the territory would be shed by the Portuguese'. It was 'unlikely that the Indonesians would take precipitate action in the next few months', but there would be a further orchestrated press campaign against Fretilin. Van den Berg thought that the 'Indonesians must have been pleased at the break between Fretilin and UDT' and that 'they would concentrate on trying to further isolate Fretilin'.[39]

According to Indonesian newsmen, the telegram to the FCO read, the Portuguese Government put forward the program Akosah had outlined to Duggan, which 'differs from an understanding the Indonesians previously thought they had reached with the Portuguese in that it involves a directly elected parliament after 1976, as distinct from a consultative body with fewer constitutional implications'. But an immediate Indonesian invasion seemed 'most unlikely'. Apodeti put out a statement that, far from objecting that Portugal was 'hurrying the pace', expressed 'disappointment that the meeting had only involved an exchange of ideas and not a decision on the process of decolonisation': it urged an immediate referendum to 'give an opportunity to the majority of the people who supported integration with Indonesia'.

---

[38] FO 810/29[63]: Minute, 4 July 1975.
[39] FO 810/29[64]: Minute by Gozney, 4 July 1975.

The Embassy's assessment was 'that this call for a referendum is tactical and designed to improve Apodeti's image as a democratic party'. Privately the Indonesians admitted that a referendum held now would produce a majority for independence. Apodeti banked on a refusal, which would give the Indonesians 'time to swing local opinion in favour of integration, a process at which they are expert'. The Indonesians also saw tactical advantage in Fretilin's refusal to attend: 'it appears to brand the independence party as unconstitutional'.

Such 'cosmetic points' would be useful if the Indonesians decided to intervene. They would do so if necessary, 'since their overriding priority is that Timor should be joined to Indonesia one way or the other. But such excuses would take time to mature', and the Embassy believed 'that they would still greatly prefer a peaceful solution'. They had, moreover, formally said that they had no intention to invade; 'It would be uncharacteristic of them to act quickly and decisively to reverse this. Their present policy is to keep things as quiet as possible within the ASEAN area.'[40]

In London Vítor Alves called on the Minister of State at the FCO, Roy Hattersley. One party at the talks wanted integration, he said, one independence. 'The majority of the inhabitants however, many of whom lived in the mountains, wished to remain associated with Portugal which was not the wish of the Portuguese Government.' If the assembly to be elected in October 1976 wanted to remain associated with Portugal, the Portuguese Government would 'discuss this question' with it, but it intended to end Portuguese sovereignty by 1978. Alves saw no future for an independent Timor: it was

> too small and backward and half of the island was Indonesian. He felt the Australian Government would be happy to see Timor integrated with Indonesia, but the Portuguese Government would see that the Timorese were allowed to determine their own future.

About 80% still wished 'at this moment' to retain links with Portugal. Portugal did not want to maintain them, 'both because of the cost of maintaining an army there…and because the Portuguese people no longer wished to have colonies'.[41]

---

[40] FCO 15/1704[50]: Telegram, 4 July 1975, 244.
[41] FCO 15/1704[48]: Record of call, 4 July 1975.

Gordon Duggan, Head of Chancery in Jakarta, but also accredited to Portuguese Timor as British Consul, visited the territory from 2–9 July. He outlined the draft constitution put to the Macau conference. The administration in Dili, he reported, hoped the promulgation of the law when approved in Lisbon would be 'an important step towards the removal of political uncertainty within and concerning the territory'. It wanted arrangements that would help to 're-constitute the middle levels of authority…between the village chiefs and the Administration, the colonial system having in practice broken down with party representatives undermining the position of the provincial Administrators'. It also hoped 'that the announcement of a clear and progressive advance to self-determination' would give foreign investors confidence.

The Governor told Duggan that he had tried to get the parties to agree to a scheme not very different before Macau. While Fretilin had endorsed it, he felt 'that their boycotting of the Conference left them in a good tactical position from which they could repudiate what was proposed in the Constitutional Law'. UDT and Apodeti 'professed themselves satisfied with Macau'. The former thought it would have been better if Fretilin had attended. The Apodeti secretary-general appeared not unhappy: the scheme ignored Fretilin demands for *de jure* independence, made no proposals for a provisional government, 'though the change is essentially one of nomenclature', and 'kept the door to integration open'.

Duggan thought the prospects 'gloomy'; it would be 'surprising' if the future were decided 'peacefully'. The Administration wants 'time and tranquillity' to try to settle its problems, 'politically if its preparation of the inhabitants for self-determination is to succeed and economically if the territory is to be given some basic infrastructure and some possibility of a developing economic structure'. It was unlikely to get either. Bitterness and rivalry had built up among the political parties; further clashes could occur at any time, but particularly in the excitement of an election campaign. The economy would continue to be 'dangerously over-dependent' on coffee. 'The odds against an oil or minerals miracle are lengthened even further by the reluctance of the exploration companies to commit funds as yet.' The Administration admitted the difficulties. It had the advantage of the 'genuine regard' of the inhabitants. But it had 'no success in implanting the thought…that economic circumstances in Portugal might require them to leave the territory to its own best devices, perhaps at short notice; the inhabitants simply refuse to accept the possibility'.

While the territory was ill prepared, 'politically, economically and mentally', to stand on its own feet, it was likely that the assembly elected in 1976 would vote for independence. The Administration would probably accept. 'The case for integration into Indonesia may have a sound logical basis but there is an emotional tide for independence and against the Indonesians who cannot, in any case, really be considered to have played their hands well.' Whether the Indonesians would accept would be answered in Jakarta.

Duggan speculated on the attitude of the armed forces in Timor, which, like those in Portugal, had political views and structures. The Timorese soldiers, especially the sergeants, would, he thought, stay loyal to their Portuguese officers while they remained in the territory. 'The real test of their loyalty would arise should the Administration have to call on them to intervene and hold the ring should the parties come to blows.' After independence, the sergeants, seeing themselves as 'guardians of the territory's nationalism', might not tolerate any confusion that arose from inter-party rivalry. 'A *coup d'état* cannot be ruled out after self-determination.'[42]

The chances of unrest and of a coup Ambassador Ford 'rated high'. Indonesian media, with official backing, played up incidents such as the clash between party supporters on 28 June. 'If the Indonesians want to find excuse to intervene they should have little difficulty.' For the moment, however, he was prepared to believe their public statements 'that they hope the territory's future will be settled by peaceful means'. Trouble was, however, 'almost certainly on the horizon': the Indonesians wanted integration, the Timorese independence. At most the Indonesians had three years to persuade the people to opt for integration; at worst they would be faced by a coup by military leaders committed to independence. Neither Lisbon nor Dili could do anything effective against a coup.

'Duggan saw no evidence that either the Russians or the Red Chinese were yet stirring the pot', though 'any increase in Soviet influence in Lisbon might increase the chances that the former will seek to exploit the situation'. Even without such intervention, however, 'the territory seems likely to become steadily more of a problem child, and the arguments in favour of its integration into Indonesia are all the stronger'. It was still in Britain's interest 'to steer clear of becoming involved in its future', but

> developments in Lisbon...seem now to argue in favour of greater sympathy towards Indonesia should the Indonesia[n] Government feel forced to take strong action by the deteriorating situation in

---

[42] FCO 15/1704[54]: Visit to Portuguese Timor, 2–9 July 1975, enclosed in Ford to Male, 14 July 1975.

Portuguese Timor. Certainly as seen from here it is in Britain's interest that Indonesia should absorb the territory as soon and as unobtrusively as possible; and that if it comes to the crunch and there is a row in the United Nations we should keep our heads down and avoid siding against the Indonesian Government.[43]

The civil war in Timor

The disorder did not come about quite as the British Embassy expected. The absence of Fretilin from the talks in Macau and the persuasion of Komodo operatives increased UDT's suspicion of their rivals. A radicalised Fretilin might provoke Indonesian intervention. Ali Murtopo confirmed their apprehension: Fretilin, he told UDT leaders Oliveira and João Carrascalão, was a communist movement with links to China and Vietnam and was planning a coup in August, and then Indonesia would intervene (Taylor 1999:49–50; Dunn 1983:167; Dunn 1995:63). At the same time a reshuffle of the government in Lisbon strengthened the communists and it was rumoured that Fretilin, backed by the PCP, would encourage Portuguese troops to carry out a coup (Hiorth 1985:26). A BAKIN agent assured UDT leaders of Indonesian support if they could prevent a left-wing government coming to power in Timor and their 'show of force' ensued. By 11 August the UDT had occupied the police headquarters, where most of the police came over with their arms. They then took over the airport and the communications centre, but did not enter the arsenal. The aim, Carrascalão said, was to rid East Timor of Communists (Taylor 1999:50; Hiorth 1985:26). Ramos Horta told reporters in Darwin that he thought the UDT had carried out the coup because the government in Portugal was 'going far left'.[44]

Early on 11 August Governor Lemos Pires called his advisers together and agreed to try negotiating with Fretilin and UDT. On 12 August a courier returned with a set of Fretilin's conditions for negotiation, signed by Nicolau Lobato, which included the release of prisoners and safe conduct for negotiators. On 13 August UDT demanded the expulsion from Timor of 'communists' in the administration and in Fretilin. Arguing that he was

---
[43] FCO 15/1704[54]: Visit to Portuguese Timor, 2–9 July 1975, enclosed in Ford to Male, 14 July 1975.
[44] *Times*, 12 August 1975.

bound by the MFA's non-interference policy, Pires claimed he was stymied. UDT arrested Fretilin members in Dili and there were reports of executions elsewhere. Jónatas and Mota left for Darwin, 'ostensibly to report to Lisbon, but largely for their own protection'. Fretilin called for armed support and on 19 August the garrisons in Aileu and Taibasse declared in its favour. The Dili barracks and arsenal were opened to Fretilin and a battle for the capital followed. Instructed by Costa Gomes that he must avoid being taken hostage (Gunn 1999:275), Lemos Pires and his staff withdrew to a suburb and then to the island of Atauro (Taylor 1999:51). They took a portable radio transmitter and 'a refrigerator stocked with beer'.[45]

The FCO heard about the initial UDT coup from Australian Defence officials then in the United Kingdom, who believed

> it is possible that action may have been precipitated by recent events in Lisbon and the rumoured arrival in Timor of Portuguese troop reinforcements. It is possible also that UDT may have acted now in order to prevent the sort of situation that exists in Angola from arising in Timor closer to the time of formal independence.

A memorandum by Lynton Jones of the FCO suggested that, if law and order broke down or an anti-Indonesian regime emerged, Indonesia might be tempted to take over, 'using the attempted coup d'état as justification for intervention'. Ministers had agreed that Britain should stay out of the 'bickering' over Timor 'as far as possible'. It agreed with Whitlam that integration was 'probably the right answer in terms of regional stability'. Ford also believed that it was in Britain's interest that Indonesia should absorb the territory 'as soon as and as unobtrusively as possible'. If it invaded, 'there could well be strong left-wing pressure [in Britain] to condemn the action of the Indonesian Government, which is already unpopular with left-wingers because of its policy over political detainees'. The FCO should 'do its utmost to avoid taking a stance at all', but if forced to, 'bear in mind the damage that criticism of Indonesia may cause to Anglo–Indonesian relations'.[46] KM Wilford agreed that in the long run it would be best if Timor became part of Indonesia, 'but NOT as a result of an Indonesian *coup de main*'.[47]

---

[45] *Times*, 29 August 1975.
[46] FCO 15/1704[56]: Memorandum, 11 August 1975.
[47] FCO 15/1704[56]: Note, 12 August 1975, on Memorandum of 11 August.

Malik had declared that Indonesia would protect the people of Timor if they wanted to join the Republic.[48] It did not want to make Portuguese Timor 'another Goa'; easily done, 'but we want the people there to decide'.[49] Yoga Sugama, head of BAKIN, briefed Woolcott on 14 August. He denied Indonesia was involved in the coup, which was 'a complete surprise', and suggested that Mota and Jónatas were behind it. He thought the situation would get worse; all Portugal had done was to send Major Antonio Soares to Timor. He hoped Indonesia did not have to act, but, if it did so, it would want Australia's understanding. Woolcott told him 'that latent fears of Indonesia in Australia would be stirred up by Indonesian intervention'. Yoga said Indonesia would have to put considerations of security ahead of international reactions and he talked of the possibility of Soviet intervention. Woolcott told him he was exaggerating.

Reporting to Canberra, the Ambassador suggested

> that our efforts to persuade Indonesia that an independent Timor need not be detrimental to their interests have been overtaken by these events. There would also seem little chance now of a protracted period of Portuguese disengagement from the territory which will permit orderly arrangements for the people of Timor to decide their own future.

If Indonesia intervened, the Australian Government must do its best to contain the damage to its relationship with that country and 'act to limit a recrudescence of latent hostility to Indonesia' at home. It should publicly emphasise that it is 'not a party principal' and that it was not in its interests 'to become deeply involved', nor be in the vanguard of critics. 'There are also no inherent reasons why integration with Indonesia might not prove more workable for the Timorese inhabitants than independence or continuing factional friction.' Australia's support for self-determination in general had to be tempered in view of its relations with Indonesia.[50]

Woolcott gave Ford an account of the conversation, which he telegraphed to the FCO. Yoga evidently did not intend to brief him, he added, and a member of staff found his BAKIN contacts 'clam-like'. A senior official told Duggan that Repelita II—the development program—was Indonesia's

---

[48] *Times*, 12 August 1975.
[49] *Times*, 15 August 1975.
[50] Cablegram, 14 August 1975, in AIPT:306–309.

top priority. 'The President had said that military intervention was to be regarded as a last resort.' He was, Ford thought, 'proceeding with his usual caution but it looks as if events may now be forcing his hand'. He doubted if any final decisions had been taken and suggested that 'if you agree that our attitude should remain as detached as practicable given our own deep-rooted convictions about democracy and self-determination, he should not try directly to seek further information at the top level from BAKIN or the [Indonesian] DFA'. He would, however, keep in close touch with the Australians.[51]

The FCO agreed that it was in Britain's interest that Indonesia should absorb Timor as soon as possible and as unobtrusively and that it should avoid siding against Indonesia if it came to the United Nations. If, however, integration took place as a result of a *coup de main*, it would put Britain 'in an embarrassing situation', particularly if the matter were, as seemed inevitable, raised in the United Nations. Britain's main aim must therefore remain to 'stay out of the bickering'. The FCO agreed that Ford should not seek information at senior levels, though he need not refuse to attend a briefing if the Indonesians decided to include Western ambassadors among those who should receive a warning of their intentions. If the Indonesian Government questioned him about British policy in the event of intervention, he should 'restate our support for the principle of self determination', and he could also say 'that we support integration into Indonesia only if this is acceptable to the inhabitants of Timor'.[52]

A week later, as Squire wrote, the situation had 'deteriorated dramatically'; the Portuguese administration had lost control and 'virtual civil war' broken out. About 1,000 European civilians and dependants and about 400 Portuguese military staff needed to be evacuated. Lisbon was sending Almeida Santos to the United Nations to seek humanitarian assistance and to explore with Secretary-General Kurt Waldheim the resolution of the political problem. Indonesia might choose to intervene, 'ostensibly to restore law and order'. British ministers had agreed that the government 'should stay out of the controversy…as far as possible. There is no British interest in the region. There are no British subjects in Timor.' If it had to take a line with the press, it should regret the breakdown of law and order and reiterate support for self-determination.[53]

---

[51] FCO 15/1704[61]: Telegram, 15 August 1975, 298.
[52] FCO 15/1704[63]: Telegram, 15 August 1975, 192.
[53] FCO 15/1705[70A]: Minute by Squire, 22 August 1975.

Indonesia now talked of a new Angola rather than a new Goa.[54] It offered to assist Portugal in the restoration of law and order. Its request for international help, the Portuguese Government indicated, related to evacuation. There was, however, talk of a good offices committee. '[W]e would only wish to serve if the idea of a committee were acceptable to Indonesia', Canberra told Jakarta; '[and] if Indonesia were agreeable to our doing so and if we were in company with Indonesia and some other regional countries'.[55]

Against the recommendation of the more hawkish of his advisers, Suharto had twice ruled out intervention, the British Embassy reported on 25 August: he was 'still worried both about the principle of intervention and about its appearance'. But the Australian and United States ambassadors believed he would invade at once if the Portuguese specifically asked. 'Delay was dangerous.' If the situation worsened, it would be more difficult to restore law and order. 'Conversely if either Fretilin or UDT were seen to come out on top, it would be more difficult to justify intervention.'

The American Ambassador, John Newsom, doubted that the Portuguese would invite Indonesian intervention. In Lisbon there were suggestions that the Indonesians had prompted UDT to start the disturbances. 'If the Portuguese left wingers regarded the whole episode as an Indonesian plot to put down the left wing Fretilin, they would not be likely to give cover for an Indonesian invasion.' He had himself told the Indonesians they must decide for themselves. 'He had taken the Indonesians through the US law which led to the suspension of arms supplies to Turkey.' That statement would be important to them, since they were so dependent on American arms. Speaking to the British, Newsom thought Congress would 'swallow intervention provided that it was quick, has a colour of a police action and particularly if the Portuguese asked for it: but that if it was long drawn out and could be made to look like aggression, suspension was very possible'.[56] Woolcott reported a similar comment (Taylor 1999:55).

Antonio Soares, despatched from Lisbon on 13 August, reached Bali on 15 August, but was held up by immigration officials and then told he could not travel further. He returned to Lisbon (Taylor 1999:53). Almeida Santos, though no longer Minister for Overseas Territories, went to New York.[57] According to the United Kingdom Mission, he talked of humanitarian assistance, but also

---

54 *New Zealand Herald*, 22 August 1975.
55 Cablegram, 25 August 1975, in AIPT:339–40.
56 FCO 15/1705[72]: Telegram, 25 August 1975, 315.
57 FO 810/29[122]: Minute by Duggan, 29 August 1975.

stressed the need to mediate between UDT and Fretilin. 'He did not issue a formal invitation, and we doubt whether the Portuguese will do so given the tepid response to his exploratory talks.' Waldheim told him he had no authority from the General Assembly to send a mission and that the Security Council was not seized of the matter. The only possibility was that the Committee of 24 might send a mission in response to a request from the administering power. Over the weekend Santos had informal discussions with the executive bureau of the committee and proposed a mission that included Australia, Indonesia, Portugal and two other countries in the region, perhaps New Zealand and the Philippines, though they were not members of the committee. 'The proposal was greeted coolly' and Salim of Tanzania, the chairman, doubted if a mission could even enter Timor. The bureau was also concerned by the lack of precise terms of reference. A mission could of course mediate, 'but the unstated assumption is that the committee would only agree to such terms of reference if they were acceptable to both Australia and Indonesia'. It was unlikely that the Portuguese would formally request a mission and 'still more unlikely' that the committee would take up the invitation.

The Foreign Minister was sending a further letter to Waldheim, the Mission added, calling for his good offices. The impression of the United Kingdom mission was that the Portuguese had 'washed their hands' of Timor, and were 'looking desperately for some way of "internationalising" the problem, failing which they will countenance Indonesian intervention'. Almeida Santos, it seemed, would shortly leave for Southeast Asia, 'where he may seek to involve Timor's neighbours directly without pressing for a UN umbrella'.[58]

The letter related to evacuation, the embassy in Jakarta reported. The ships Indonesia was sending were, the Australians believed, in accordance with the request and not an invasion fleet. But they and the Americans thought that the Portuguese President would shortly make 'a new direct appeal to Indonesia to restore order. ...This would be a green light for immediate invasion'. The Indonesians would wait for an appeal. But 'the external political obstacles to an Indonesian invasion' were being 'whittled away'. Whitlam's statement in the House of Representatives on 26 August—that Australia was not a 'party principal', though willing to help in a humanitarian sense, that Portugal could not wash its hands of Timor and that the future of Timor, in many ways 'part of the Indonesian world', was 'a matter of great importance to Indonesia'[59]—

---

[58] FCO 15/1705[74]: Telegram, 26 August 1975, 922.
[59] FCO 15/1705[78]; UK telegram from Canberra, 27 August 1975, 777; also, slightly abbreviated, in Meaney (1985:774–776 and partly in *New Zealand Herald*, 27 August

was not 'a direct clearance for an invasion', but in Jakarta it was 'plausibly being interpreted as a non obstat'. The American Embassy's assessment was 'that developments in the UN and on the ground would already be enough to prevent severe Congressional reactions to a quick invasion'.[60]

Almeida Santos arrived in Jakarta late on 28 August and spent most of the next day in discussions with the Indonesians, especially acting Foreign Minister Mochtar Kusumaatmadja. He also saw Woolcott and the Head of Chancery at the British Embassy secured an account from his counterpart in the Australian Embassy. Apparently Santos had powers to negotiate an arrangement with the Indonesians under which Portugal would invite a group of countries, possibly including Malaysia and Australia, to

> assist in the humanitarian task of seeking to restore peace in Portuguese Timor: all the armed forces personnel committed to the operation would come from Indonesia. The aim would be to establish a body in the territory made up of representatives from each of the countries ... to take administrative control.

Almeida Santos, the Australian Embassy thought, had no intention of inviting Indonesia to go in alone. The arrangement appeared, however, to be 'something of a cloak for an Indonesian action'.[61]

Almeida Santos left for Australia. The talks, Mochtar told a press conference, were disappointing; the Portuguese had 'rejected several points in the draft proposals'. Ford concluded:

> Unless the Indonesians are to destroy their carefully prepared respectable position, they now seem to have painted themselves into a corner over intervention. They can only await the return of Santos, with little hope that he will give them the go-ahead then...The Indonesian dilemma... has been increased by the visit.[62]

Dr Girão, the Portuguese Chargé, gave Duggan details of the talks with Mochtar on August 29. The Portuguese proposals covered a multinational military force, entering Timor simultaneously with a multinational admin-

---

1975.
[60] FCO 15/1705[76]: Telegram, 27 August 1975, 319.
[61] FCO 15/1705[86]: Telegram, 29 August 1975, 323.
[62] FCO 15/1705[91]: Telegram, 1 September 1975, 326.

istrative authority and withdrawing when the situation had settled down. 'Portugal's ultimate responsibility and control of the colony must be made manifest.' The Indonesians, Girão thought, had expected Santos to ask them to go in and were disappointed. 'They insisted that there should be elections in the territory before its constitutional future was decided and they insisted also that Indonesian troops only should be used in the military operation.' The first round of talks in the afternoon was adjourned and the second lasted only 15 minutes 'when Dr Santos (after a telephone call to Costa Gomes in Lisbon) refused to negotiate further, saying he must go on to consult Australia'.

Girão told Duggan that 'Portuguese handling of the Timor problem had to be seen in the context of what was happening inside Portugal itself'. Almeida Santos was 'continually looking over his shoulder and…trying to avoid taking the responsibility for any Agreement that might be reached'. He insisted that all the Portuguese involved should sign any agreement. Girão told Duggan 'that the left-wing forces in Portugal could not give Timor away to the Indonesians for fear of recriminations from their opponents and also for fear that Fretilin supporters would be massacred'.[63] In Lisbon the 'moderates', as the founders of the MFA now seemed, were reasserting themselves and, supported by the Socialists, they indeed drove out Prime Minister Vasco Gonçalves at the end of August (Bruneau 1984:54–57).

In Canberra Almeida Santos had four hours of talks with Whitlam, as Acting Foreign Minister, and Defence Minister Morrison. The DFA told the British High Commission that Santos had explained the proposal for a four-nation joint authority and a predominantly Indonesian task force and had made it clear that the 'Portuguese could not accept Indonesian proposal that task force should precede establishment of joint authority. Indonesian intervention could only be at request of joint authority, co-ordination of which would be in the hands of Portuguese Governor.' He feared Indonesians would massacre Fretilin supporters if not controlled by the joint authority and he could not accept derogation of Portuguese authority. The task force was to restore law and order and permit the return of the Governor. Whitlam said Australia could not participate in the joint authority if its first act were to invite Indonesia to send a military task force, adding that 'Australia had no wish to assume Portuguese colonial responsibilities'.[64] According to Renouf (1979:445–446), the DFA saw some advantages in the Portuguese proposal, but Whitlam did not.

---

[63] FO 810/29[128]: Minute by Duggan, 5 September 1975.
[64] FCO 15/1705[92]: Telegram, 2 September 1975, 795.

In the House of Representatives Whitlam ruled out sending a peacekeeping force to Timor, but he left some of his options open. The Government would consider positive proposals after Almeida Santos had had further discussions in Timor and Indonesia. His hope, Hewitt thought, was that Santos might be able to bring the three parties together. The DFA doubted if that was practicable and believed some kind of peacekeeping force would be needed:

> The Australians clearly dislike the proposal for a four nation joint authority which would buy Australia into helping to solve a matter of primary concern to Portugal, particularly as the Portuguese seem to envisage the joint authority as a transitional arrangement to permit the re-establishment of their own authority.

Any peacekeeping force would need United Nations' authority, the Australians considered. If it were given, they might contribute a police contingent, but even that would draw Australia into the Timor question more closely than Whitlam and DFA officials appeared to wish.[65]

An Indonesian Ministry of Foreign Affairs official told Duggan in Jakarta that the main points of difference between Santos and Mochtar had been over the composition of the military force and the Indonesian proposal that it should be given time—say five to six months—to re-establish law and order before the joint authority took charge. He was pessimistic about Santos' further round of talks in Jakarta, as was the Australian Embassy. Its assessment was 'that the exchanges are now not unlike a game of poker with Santos refusing to budge on essentials in the hope that Indonesia will intervene and relieve Portugal of all responsibility'.[66] The basic problem, the *Far Eastern Economic Review* suggested, was 'that no love is lost between Indonesia and Portugal'.[67]

Though now dominant, Fretilin did not at this time intend to declare independence. A Portuguese presence was a means of deterring Indonesian invasion (Hill 1978:174). The secretary, Alarico Fernandes, stated: 'FRETILIN…intends to provide stable civil administration until the Portuguese colonial administration resumes its responsibilities in this territory' (quoted in Hill 1978:183). The Portuguese flag was still flown, but Fretilin's success prompted reports that it would declare independence and that Almeida Santos might negotiate over recognition. UDT leaders,

---

[65] FCO 15/1705[102]: Hewitt to Jones, 4 September 1975.
[66] FCO 15/1705[100]: Telegram, 5 September 1975, 333.
[67] *Far Eastern Economic Review*, 12 September 1975.

Mochtar told Ford on 8 September, had sent a message seeking Indonesian support and offering to declare independence, indicating in their declaration a willingness to consider integration. Suharto had refused to agree. The Indonesian Government would not deviate from its established line—the people must determine their own future. Only in that way 'would people forget the way in which Indonesia behaved under President Sukarno and believe what they said when they denied having any territorial ambitions. This credibility was particularly important so far as the country's future relationship with Malaysia was concerned.' If Almeida Santos had talks with Fretilin, Indonesia would consider the outcome 'illegal'.[68]

Almeida Santos arrived back in Jakarta on 10 September. Mochtar refused to discuss Timor with him, on the ground that since Gonçalves' resignation there was no government in Lisbon. Instead he met the secretary of the Political Directorate, Mrs Laurens Wiryoseputro.[69] The Indonesians rejected any transfer of power to Fretilin and demanded that UDT and Apodeti be included in talks.[70] Almeida Santos proposed a meeting of the three parties in Macau on 20 September, maintained that Portugal would carry out its decolonisation with the full participation of the population, and declared his conviction that an agreement could be reached. Ramos Horta, who had been in Australia, had gone to Timor to try to sell the idea to Fretilin, while Santos hoped to meet UDT and Apodeti leaders on the borders of West Timor. Ramos Horta, the Australians said, had not yet convinced his party: Fretilin would like to negotiate alone. Meanwhile, Ford reported, President Suharto was coming under increased pressure from the hawks:

> He still seems to be standing firm though he is perhaps more isolated from his main military supporters on this issue than he has been on any other issue since he successfully stood out in 1966 for a patient and cautious policy in effecting the succession to President Sukarno.

There were increasing movements in the border area, apparently by 'irregular units of the Indonesian armed forces in the guise of UDT and Apodeti supporters'. Suharto was aware of the activity, which suggested he was keeping open his option to intervene.[71]

---

[68] FCO 15/1705[103]: Telegram, 9 September 1975, 338.
[69] *New Zealand Herald*, 12 September 1975.
[70] *Times*, 12 September 1975.
[71] FCO 15/1705[106]: Telegram, 12 September 1975, 342.

The Indonesians saw the new talks with Almeida Santos as a failure, the British learned from the Australians. They still hoped for a political solution and, if a meeting in Macau were set up, would ensure that the pro-Indonesian parties did not sabotage the initiative. Increasingly, however, they were looking to a military solution, although it still did not involve overt intervention. 'Instead they plan to step up clandestine intervention designed to look like popular uprisings by UDT and Apodeti supporters', which might defeat Fretilin, or at least support the thesis that Timor was in chaos and so help to justify overt intervention. According to the Australians, Suharto had told Yoga Sugama that for the moment clandestine activities should not go beyond the present level. A planeload of Australian journalists and politicians was due to visit Timor, apparently at Fretilin's request, to investigate allegations of Indonesian intervention.[72]

In Timor, as in the African colonies, the end of the Portuguese Empire prompted disputes among the would-be successors, which Indonesia's covert operations encouraged. The result was not, however, what Indonesia expected—a civil war from which Fretilin came out on top. The Portuguese had, so the Indonesians thought, sanctioned their political intervention, arguing that, over a period of preparation, they might be able to strengthen the pro-Indonesian elements. Now the policy had failed, the Indonesians had to consider the alternatives. Though allegedly concerned about the advance of the left in Portugal and the success of the Communists in Indochina, Suharto was still unwilling to proceed with overt intervention on a unilateral basis, an important motive being his wish to dissociate Indonesia, now the leading member of ASEAN, from the aggressive policies his predecessor had adopted. The British stood aside, though prepared to accept integration provided it was not achieved by force and in denial of self-determination. Although their strategic interest in the region was now greater than Britain's, the Australians also stood aside. Half-heartedly Australian officials pursued a policy that sought to reconcile Indonesia to outcomes other than incorporation, which ran up against not only the changes within Timor but also the attitude of their Prime Minister and his chosen ambassador. Well aware of covert intervention—indeed bought into it—the Australians avoided public reference to it. When it became more open, they said and did as little as possible.

---

[72] FCO 15/1705[115]: Ford to Squire, 15 September 1975.

Chapter Eight

The Incorporation of Timor

Indonesia's covert intervention was stepped up so far that it became open. It still did not suffice and Indonesia was finally to resort to invasion in December 1975. That did not solve its Timor problem either, as the ripe plum did not fall into its hands. It failed to secure even the measure of United Nations sanction it had secured in respect of West Irian and it met a bitter resistance that prompted its forces to adopt a level of violence that was to be quite counterproductive. In this phase the British were still predominantly observers, but at the United Nations they helped to preserve the possibility of self-determination—less because of an intrinsic interest in Timor than because of the implications for the decolonisation of parts of its own empire. But that was ultimately to help in the de-integration of East Timor in the 1990s and thus in the creation of what had generally been deemed an impossibility, an independent state.

Balibo

The Taiwan Vice-Consul thought that UDT had thrown its initial victory away. By 18 August it had been in control except for some Fretilin pockets, but then it organised a force to attack the Fretilin stronghold of Aileu and left Dili unprotected, which gave Fretilin its opportunity. It secured control without much fighting and reports of atrocities were generally exaggerated.[1] In early September regional centres of UDT support surrendered and the bulk of UDT's troops were trapped at Batu Gade. On 24 September 500 soldiers, 2500 refugees and 19 captive Portuguese soldiers crossed into West Timor, allowed in on condition that they signed a petition calling for integration which had been drawn up by Lopes da Cruz, who had

---

[1] FO 810/29[160]: Minute by Duggan, 17 October 1975.

broken with Carrascalão in August. BAKIN, Taylor suggests, had expected the coup to produce a prolonged conflict. It had over-estimated UDT's strength, as it had earlier overestimated that of Apodeti. Fretilin's rapid victory forced BAKIN to rethink its strategy, hence the petition. Most of the refugees were against integration, but had little option but to sign it (Taylor 1999:51–53).

Still at this point Indonesia undertook no overt intervention, with or without Portuguese sanction, but Operasi Komodo was stepped up. Early in October there were reports of a military build-up: troops were sent to Atambua, aircraft positioned at Ampenan, and naval forces off Dili comprised at least two destroyers and two submarines. Ford mentioned to Ali Murtopo the hope that the future of the colony would be decided by self-determination—Fretilin's reported excesses might encourage a vote for integration—and stressed the dangers of overt intervention. Murtopo gave no indication that Suharto had changed his attitude. But, Ford thought, the hawks in HANKAM might expect further incidents in the following few days that would finally persuade him to do so.[2] The build-up increased, but the Australians, Ford reported, still saw it in the context of 'a stepped-up clandestine operation'. The pressure on the President must, however, be growing.[3]

The President had on 25 September again ruled out overt intervention, Duggan wrote on 13 October. Akosah in the Asia and Pacific Directorate of the Foreign Affairs Department, and Sudio Gandarum, of the European Directorate, 'admitted quite freely that they are at a loss to know how to proceed'. The clandestine operation provided propaganda about Fretilin atrocities and gave substance to the view, which was 'becoming increasingly difficult to maintain', that it had not yet won full control. But it seemed

> little more than a policy of *faute de mieux*; by its nature it has to be limited; until the President lifts his veto on overt action, no effective military use can be made of any Fretilin provocation on the border, however well staged.

Department officials were casting round for a way of opening up the diplomatic front and their only hope appeared to be that the Portuguese would honour Santos' suggestion that there should be a meeting of all three parties. At the United Nations Melo Antunes had made some reference to

---

[2] FCO 15/1705[124]: Telegram, 4 October 1975, 375.
[3] FCO 15/1705[131]: Telegram, 17 October 1975, 385.

a conference and Lemos Pires, who had been in Lisbon, told an Australian official in Darwin that Portugal would seek multi-party talks.[4] Now that Almeida Santos had agreed to negotiate with the three parties, official Indonesian sources said that intervention was 'unnecessary'.[5]

Woolcott had continued to advise what he called a pragmatic policy. That more or less coincided with the views of the Australian Prime Minister. Senator Willesee's attitude still differed. He had tended, as Woolcott put it, 'to put the main emphasis on a proper act of self-determination'.[6] Before the August coup he had agreed that Australia had a long-term interest in 'a close, co-operative relationship with Indonesia', but added that 'any Indonesian action which appears to subve[r]t a process of self-determination will make it difficult to further pursue this aim in the short run'.[7] After the coup and the Fretilin takeover, Woolcott argued that there would never be a proper act of self-determination. Australia should accept the alternatives—a *de facto* Fretilin government under Indonesian pressure or integration.[8]

Australian policy 'must also take account of *principle* as well as of the need for good relations with Indonesia', Renouf wrote on 7 October. He did not believe that what Whitlam had said to Suharto in Townsville was meant to convey a *carte blanche*:

> The Government has never accepted Indonesian claims that an independent Portuguese Timor could pose a threat to Indonesia. In addition, the element of self determination has also remained an important plank in Australian policy and was also conveyed to President Suharto in Townsville.

Fretilin was in control and Indonesia would have to allow for that. Indonesia's moment for action was at the end of August, but it hesitated and now intervention would have much less international support. The problem for Australia, Renouf though, was compounded

> because of the keen interest of our public opinion in the outcome in Portuguese Timor and the certainty that as Indonesian involvement

---

[4] FCO 15/1705[134]: Duggan to Jones, 13 October 1975.
[5] *Financial Times*, 13 October 1975.
[6] Woolcott to Willesee, 17 April 1975, in AIPT:253.
[7] Willesee to Woolcott, 7 July 1975, in AIPT:285–287.
[8] Cablegram, 17 September 1975, in AIPT:420–421.

escalates, knowledge of it will become increasingly public, leading to domestic pressure for the Australian government to dissociate itself from Indonesian policy in Timor.

He felt that Australia's policy was being 'overtaken by events. Between them Portugal and Indonesia had made a mess of things.' Ministers would soon have to consider 'whether we sit tight and allow the mess to drift on getting more messy or do we change course and if so, how?'[9]

Renouf told the British High Commissioner, Sir Morrice James, that the official policy of self-determination and Whitlam's statement to Suharto were the horns of a dilemma: the DFA had hoped against hope that they could be reconciled, though that was 'never realistic'. Suharto had opposed intervention; now the objective could not be attained with minimum force. Covert efforts had been 'a sorry mess'. Fretilin was in control, Moçambique and Guyana were stirring in its favour at the United Nations, and there was chaos in Lisbon. Renouf thought Australia would move towards leaving the question to the United Nations. James said Australia would have to show its hand and Renouf shrugged.[10]

The line consistently taken by Whitlam, Hewitt had reported, was being challenged by Willesee, who had returned from New York. He thought that the pro-Fretilin line taken by the press, by the left wing of the ALP and by the National Union of Students, largely responsible for a demonstration at the Indonesian Embassy in Canberra, called for a modification of Australia's stance, and, if need be, 'a clear message to Indonesia that Australia could not countenance Indonesian interference in affairs in Timor'. Hewitt could not see Willesee 'winning this battle' with Whitlam, particularly as the relevant branch of the DFA stressed the need for close relations with Indonesia.[11]

Renouf's thoughts seemed to be close to Willesee's, he now commented. There was infighting within the DFA and between Ministers and overseas posts. The relevant branch in the DFA did not agree with Renouf that a change of policy was needed. Whitlam was probably still not convinced that his line had been overtaken by events, Hewitt thought.[12] In fact, as

---

[9] Cablegram, 7 October 1975, in AIPT:446–447.
[10] FCO 15/1705[139B]: Note for record, 13 October 1975, in Hewitt to Squire, 17 October 1975.
[11] FCO 15/1705[128]: Hewitt to Jones, 10 October 1975.
[12] FCO 15/1705[139B]: Hewitt to Squire, 17 October 1975.

news arrived that Indonesia was stepping up its intervention, the DFA instructed Woolcott to express the Australian Government's 'extreme disappointment that the Indonesian Government has in the end seen it as being necessary to resort to large-scale military intervention'. He was also to say that the Indonesians might well be underestimating 'the political strength and will of FRETILIN and the degree of resistance FRETILIN is likely to mount'.[13] Woolcott questioned the instructions; meanwhile he would allude only to 'media reports' of intervention.[14] His meeting with Malik was 'unhelpful'.[15]

If Indonesia took over by force, Britain would resist the pressures that would build up for oral condemnation and termination of aid, the Australian High Commission had reported PJE Male, Assistant Under-Secretary of State at the FCO, as saying. A British statement would be issued, drawing attention to Indonesia's patience, denying that Timor was a British problem, and suggesting that neighbours were not concerned.[16] Within the Office Male now expressed the hope that Australia's line would be one with which Britain could associate itself. 'We have no need meanwhile to take a position on the merits of a disputed settlement. Nor…is there any merit in seeking to evolve a contingent policy for discussion with the Australians.'[17] 'The interest is Australian', Goronwy-Roberts commented; 'Our interest is in supporting them if at all possible.'[18]

Batu Gade had fallen to Fretilin forces on 24 September,[19] but was retaken on 7 October by the UDT, backed by 200 Indonesian commandos (Dunn 1983:228), and Fretilin failed to regain it.[20] News reports on 17 October said Balibo and Maliana had been captured by anti-Fretilin forces, including Indonesian troops from across the border.[21] By 24 October the forces were on the edge of Maubara. Suharto, the Australians said, had authorised the stepping-up of military activity. The aim was the encirclement of Dili by 15 November, the collapse of Fretilin, negotiations with UDT and Apodeti, handover to Indonesia the following year. The Australians were embarrassed

---

[13] Cablegram, 17 October 1975, in AIPT:480.
[14] Cablegram, 19 October 1975, in AIPT:487–488.
[15] Cablegram, 19 October 1975, in AIPT:488–491.
[16] Cablegram, 2 October 1975, in AIPT:443.
[17] FCO 15/1705[W39b]: Minute, 22 October 1975.
[18] FCO 15/1706[151]: Minute, 22 October 1975.
[19] *New Zealand Herald*, 9 October 1975.
[20] *New Zealand Herald*, 15 October 1975.
[21] FCO 15/1705[131]: Telegram from Jakarta, 17 October 1975, 385.

at home, Ford remarked. The American Ambassador had said on 21 October that Timor was high on the list of places where the United States 'do not want to comment or to get involved. I am sure we should continue to follow the American example.'[22]

Five journalists had been killed at Balibo on 16 October, two of them, Ford reported, British-born. They were killed, 'almost certainly inadvertently', in the course of attacks by UDT/Indonesian forces and their bodies probably burned. Malik had agreed to enquire, but the Indonesians had refused further requests for information. Ford had suggested that it was pointless to go on asking. No protests would produce the bodies: probably the local commander panicked when he found that he had killed them. The journalists were in the war zone of their own choice. But the Australian Embassy was pressed by Canberra.[23] The question has remained a matter of controversy in Australia, recently brought back to public notice by an inquest in Sydney in 2007 and by the publication of Jill Jolliffe's *Balibo* in 2009. The film, *Balibo*, of the making of which Tony Maniaty's *Shooting Balibo* (2009) gives an unduly self-regarding account, surely contains too much fiction to contribute to the search for truth or justice. It seems clear that there was nothing inadvertent about the killings. Perhaps the Indonesians hoped to deter others from reporting their intervention. The FCO at the time agreed with Ford's view.[24]

In the Ministry of Foreign Affairs in Jakarta, Duggan reported, Akosah was optimistic that the anti-Fretilin forces would be in Dili by 1 November. Contacts in BAKIN differed and the Australian Embassy did not speak with one voice. 'The American Embassy simply take the line that they are not in a position to judge; and go on to say with some satisfaction that they are under no pressure from the State Department to try to do so either.' Presumably, Duggan thought, the military dilemma was that the road to Dili from Bobonaro was 'long and difficult'. The short northern road, best for a seaborne attack, did not, on the other hand, reach the border, and using it would 'endanger the Indonesian cover story'. There was no evidence that the President had yet decided to risk that. He had given the green light for stepping up the covert operation, but not for overt action.[25]

---

[22] FCO 15/1705[144]: Telegram, 24 October 1975, 393.
[23] FCO 15/1705[145]: Telegram, 24 October 1975, 394.
[24] FCO 15/1706[158]: Telegram, 28 October 1975, 253.
[25] FCO 15/1706[161]: Duggan to Jones, 27 October 1975.

The Australian Embassy, Duggan felt, was less reliable than it had been. It had little success in extracting information on the fate of the journalists at Balibo and had come under some pressure as a result of the boycott of Indonesian vessels by dockers in Melbourne and Sydney. Inevitably there was a tendency as a result for the Embassy 'to hope that matters on the ground will be resolved as soon as possible'. At a dinner for Sir Michael Palliser, Woolcott gave an account of his exchanges with DFA in Canberra on the delivery of a message to the Indonesians. In the coming weeks, Duggan thought, the Australian Embassy would be an even less reliable source of information, particularly if there were signs that Timor was going to be an issue in the Australian constitutional crisis[26] provoked by Whitlam's clash with the Senate.

The Indonesia–Portugal talks in Rome

Duggan also alluded to the statement Willesee had made on 30 October, which indicated that the Government had expressed its 'extreme disappointment' over Indonesian military intervention and urged the Indonesian authorities to reaffirm their commitment to self-determination. It was glad to hear that the Foreign Ministers of Portugal and Indonesia would meet in Rome and hoped that the three parties could be brought together. The matter could not be settled by force. The Australian Government was doing what it could 'to get all the parties round the table for talks'. It was prepared to offer a venue.[27] Was the statement a shift in Australia's policy? Duggan asked a member of the Embassy staff. Only in respect of offering an Australian venue, he replied.[28]

The Indonesians were working out their position for the Foreign Minister talks to be held in Rome on the assumption that they will be in Dili by 1 November, Duggan had gathered. Much would depend, Akosah said, on the position the Portuguese took. Unless they showed themselves

> extremely forthcoming in their willingness to accept responsibility for Timor and to assist positively in attempts to secure a return to proper constitutional processes, the Indonesians would make it plain through some very hard speaking that they could not accept the continuance of

---

[26] FCO 15/1706[176]: Duggan to Jones, 3 November 1975.
[27] Draft, 29 October 1975, in AIPT:530–532; the statement is in Meaney (1985:776–778).
[28] FCO 15/1706[176]: Duggan to Jones, 3 November 1975..

the existing situation and that they would be left with no choice but to throw their full support behind UDT and Apodeti, particularly if Dili had fallen, in an operation intended to restore law and order in the territory...A small group of Indonesians, in Indonesian uniform, would join the UDT and Apodeti forces in Dili to assist them. Once law and order had been restored, the territory would formally be put back into the hands of the legal authority, namely Portugal, but within 4–6 months a referendum or general election on the territory's constitutional future would have to be organised. The implication is that consensus would be for integration into Indonesia.

The timetable envisaged at Macau, Akosah indicated, was 'no longer acceptable'.[29] Dili was not, however, in the hands of anti-Fretilin forces when Melo Antunes and Malik met in Rome on the first two days of November.

In Lisbon a new provisional government had at last been installed on 19 September, though it continued to face crisis throughout the following weeks. Headed by Pinheiro de Azevedo, it included five military moderates (Bruneau 1984:74), among them Melo Antunes. Only Fretilin had responded to the call for talks among the three parties.[30] At the United Nations General Assembly in October Melo Antunes proposed talks involving Portugal, Indonesia and the three parties. Indonesia agreed to talks, but only on condition that the United Nations would not intervene and the parties were not present. Under pressure to secure the release of the captured Portuguese soldiers taken to West Timor, Melo Antunes accepted, influenced, he said, by an assurance from Malik 'that, if the outcome of the meeting were acceptable to Indonesia, he would be able to restrain the generals from an outright invasion' (Dunn 1983:265–266).

According to the joint press statement the Foreign Ministers issued after their Rome talks, they 'affirmed their fidelity to the principles of decolonisation and of respect for the will of the people of Portuguese Timor'. They agreed that the responsibility for decolonisation lay with Portugal, the legal authority, and that it should make every effort to bring about an 'act of self-determination'. They also agreed it was urgently necessary to restore peace and order and 'allow the population to settle its own destiny'. A meeting between Portugal and the three parties was to be held as soon as possible. The Ministers also discussed the question of refugees in West

---

[29] FCO 15/1706[161]: Duggan to Jones, 27 October 1975.
[30] *Times*, 7 October 1975.

Timor and specifically the 23 Portuguese held by UDT, and they 'shared the view that in bringing about the decolonisation of Portuguese Timor it was essential to safeguard the legitimate interests of the countries in the area'. They agreed to maintain close co-operation. Neither Malik nor Antunes, the Indonesian Ambassador in Rome hinted, wanted the intervention of the United Nations or any outside power.[31]

Malik gave Woolcott an account of the Rome talks. There was an inconclusive discussion about a venue for the multi-party talks. The Portuguese had subsequently suggested Australia from 15 to 20 November and Woolcott believed his Government would propose Darwin as the venue, provided all parties agreed to attend. Indonesia thought that Australia could help to get Fretilin to attend and Woolcott again believed his government would make a favourable response, provided that it did not come to be regarded as Fretilin's sponsor. Finally Woolcott had asked Malik if the Rome meeting marked a shift in Indonesian policy. It had favoured integration. What would its attitude be if an act of self-determination produced a Fretilin government? Malik said he had made it clear that Indonesia's preference was integration, 'but if Fretilin won the support of the majority of the people, Indonesia would accept this, provided that Fretilin did not obtain control through force of arms'. Privately, Malik said, Melo Antunes had told him that integration would be the most satisfactory result, provided that it reflected the will of the Timorese.

The main gain the Indonesians had made at Rome, Ford concluded, was that Portugal did not go for internationalisation. He thought they had not given up 'hope of eliminating or minimising Fretilin's strength through their clandestine operations on the ground'. He doubted that they believed that it would be sufficiently reduced by 15 November to be prepared to make concessions to the pro-Indonesian parties. 'Perhaps the best scenario for Indonesia would be if Fretilin once again refused to attend, as they did the Macau meeting in the summer. This would damage Fretilin's international image and give Indonesia time to complete the covert operation.' The worst result for Indonesia would be for Fretilin to attend and dominate, 'perhaps with the connivance of the Portuguese'. But the meeting in Rome might have generated enough trust to discount that.[32]

UDT and Apodeti agreed to talks 'with alacrity'. Fretilin was reportedly 'wary…It would face losing de facto control of the most important part of

---

[31] FCO 15/1706[177]: A Brooke Turner to ML Hutchinson, 7 November 1975.
[32] FCO 15/1706[178]: Telegram, 10 November 1975, 412.

East Timor', Hamish McDonald wrote, 'and a new political fight in which Indonesia's hand would be immensely stronger'.[33] The Rome communiqué was a 'sell-out'. Fretilin would be outvoted by the other parties, both of which were now for integration (Dunn 1983:267).

The Australian Government, RM Sands reported from the British High Commission on 14 November, had agreed to the Portuguese request to provide a venue for the talks and the offer would not be withdrawn, since the caretaker government installed after Whitlam's dismissal was bound not to change policy. The DFA's information was that UDT was not keen on an Australian site, since its leaders thought the Australian press pro-Fretilin and suspected Australians were helping that party. Fretilin had accepted the idea of talks, but did not wish to talk to Apodeti or UDT. The DFA thus thought it would be some time before the talks were held, if they ever were.[34]

Duggan reported that it was one faction of Fretilin that refused to have anything to do with the other parties. The Australians, he added, did not apparently intend to take up Malik's suggestion that they should help to get Fretilin to the meeting. If, however, Ramos Horta turned up in Canberra and asked for their views, they would say they hoped all parties would attend. The fifteenth of November, the next 'target' date for the fall of Dili, had passed, Duggan noted on 17 November. The Information Minister, Mashuri, spoke openly of the help Indonesia was giving to anti-Fretilin troops.[35]

On 25 November Ramos Horta called on the British High Commission in Canberra, along with Alarico Fernandes, and met the Head of Chancery (Barder), Easey and Sands. Fretilin had reports that an Indonesian warship had shelled Atabae on 24 November. Indonesian troops had been involved in East Timor for more than a month. Fretilin believed Indonesia would begin an all-out offensive on 29 November. All but 1% of Timor was controlled by Fretilin, he said, thanks to 'mass support'; it had only 3,000 troops, its opponents many more. 'Fretilin was willing to talk to the Portuguese (whose sovereignty in East Timor they recognised) in Darwin, but the continued postponement of the proposed talks might result in a unilateral declaration of independence by Fretilin.' UDT and Apodeti had lost the war and 'had no place at the international negotiating table', but Fretilin would negotiate with other parties if the Indonesians withdrew

---

[33] *Financial Times*, 20 November 1975.
[34] FCO 15/1706[186]: Sands to Jones, 14 November 1975.
[35] FCO 15/1706[188]: Duggan to Jones, 17 November 1975.

their forces. 'They would even talk with the Indonesian Government if the latter ceased their intervention.' A message to Malik to that effect had not been answered. Barder gave Ramos Horta a copy of a statement Minister of State David Ennals made in the House of Commons on 6 November, which referred to the proposal that Portugal would arrange talks with all the political groups and stated that Britain would favour a solution based on self-determination.[36]

The British officials were 'struck' by Ramos Horta's 'lack of precision' on Indonesian involvement:

> He seems to have accepted that he could not prove intensive physical presence on the ground, since he spoke mainly of air, sea and cross-frontier bombardment, plus training, supply and base facilities provided for anti-Fretilin forces on the Indonesian side of the frontier.

His willingness to negotiate with other parties would clearly be in terms of an attempt at 'reconciliation' after Fretilin had been recognised as the government 'in some kind of post-colonial era, whether fully or partially independent'.[37]

Over in Jakarta, Woolcott had found Murdani 'under some strain' on 25 November. The 'covert' involvement had not so far been sufficient to bring the matter to 'a speedy conclusion'; yet, as time slipped by, Indonesia's denials became less credible. The President was 'still unwilling to agree to large scale Indonesian intervention or to admit involvement'. Murdani and Yoga were 'trying to find a way to convince the old man' that Indonesia 'ought to move in'.[38] On 28 November the Australian Embassy discussed with Tjan and Liem Bian Kie the possibility that Fretilin might soon declare independence. 'They were not surprised to hear this. In fact they gave the distinct impression they expected FRETILIN to make such a move and would not be unhappy about it.' It would introduce a new factor into a situation that was something of a stalemate. Indonesia would point out to Portugal that the declaration was contrary to the Rome agreement and ask it to take action. Fighting would continue and Timor would become a 'no-man's land'.[39]

---

[36] FCO 15/1706[203]: Minute by Sands, Call by Horta, 17 November 1975.
[37] FCO 15/1706[203]: Sands to Jones, 28 November 1975.
[38] Cablegram, 27 November 1975, in AIPT:584–586.
[39] Cablegram, 28 November 1975, in AIPT:586.

Taylor (1999:63–64) records Fretilin's next move:

> Sensing that an independent state might have a more successful chance of appeal to the UN if it did not have to rely on its mentor in Lisbon, and persuaded by the intense feeling from the military front that, if soldiers were going to die, they would prefer to do so for a country which was actually theirs, the Fretilin administration transformed itself into the Democratic Republic of East Timor on 28 November.

The decision had followed weeks of debate within Fretilin. The fall of Atabae the previous day had given it 'new urgency. ...Ways had to be found to break through the diplomatic silence and indifference with which Indonesia's allies had shrouded its aggression.'

The decision marked the victory in the debate of the leaders of the Fretilin army, Forças Armadas da Libertação Nacional de Timor-Leste (Falintil), the defeat of internationalists like Ramos Horta, and the emphasis Rogerio Lobato put on self-reliance. Angola's declaration of independence on 11 November was another factor; it had been recognised by 30 countries. Mari Alkatiri secured some pledges of recognition for an independent Timor, though he warned that Timor was not Angola (Dunn 1983:270,273; Hill 1978:201–202). The decision was, in Hiorth's view, a 'mistake' (Hiorth 1985:31). It was a provocation that, as Liem and Tjan indicated, was not unwelcome. The Indonesians invaded. But Fretilin built both on the traditional kinship alliances and on a nationalist ideology and it had enhanced its support dramatically in the months after the August coup (Taylor 1995:33–34). It could not outface Indonesia in the short term; in the long term the prospects might be different.

The Indonesian invasion

Following a meeting chaired by Suharto, Mashuri deplored Fretilin's unilateral declaration of independence (UDI) and expressed regret at the attitude of the Portuguese Government, which appeared to approve of Fretilin's action. 'Indonesia had come to the conclusion that the Portuguese Government had made use of the Rome understanding as a cloak to conceal its real political aims' and considered East Timor 'a no-man's land'. Minister Crespo had apparently told the Indonesian Ambassador of the move before it happened. He also spoke of withdrawing the troops from Atauro—which the Indonesians saw as 'Portugal washing its hands of Timor as it did of

Angola'—and of taking the question to the United Nations—which they considered contrary to the Rome agreement). They were apprehensive lest anyone recognised Timor's independence. Despite the 'no-man's land' reference, it was still thought, the British Embassy in Jakarta reported to the FCO, that the President's veto on overt intervention would continue, though support for UDT/Apodeti would increase.[40]

Australia declared that it did not recognise the UDI but was bound still to recognise Portuguese sovereignty; it sought the resolution of conflict through peaceful means through which the will of the people could be expressed.[41] The new 'President', Francis Xavier do Amaral, sought British recognition. There were reports, Jones wrote, that Moçambique and the MPLA in Angola had extended recognition. Fretilin claimed that Guinea-Bissau and two dozen other countries would follow suit, although that seemed 'most unlikely'. The Soviet Union would not want to set its relations with Indonesia back. Members of the Chinese Embassy, Lin Hsiang-ming and Cheng Yao-men, had called to say that the People's Republic of China would not recognise Fretilin's UDI.[42] The remaining parties had declared integration on 30 November.[43] Both the declarations had been denounced by Portugal, which, in a letter to the United Nations Secretary-General, had accepted responsibility for Timor but 'inability to affect circumstances there'. Indonesia had stepped up military support for the parties opposing Fretilin. Malik had said at Atambua that the time for diplomacy had ended. He said, if they were not women, the parties would fight. He came to bring the spirit of the fighting cock.[44]

Jones drew attention to the parliamentary question of 6 November to which Ennals had been responding. Would Britain recognise a provisional government of East Timor? Britain had frequently expressed support for attempts by Portugal and Indonesia to reach a negotiated solution and that should continue to be its attitude. If asked, the FCO News Department should state unattributably that it would not be replying to the request for recognition and, on the record, say that Britain regarded the territory as the responsibility of Portugal, that it favoured continued attempts to reach a solution on the basis of self-determination, and that the party claiming

---

[40] FCO 15/1706[202]: Telegram, 1 December 1975, 437.
[41] FCO 15/1760[202]: Telegram from British High Commission, 1 December 1975, 980.
[42] FCO 15/1706[206]: Minute by Goldsworthy, 2 December 1975.
[43] *Times*, 2 December 1975.
[44] FCO 15/1706[210]: Duggan to Jones, 2 December 1975.

independence did not in any event meet its criteria for recognition.[45] Jones' position was endorsed by his superiors.

A guidance telegram stated, for the information of officials only, that it remained Britain's

> prime aim to keep out of the controversy surrounding Timor as far as possible. East Timor is economically weak and could become a source of instability within the Indonesian Archipelago. In the wake of Vietnam we wish to see a period of prolonged stability in the region.

Integration would make good sense, but Britain hoped it would come about through an act of self-determination not 'crude annexation'.[46]

The Indonesian Government issued a statement on 4 December. Indonesia had from the start supported Portugal's decolonisation policy, it declared. An orderly process implied a guarantee that all could express their views. Indonesia objected 'most strongly' to Fretilin's one-sided action and would

> take the necessary steps to guarantee the security of the national region, to guard the sovereignty of the state and to protect the people against disturbances from the outside. On the basis of anti-colonialism and humanitarianism, the Government and people of Indonesia have a moral obligation to protect the people in the region of Timor so that the process of decolonisation is achieved in accordance with the ideals and wishes of all the people of Portuguese Timor.[47]

Woolcott was summoned to the Ministry of Foreign Affairs on 4 December. The Director-General of Political Affairs, accompanied by Adenan of the Asia and Pacific Directorate, told him that Indonesia might have to intervene to restore conditions under which an orderly process of decolonisation could be carried out and said it would look for Australia's understanding. Indonesia would conduct an act of self-determination and some United Nations involvement in that was not ruled out. A Ministry of Foreign Affairs official told the British Head of Chancery that Indonesia had to act quickly lest Fretilin establish itself and gain more recognition. 'He said Indonesia was no longer worried about the international reaction as

---

[45] FCO 15/1706[210]: Minute, 2 December 1975.
[46] FCO 15/1707[253]: Guidance telegram, 5 December 1975, 213.
[47] FCO 15/1706[219]: Telegram, 5 December 1975, 446.

Indonesia now had good legal reasons for taking action, the purpose of which was to restore law and order and to arrange for an act of self-determination'. Nothing would happen, he thought, till the visiting President Ford had left Jakarta on 6 December. Suharto seemed, the British Ambassador reported, to have lifted his veto on overt action. The military aim would probably be to take Dili quickly from the sea.[48]

Jones now developed a line for Britain to take in the event of an Indonesian invasion. It should regret the breakdown of negotiations for a peaceful solution and express the hope that Indonesia would take note of 'the international desire, which we share, to see progress towards decolonisation on the basis of self-determination'. Britain noted the statements to that effect in the declaration of 4 December. 'The people of Timor have not yet been consulted although they have been the prime sufferers so far. We hope they will now be given the opportunity to express their wishes concerning their future.' An unattributable part of the line was that Fretilin's UDI led to the breakdown of negotiations. If pressed, British spokesmen could say that it was for the parties 'most closely involved' to consider whether the matter should go to the Security Council.[49] A motion before the General Assembly's Fourth Committee appealing to the political parties to resume talks was postponed on 5 December. Meanwhile Fretilin had announced its intention to send a delegation to New York.[50]

In the early hours of 7 December—a day already living in infamy— Indonesian ships bombarded the coast east and west of Dili. Then paratroopers landed to secure a landing ground for the marines who followed. Most of the Fretilin forces retreated into the hills. The Indonesian advance 'stalled in the suburbs'. Civilian casualties were high 'and there were many reports of summary executions and massacres'. The two Portuguese corvettes off Atauro watched Dili burn, then left for Darwin (AIPT:603; Dunn 1983:283–286). The Indonesians, Ambassador Ford suggested, had acted as expected, the only surprise being 'the extent of their overt intervention'. The Embassy attributed it to Fretilin's UDI, coupled by reports of Russian and Cuban intervention in Angola, to the cost of maintaining 30–40,000 refugees in West Timor, and to the short time available between President Ford's visit—he and Kissinger had left

---

[48] FCO 15/1706[218]: Telegram, 5 December 1975, 445.
[49] FCO 15/1706[221]: Memorandum, British Response in the Event of Indonesian Invasion of Dili, 5 December 1975.
[50] FCO 15/1706[222]: Telegram from United Kingdom Mission, 6 December 1975, 2103.

less than 24 hours earlier (Dunn 1983:282)—and the Australian elections on 13 December.

British interests would be best served, the Ambassador continued to believe, 'by comment *in as low a key as possible*'. Kissinger was reported as saying that the United States did not recognise Fretilin and 'understood' Indonesia's position, and the United States Ambassador said the two Presidents had not discussed Timor. The caretaker government in Canberra, Woolcott said, had been 'equally cautious'. Unless instructed, Ford did not intend 'to go into bat with the Indonesian Government'. If what the Indonesians had told Woolcott was 'a fair guide', the Indonesians would allow some form of international inspection of an act of self-determination. If they did, the British Government should promote the process, while recognising that, as with West Irian, the final outcome was 'not likely to be in doubt'. The Ambassador suggested that Britain's line should also include expressing an 'understanding' of Indonesia's position.[51]

In fact the two Presidents had discussed Timor. Gerald Ford had said that, if Suharto had to take 'rapid and drastic action', the United States would understand (quoted in Scott 2005:112). The Secretary of State, Henry Kissinger, was irate when an American diplomat mentioned that Indonesia was using weapons supplied for self-defence: 'I know what the law is but how can it be in the US national interest to…kick the Indonesians in the teeth?' (quoted in Scheiner 2000:118).

The FCO agreed with Ambassador Ford that Britain's interests would be best served by 'keeping comment in as low key as possible'. The line he suggested, however, might be regarded as 'too complaisant towards the Indonesians—especially in view of the Portuguese severance of relations with Jakarta'. It would be helpful to know whether the United States and Australia would continue to deal with the matter in a low key and also to hear the reactions of Singapore, Malaysia and Japan.[52]

The British at the UN

The United Kingdom Mission in New York thought that the postponement of the vote in the Fourth Committee and the knowledge that Fretilin representatives would shortly arrive in New York had been major factors in provoking intervention. At the United Nations the Portuguese intended to

---

[51] FCO 15/1706[223]: Telegram, 8 December 1975, 447.
[52] FCO 15/1707[232]:.Telegram to United Kingdom Mission, 8 December 1975, 1073.

go to the Security Council two days after the Fourth Committee voted on 8 December. The Mission reported that the 'atmosphere had turned ugly. There is widespread bitterness at what is regarded as Indonesian duplicity. Those Africans who have supported self-determination in Belize and the Sahara will demand it for Timor too, whether or not they recognise Fretilin.'[53]

The United Kingdom, in the person of Ivor Richard, its Ambassador to the United Nations, was current president of the Security Council. He consulted the Indonesian and Portuguese ambassadors at the United Nations. He told Sani that the Portuguese apparently wanted a mission or a representative of the Secretary-General to visit Timor shortly. Sani thought a visit to Timor might raise problems of security. Richard then told the Portuguese Ambassador that an immediate mission could take place only with Indonesia's co-operation. Perhaps a short visit could be followed by the conference of parties that Portugal still wanted. He commented on

> an air of unreality about this discussion. The Portuguese ambassador said that it was hard for his government to accept the presence of Indonesian troops and certainly he could not defend their presence, when he spoke in the Security Council. At the same time, I gained the impression that he did not expect them to leave.

Even if the Security Council called for an Indonesian withdrawal, Richard reported, the Portuguese would have to 'swallow the pill of a continuing Indonesian de facto presence'.[54]

At the Fourth Committee on 8 December the Australian Ambassador read out a statement issued on 7 December by the spokesman for foreign affairs in the caretaker government, Andrew Peacock, omitting a paragraph regretting that Australia had not played a more positive role earlier. A new text was tabled on 9 December. Overnight, the United Kingdom Mission gathered, caretaker Prime Minister Fraser had instructed the Australian Mission to vote in favour of a draft, amended by Guinea-Bissau, strongly condemning Indonesia and demanding the withdrawal of its troops. An alternative Asian draft, expected to be supported by India, Iran, the ASEAN countries other than Singapore, and possibly Japan, avoided such clauses and called for a fact-finding mission. Richard thought that draft more realistic,

---

[53] FCO 15/1707[236]: Telegram, 8 December 1975, 2138.
[54] FCO 15/1707[239]: Telegram, 9 December 1975, 2148.

but it would be unwise for Britain to vote for a text that did not mention withdrawal and he believed it should abstain in both cases.[55]

The FCO agreed. Supporting the Guinea-Bissau text would be contrary to the low-profile approach. Supporting the Asian text 'might store up trouble for us...as it makes no mention of the need for Indonesian withdrawal (which we would not advocate for wider reasons)'. Abstaining would leave Richard with a freer hand while chairing the Security Council debate,[56] which Male thought important. Lord Goronwy-Roberts wished it had been possible to support the Asian text,[57] but, as the FCO told Richard, Britain might wish to insist on a withdrawal clause in the event of an invasion of Belize,[58] claimed by neighbouring Honduras.

The Indonesian Ambassador called on Goronwy-Roberts on 10 December to explain his government's action. The Minister of State said his Government was 'deeply concerned' at it and regretted it, but what the Ambassador said about the future conformed with Britain's hopes. 'There should be a speedy end to hostilities, and a withdrawal of Indonesian troops...at the earliest possible opportunity'. That should lead to a situation where the Timorese would be given 'a genuine opportunity to exercise their right of self-determination'. The world must be left in no doubt that they had expressed their view 'freely and openly', so the process had to involve 'an act of formal, comprehensive consultation with the people of the territory, which could best be conducted by an international authority, such as the UN'. Indonesia would have to accept whatever decision the Timorese reached. Goronwy-Roberts was glad to hear that Indonesia was thinking along these lines and noted that Malik had spoken of a genuine act of self-determination. In speaking to the press or in Parliament, he would propose to say that he had welcomed Indonesia's commitment towards self-determination. He advised the Ambassador to emphasise that Indonesia had intervened to restore law and order and 'to pave the way for a genuine act of self-determination'.[59] The FCO hoped to deflect the call for a debate in the Commons made in an Early Day Motion by 104 Labour MPs and one Conservative.[60]

Singapore, it was reported, had declined to sponsor the Asian resolution, though it was expected to vote in favour, as '[n]ot surprisingly it seems

---

55   FCO 15/1707[243–245]:Telegrams, 9 December 1975, 2157–2159.
56   FCO 15/1707[248]: Memorandum by AH Simons, 10 December 1975.
57   FCO 15/1707[248]: Minutes, 10 and 11 December 1975.
58   FCO 15/1707]265]: Telegram, 11 December 1975, 1088.
59   FCO 15/1707[272]: Record of conversation, 10 December 1975.
60   FCO 15/1707[252]: Memorandum by Simons, 10 December 1975.

unlikely that Singapore will want to rock the ASEAN boat'.⁶¹ In Kuala Lumpur the Under-Secretary, Khor, indicated that Malaysia's view was that, provided that self-determination went ahead, integration was the best solution. The Prime Minister's principal private secretary had told the British High Commissioner on 8 December that Razak's only criticism had been that the Indonesians 'had not acted firmly earlier'.⁶² Earlier it had been suggested that one reason for Suharto's caution had been his anxiety not to alarm the Malaysians.

At the Fourth Committee meeting on 10 December, India introduced the Asian draft, saying that it implied Indonesia's withdrawal and continued Portuguese participation in Timor's self-determination.⁶³ The following day, however, the Committee voted for the African draft (69 votes to 11, with 43 abstentions). Some had wanted to go further in exculpating Indonesia. 'If there was a fire next door', Saudi Arabia claimed, 'the neighbours had a perfect right to put it out.' But it was clear that the Asian draft would not succeed and India did not press it to the vote. Australia voted for the African draft; the use of force, its Ambassador declared, was 'not appropriate'. It would, however, seek amendments in the plenary session, designed to avoid explicit condemnation of Indonesia by referring to 'foreign armed forces'.⁶⁴

That Britain could accept, inasmuch as it did not directly criticise the Indonesians, but thought that

> in practical terms, it would be unhelpful in that, if the Indonesians withdraw soon, Fretilin would be likely to take over or there would be an upsurge in the civil war. In these circumstances, an exercise in self-determination for the people of Portuguese Timor would be unlikely.

Richard should therefore abstain, unless that meant the United Kingdom delegation became isolated from the majority of the nine European Economic Community countries, the United States and New Zealand.⁶⁵ The Australians in any case failed to secure their amendments.⁶⁶ The

---

⁶¹ FCO 15/1707[247]: Telegram from Singapore, 10 December 1975, 719.
⁶² FCO 15/1707[250]: Telegram, 10 December 1975, 441.
⁶³ FCO 15/1707[257]: Telegram, 10 December 1975, 2176.
⁶⁴ FCO 15/1707[266–267]: Telegrams, 11 December 1975, 2190–2191.
⁶⁵ FCO 15/1707[275]: Memorandum by Simons, 12 December 1975; FCO 15/1707[277A]: Telegram to United Kingdom Mission, 12 December 1975, 1096.
⁶⁶ FCO 15/1707[278]: Telegram, 12 December 1975, 2202.

United Nations General Assembly deplored Indonesia's intervention (72 votes to ten, with 43 abstentions),[67] the abstainers including Singapore.

The Indonesians were not worried by what the Australians said in New York, Akosah told the British Head of Chancery—Woolcott had delivered a message from Fraser 'to the effect that what was being said in Australia… was only for the purposes of the election campaign'. Duggan 'subsequently wheedled out of highly embarrassed member of Australian Embassy staff [Taylor] confession that there had indeed been a message from Mr Fraser', orally passed some weeks ago, known only to three people in the Embassy. At first Taylor had 'blanched visibly', then he had rung back. The substance was that Fraser wanted close personal contact with Suharto and attached great importance to relations with Indonesia. There was some reference to Timor, but the staff member was not specific. The Embassy was very apprehensive of a leak and the possible political reaction in Australia. The Minister, Malcolm Dan, told Stuart it was because Fraser had assured the Governor-General 'that no foreign policy initiative would be taken during the interregnum'. Presumably that was why Australia felt free to take a tough line at the United Nations, 'having warned the Indonesians in advance to pay no attention'.[68]

The exchange was presumably a reference to the telegram to Woolcott of 20 November, conveying a message from Fraser. If returned in the general election on 13 December, he would want to build up relations. He recognised Indonesia's need for 'an appropriate solution' of the Timor problem. He would want his Foreign Minister to make an early visit to Jakarta. In the meantime ministers would not receive Ramos Horta or any representative of Fretilin.[69] Woolcott delivered it on 25 November. He thought it had a good effect. Suharto might expect the Government to take steps after the election to moderate the growth of hostility in Australia.[70]

The British High Commission in Canberra had noted at the time some difference between the attitudes of Fraser and Peacock. In a speech at Darwin the former had called Fretilin communist. Peacock had not met Ramos Horta on his visit, but said it was simply because they were in different parts of Australia. Sands thought the difference echoed the dichotomy between

---

[67] *Times*, 13 December 1975.
[68] FCO 15/1707[276]: Telegram from Jakarta, 12 December 1975, 453; FO 810/29[280]: Minutes by Duggan, Stuart, 12 December 1975.
[69] Telegram, 20 November 1975, in AIPT:598.
[70] Telegram, 12 December 1975, in AIPT:598–599.

Whitlam and Willesee; the Foreign Ministers were 'rather more even-handed' than the Prime Ministers.[71]

In any case the Australian ploy, if such it was, had not been received as Stuart suggested. The Indonesians reacted with disappointment, as a statement by Mashuri put it, and that was directed neither at Sri Lanka, which had in the event changed its vote, nor at Singapore, which had abstained. Woolcott feared that Australia's role had made it look like a party principal. He thought its negative vote had set back relations with Indonesia, might prevent Australia's playing an effective role on Timor in the future, and could stir up anti-Indonesia sentiment in Australia.[72]

The Security Council proceedings

The Security Council met on 15 December. The Portuguese delegate insisted Portugal was still the administering power and that it was inadmissible for Indonesia to take the law into its own hands. The United Nations should help to ensure the holding of a conference involving Portugal and all the political parties and to organise and supervise an act of free choice, condemn Indonesian aggression and call for the withdrawal of all invasion forces. Indonesia, said Anwar Sani, had been confronted by chaos caused by Fretilin and by Portugal's abdication. It was ready to co-operate with the United Nations and countries of the region to enable the Timorese to exercise their right to self-determination. Ramos Horta appeared under Rule 39, which allowed the Security Council to invite persons to attend in order to provide information. The violence in Timor started with the UDT coup, he said. The Indonesians had expected to step in, but had been surprised by Fretilin's strong resistance. It had been the *de facto* government since September. The United Nations should call for Indonesia's withdrawal and send a fact-finding mission. Khir Johari of Malaysia said Portugal should seek the assistance of countries in the region in discharging its responsibilities. The United Nations should send a mission to assess the situation and make recommendations.[73]

Next day China condemned Indonesia's action. UDT, said Carrascalão, had broken with Fretilin because Ramos Horta and others had been PIDE informers, and it had staged its coup because it had information

---

[71] FCO 15/1706[203]: Sands to Jones, 28 November 1975.
[72] Cablegram, 15 December 1975, in AIPT:629–631.
[73] FCO 15/1707[298]: Telegram, 15 December 1975, 2218.

that Fretilin had been about to stage a coup. When Fretilin took power, many UDT supporters had been killed. UDT had opted for integration. Gonçalves said Apodeti had always stood for integration, and Martins for *Klibur Oan Timor Asuwain (*KOTA), a small party, said Portugal had done nothing to prepare Timor for independence. Ralph Harry, the Australian representative, said the first step was a ceasefire. Some United Nations presence was needed before the self-determination process could begin. The Secretary-General might be asked to appoint a special representative to consult the parties principally concerned and recommend action. Alternatively, if hostilities ended quickly, the Committee of 24 might assume responsibility. He supported the Malaysian view that the countries of the region might have a special responsibility for assisting the administering power.[74]

Before the Security Council met again on 18 December, France, the United States, Italy and the United Kingdom had an informal meeting to discuss possible draft resolutions 'and in particular what degree of UN involvement we would find acceptable'. While it was agreed Indonesia would undoubtedly absorb Timor, 'there must be some form, however muted, of self-determination'. A two-stage package might be best. First, the Security Council would request a representative of the Secretary-General to visit Timor, report on the situation and make recommendations 'on the way in which a future act of self-determination (or consultation of local opinion) could be effected'. Indonesian troops, or 'volunteers' as they were called, would still be there, but the terms of reference could make it clear that the Council still recognised Portugal as the administering power. The second stage, post-report, would consist of consultations in New York about the creation of a temporary administration under which an act of self-determination would be conducted. By then Indonesia's control would have been consolidated and it 'would not object unduly to an act of self-determination or a consultation of village councils which would probably result in a heavy vote for integration with Indonesia'. The Australians thought it was a plausible package. The Guyana and Tanzania representatives raised the question whether a representative could properly visit Timor while it was under Indonesian control. The choice, the British replied, was 'half a cake or none'.[75]

---

[74] FCO 15/1707[309]: Telegram, 16 December 1975, 2223; Harry's text is in Cablegram to Canberra, 16 December 1975, in AIPT:637–638.

[75] FCO 15/1708[311]: Telegram from New York, 17 December 1975, 2231.

In Jakarta the deputy head of the Asian and Pacific Directorate gave the British Head of Chancery some account of the Ministry of Foreign Affairs' thinking on the next steps. Indonesia, he said, had an open mind over a visit by a representative of the Secretary-General, but any approach had to be made to the provisional government in Dili which would naturally consult Jakarta and a reply might take up to a month. An act of self-determination was necessary. He spoke of a United Nations observer team, including an African representative, probably from a former Portuguese colony, an Asian one, perhaps from Indonesia or Malaysia, and one from the Southwest Pacific, for example New Zealand. 'The ascertainment would be on the lines of that for West Irian, with the opinion of the territory's nine districts being considered and it would not involve anything more direct like a general election.' Asked about a call to withdraw troops, he said Indonesia might be able to get some 'volunteers' from Java out, but many from West Timor were indistinguishable.[76]

The tactical situation in New York, Ambassador Ford appreciated, was likely to dictate the form of any Security Council resolution. He was also sure that Britain should try to keep out of the controversy, as the guidance telegram suggested. 'The Australians have gained nothing from their involvement, indeed they have lost by it.' There was no reason to defend the Indonesians. 'Their handling of the international debate continues inept, even dishonest: and their underlying motives, while primarily defensive, are also at least partly imperialist.' Britain had, however, an interest in 'a stable Indonesia, an effective South East Asian grouping, and the avoidance of futility in the UN'. It was therefore worth considering whether any of the United Nations initiatives so far canvassed had 'a chance of helping the situation on the ground', and if so whether Britain could offer 'any discreet help'.

The most promising notion was regional involvement along the lines suggested by Australia and Malaysia, but Indonesia would clearly only accept a preliminary visit by a representative of the Secretary-General and 'the final presence of an international group to give respectability to an act of integration dressed up as self-determination'. There was no place for 'any continuing UN or ASEAN sponsored presence or co-administration'. Nor, given the current uncertainty in the Australians' foreign policy, should Britain, however discreetly, back the ideas Harry floated in the United Nations lest they backed down and left it out on its own. The Australian

---

[76] FCO 15/1708[313]: Telegram, 18 December 1975, 461.

Embassy had already warned Canberra of the 'unreality' of the ideas. Britain should 'steer clear of initiatives'. It should concentrate on achieving the best it could hope for, 'a plausible act of self-determination which does not embarrass the UN'.[77]

At the Security Council on 18 December, after speeches from Tanzania, Guinea-Bissau, the Soviet Union, and Japan, Galvão Teles declared that Portugal was ready to resume its responsibilities as administering power. It proposed the despatch of a special representative of the Secretary-General to report on the situation and propose measures for restoring peace. The Portuguese Government would send military and naval forces to keep the peace until decolonisation had been completed—'a bit late in the day', ran a marginal FCO comment—provided Indonesia withdrew its forces and undertook to refrain from further intervention. After the representative had reported, Portugal would endeavour to organise under United Nations auspices a conference of the Timorese parties, attended by observers from other countries in the region, 'to decide how the territory should be administered until the act of self-determination'. During that period Portugal would be responsible with its own troops, in collaboration with the United Nations, for the maintenance of peace and security. If the United Nations preferred a force of contingents from different states, including states in the region not parties to the conflict, Portugal would participate, provided it was in command.[78]

In the afternoon the non-aligned members of the Council circulated a preliminary working paper, representing, Richard thought, the lowest common denominator of agreement. It noted the General Assembly call for a fact-finding mission, deplored Portugal's abdication of its responsibilities and Indonesia's armed intervention, called for Indonesia's withdrawal, called upon Portugal, in co-operation with the United Nations, to take effective measures to ensure the exercise of self-determination, and requested the Secretary-General to implement the resolution and report.[79] The draft, Richard noted, left open the question of an interim administration if and when the Indonesian troops withdrew. It gave the Secretary-General a restricted mandate, no doubt because the Chinese would object to a visit by his representative while the territory was under Indonesian control.

Representatives of Britain, France, Italy, the United States and Sweden had a short meeting to discuss the draft. They agreed that it was too hard on

---

[77] FCO 15/1708[314]: Telegram, 18 December 1975, 462.
[78] FCO 15/1708[316]: Telegram, 18 December 1975, 2234.
[79] FCO 15/1708[326]: Telegram, 18 December 1975, 2236.

Portugal, by comparison with Indonesia. There was no call for a ceasefire, apparently, according to the Guyanese, because some of the non-aligned thought the parties should be allowed to fight it out. The paragraph on the Secretary-General, it was felt, should be amplified: he should be asked to appoint a representative to contact the parties concerned and report back to the Security Council. The Chinese might object, but would not receive much support. The non-aligned would probably welcome Western attempts to improve the text. Richard sought broad authority from the FCO to offer amendment to the non-aligned along these lines. 'We shall, of course, as President continue to play an inconspicuous role ourselves.'[80] That authority was secured.[81]

The Council met informally to consider the non-aligned working paper. Then members held informal discussions and in the afternoon the non-aligned and Western groups produced versions that narrowed the gap. Richard then invited the groups to meet and they agreed on a text, which 'regretted' Portugal's failure and 'deplored' Indonesia's intervention. It recognised Portugal as the administering power, but, given the views of Australia and Indonesia, confined its role to that of collaborating with the United Nations. It encouraged the Secretary-General to make recommendations, although that had been questioned by the non-aligned, who made a distinction between the Security Council's role in maintaining peace and security and the General Assembly's in decolonisation. He was to send a representative to East Timor 'for the purpose of making an on-the-spot assessment of the existing situation and of establishing contact with all the parties in the territory and all states concerned to ensure the implementation of the resolution'. Taking into account the report of his special representative, he was to submit recommendations to the Security Council. Meanwhile, as Richard pointed out, Indonesian troops would no doubt remain and the UDT–Apodeti administration consolidate itself; it was not suggested that they should withdraw before the representative's visit.

Richard planned informal consultations on 22 December, followed by formal adoption. There might be last-minute objections from the Chinese, but Richard thought it would go through. The Americans had said little, but were pleased with the text, 'subject to any views the Indonesians may have on it'. He believed Britain should vote for it on the assumption that France and Italy did. 'It would be hard not to do so after our extensive

---

[80] FCO 15/1708[320]: Telegram, 18 December 1975, 2235.
[81] FCO 15/1708[325]: Telegram, 19 December 1975, 1116.

consultations and the formulation of a common working paper.' In explaining the vote he suggested 'that we dwell on the future rather than the past, reaffirm our view that there should be some form of consultation of local opinion and stress the importance of the Secretary-General's role and the assistance which the UN can provide'.[82] The suggestions were approved[83] and the resolution was adopted on 22 December.[84] Ramos Horta welcomed it, but wanted urgency. The invading forces had already killed 2,000 women and children.[85]

The Australian representative, as the British High Commission in Canberra had been told, had been instructed that the only substantive action required of the Security Council was the appointment of the special representative to consult and investigate in Timor. Djajadiningrat of the Indonesian Ministry of Foreign Affairs had stated that a United Nations transitional administration was a possible option. But the Australian DFA suspected that Indonesia would want it to comprise 'compliant regional countries likely to rubber-stamp decision for integration', and did not want Australia to be made 'internationally or domestically accountable for Indonesian actions by participating in such a body'. Lance Joseph, head of the Southeast Asia branch, said that the Australian vote for the General Assembly resolution, 'largely for domestic reasons', was a high point in Australian activity and that 'Harry's instructions would now be to pull back and play more unobtrusive role'. The Australians hoped that the representative would not be in an undue hurry to visit or report, as 'Indonesians needed time'.[86]

Joseph expected the new government in Australia to continue civil and military aid to Indonesia without announcing it. He understood that Kissinger had instructed the United States Embassy in Jakarta to cut down reporting, 'since he was anxious to avoid any US involvement, or even excessive interest in the question of Timor'. Sympathy in Congress might lead to demand for a reduction or suspension of aid to Indonesia. 'Joseph thought pressure of this kind was much likelier in Australia; but he was fairly sure that such pressures would not be so intense that it would prove impossible to keep Australian aid to Indonesia at its intended level.'[87]

---

[82] FCO 15/1708[327, 328]: Telegrams, 20 December 1975, 2240, 2241.
[83] FCO 15/1708[332]: Telegram, 22 December 1975, 1122.
[84] FCO 15/1708[337]: Telegram, 22 December 1975, 2246.
[85] FCO 15/1708[344]: Telegram, 23 December 1975, 2248.
[86] FCO 15/1708[326]: Telegram, 19 December 1975, 1023.
[87] FCO 15/1708[339]: Barder to Simons, 22 December 1975.

A British retrospect

In the new year the British Embassy in Jakarta prepared an account of what had taken place to be incorporated in a despatch to the FCO. Andrew Stuart began the process. For whatever reason—fear of insecurity, of a left-wing government, of separatism—the Indonesians decided on a takeover, and, if the Australians were right, had decided long before August 1975. They were fortunate that the Macau and Rome agreements were not implemented. Or perhaps they hoped 'that, over a long period of controlled decolonisation, they would have time to swing the political situation inside Timor their way'. The August UDT coup and the Fretilin counter-action provided a chance of direct intervention, which they let pass. Apparently the Indonesians thought the Portuguese would invite them in, but that was 'never on'. There might also have been 'a genuine hesitation to be seen to take the law into their own hands'.

The President decided on clandestine intervention, which 'was a mistake because it failed'. With the UDT the Indonesians moved to direct intervention.

> They had plenty of time to plan the politics and logistics of this, but both were bungled…The military invasion was badly handled. On the political front the denial that Indonesia had participated in the invasion, except with volunteers, may have been the logical continuation of the clandestine phase; but it was politically inept, not least because it prevented Indonesia from defending itself properly in the UN.

It also made the government, especially Malik, appear 'brutal and cynical'.

The Indonesians had a case for direct intervention, Stuart continued. They could have argued that Portuguese 'scuttle' had left 'an intolerable situation on their doorstep' and that they had to restore order and allow people to exercise self-determination. That would have been more plausible in August, when there was 'a genuinely chaotic situation'. By December it was 'less convincing'. Contrast Angola: it was one reason, 'apart from double standards', why Indonesia was censured and Cuba, which intervened in Angola, was not. It would still have been possible to admit and defend intervention in December, however, but for 'the over-complication of the Javanese mind'.

The United Kingdom and the United States emerged, Stuart thought, without damage to their interests in Southeast Asia, but the Australians did not. Their actions were 'an example of inconsistent meddling without the power to influence events. ...For perhaps the first time they have reacted like a great power with direct interests to protect in an overseas situation. Their diplomatic and governmental machine has not been up to it'.

For the Indonesians the gain was negative, as they had absorbed a trouble spot. The regime had been damaged and Timor had been and would be costly. If they continued to underestimate the strength of international opinion or if mopping-up went badly wrong, there could be an 'even more serious' result 'in terms of internal instability and international disapprobation'.[88]

Reading Stuart's draft, Ambassador Ford questioned whether the Australians were right in believing that Indonesia had decided on incorporation long ago. His impression was that the President would have been 'content to accept a long transition period provided that the Portuguese had been willing to conduct themselves responsibly'. He also thought that intervention in August would have aroused the same emotions in New York as in December and that the reaction in the United Kingdom would have been 'more violent'. Regarding Indonesia's gain as negative was overdoing it; if Fretilin had established a hostile government and made Timor a home for dissidents, that would have been 'more costly'. The Ambassador thought Timor might prove 'a dead issue'.[89]

The final despatch emphasised the low profile of the Russians. The Australians, it said, 'lacked the political guts to stay out or to intervene effectively'. In August Australia and New Zealand might have persuaded Portugal to set up some joint body to restore order and administer 'a programme of orderly decolonisation acceptable to Indonesia'.[90]

If Indonesia's intention was to occupy Timor, Murray Simons commented at the FCO, the best opportunity for 'a clean operation' was in August. It might then have been possible to claim that Indonesia was restoring law and order following Portugal's abdication. 'As it was, the decision to try for the long haul led to the need for a full-scale invasion in circumstances where FRETILIN had consolidated its hold and could claim to represent the majority of the population.' Simons was glad that Ford thought that the FCO had followed the right course. It was not always easy, since 'certain sources' pressed for a 'forward' policy in support of Fretilin. 'Had we yielded to this it would not have been possible for Mr Richard to play his admirable

---

[88] FO 810/30[53]: Minute, 9 February 1976.
[89] FO 810/30[53]: Minute, 10 February 1976.
[90] FCO 15/1712[138]: Ford to Callaghan, 15 March 1976.

(and admirably successful) role at the United Nations.'[91] Britain had indeed stood apart throughout the crisis: it now had no strategic interests in Southeast Asia beyond regional stability. But the United Nations resolutions it helped to secure were to have a long-term significance for Timor.

The Guicciardi report

In February Geoff Edge, the MP who had raised the parliamentary question on recognition in early November, sought to bring Ramos Horta, Minister for External Relations in the 'self-declared' Democratic Republic of East Timor, to meet Lord Goronwy-Roberts, the Minister of State at the FCO. He had been 'travelling for some time seeking support' and probably wished to gain sympathy for his cause. If received by a Minister, he would seek to portray that as a British recognition of the Fretilin government, AK Goldsmith of SEAD pointed out. Britain's policy had been 'to avoid becoming involved…as far as possible'. At the United Nations its role had mainly been to restate support for self-determination; in late November it had decided not to recognise UDI. Receiving Ramos Horta would 'imply a greater degree of interest in the problem than we have', give a degree of recognition not so far given, and damage relations with Indonesia, 'in any case…slightly strained as a result of our support for the recent UN Security Council resolution'. Customarily ministers had declined to receive self-proclaimed Ministers from countries Britain did not recognise. Officials might, however, see him if he wished.[92] Goronwy-Roberts agreed with the principle. 'In this case I think we should offer Mr Horta the opportunity of seeing officials, indicating that I am not available rather than adducing the principle'.[93]

On 11 February Simons and Jones met Ramos Horta, Edge, John Taylor of the British Campaign for an Independent East Timor and Chris Farley of the Bertrand Russell Peace Foundation. Ramos Horta said there were 20,000 Indonesian troops in East Timor, but the people were holding them at bay, because they 'were not prepared to accept defeat. If necessary they would join forces with the independence movements of the South Moluccas and West Irian; the fight against Indonesian aggression would spread across the Archipelago.' He expected Britain to use its influence to get the Indonesians

---

[91] FCO 15/1713[147]: Simons to Ford, 25 March 1976.
[92] FCO 15/1710[47]: Memorandum by Goldsmith, 4 February 1976.
[93] FCO 15/1710[47]: Minute, 4 February 1976.

out and paid tribute to the Balibo Englishmen. Simons drew attention to the resolution adopted when Britain chaired the Security Council. The report by Vittorio Winspeare Guicciardi, the Secretary-General's representative, was awaited; then the British Government would decide on its action.

> We could best make our views effective by working through the Security Council and not by trying to apply unilateral pressure. It would in any case be wrong to interpose new measures while the UN procedure, which we had helped set up, was still working.

A decision on recognition, Simons concluded, would be taken only after an act of self-determination.[94]

Late in February Guicciardi was finalising his report and Secretary-General Waldheim considering his recommendations. Waldheim told Richard he was discussing a suggestion that Guicciardi should chair a meeting in Geneva of all the parties concerned, ie Portugal, Indonesia, the provisional government and Fretilin, 'to try to work out a solution'. The Portuguese were much in favour. He had no answer from the Indonesians, who had also not answered over withdrawal, merely saying that they would withdraw when the provisional government considered that the situation allowed it. Waldheim wondered whether he should include the idea of a meeting in his report. 'He himself thought it might be better if he did not.' Richard agreed, but thought he might put it forward in his oral report to the Security Council, which 'might then give a focus to the meeting and enable the Council to work for a resolution calling for such a meeting'. Waldheim agreed.[95]

Waldheim had phoned Malik, Imrod Idris of the International Organisations directorate at the Indonesian Department of Foreign Affairs told Ambassador Ford. The Foreign Minister did not see how the parties in the provisional government—set up in December, with Arnaldo Araujo as Governor and Lopez da Cruz as Deputy Governor (Hill 1978:210)—could sit down with Fretilin representatives living outside Timor 'who no longer represented the populace'. Later the Indonesian Government told Guicciardi that, as it was not a party to the conflict, participation would be inappropriate, but he might see representatives of both governments and all the parties individually in Geneva 'and thus carry out an informal

---

[94] FCO 15/1710[71]: Record of conversation, 11 February 1976.
[95] FCO 15/1711[106]: Telegram from New York, 27 February 1976, 284.

consultation'. Ford noticed a discrepancy between the Indonesian Government's reference to an act of self-determination and the provisional government's talk of a *de facto* integration. The latter would create 'a most unfavourable impression'. Idris said the provisional government had been persuaded to accept an act of self-determination,[96] but it had told Guicciardi that the people had exercised their right already and considered themselves part of Indonesia.[97]

The Secretary-General's report was circulated mid-March with Guicciardi's annexed to it.[98] The former only noted that the parties had expressed their readiness to consult with Guicciardi and suggested that the consultation should be continued on the understanding that any developments should be reported to the Security Council. Guicciardi gave an account of his mission and the difficulties it faced. 'He goes no further', as Richard put it, 'than to identify one common element in the divergent views of the parties, namely the need for consultation, which he describes as "a slender common assumption", on which it may be possible to build.' Unless Waldheim made further points in his oral presentation, the mission would not have provided guidance for the Security Council's next steps. The non-aligned were likely to take a strongly anti-Indonesian line. Salim Ahmed Salim of Tanzania, chair of the Committee of 24, had described the visit as a farce and ruled out United Nations endorsement of an act of self-determination in the presence of Indonesian troops. He quoted African views on the inviolability of colonial borders. If Fretilin were clearly defeated, the non-aligned might in the longer term accept the *fait accompli* and settle for a limited consultation. 'There are still memories, however, of the way in which the West Irian exercise turned out,' Richard added, 'with Indonesia nominating representatives who then rubber-stamped the territory's absorption into Indonesia. We judge that UN opinion is not yet ready for a repetition of this exercise.'

There were few ideas in New York about what the Security Council might do in the short term, Richard continued. 'Australians have warned us that their freedom of manoeuvre is greatly restricted by the strength of anti-Indonesian feeling on Timor from both right and left wings.' The Chinese would be guided by the non-aligned. The Indonesians had no instructions.

---

[96] FCO 15/1711[115]: Telegram, 9 March 1976, 72.
[97] FCO 15/1711[116]: Araujo to Guicciardi, given by Idris to Ford, in telegram, 9 March 1976, 73.
[98] FCO 15/1712[130]: Report, 12 March 1976.

The best they could expect was strong disapproval and a further call for withdrawal within a specified period. By then indeed the provisional government might be able to organise an 'act of self-determination'.

What line should Britain follow? 'I assume that you do not want us to become involved in the argument over Timor, nor to embarrass Indonesia, but that the UK has a general interest in upholding the principle of self-determination.' Richard suggested that, with Western Council members and Japan, it should work for 'a reasonably mild resolution' on withdrawal, arguing that condemnation might only prompt an early move towards popular ratification, that it should endorse the suggestion of further consultations under the Secretary-General's aegis, and that it should have it established that those should not exclude discussion of the modalities of an act of self-determination on the understanding that Indonesia would first have to withdraw its troops.[99]

The FCO agreed with this line, but suggested that, if the resolution stressed withdrawal, it would prompt the Indonesians to reiterate that they were there at the invitation of the provisional government and could not leave unless it so wished. That would lead to 'an unfruitful argument'. The stress might rather be on consultations 'conducted with a view to securing agreement on the modalities of an act of self-determination on the understanding that Indonesian troops should be withdrawn before this act occurs'. The Indonesians still seemed to favour some kind of act of self-determination. 'It might therefore be marginally easier for them to agree to withdrawal in this context.' What would the reaction be to suggesting token withdrawals, preferably before the Security Council met?[100]

In Jakarta Imrod Idris had told the Counsellor that the withdrawal of some 'volunteers' was being considered. The provisional government argued against it, as it would only encourage demands for complete withdrawal. Timor was part of Indonesia, the government said, and they were needed to maintain law and order. Imrod Idris had argued that something needed to be done to meet the United Nations resolution. On a personal basis the Counsellor raised the idea of a timetable, but there was no chance of that. It would bring about the collapse of law and order and make 'an act of free choice' impossible. The Indonesians expected to complete that in two and a half months, it seemed. They hoped the West would 'continue to try to keep the temperature down'.[101]

---

[99] FCO 15/1712[132]: Telegram, 17 March 1976, 377.
[100] FCO 15/1712[137]: Telegram, 18 March 1976, 189.
[101] FCO 15/1712[134]: Telegram, 19 March 1976, 85.

As for tactics in the United Nations, the Jakarta Embassy doubted whether the form of any United Nations resolution would affect the Indonesian timetable. It would complete the 'act of free choice'. The United Nations would thereafter have the choice 'either of accepting the fait accompli or of an indefinite stalemate'. The best United Nations resolution would therefore be

> one which avoids committing us to an eventual stalemate. Thus the less it concentrates on prior withdrawal of troops and the more on an act of free choice the less the eventual embarrassment, and also possibly the greater the chance of influencing the nature of that act (UN participation etc.).[102]

Indonesia announced some troop withdrawals. That, Richard thought, would have 'a certain favourable impact', but he considered that the non-aligned would still insist on a resolution emphasising withdrawal, while the Western interest lay in 'making the wording of any such resolution as flexible as possible'. A delegation from the provisional government had now arrived. The United States assessment was that, if it lobbied members of the Security Council successfully, there might be a chance of securing a resolution that admitted withdrawals were taking place, called for their completion and endorsed consultations through Guicciardi on an act of self-determination. Informally, according to this scenario, members of Council would ultimately accept the validity of an act of the kind the provisional government envisaged, ie ratification of integration by a 'representative' council.[103]

The United States initiative, the British Embassy in Jakarta thought, was reflected in the draft of the speech Sani was to give, which Idris discussed with the Counsellor at the British Embassy. It would include agreeing to renewed discussions among the parties, endorsing Guicciardi's return to Timor, supporting a United Nations presence in the act of self-determination, and welcoming the announcement that some 'volunteers' had been returned.[104] In New York a week later Sani told Richard that the Fretilin threat had been 'all but disposed of' and volunteers were being withdrawn. The Council 'should recognise the realities of the situation'. Richard suggested that, in addressing it, Indonesia and the provisional government should do all they could to facilitate the task of those in favour of a realistic resolution, giving

---

[102] FCO 15/1712[135]: Telegram, 19 March 1976, 86.
[103] FCO 1713[146]: Telegram, 24 March 1976, 425.
[104] FCO 15/1713[153]: Telegram, 1 April 1976, 98.

details of the withdrawals and avoiding conveying the impression that they intended to go ahead with plans for consulting the people without reference to views expressed in New York. Some might argue that the provisional government had no right to invite United Nations observers to the planned representative assembly: 'they should confine themselves to giving a general welcome to UN observers'.[105]

The Japanese delegation put forward a working paper which reaffirmed the Timorese right to self-determination, expressed the belief that conditions should as soon as possible be established to permit the exercise of that right, called on the Indonesian Government, in compliance with the December resolution, to complete the withdrawal of its forces without delay, requested the Secretary-General to have his special representative complete his assignment, including a possible further visit to the territory, and to submit recommendations taking account of his report.[106] The British delegation, like the American, thought the non-aligned might accept the draft if a paragraph were added that regretted Indonesia's non-observance of the December resolution and if it were toughened elsewhere, for example by setting a date for withdrawal. 'Another potential difficulty is that there is no direct reference to the administering power.' The British delegation thought they could support it; it emphasised self-determination, though in general terms, and was 'realistic' on Indonesian withdrawal.[107] The FCO agreed.[108]

The delegation did not propose to intervene in the debate, but saw advantage in making an explanation of its vote. Britain should speak with the same voice on self-determination for the Timorese as for the inhabitants of its own dependent territories, because of 'signs that in view of our recent lobbying on self-determination for the Falklands, our views on Timor will be watched closely'. The delegation could support the continuance of Guicciardi's mandate and 'could state that our prime concern is that the Timorese should be able freely to decide their future'. Calling for withdrawals in terms of the December resolution,

> we need not specify whether or not they should go before or after the act of self-determination. We might admit that the act of choice will have to be appropriate to the primitive stage of political development

---

[105] FCO 15/1713[165]: Telegram, 9 April 1976, 566.
[106] FCO 15/1713[175]: Telegram from New York, 13 April 1976, 593.
[107] FCO 15/1713[174]:.Telegram, 13 April 1976, 592.
[108] FCO 15/1713[177]: Telegram, 14 April 1976, 297.

reached in Timor, but should emphasise that the assembly should be chosen in a way which would permit the fullest possible exchange of views on the future of the territory.[109]

The FCO agreed in general, but it was 'quite likely' that the act would find in Indonesia's favour. 'We risk being accused of conniving at a sham unless sizeable Indonesian withdrawals appear to have taken place first—notionally in order to permit the "act" to take place fairly.' The delegation need not specify that all Indonesian personnel should leave before the 'act', but it could make the point that without a sizeable withdrawal it would be hard to maintain convincingly that there had been 'no impediments to the expression of the popular will'.[110]

The non-aligned, with Romania and Pakistan, had produced a draft resolution based on the Japanese working paper, but including a call for Indonesia to withdraw all its forces 'immediately and unconditionally'.[111] The co-sponsors, Guyana and Tanzania, agreed to modify that, Sani indicating that, if the Council called for immediate and unconditional withdrawal, Indonesia would not be able to accept a further fact-finding mission by Guicciardi.[112] The phrase now read: 'to withdraw without further delay all its remaining forces'.[113] China and Benin, however, insisted on removing the word 'remaining', on the ground that it 'gave unwarranted credence to Indonesia's claim to have begun withdrawal'. Removing the word at that stage cast doubt on Indonesia's word and Sani feared his government might withdraw any offer of co-operation with the United Nations. The Japanese were planning an amendment to restore 'remaining'. If they failed, the United States planned to abstain, because they 'would be helping to create a dangerous precedent if [they] were to acquiesce in a Chinese demonstration of their ability to bring the non-aligned to heel'. That was an argument for Britain also to abstain, but, even if Britian's abstention were accompanied by a strong explanation, it would give rise in debates on Belize or the Falklands to the contention that it had not practised what it preached.[114]

After phoning London, the United Kingdom delegation voted for the Japanese amendment. When it was lost, the United Kingdom voted for the

---

[109] FCO 15/1713[184]: Telegram, 15 April 1976, 611.
[110] FCO 15/1713[187]: Telegram, 20 April 1976, 308.
[111] FCO 15/1713[182]: Telegram, 15 April 1976, 610.
[112] FCO 15/1713[188]: Telegram, 20 April 1976, 618.
[113] FCO 15/1713[189]: Telegram, 20 April 1976, 619.
[114] FCO 15/1714[193]: Telegram, 21 April 1976, 622.

resolution, which was adopted (12 votes to none, with two abstentions). Gonçalves, representing the provisional government, regretted that it took account neither of the start that had been made with the withdrawal of volunteers nor of the advanced state of preparations for an act of self-determination. His government would co-operate and welcome Guicciardi. Sani said the volunteers would leave in accordance with the wishes of the provisional government and Indonesia would be guided by it in respect of a further Guicciardi visit.[115] Britain's explanatory speech urged substantial withdrawals as a matter of urgency so that self-determination could be carried out fairly. In that respect, 'procedures suited to the local circumstances should be used', as some speakers had suggested. 'We would hope that as many as possible of the members of a representative assembly will be chosen by popular vote, and that the different options for the political future of the territory will be canvassed widely during the selection of representatives.'[116]

'The non-aligned showed welcome realism', JC Thomas of the United Kingdom Mission commented. Generally they recognised 'the importance of securing the co-operation of Indonesia and a widely supported resolution'. The 'flurry' over the word 'remaining' was provoked by China. 'Muslim solidarity played an important role' and Libya and Pakistan did not support the extreme resolution. The Swedish delegation had said the night before that 15 condemnatory votes would be the best way of extracting Indonesia from Timor, but that they would 'go along with what we regarded as realistic wording'. Next day, however, the Swedish vote was cast against the Japanese amendment and was decisive in its defeat. It was clear that the speeches of the provisional government's representatives were written for them. Ramos Horta claimed they were prisoners of the Indonesians, their families hostage. A conversation with Carrascalão suggested 'that leanings towards independence still exist, particularly with ex-UDT people. ...There may after all be some debate, in connection with the proposed Representative Assembly, of the alternatives to integration within Indonesia'.[117]

Malik sent the Foreign Secretary a message thanking him for 'understanding' Indonesia's position and giving 'support'. It was regrettable that, despite Britain's efforts, a more realistic resolution was not adopted, but Indonesia would co-operate as far as possible and he looked for continued support. Jones recommended an answer, as Britain might have to vote against

---

[115] FCO 15/1714[195]: Telegram, 22 April 1976, 627; *Times*, 23 April 1976; Dunn (1983:361).
[116] FCO 15/1714[196]: Telegram, 22 April 1976, 628.
[117] FCO 15/1714[202]: Thomas to Simons, 28 April 1976.

Indonesia again. Britain attached great importance to self-determination, it read, and was glad that the Indonesian representative had been able to give assurances that his country would abide by the decision of the Timorese. It also welcomed the beginning of the withdrawal of Indonesian forces. The reply also noted the assurance of co-operation. Britain's attitude would continue to be guided by the principles it outlined, 'and I am confident', it continued, 'that this should mean that we will be able to lend you all possible support. We continue to attach high importance to the continuance of the excellent relations existing between our two countries'.[118] The Embassy in Jakarta was concerned over leaks and, at its suggestion, the penultimate phrase was altered: 'In the light of your assurances, I am confident that we should be able to maintain the degree of understanding and support between our delegations to which you have referred so appreciatively'.[119]

Witnessing self-determination

Contacts in the Department of Foreign Affairs and CSIS in Jakarta suggested that an international party might be invited to visit Timor in early June to observe the regional bodies that would send delegates to the assembly in Dili that in turn would forward the pro-integration resolution to Jakarta. Diplomats in Jakarta, not necessarily ambassadors, would be invited, also United Nations representatives and possibly members of the international press. The Dutch Embassy, recalling West Irian, thought its government would refuse to be associated with 'such a sham'. It was also concerned about 'the affront to Portuguese sovereignty' and the implication that individual countries, as distinct from the United Nations, had some *locus standi*. At Counsellor level, the New Zealand, Australian and Japanese embassies took a more pragmatic view: 'having talked about the importance of popular participation in the act of self determination, it would be difficult for them to refuse to observe this.' Ambassador Ford thought the embassies might take part if the United Nations led or sponsored the group. He suggested that the European Economic Community (EEC) and Western embassies should co-ordinate a response.[120] The FCO took up the idea: the EEC countries were

---

[118] FCO 15/1714[205]: Minute by Jones, 28 April 1976; FCO 15/1714[217]: Telegram, 4 May 1976, 74.
[119] FCO 15/1714[218, 219]: Telegram from Jakarta, 5 May 1976, 129; telegram to Jakarta, undated, 77.
[120] FCO 15/1714[234]: Telegram, 14 May 1976, 148.

told that, if the Indonesians did not propose United Nations participation, it would in the United Kingdom's view be in order to suggest it to them.[121]

The visit, the Australians learned, was timed for 31 May—one long day—and would focus on witnessing the decision in Dili rather than the selection of representatives. Guicciardi had already told the Indonesians that he could not accept an invitation as long as Indonesian troops were present. Apparently the Committee of 24 would have considered a visit if it had been to observe the selection of representatives, but the representatives had all been selected and Indonesia simply wanted observers of the final act. The DFA in Canberra, Richard was told in confidence, was recommending against accepting the invitation. Given Britain's interest in upholding the principle of self-determination, Richard thought it should be 'wary' of accepting one. 'There is already a danger that we will be accused of inconsistency in advocating self-determination for Belize and the Falklands, while being lukewarm on the application of the principle to Timor and the Sahara.' Britain should seek EEC agreement to a joint refusal of the invitation in the likely absence of United Nations participation.[122]

Simons thought the FCO should try that.[123] Male agreed:

> I think we should come under greater criticism were we to send someone as Indonesian stage props to 'observe' an act of self-determination than if we declined an invitation, which would at least enable us to receive some first-hand account of conditions.

'Let us try', wrote Goronwy-Roberts, 'and if we fail look at it again'.[124]

In Jakarta, Woolcott told Ford that Murdani had left him in no doubt that the invitations for 31 May would go ahead. Delegates would meet in Dili and pass a resolution affirming their desire for integration. That resolution would be passed to the provisional government and put to the Indonesian parliament. At the end of June the parliament would send a delegation to East Timor 'to investigate whether the resolution and those who had passed it in Dili were representative of the opinion and people of East Timor'. That delegation, it was hoped, would be accompanied by foreign ambassadors

---

[121] FCO 15/1714[239]: Telegram to Coreu Luxembourg, 17 May 1976.
[122] FCO 15/1714[243]: Telegram, 18 May 1976, 788. In November 1975 King Hassan of Morocco had mobilised 350,000 Moroccans to cross into Spanish Sahara (Pinto Leite 2000:171).
[123] FCO 15/1715[247]: Memorandum, 20 May 1976.
[124] FCO 15/1715[247]: Minutes, 20, 21 May 1976.

and United Nations representatives. On the assumption that the delegation found that opinion favoured integration, the resolution would be accepted by parliament, and the President would refer to it in his Independence Day speech in August.

Ford called on Malik's secretary, Sumario. What Woolcott had gathered, he said, did not square with an earlier statement by Malik, that a final act of self-determination might be at the end of the year after the General Assembly meeting. Sumario said the question was being discussed at the highest level and he would contact Malik and get in touch afterwards. Speaking personally, Ford said that a 'rushed operation' on 31 May would not help Indonesia's friends at the United Nations. It would be much better if instead it provided 'an opportunity for some responsible observers to see for themselves on the spot in East Timor the difficulty of running a meaningful one-man, one-vote operation and the way in which the "representatives of the people" had been selected'.[125]

Sumario told Ford on 25 May that arrangements were going ahead. The monthly lunch of the EEC ambassadors revealed that none had received instructions, but each saw an objection to accepting an invitation from the provisional government. The consensus was that only if the provisional government passed the invitation through the Security Council and the Council members decided their ambassadors should accept it, would acceptances not involve some form of recognition of the provisional government. On 26 May a note from the Indonesian Department of Foreign Affairs conveyed the invitation of behalf of the provisional government and expressed the hope that the reply could be sent to its liaison office in Jakarta. Ford proposed neither to acknowledge the note nor send an answer.[126] The FCO agreed.[127]

Twenty-eight members representing 13 regencies met on 31 May and unanimously approved a petition for integration. The ambassadors of India, Saudi Arabia and Iran were present, along with the chargé for Nigeria and representatives of Malaysia, Thailand and New Zealand. The Americans had been instructed they could go if the Australians did, and the Japanese if either did. None of them went.[128] Peacock decided against it, 'essentially

---

[125] FCO 15/1715[253]: Telegram, 24 May 1976, 155.
[126] FCO 15/1715[256]: Telegram, 26 May 1976, 160.
[127] FCO 15/1715[257]: Telegram, 26 May 1976, 92.
[128] FCO 15/1715[271]: Telegram, 1 June 1976, 171; cf Cablegram to Canberra, 30 May 1976, in AIPT:771–772.

because we know that the procedures being followed in Dili do not match up to the standards which would be generally acceptable in Australia'.[129] ASEAN solidarity crumbled: neither Singapore nor the Philippines were represented.[130] Alison Stokes, the New Zealand Counsellor, found the proceedings flawed. Only one option was offered and how the representatives had been selected was not apparent.[131]

Indonesia proceeded to invite the embassies to send observers along with the parliamentary fact-finding mission. This time, Simons noted, the invitation was from Indonesia and not the provisional government, so Britain could not 'adduce non-recognition as a reason for not accepting'. The lack of United Nations involvement was, however, still a valid factor. The United Nations was unlikely to participate even if invited. Other countries might, possibly even the United States and Japan. He continued:

> If we are conspicuous by not attending, the Indonesians would doubtless take this amiss, but they have known of our unhappiness at the way matters were developing. Nonetheless, we do not want to fall out with them; this could happen if they got wind of the fact that it was we who acted as 'whippers-in' for countries declining their invitation.

By attending, however, Britain would become associated with the incorporation of East Timor.

> That is why we (and others) are being invited: the element of blackmail should not be overlooked. But we may be held to have undermined UN authority by associating ourselves with a procedure which ignores the recommendations of two Security Council resolutions (which, it is true, pay no regard to the unrealism of conducting an 'act of self-determination' in a primitive territory).

Simons thought the invitation should be declined 'as a consequence of the failure to associate the UN with the proceedings. (There is an important UK point here, connected with our attachment to the proper conduct of self-determination exercises; we have Belize and the Falklands in mind.)' But

---

[129] Cablegram, 28 May 1976, in AIPT:770–771.
[130] FCO 15/1715[280]: Jones to Wallace, 4 June 1976.
[131] Cablegram from Wellington, 2 June 1976, in AIPT:772–773.

Britain should try to avoid being isolated. It could canvass opinion at the EEC's Asian Working Group on 15 June.[132]

The Working Group agreed that all members should decline the invitation.[133] Malaysia and the Philippines were among the countries that agreed to attend; Singapore and Papua New Guinea were not. New Zealand did not 'repeat its near solo performance'. Guicciardi would not be there, despite the efforts Australia had made and Australia decided not to attend after all.[134] No attempt was made by the mission on its one-day visit on 24 June to ascertain whether the Timorese wanted integration or independence (AIPT:795n).

Suharto approved integration at a cabinet meeting on 30 June. The indications, Ford reported on 15 July, were that the legislative process would be completed that day and presidential approval given on 17 July. He continued:

> Thereafter Indonesia will regard East Timor as an integral part of the state and take the line that any further UN action is unjustified intervention in Indonesia's internal affairs. The Army have been making the running here in the determination of this programme and are going to brook no interference.[135]

It had been expected that incorporation would be announced on Independence Day, 17 August, but the process had been speeded up in order to present the world with a fait accompli (Dunn 1983:300).

New Zealand's Foreign Minister, Brian Talboys, had written to Malik on 8 July, urging that the United Nations should be associated with the process before final integration so that self-determination would have wide acceptability and advocating that Guicciardi pay his second visit.[136] Ford did not think 'that there is scope for us to influence the Indonesians further over East Timor' and thought it was in Britain's interests 'as far as possible to keep out of the issue'. The New Zealand initiative seemed 'particularly half-baked over timing' and unlikely to achieve anything 'other than unnecessarily incur Indonesian ill-will'.[137]

---

[132] FCO 15/1715[288]: Memorandum, 11 June 1976.
[133] FCO 15/1716[296]: Telegram to Jakarta, 15 June 76, 112.
[134] Cablegram to Peking, 21 June 1976, in AIPT:795–796.
[135] FCO 15/1716 [345]: Telegram, 15 July 1976, 235.
[136] FCO 15/1716[339]: Telegram from Wellington, 9 July 1976, 222.
[137] FCO 15/1716 [345]: Telegram, 15 July 1976, 235.

Goronwy-Roberts had been inclined to think there would be advantage if the Security Council send Guicciardi back. But, as Goldsmith wrote, SEAD would have recommended against that even without Ford's latest report. Waldheim, it was clear, was concerned lest a further visit might give rise to allegations that the United Nations was condoning Indonesian aggression. If Britain wished actively to promote a visit, it would have to approach the Secretary-General, which would probably be 'unproductive', or call a Security Council meeting. 'To take an initiative of this sort would run counter to our previous "low-profile" policy. Would the advantages outweigh the drawbacks?' When he received the Indonesian Ambassador in December 1975 Lord Goronwy-Roberts had stressed his hope for a genuine opportunity for self-determination, 'preferably under international auspices'. A second Guicciardi visit, before or after Indonesia's declaration of integration, could not be 'a convincing substitute'.

Even if Indonesia allowed it, 'his report would probably be confined to the conclusion that Indonesia was now effectively in total control'. Britain and the other Security Council members would then have to decide whether to accept that as 'satisfactorily closing the Timor question'. That might mean facing

> an awkward decision. Acceptance of the principle that a UN representative could legitimise a military takeover could constitute a dangerous precedent in the light of the analogous situations we might one day face in connection with Belize, the Falkland Islands and Gibraltar.

In the absence of another mission, the international community would come to accept the reality of East Timor's inclusion in Indonesia, 'as it came to accept Chinese action in Tibet and Indian action in Goa'. It was not in Britain's interest to take any initiative.[138] 'The Indonesians have ignored our advice and behaved badly over Timor', Hugh Cortazzi agreed, but Britain had nothing to gain by an initiative and something to lose. 'The Indonesians will get away with incorporation and the world will accept it. We need not publicly condone their actions.' Goronwy-Roberts agreed.[139]

A telegram to Jakarta, agreeing with Ford's stance, indicated that the News Department would say that the question of legal recognition did not

---

[138] FCO 15/1716[346]: Memorandum, 15 July 1976.
[139] FCO 15/1716[346]: Minutes, 15, 18 July 1976.

arise.¹⁴⁰ That could be taken to mean, the Mission in New York commented, that the Timorese had had an acceptable form of self-determination. Britain should say that Timor's status was 'unclear', like that of Western Sahara.¹⁴¹ The FCO agreed.¹⁴²

'Geographical tidiness and Javanese imperialism look like winning the day', the London *Times* had commented.¹⁴³ In the end they did not do so. Timor turned out not to be the ripe fruit waiting to fall into Indonesia's hands. Hoadley's earlier forecast was a better one. An independent government, he had written after his visit in December 1974, would be better able to deal with possible intra-Timor strife. An Indonesian-run government would have 'a harder time of it', and imposing Indonesian rule, far from avoiding strife, might instead create it, with Indonesia as the target of a unified Timorese struggle for independence.

> Indonesian military forces could no doubt contain the disturbances and disperse the rebels for a time, but one can visualise the problem festering for years as it still is in West Irian and Kalimantan. The inefficiency of this sort of governance must be set against the hypothetical gain in security (Hoadley 1975:26).

In the event continued resistance in Timor, in part provoked by the methods of the Indonesian military (ABRI), helped to prevent its effective incorporation.

The uncertainty of the territory's status was also a factor in its undoing, however. The mixture of force and diplomacy, a recipe Indonesia used more than once, could be used against it. Once inordinately proud of the empire they had acquired, the Portuguese sought to regain some pride in the manner of leaving it. In 1980, still in United Nations terms the administering power, Portugal proposed talks with Indonesia, Timorese political groups, and other interested countries (Dunn 1983:371). In 1982 a United Nations General Assembly resolution based on a Portuguese initiative, passing 50 votes to 46, with 50 absentions, called on the Secretary-General to intervene (Dunn 1983:366). It was not only the struggle of Fretilin and Falintil that kept the struggle going, though it took ABRI's own blunders, such as the Santa Cruz massacre of 1991, to ensure the success of diplomacy.

---

¹⁴⁰ FCO 15/1716[347]: Telegram, 19 July 1976, 138.
¹⁴¹ FCO 15/1716[349]: Telegram, 19 July 1976, 1120.
¹⁴² FCO 15/1716[351]: Telegram, 20 July 1976, 551.
¹⁴³ *Times*, 9 December 1975.

What effect had Britain's policy had? After its withdrawal from Singapore it no longer took a lead in policy-making in Southeast Asia. It put a premium on stability and tried to maintain good relations with the Suharto regime, despite its poor human rights record. It sought to take a low profile over the Timor crisis of 1974–6, but it had an interest in self-determination, since it had itself a number of minor dependencies that larger neighbours might seek to swallow up. At the United Nations, therefore, it put its influence and its diplomatic skill behind resolutions that avoided endorsing Indonesia's methods of incorporation. Its policy towards Timor was determined, as in the previous decades, by its interests elsewhere, but was not without an impact.

Epilogue

The Timorese people were to play a major role in finally securing the independence of Timor Leste and so making it no longer one of the exceptions to the general rule that the states of the postcolonial world inherited the frontiers of the colonial world, no matter what their inconvenience or irrelevance. The attitude of outside powers, in particular of the United Nations, was also crucial, but they no longer dominated the history of the territory.

That had not earlier been the case. Timor's history and that of its people had been profoundly affected by the interests of outsiders and those affected not only by their interest in Timor but also by their interests in other parts of the world. Those, too, changed over time, as indeed did the strategic significance of the island. Not only is history a mutable factor, but geography is too.

Timor was significant in the early years of the Portuguese venture in Asia for its trade in sandalwood, part of what was then an Asia-wide trade, the creation and maintenance of which was the task of the Estado da India. The success of the Dutch did not eliminate the Portuguese from Asia, but it diminished and fragmented their trade and drove them back into Timor as a kind of remote outpost linked with Macau, which they also retained.

The growth of the Dutch empire in the 19th century took place, with Britain's complaisance, at the expense of the Indonesian rulers, but not at the expense of the Portuguese, Britain's long-term allies, with whom the Dutch reached a reluctant deal. The advance of other imperial powers in the late 19th century, in particular Germany, prompted the existing powers to strengthen their claims under the rules of the Berlin conference of 1884-5. It also prompted concern lest minor powers, such as Spain or Portugal, might prove unable to sustain their empires under the pressure of the new imperialism. The Dutch regulated their frontiers with Portugal and secured the reversion of its bifurcated territory in Timor.

Timor's position was also changed—as was that of the remoter parts of the Dutch empire in the archipelago and in New Guinea—by the creation of British colonies in Australia, which were to be formed into a federation, the Commonwealth of Australia, in 1901. Islands that had seemed to be on the periphery of European interests were now strategically important to the government of the southern continent. Another state had an interest in the fate of the Timorese and their territory, one that was thinly populated and nervous about its security. The Japanese invasions underlined that concern and its commitment to Papua New Guinea.

The neighbours of the Timorese emerged from the colonial pattern before they did. The process reveals, as this book has shown, both continuities and discontinuities. Salazar's New State retained its colonial territories as long as possible, if not longer, and his post-1974 successors found it difficult to retain some sense of post-imperial responsibility. In 1941 the Dutch were anxious to step in, partly because they had always been anxious to do so and partly because of the Japanese threat; their Indonesian successors stepped in because they had always been anxious to do so and could point to the advance of communism in mainland Southeast Asia, if not in Portugal itself and Timor, too. Australia put in troops with the Dutch in 1941 and did something to encourage the Indonesians in 1974–5.

What they did was and remains deeply controversial. It has been and is open to investigation through the archives as well as through newspapers and other public documents. The same is not true in respect of Indonesia, but it is true in respect of Britain, whose policy has been the main focus of the present work. Though its archives have been used to explore the death of the journalists at Balibo in October 1975, they have not hitherto been used for a fuller discussion of that policy.

Britain's involvement changed over time, though it, too, had some enduring features. One of those was the long relationship with Portugal, originally based on a medieval alliance that, not quite lost in the mists of antiquity, still had some pull. It was useful to Portugal when it sought to evade the unwelcome embrace of the Kaiser. It was useful to Salazar when he sought to sustain neutrality in Hitler's war without alienating Britain. Britain wanted access to the airfields of the Azores. Invoking the treaty, however, ran up against the actions of the Australians, to whom, of course, the British were also committed.

Post-war the British were concerned also to develop a positive relationship with the new state of Indonesia, prompted not only by their commercial interests and their belief that the future of Southeast Asia lay with nation states, but also by their concern for the security of Singapore and Malaysia, for which they bore a major responsibility till the mid-1960s. They were concerned by the growing violence of Indonesia's campaign to secure West Irian—not transferred by the Dutch in 1949, when they accepted the Republic's independence—and sought to prevent its becoming a war. But they also became concerned lest Indonesia then moved on territories that had never been part of the Dutch colonial empire, their protectorate Brunei, their colonies, Sarawak and Sabah, and Portuguese Timor.

Even in the early 1960s, however, they recognised that they could offer their ancient ally little help if Indonesia resorted to violence. They themselves became embroiled in the defence of Malaysia into which Sarawak and Sabah had been incorporated. When the Sukarno system collapsed in 1965 and Indonesian confrontation ended in 1966, they were quick to announce their long-contemplated withdrawal from Singapore. With that their strategic interests in the region ceased.

In the 1974–5 crisis over Timor, precipitated by the revolution in Portugal, the British sought to limit their involvement and to adopt a low profile. Relations with Indonesia and with Australia were more important than the fate of the Timorese. But once more their policies were affected by an outside factor. They had an interest in ensuring that the incorporation of the territory in Indonesia—which seemed inevitable, if not desirable—was done with some proper respect for the principle of self-determination. In their minds was the fate of remnants of the British Empire—Honduras, the Falklands, Gibraltar—whose future should not necessarily be simply determined by their hungry neighbours. They thus contributed to the United Nations resolutions that in the event were to stand in Indonesia's way and offer Timor a way back.

The United States had helped Indonesia secure West New Guinea and it turned a blind eye on Portuguese Timor. Indonesia should quickly get it over with, which, of course, it notably failed to do. The British papers add to our knowledge of Suharto's hesitation as well as Australia's ambivalence and Portugal's confusion. Whether earlier action would have led to more complete success cannot, of course, be determined, but Suharto's forces proved themselves as inept as they were violent and contributed to the resistance they continued to face.

Throughout this part of the story, West New Guinea is in the mind of the historian, as it often was in the minds of the historical actors. There Sukarno had succeeded by stopping short of outright invasion and by deploying diplomacy and his successor was able to benefit from an act of free choice that the United Nations sanctioned. In East Timor Suharto resorted to invasion, demonstrating the incapacity that, as commander, he had himself feared during the West Irian campaign. He went through the routine of an act of free choice, but it won no United Nations sanction. His opponents were ultimately able to deploy the mixture of force and diplomacy with which

Sukarno had succeeded and to create what he, like others, had argued was impossible, an independent East Timor.

Men had other precedents in mind too. Had not the rounding-out of Netherlands India been an object of the Dutch as the rounding-out of the successor state was an object of the Indonesians? Would not the Australian intervention in the 1990s recall that of nearly 60 years earlier? Time teases historians in other ways as well: Ben Anderson (1995:141) reminds us of the 'conjunctures'.

Suppose Sukarno had turned to Timor after Irian. He would surely have fared in the United Nations better than his successor did, since there were then few African members insistent on inheriting colonial frontiers. Suppose, despite his anxiety not to renew the reputation Sukarno had given Indonesia during the West Irian and Malaysia crises, Suharto had intervened more promptly, as the Malaysians in fact wished, and before Fretilin established itself: he might have been more successful, as the British diplomats in Jakarta speculated. Would the United States have turned so blind an eye on Timor— have been so accepting of Suharto's argument that it was unviable and the supporters of its independence 'almost Communists' (Cotton 2004:37)—if it had not been alarmed by the extent of communist triumphs on the mainland in 1975 and by the apparent trend to the left in Portugal? Would the British have been more active—at least on the diplomatic front—if the crisis had happened earlier or if the Australians had not been led by Whitlam and adopted his stance? If they had been and if they had secured a more genuine act of self-determination, Timor might, of course, have become permanently a part of Indonesia and there would have been no Timor Leste.

Bibliography

Unpublished Sources from the National Archives, Kew, United Kingdom

Cabinet Office records: CAB 65, 66, 79, 121
Dominions Office and Commonwealth Relations Office General correspondence: DO 35
Foreign and Commonwealth Office records: FCO 15, 24
Foreign Office records: FO 115, 371, 810, 972
War Office records: WO 208

Published Records

Documents on Australian foreign policy 1937–49 [AFPD], Australian Government Publishing Service, Canberra.
Documenten betreffende de buitenlandse politiek van Nederland 1919–1945. Periode C, 1940–1945 [DBPN], Nijhoff, The Hague.
Dez anos de política externa 1936–1947 [DAPE], Imprensa Nacional, Lisboa.
Dorling, P (ed) 1994, *Diplomasi Australia and Indonesia's Independence*, Australian Government Printing Service, Canberra.
Way, Wendy (ed) 2000, *Australia and the Indonesian incorporation of Portuguese Timor, 1974–1976* [AIPT], Melbourne University Press, Carlton, Vic.

Secondary Works

Andaya, LY 2010, 'The "informal Portuguese empire" and the Topasses in the Solor archipelago and Timor in the seventeenth and eighteenth centuries', *Journal of Southeast Asian Studies* 41(3).
Anderson, Ben R O'G 1995, 'East Timor and Indonesia: some implications' in Carey, Peter and G Carter Bentley (eds), *East Timor at the crossroads*, University of Hawaii Press, Honolulu.
Birmingham, David 1993, *A concise history of Portugal*, Cambridge University Press, Cambridge.
Bowen, Wayne H 2006, *Spain during World War II*, University of Missouri Press, Columbia, MO.
Bruneau, Thomas C 1984, *Politics and nationhood in post-revolutionary Portugal*, Praeger, New York.
Callinan, Bernard J 1953, *Independent company: the 2/2 and 2/4 Australian Independent Companies in Portuguese Timor, 1941-1943*, Heinemann, Melbourne.
Cardoso, Luís 2002, *The crossing*, Granta, London.

Carey, Peter and G Carter Bentley (eds) 1995, *East Timor at the crossroads*, University of Hawaii Press, Honolulu.
Cotton, James 2004, *East Timor, Australia and regional order: intervention and its aftermath in Southeast Asia*, Routledge, London.
Coward, Barry 2003, *The Stuart Age: England 1603-1714*, Longman, London.
Crocombe, RG 2007, *Asia in the Pacific Islands: replacing the West*, University of the South Pacific, Suva.
Dalrymple, Rawdon 2003, *Continental drift: Australia's search for a regional identity*, Ashgate, Aldershot.
Dalziel, RM 1975, *The origins of New Zealand diplomacy*, Price Milburn, Wellington.
Disney, AR 2009, *A history of Portugal and the Portuguese Empire*, Cambridge University Press, Cambridge.
Dunn, James 1983, *Timor, a people betrayed*, Jacaranda, Brisbane. Reprinted in 2003 with some additions as *East Timor: a rough passage*, Longueville, Double Bay.
— 1995, 'Timor in international perspective' in Carey, Peter and G Carter Bentley (eds), *East Timor at the crossroads*, University of Hawaii Press, Honolulu.
Easter, David 2004, *Britain and the confrontation with Indonesia 1960-66*, Tauris Academic Studies, London and New York.
Edwards, Peter 1983, *Prime ministers and diplomats: the making of Australian foreign policy, 1901-1949*, Oxford University Press, Melbourne.
— with Gregory Pemberton 1992, *Crises and commitments: the politics and diplomacy of Australia's involvement in Southeast Asian conflicts 1948-1965*, Allen and Unwin, North Sydney.
Esteves Felgas, Hélio A 1956, *Timor Português*, Agência Geral do Ultramar, Lisboa.
Farram, Steve 2004, 'From "Timor Koepang" to "Timor NTT": a political history of West Timor, 1901-1967', PhD thesis, Charles Darwin University.
Fields, Rona M 1975, *The Portuguese Revolution and the Armed Forces Movement*, Praeger, New York.
Förster, Stig, Wolfgang Mommsen and Ronald Robinson (eds) 1988, *Bismarck, Europe and Africa: the Berlin Africa Conference 1884-1885 and the onset of partition*, Oxford University Press, Oxford and New York.
Frei, Henry P 1991, *Japan's southward advance and Australia: from the sixteenth century to World War II*, Melbourne University Press, Carlton, Vic.
— 1996, 'Japan's reluctant decision to occupy Portuguese Timor', *Australian Historical Studies* 107.
Goto Ken'ichi, 2003, *Tensions of empire: Japan and Southeast Asia in the colonial & postcolonial world*, Centre for International Studies, Ohio University, Athens, OH and Singapore University Press, Singapore.
Grenville, JAS 1964, *Lord Salisbury and foreign policy*, Athlone Press, London.
Gunn, Geoffrey C 1988, *Wartime Portuguese Timor: the Azores connection* (Centre of Southeast Asian Studies, Monash University, Working paper 50). Reprinted in 2000 in Geoffrey C Gunn, *New World hegemony in the Malay world*, Red Sea Press, Lawrenceville, NJ and Asmara.

— 1999, *Timor Loro Sae: 500 years*, Livros do Oriente, Macau.
Gusmao, Xanana 2000, *To resist is to win!: the autobiography*, Aurora, Richmond, Vic.
Hainsworth, Peter and Stephen McCloskey (eds) 2000, *The East Timor question*, IB Tauris, London and New York.
Hastings, Peter 1975, 'The Timor problem', *Australian Outlook* 29(1), 29(2) and 29(3).
Henry, Adam Hughes 2010, *Independent nation: the evolution of Australian foreign policy 1901-1946*, Charles Darwin University Press, Darwin.
Hensley, Gerald 2009, *Beyond the battlefield*, Penguin Viking, Auckland.
Hill, Helen 1978, 'Fretilin: the origins, ideologies and strategies of a nationalist movement in East Timor', MA thesis, Monash University. Published with some additions in 2002 as *Stirrings of nationalism in East Timor: Fretilin 1974-78*, Otford Press, Otford, NSW.
Hiorth, F 1985, *Timor past and present*, James Cook University, Townsville, Q.
Hoadley, J Stephen 1975, *The future of Portuguese Timor: dilemmas and opportunities* (ISEAS Occasional Paper 27), Institute of Southeast Asian Studies, Singapore.
Hussainmiya, BA 1995. *Sultan Omar Ali Saifuddin III and Britain*, Oxford University Press, Kuala Lumpur.
Jolliffe, Jill 1978, *East Timor nationalism and colonialism*, University of Queensland Press, St Lucia, Q.
— 2009, *Balibo*, Scribe, Carlton North, Vic.
Jones, Matthew 2002, *Conflict and confrontation in South East Asia 1961-1965*, Cambridge University Press, Cambridge.
Krieger, Heike (ed) 1997, *East Timor and the international community*, Cambridge University Press, Cambridge.
Langhorne, R 1977, 'Great Britain and Germany, 1911-1914' in Hinsley, FH (ed), *British foreign policy under Sir Edward Grey*, Cambridge University Press, Cambridge.
Leadbetter, Maire 2006, *Negligent neighbour: New Zealand's complicity in the invasion and occupation of Timor-Leste*, Craig Potton, Nelson.
Lee, David 1997, 'The origins of the Menzies Government's policy on Indonesia's confrontation of Malaysia' in Cain, F (ed), *Menzies in war and peace*, Allen and Unwin, St Leonards, NSW.
McIntyre, W David and WJ Gardner (eds) 1971, *Speeches and Documents on New Zealand history*, Clarendon Press, Oxford.
McLean, D 2003, *The prickly pair: making nationalism in Australia and New Zealand*, University of Otago Press, Dunedin.
Mackie, JAC 1974, *Konfrontasi*, Oxford University Press, Kuala Lumpur.
Maniaty, Tony 2009, *Shooting Balibo: blood and memory in East Timor*, Viking, Camberwell, Vic.
Meaney, N (ed) 1985, *Australia and the world. a documentary history*, Cheshire, Melbourne.
Mommsen, WJ 1988, 'Bismarck, the Concert of Europe, and the Future of West Africa, 1883-1885' in Förster, Stig, Wolfgang Mommsen and Ronald Robinson (eds), *Bismarck, Europe and Africa: the Berlin Africa Conference 1884-1885 and the onset of partition*, Oxford University Press, Oxford and New York.

Ogg, David 1963. *England in the reign of Charles II*, Oxford University Press, London. Originally published 1934.

Pélissier, René 1996, *Timor en guerre: le crocodile et les Portugais*, Pélissier, Orgival.

Pinto Leite, Pedro 2000, 'East Timor and Western Sahara: a comparative perspective' in Hainsworth, Peter and Stephen McCloskey (eds), *The East Timor question*, IB Tauris, London and New York.

Renouf, Alan 1979, *The frightened country*, Macmillan, Melbourne.

Rosas, Fernando 2002, 'Portuguese neutrality in the Second World War' in Wylie, Neville (ed), *European neutrals and non-belligerents during the Second World War*, Cambridge University Press, Cambridge.

Rotter, Andrew J 2000, *Comrades at odds: the United States and India*, Cornell University Press, Ithaca, NY and London.

Russell, PE 1955, *The English intervention in Spain and Portugal in the time of Edward III and Richard II*, Clarendon Press, Oxford.

Saltford, John 2003, *The United Nations and the Indonesian takeover of West Papua*, RoutledgeCurzon, London and New York.

Scheiner, Charles 2000, 'The United States: from complicity to ambiguity' in Hainsworth, Peter and Stephen McCloskey (eds), *The East Timor question*, IB Tauris, London and New York.

Scott, David 2005, *Last flight out of Dili*, Pluto, North Melbourne.

Singh, Bilveer 2002, *Defense relations between Australia and Indonesia in the post-Cold War era*, Greenwood, Westport, CT.

Sobel, Lester A (comp) 1976, *Portuguese Revolution*, Facts on File, New York.

Stone, Glyn 1994, *The oldest ally: Britain and the Portuguese connection, 1936-1941*, Boydell, Woodbridge.

Tarling, N 1996, *Britain, Southeast Asia and the onset of the Pacific War*, Cambridge University Press, Cambridge.

— 2008, *Britain and the West New Guinea Dispute, 1949-1962*, Mellen, Lampeter.

— 2011, *Britain and the neutralisation of Laos*, NUS Press, Singapore.

Taylor, AJP 1954, *The struggle for mastery in Europe*, Clarendon Press, Oxford.

Taylor, John G 1995, 'The emergence of a nationalist movement' in Carey, Peter and G Carter Bentley (eds), *East Timor at the crossroads*, University of Hawaii Press, Honolulu

— 1999, *East Timor, the price of freedom*, Zed, London.

Telkamp, Gerard J 1979, 'The economic structure of an outpost in the outer islands of the Indonesian archipelago: Portuguese Timor 1850-1975' in van Anrooij, Francien et al (eds), *Between people and statistics*, Nijhoff, The Hague.

Thorne, C 1978, *Allies of a kind*, Hamish Hamilton, London.

— 1988, *Border crossings*, Blackwell, Oxford.

Toynbee, Arnold and Veronica M 1956, *The War and the neutrals* (Survey of international affairs, 1939-1946), Royal Institute of International Affairs and Oxford University Press, London.

Wigg, Richard 2005, *Churchill and Spain: the survival of the Franco Regime*, Routledge, London and New York.

Index

Addison, Lord 119, 120
Afonso de Albuquerque 117, 118
African liberation movements 176–80
African Party for the Independence of Guinea and Cape Verde (PAIGC) 176, 177, 185, 195
Akosah 205–6, 225, 231, 233, 242–3, 244, 260, 264, 265, 266, 278
Allen, Roger 99
Almeida Santos, António de 196, 200–10, 218, 230, 236, 240, 241, 251, 252–3, 254–8, 260–1
Alves Aldeia, Fernando (Governor, Portuguese Timor) 186, 188
Alves, Vítor 177, 218, 236, 240, 241, 242, 245
Amaral, Francisco Xavier do 134, 168, 185, 271
American–Portuguese relations 97–8, 101–2
Anderson, Ben 306
Anderson, Sir John 26, 35
Anglo–German agreements, in 1898/99 5, 6, 7
Anglo–Portuguese alliance
  Azores Agreement of 1943 79–91
  during age of imperialism 3–7
  during Second World War 11–12, 15
  and Indonesian ambitions to claim to Portuguese Timor 129, 139, 142–7, 152, 155, 158–9, 164–7
  origins 3–4
Angola 1, 4, 6, 117, 136, 138, 153, 159, 164, 176, 177, 178, 180, 218, 249, 270, 271, 285
Angola (troop ship) 113
Antara (Indonesian news agency) 140, 222, 233
Antunes, Colonel (Commander of Portuguese forces) 60
Apodeti (Associação Popular Democrática Timorense) 134, 185–6, 189, 190, 208, 225, 228, 229, 230, 234, 236, 237, 238, 239, 243, 244–5, 246, 257, 258, 260, 263, 266, 267, 268, 271, 280, 283
Araujo, Arnaldo 288
Arriens, Jan 171, 183, 186, 187, 191, 192, 193, 207
Association of Southeast Asian Nations (ASEAN) 167, 168
ASTD (Associação Social-Democrata Timorense) 185, 186, 189, 190, 208, 209
Australia
  agreements protecting post-war interests in Timor 85–6, 112, 119, 126, 129
  aid to Timor 205, 220, 221
  ambitions for post-war regional sphere of influence 86–7, 103, 108
  assessment of political situation and prospects in Timor 189–92
  concerns over an independent Timor 181–5, 192, 221
  concerns over Indonesian claim to West New Guinea 128, 129
  constitutional crisis 265
  consular representatives for nearest neighbours 126
  consulate in Portuguese Timor 126, 127, 128–9, 167–8, 174, 183, 220
  economic interests in Portuguese Timor 128
  guerrilla warfare by troops in Portuguese Timor 37, 72–8, 112, 131
  Japanese surrender of Timor 109, 112–17, 118–23
  landing of troops in Portuguese Timor 14–25, 28–31, 62–3
  opposition to Indonesian military intervention in Portuguese Timor 138, 139, 141, 149–50, 151, 152–3, 156–7, 211, 220–1, 222–4, 265
  policy of non-involvement in future of Portuguese Timor 211–14, 220
  proposal to send troops to defend Timor 9–10
  proposed administration of Timor 37–8, 111
  proposed occupation of Portuguese Timor 112–13, 123, 124
  public opinion over Indonesia and future of Timor 150, 191, 194, 195, 199–200, 207, 213, 222, 227, 237, 239, 261–2
  refusal to recognise Fretilin's UDI 271
  response to civil war in Timor 255–6, 258, 261–3
  response to Indonesian invasion of Timor 275–6, 277, 278–9
  response to regime change in Portugal 179–81

security concerns over stability of
region 8–9, 41, 85–6, 92, 205, 208, 235
statement to UN regarding Indonesian
invasion of Timor 275–6
support for independent Timor 236
support for integration of Timor into
Indonesia 149, 155, 159–60, 184, 188,
192, 194–5, 197–9, 201–2, 212, 216,
217, 220, 262
support for Portuguese sovereignty over
Timor 22, 81–3, 91–2, 271
support for principle of self-
determination 138, 150, 153, 171–2,
188, 192, 194–5, 198, 199, 201–2,
203–4, 211, 212, 213, 215, 216, 217,
220, 221, 223, 227, 232, 235, 261, 262
visit by Suharto 234, 237–9
Whitlam visit to Java 194–200
withdrawal of troops from Portuguese
Timor 114, 121
Australia–New Zealand agreement of
1944 79, 86–7, 91, 103
Australian–Indonesian relations, over future
of Timor 184, 187–8, 191–2, 193–4,
199–200, 211, 212, 214, 220, 222–3, 232,
235, 237–9, 278–9
Australian–Portuguese relations
dispute over seabed and oil rights 181, 182
over future of Portuguese Timor 153,
161–2
proposed training cadre of Portuguese
officers in Australia 105–8
reciprocal diplomatic missions 108
tensions over Australian troops in
Portuguese Timor 114–15
tensions over Portugal's colonial
policies 171–2, 173–4
Azores
Anglo-Portuguese Agreement
(1943) 79–91, 100
as British base 79–91
British interest in 8, 10, 37, 43, 79
NATO's need for bases 151
as part of Portuguese Empire 1, 8, 10
Santa Maria facilities 79, 91, 95, 97–8,
99, 100–1, 103, 106, 219
Santa Maria–Timor agreements 100–11,
106, 110, 120, 125
threat of Nazi occupation 8, 45
US interest in 8, 10, 79, 87–8, 91, 95,
97–8, 99, 100–1

BAKIN (Badan Koordinasi Intelijen
Negara) 183, 186, 195, 206, 239, 248, 250,
251, 260, 264
Balfour, John 46–7
Barder, BL 189, 203, 210, 211, 268, 269

Barnard, Lance 220
Bartolomeu Dias (sloop) 113, 114, 117
Barwick, Sir Garfield 150, 152, 181
Beale, Sir Howard (Australian Ambassador,
Washington) 149, 150–1
Beaven, John 188, 205, 206, 209–10
Bennett, John Sterndale 24, 31–2, 34–5, 38,
41, 42, 44, 59, 66, 96, 99
Berlin Africa conference (1884–5) 4
Bevin, Ernest 119, 120, 122
Bianchi, João de (Portuguese Ambassador,
Washington) 126
Bland, Sir Neville 105
Brash, Robert 131, 132
Brimelow, Alison 196
Britain
attitudes and assessments regarding future
of Portuguese Timor 227–32
policy towards Portuguese Timor xii,
xiv–xv, 142–7, 164, 214–16, 228, 247–8,
251, 263, 287, 302, 304–5
refusal to recognise Fretilin's UDI 271–2
relations with Dutch 12–13
response to civil war in Timor 249, 251,
258
response at UN to Indonesian invasion of
Timor 274–9, 287
retrospective account of Indonesian
invasion of Timor 285–7
support for Portuguese declaration of
war 87–8, 99
support for Portuguese Empire xiii
support for Portuguese neutrality 7–8
support for self-determination 217, 228,
259, 271, 273, 287, 290, 292, 296
see also Anglo–German agreements;
Anglo–Portuguese alliance; British–
Portuguese relations
British Chiefs of Staff (COS) xv, 8, 10
British Commonwealth Relations Office
(CRO) xv
British Dominions Office (DO) xv
British Foreign and Commonwealth Office
(FCO) xv
British Foreign Office (FO) xv
British–Portuguese relations
attempts to restore relations with
Salazar 25–36, 42, 47, 53, 59
responses to threat of Japanese attack on
Timor 10–15, 21, 22, 50–1
tensions over Goa and Angola 153, 164
tensions over landing of Australian and
Dutch troops 15–25, 39–40
Brooke, Sir Alan 43
Brooke-Popham, Sir Robert 12
Bruce, Stanley 29, 30, 44, 45, 48, 52, 107–8,
111–12, 116, 119

Brunei rebellion   139, 146–7, 148
Burton, John   127

Cable, James   137, 162
Cabral, Amílcar   176
Caccia, Sir Harold   146–7
Cadogan, Sir Alexander   11, 13, 45, 67, 71, 74, 76, 80, 89, 90, 105, 111, 121, 123
Caetano, Marcelo   175, 176, 177, 178
Cairo conference (1943)   85, 87
Callinan, Bernard   78
Campaign for the Independence of East Timor   213
Campbell, Sir Ronald (British Ambassador, Portugal)   13, 14, 15, 17, 19–21, 23–8, 30, 32–4, 35, 37–9, 42, 45–6, 48–53, 55–9, 62–6, 68–74, 83–4, 90–2, 93–4, 96, 98, 101–3
Campinos, Jorge   198, 202, 236
Cape Verde islands   1, 40, 61, 88, 89, 142, 153, 176, 185
Carmona, António Óscar Fragoso (President, Portugal)   46
Carnation Revolution   xi, 175, 177–8, 185, 217
Carrascalão, João   248
Carrascalão, Mario   185, 248, 260, 279, 294
Carrascalão, Oliveira   248
Carvalho, Ferreira de   16, 22
Centre for Strategic and International Studies (CSIS) (Jakarta)   172, 186, 188, 200–1, 233, 295
Chiba Shinichi   70
Churchill, Winston (Prime Minister, Britain)   54, 80, 81, 82, 85, 93, 112
Clark, Gerald   203, 208–9
Clarke, Ashley   13, 15, 17, 38, 48, 52, 53, 55, 64–5, 68, 71, 89, 96, 110, 117, 118
Colombo Plan   128
Combs, Willis (British Ambassador, Jakarta)   197, 230, 231
Cooper, Duff   14, 18
Cooper, Frank   202, 236
Cortazzi   300
Costa Branco, JN de (Capt)   127
Costa Gomes, Francisco da (President, Portugal)   177, 202, 218, 219, 224, 249, 255
Costa, Silva (Capt)   91
Cousins, Ian   203
Cranborne, Lord   16, 30, 40, 86
Cross, Sir Ronald   85
Cruz, Magalhães   196
Cunhal, Álvaro   219
Curtin, John (Prime Minister, Australia)   16, 22, 29, 31, 50, 81, 238

Dai Nippon Airways   9

Dan, Malcolm   278
decolonisation
  of Portuguese Empire in Africa   138
  Portuguese policy   218
  Portuguese program for Timor   224, 230, 236, 237, 238, 242, 243–4, 266
  spread of   127–8
Delgado, Humberto (General)   178
Democratic Republic of East Timor   270
Detiger, W (Lt Col)   22
Duarte, Silva (Capt)   188, 189
Duggan, GA   216, 225–6, 228, 229, 231, 233–4, 239, 240, 241, 242, 243, 244, 246–7, 254, 255, 256, 260, 264–5, 268, 278
Dunn, James   163, 167, 183, 189, 195, 203–4, 210–11
Dutch Timor *see* West Timor
Dyke, Brigadier   124

East Timor *see* Portuguese Timor; Timor Leste
Easter, David   148
Eden, Anthony (UK Foreign Secretary)   10–11, 12, 38, 39–40, 48, 52, 54–5, 64, 67, 71, 75, 81, 85, 88, 92–3, 103, 107, 112
Edge, Geoff   287
effective occupation, as indicator of sovereignty   4
Ennals, David   269, 271
Etherington-Smith, Gordon   141, 142
Evans, GC   181
Evatt, HV (Foreign Minister, Australia)   78, 81, 85–6, 103, 112, 115–16, 117, 118, 119–24, 126, 128

Falintil (Forças Armadas da Libertação Nacional de Timor-Leste)   270, 301
Farley, Chris   287
Feakes, GB   184, 191–2, 193, 199, 211, 212, 221, 238
Fernandes, Alarico   256, 268
Fernandes, Esteves (Portuguese Ambassador, Japan)   60, 62
Field, Richard   169, 170, 172–3, 195
Fields, Rona   177–8
Ford, Gerald (President, US)   219, 273, 274
Ford, JA, (British Ambassador, Jakarta)   241, 247, 249, 250–1, 254, 257, 260, 264, 267, 273–4, 281, 286, 288–9, 295, 296–7, 299–300
Forsyth, WD   124
Foulds, LH   9
Fraser, Malcolm (caretaker Prime Minister, Australia)   275, 278
Fraser, Peter (Prime Minister, New Zealand)   86
Fremilo   168, 185, 218

Frente Nacional de Libertação de Angola (FNLA) 218
Fretilin (Frente Revolucionária de Timor-Leste Independente) 134, 185, 199, 213, 217, 222, 224–5, 226, 229, 234, 236, 238, 239, 240–1, 243, 244, 245, 246, 248–9, 252, 255, 256, 257, 258, 259–60, 261–3, 266, 267–72, 273, 274–5, 277, 278, 279–80, 287, 289, 291, 306, 285286
Fry, Sir Leslie (British Ambassador, Jakarta) 135, 140, 145
Furlonger, Bob 187, 191, 192, 193, 197, 198, 199, 202, 206, 207, 235

Gallman, WJ 125
Gan 166, 167
Gandarum, Sudio 260
Garran, IP 95, 97, 101, 104, 118–20, 122
Gerakan Timor Merdeka 163
Gerbrandy, Pieter Sjoerds (Prime Minister, Netherlands) 18, 103
Girão (Portuguese Chargé) 254–5
Goa xii, xiv, 1, 128, 133, 136, 140, 141, 145, 151, 153, 161, 164, 211, 300
Goldsmith, AK 287, 300
Gonçalves, Francesco Rebelo (Major) 185
Gonçalves, Vasco dos Santos (Prime Minister, Portugal) 202, 217, 218–19, 255, 257, 280, 294
Gonçalves Zarco (sloop) 64, 117
Goronwy-Roberts, Lord 228, 263, 276, 287, 296, 300
Gozney, RH 244
Grey, Sir Edward 6
guerrilla warfare, Australian troops in Portuguese Timor 37, 72–8
Guicciardi report 287–95
Guicciardi, Vittorio Winspeare 288, 289, 294, 296, 299, 300
Guinea–Bissau 176, 185, 195, 218, 224, 225, 271, 275, 276, 282
see also Portuguese Guinea

HANKAM (Indonesian Defence and Security Ministry) 207, 233, 260
Harriman, Averell 137, 151, 152, 155
Harry, Ralph 280, 281, 284
Harvey, Oliver 104, 107, 112–13, 125
Hastings, Peter 126, 223
Hattersley, Roy 245
Hebblethwaite, SH 9
Heppel, RP 134, 135
Hewett, Gavin 189
Hoadley, Steve 224, 301
Home, Lord (Foreign Secretary, Britain) 142, 145–6, 147, 148, 164
Hood, John 120, 121–2, 124

Hull, Cordell 86

Idris, Imrod 288, 289, 290, 291
Indochina
  communist victories 217, 219
  Japanese invasion 8
Indonesia
  acquisition of West New Guinea xiv, 139–40, 142, 168
  arms supplies 135, 142, 143, 144, 145
  BAKIN (Badan Koordinasi Intelijen Negara) 183, 186, 195, 206, 239, 248, 250, 251, 260, 264
  border incidents with Portuguese Timor 140, 142, 168–9, 170, 173
  campaign for assimilation of Timor 209–10, 226
  claim to West New Guinea 109, 128, 129, 130, 134
  complicity in Brunei revolt 139, 146–7, 148
  confrontation of Malaysia 147–67, 174, 201
  confrontation of the Netherlands 135
  covert intervention in Timor 171, 175, 179, 186–7, 191, 192, 193, 195, 200, 236, 258, 259, 260, 264, 267, 269, 285
  emergence of independent nation 126
  HANKAM (Indonesian Defence and Security Ministry) 207, 233, 260
  ideas for 'Greater Indonesia' 129, 135, 148
  incorporation of Timor xiv, 295–302
  interest in Portuguese Timor during Suharto regime 168, 170–1, 181, 184, 186, 196, 200–1
  interest in Portuguese Timor during Sukarno regime 129, 130–1, 134–7, 140, 142, 149, 154, 157–8, 162–4, 168
  invasion of Portuguese Timor 259, 270–4
  military intervention in Portuguese Timor 259, 263–5, 268
  Operasi Komodo 222, 225, 240, 248, 260
  PKI (Communist Party) 154, 168, 172
  plan for military takeover of Portuguese Timor 207–8, 210–11, 220–1, 222, 225, 226, 230, 232, 233, 236, 237, 238, 260
  policy of co-existence with Portuguese Timor 170, 172, 174
  relations with Australia 184, 187–8, 191–2, 193–4, 199–200, 211, 212, 214, 220, 222–3, 232, 235, 237–9, 278–9
  relations with Portugal 202–3, 205–8, 230, 231, 236–7, 242–3, 256, 270–1

relations with US   143, 147, 149, 157, 274, 284
response to civil war in Timor   254, 256, 257–8
security concerns about an independent Portuguese Timor   173, 183–4, 186, 187, 194, 195, 196, 201, 206, 209, 210, 211, 219, 223, 225, 226, 231
support for Apodeti Party   230, 238, 271
support for liberation movement in Timor   168, 169, 170, 171, 174, 180
support for UDT   271
talks with Portugal in Rome   265–70
territorial expansion   139–47, 171
Indonesia Raya   169
Ito Takeo (Major-General)   62

James, Morrice   183, 262
Japan
  attack on Portuguese Timor   37, 59–72
  entry into Second World War   14
  interest in Portuguese Timor   9
  invasion of Indochina   8
  surrender   xiv, 109–26
  see also Portuguese–Japanese relations
João Belo (troop ship)   64, 68, 69
Jónatas, Costa (Major)   224, 225, 240, 249, 250
Jones, Lynton   249, 271, 273, 287, 294
Joseph, Lance   221
Joyce, HJ Jayman (Major-General)   102, 103

Kelly, Kevin (Australian Ambassador, Portugal)   182
Ken'ichi Goto   61
Khir Johari   279
Kissinger, Henry   219, 273–4, 284
Kleffens, Eelco van (Foreign Minister, Netherlands)   9, 12, 23, 24, 25, 31, 38
Kompas (newspaper)   186
Kuroki Tokitaro   9

Leandro, José Eduardo Garcia (Major)   185
Leggatt, WW (Lt Col)   19, 22, 72
Liberation Movement of Timor   157
Liem Bian Kie   195–6, 198, 200–1, 202, 207, 210, 230–1, 269, 270
Lobato, Nicolau   168, 248
Lobato, Rogerio   270
Lopes da Cruz, Francisco Xavier   239–40, 259, 288
Luns, Joseph   198
Lusaka Agreement   218

MacArthur, Douglas (General)   76, 103, 118, 120, 121
Macau   1, 11

threat of Chinese takeover   156
threat of Japanese attack and occupation   37, 65, 66, 83, 84, 92–3, 95–6, 103
Macau talks   238, 240, 241, 242, 243–8, 267
McCredie, JD   184
McDonald, Hamish   268
McLennan, AD   183, 186, 189, 193, 197, 204
Makin, Norman   126
Makins, Roger   40, 41, 59, 66–7
Malaysia
  Indonesian confrontation   157–8, 162–3, 174
  reaction to Indonesian invasion of Timor   277
  setting up of federation   147–8
Male, PJE   263, 276, 296
Malik, Adam   168, 169, 170, 172, 186, 190, 197, 198–9, 200, 202–3, 206, 209, 211, 213, 225, 233, 250, 263, 264, 266–7, 269, 271, 276, 285, 294, 297, 299
Mari Alkatiri   168, 270
Mashuri   268, 270, 279
Mathias, Dr   117–18, 122
Mattos, Teixeira de   32, 104
Mayne-Wilson, Warwick   211, 213–14
Mello Gouveia, José de   162
Melo Antunes, Ernesto de   177, 218, 260, 266–7
Menzies government   109
Menzies, Robert Gordon (Prime Minister, Australia)   138, 151, 153, 155–6, 161, 166
Michiels van Verduynen, E (Dutch Ambassador, London)   13, 23, 24, 52, 55, 56, 104
Millar, Frederick Hoyer   105, 106, 111–12, 114, 115
Minggu Chas (newspaper)   169
Moçambique   1, 4, 41, 47, 83, 102, 103, 105, 134, 142, 153, 159, 172, 173, 176, 177, 178, 180, 185, 218, 225, 262, 271
Mochtar Kusumaatmadja   254, 256, 257
Mohammed Yamin   129, 135, 148
Monteiro, Dr Armindo (Portuguese Ambassador, Britain)   10–12, 13, 15–16, 18, 23, 26, 35, 39, 46–7, 67, 72, 74–5, 76, 89–90, 92, 107
Mook, Hubertus van   85, 103
Moore, Sir Henry R. (Vice-Admiral)   43
Moroshima Morito (Japanese Minister, Portugal)   93–4, 109–10
Morrison, Bill   223, 255
Mota, Francisco (Major)   224, 225, 229, 231, 236, 240, 250
Movimento Popular de Libertação de Angola (MPLA)   218
Murdani, Benny   207, 238, 269, 296

Murtopo, Ali   195, 198, 200–10, 222, 225, 230–1, 232, 233, 234, 236, 238, 240, 241, 248, 260
Myrtle, W Evershed (Col)   11

Nagano Osami   61
Naronha, Alfredo   188–9
Nazi Germany, possible occupation of Atlantic islands   8
Nazwar Jacub   134
Nehru, Jawaharlal   136
Netherlands Indies   1, 2, 3, 116, 126, 130
Netherlands, The
   apprehension over Australian ambitions   103–4
   landing of troops in Portuguese Timor   14–25, 27–8, 39–40, 62–3
   relations with Portugal   2–3, 4, 27, 39, 104
   withdrawal of troops from Portuguese Timor   40, 53
Newsom, John   252
Nogueiro, Major   60
North Atlantic Treaty Organization (NATO)   142–5, 151, 198, 210, 219
Norweb, Henry (US Ambassador, Portugal)   90, 92, 94, 100–2

Oliver, Sir William   165
O'Malley, Sir Owen (British Ambassador, Portugal)   110, 115, 116, 117, 119, 120, 121–2
Ormsby Gore, Sir David (British Ambassador, Washington)   147, 151, 155–6, 162

Page, Earl   40, 45, 48
Pallandt, van (Netherlands Chargé, Lisbon)   12, 14, 15, 20, 23, 25, 27, 35
Palmela, Duke of (Portuguese Ambassador, Britain)   105, 107–8, 110, 111, 119, 120, 121–2, 123
Palmer, RE   196, 224
Panggabean, Maraden   206
Papua New Guinea   139, 171, 180, 187, 195, 217, 221, 225, 299, 304
Peacock, Andrew   223, 275, 278, 297
Peck, Edward   146, 166
Pereira (Portuguese Ambassador, Washington)   150–1
Petersen, JC   162
Pinheiro de Azevedo, José   266
Pires, Mário Lemos (Governor, Portuguese Timor)   224, 225, 228, 229, 233, 234, 248–9, 261
Polícia Internacional e da Defesa do Estado (PIDE)   134, 168
Portugal
   Acção Nacional Popular party   176, 185

aims of Salazar regime   6–7
Armed Forces Movement (MFA)   175, 177–8, 191, 196, 208, 209, 217, 218, 219, 222, 249, 255
army coup   6
attempted coup by Spínola   217, 218, 219
Carnation Revolution   xi, 175, 177–8, 185, 217
colonial policy   7, 20, 79, 81, 128, 149, 158, 171, 172, 176, 185, 199, 201, 202, 218
commitment to NATO   219
concern over Indonesian interest in Portuguese Timor   142, 162
decolonisation policy   218
decolonisation program for Timor   224, 230, 236, 237, 238, 242, 243–4, 266
establishment of republic   5
Estado Novo government   6, 176, 179, 218
MFA Revolutionary Council   219
neutrality in Second World War   1, 7, 20–1, 22–3, 33, 39, 46, 48, 51, 54, 59, 61–3, 64, 65, 67, 68, 70, 80, 84, 87–90, 93, 97, 99, 102, 304
opposition to colonial policy   176–8
Party Pact   219
PCP (Portuguese Communist Party)   218–19
PPD (Popular Democrats Party)   218
PSP (Popular Socialist Party)   218
regime change and African liberation movements   176–94
relations with Dutch   2–3, 4, 27, 39, 104
relations with Indonesia   202–3, 205–8, 230, 231, 236–7, 242–3, 256, 270–1
republican movement   4
request to NATO for information on arms supplies to Indonesia   142, 144, 145
request to UN for assistance on Timor   251, 253
response to civil war in Timor   251–8
support for Timorese self-determination   199, 201, 202, 203, 207, 233, 266
talks with Indonesia in Rome   265–70
unpopularity at United Nations   149, 158
see also Anglo–Portuguese alliance; Australian–Portuguese relations; British–Portuguese relations
Portugal e o futuro (Portugal and the future) (Spínola)   176, 179
Portuguese Democratic Movement   177
Portuguese Empire
   defence of territories   11, 39, 101
   defence of Timor   37–59
   extent of   xii–xiii, 1
   hold on Timor   1–2

relations with British Empire xiii, 2
relations with Dutch Empire 2-3, 4, 104
UN debate over decolonisation in
 Africa 138
see also Anglo-Portuguese alliance;
 Azores
Portuguese Guinea 176, 177, 178, 180, 185,
 195, 218, 224, 225, 271, 275
 see also Guinea-Bissau
Portuguese Timor
 1959 uprising 133-4
 alleged treatment of Pro-Indonesian
  elements 225, 232, 241
 Apodeti (Associação Popular
  Democrática Timorense) 134, 185-6,
  189, 190, 208, 225, 228, 229, 230, 234,
  236, 237, 238, 239, 243, 244-5, 246,
  257, 258, 260, 263, 266, 267, 268, 271,
  280, 283
 atrocities by Japanese 83, 94
 attachment to Portuguese flag 208
 Australian consulate 126, 127, 128-9,
  167-8, 174, 183
 Australian security concerns about 1, 8-9
 border incidents with Indonesia 140,
  142, 168-9, 170, 173
 civil war 248-60
 covert intervention by Indonesia 171,
  175, 179, 186-7, 191, 192, 193, 195,
  200, 236, 258, 259, 260, 264, 267, 269,
  285
 death of journalists at Balibo 264, 265,
  304
 declaration of independence by
  Fretelin 268, 269, 270, 271
 decolonisation program 224, 230, 236,
  237, 238, 242, 243-4
 defence by Portuguese troops 37-59, 60,
  64, 67
 desire for independence 203-4, 205,
  209, 227, 230, 239, 247
 draft constitution 246
 Dutch enclave 1, 2
 economic situation 181, 246
 emergence of political parties 175,
  185-6, 188, 190, 208, 229
 fear of Indonesian invasion 225
 fears of a *coup d'état* after
  independence 247, 248
 Forças Armadas da Libertação Nacional
  de Timor-Leste (Falintil) 270
 Fretilin (Frente Revolucionária de Timor-
  Leste Independente) 134, 185, 199,
  213, 217, 222, 224-5, 226, 229, 234,
  236, 238, 239, 240-1, 243, 244, 245,
  246, 248-9, 252, 255, 256, 257, 258,
  259-60, 261-3, 266, 267-72, 273,
  274-5, 277, 278, 279-80, 287, 289, 291,
  306, 285286
 Fretilin victory 259-60, 261, 268
 guerrilla warfare by Australian
  troops 37, 72-8, 112, 131
 hold by Portuguese during 17th-19th
  centuries 1-2
 indigenous liberation movement 183
 Indonesian-backed 'liberation'
  movements 157, 163
 infrastructure 132, 173, 189, 246
 introduction of Legislative
  Assembly 176, 209
 invasion by Indonesia 259, 270-4
 Japanese attack 37, 59-72
 Japanese occupation 61, 83, 90, 103
 Japanese threat 9-14, 63
 landing of Dutch and Australian
  troops 14-25
 Macau talks 238, 240, 241, 242, 243-8,
  267
 military intervention by Indonesia 263-
  5, 268-9
 post-war administrative strucure 132
 referendum postponement 209
 referendum proposed for March
  1975 186, 188-9, 193, 199, 205
 refugees in West Timor 222, 225, 226,
  232, 241, 259, 260, 266-7, 273
 restoration of Portuguese authority 109,
  110, 111, 121
 self-determination for xiv, 195, 198
 strategic importance xiii-xiv, 43
 UDT coup 248-9, 252, 260, 279
 UDT (União Democrática
  Timorense) 185, 190, 208, 222, 224,
  225, 226, 229, 234, 238, 239-40, 241,
  246, 248-9, 252, 253, 256, 257-8,
  259-60, 263-4, 266, 267-8, 271,
  279-80, 283, 285
 UDT-Fretlin coalition 222-6, 240,
  241, 243
 UDT-Fretlin transition program to
  independence 222, 224, 229, 234, 240
 unrest among educated elite 168
 witnessing of petition for
  integration 259-60, 295-302
Portuguese-Japanese relations
 attempts to mitigate effects of Japanese
  occupation 83
 concerns over arrival of Portuguese troops
  in Timor 69-72
 and Portugal's neutrality and
  sovereignty 61, 62-3, 70-1, 109-10
 proposal for Japanese withdrawal from
  Timor 78, 93-4, 95, 96-7
Price, Colonel (COS Secretary) 32, 84

Pritchett, Bill 221
Profumo, John 135

QANTAS 9

Ralph, Richard 196
Ramos Horta, José 168, 185, 186, 190, 199, 211, 212, 213, 225, 239, 240, 243, 248, 257, 268, 269, 270, 278, 279, 284, 287, 294
Renouf, Alan 181, 182, 183, 192, 195, 197–8, 203, 223, 225, 261–2
Richard, Ivor 275–6, 277, 282, 283, 286, 288, 289–90, 291, 296
Richardson, Michael 172, 211
Roberts, Frank 10, 12, 44, 45, 68, 80, 87, 89, 95, 97, 98, 101, 103
Rodrigues, Barros (Col) 11
Roosevelt, FD (President, US) 8, 80, 82, 83
Ross, David 9, 22, 59, 73–8
Ross, Sir Archibald (British Ambassador, Lisbon) 151, 156, 166

Sabir 210–11
Salazar, Dr Antonio de Oliveira (Prime Minister, Portugal) 6
   on Australia's role in Timor 126
   on the Azores 8, 79–82, 100–2
   colonial policy 7, 151, 161–2
   death 175, 176
   on defence of Timor 13, 34, 38, 39, 42, 47, 51–3, 57, 63, 78
   embargo on wolfram 91
   on Japanese surrender 109–10
   negotiations with Japanese 93–5, 103, 109–10
   neutrality of Portugal 1, 7, 84, 90, 92, 304
   political situation 48
   as Prime Minister 6
   reaction to Dutch and Australian troops in Timor 20, 23, 25, 46, 51
Salim Ahmed Salim 289
Sampayo, Dr Teixeira de 8, 12, 20–1, 25–6, 27, 28, 33–4, 38–9, 46, 50–3, 56–8, 62, 63–4, 65, 69–71, 73–4
Sands, Richard 173–4, 268, 278
Sani, Anwar 237, 275, 279, 291, 293, 294
Santa Cruz massacre 301
Santos Gonçalves, Vasco dos 217
Santos, Hugo dos (Major) 208–9
Sargent, Sir Orme 15, 17, 21, 23–4, 31, 107
Satari 183
Scott, David 36
Scott, Robert 130
Seara (newspaper) 168
Second World War
   landing of Dutch and Australian

   troops 14–25
   Portuguese neutrality at outset of war 1, 7
   pre-empting the Japanese threat 9–14
Seda, Frans 198, 202
Selby, RW 140
self-determination
   Australian support for principle 138, 150, 153, 171–2, 188, 192, 194–5, 198, 199, 201–2, 203–4, 211, 212, 213, 215, 216, 217, 220, 221, 223, 227, 232, 235, 261, 262
   British support for principle 217, 228, 259, 271, 273, 287, 290, 292, 296
   in Portuguese Timor xiv, 150–1, 159, 160, 175, 177, 182, 184, 185, 188, 189, 191, 192, 193, 194, 195, 197, 198–9
Selkirk, Lord 148
Shann, Mike 141, 145, 147, 149, 154
Simmons, Murray 286
Sinar Harapan (newspaper) 170, 186, 229
Singapore xiii, 37, 60, 126, 139, 147–8, 166–7, 274, 275, 276–7, 278, 279, 298, 299, 304, 305
Soares, Antonio (Major) 250, 252
Soares, José Fernando Osório 186
Soares, Mário 176, 177, 185, 199, 200, 218, 230
Sofala 117, 118
Spender, Percy 126, 128, 129, 130
Spínola, António Sebastião Ribeiro de (General) 176, 177, 179, 180, 190, 202, 207, 217–19, 224
Squire, CW 227, 251
Staples, Justin 136, 137
Stephenson, Sir J 124
Stokes, Alison 298
Straaten, NLW van (Commander) 22
Strang, William 41, 45, 130
Stuart, Andrew 244, 278, 279, 285–6
Suara Karya (newspaper) 186
Subandrio (Foreign Minister, Indonesia) 134–5, 138, 148
Sudharmono 225
Sugama, Yoga 206, 250, 258
Sugiyama Hajime 61
Suharto (President, Indonesia) xvi, 139, 167, 168, 172, 187, 192, 193, 194, 195, 197, 199, 205, 209, 217, 222, 225, 231, 232, 233, 234, 237, 239, 252, 257, 258, 261, 262, 263, 270, 274, 277, 278, 299, 302, 305, 306
Sukarno (President, Indonesia) xvi, 109, 129, 134, 135, 136, 139, 146, 148, 149, 150, 154, 157–8, 161, 163–5, 167, 168, 174, 196, 257, 305–6
Sumario 297
Sunarso, Colonel 186

Syukur, John   186

TAA   173
Talboys, Brian   299
Tange, Sir Arthur   138, 149, 150, 159
Taylor, Alan   216, 228–30, 240, 260, 270, 278
Taylor, John   287
Teles, Galvão   282
Thomas, JC   294
Thomaz, Américo (President, Portugal)   177
Timor
 historical impact of interests of outsiders   303–4
 see also Portuguese Timor; Timor Leste; West Timor
Timor Leste   xi, 259, 303, 306
'Timor Trough' principle   180
Timorese Democratic Union (UDT) *see* UDT (União Democrática Timorense)
Tjan, Harry   186–7, 191, 192, 193, 198, 202, 206–7, 230, 269, 270
Tjarda van Starkenborgh-Stachouwer, AWL (Gov-Gen, Dutch East Indies)   13, 18, 32, 38, 54
Togo Shigenori   61
Tojo Hideki (Prime Minister, Japan)   61
Toohey, Brian   171
Trident Conference (Washington, 1943)   80
Tunku Abdul Rahman (Prime Minister, Malaya)   136

U-boats, threat in Atlantic   79, 80, 81
UDT (União Democrática Timorense)   185, 190, 208, 222, 224, 225, 226, 229, 234, 238, 239–40, 241, 246, 248–9, 252, 253, 256, 257–8, 259–60, 263–4, 266, 267–8, 271, 279–80, 283, 285
União Nacional para Independência Total de Angola (UNITA)   218
Union of Timor Republic   163
United Nations
 debate over decolonisation of Portuguese Empire in Africa   138
 Fretilin delegation   273, 274
 Guicciardi report   287–95
United Nations General Assembly - Committee of 24   153, 154, 155, 161, 173, 182, 237, 241, 253, 280, 289, 296
United Nations General Assembly - Fourth Committee, response to Indonesian invasion of Timor   273, 274, 275–8
United Nations Security Council
 Portuguese request for mission to Timor   274, 275
 proceedings over Portuguese Timor   279–84

United States
 interest in Azores   8, 10, 79, 87–8, 91, 95, 97–8, 99, 100–1, 103, 106, 219
 relations with Indonesia   143, 147, 149, 157, 274, 284

Vasconcelos Ruas, OF de   127
Vieira, Lopes   137
Vincent, Tony   204, 205
Vintras, RE de T (Wing Commander)   11
Viva, Susa (Commandant)   11

Waldheim, Kurt   251, 253, 288, 289, 300
Waller, Sir Keith   159, 161, 162
Wardell, AW (Brigadier)   120
Warner, Fred   137, 140, 142, 144, 145–6, 148
Wavell, General Sir Archibald   48, 49, 50, 54, 59
West New Guinea
 Indonesian acquisition of   xiv, 139–40, 168
 Indonesian claims to   109, 128, 129, 130, 134
West Papua *see* West New Guinea
West Timor
 Australian offer to administer   127
 Japanese occupation   73
 nationalist agitation   127
 refugees from Portuguese Timor   222, 225, 226, 232, 241, 259, 260, 266–7, 273
White, HD   127
Whitlam, Gough   170, 175, 192, 193, 194–200, 203, 204–5, 211, 212, 214, 215–16, 220, 222, 223, 227–8, 231, 232, 233, 234, 237, 239, 249, 253, 255–6, 261, 262, 265, 279, 306
Whittaker, FJ   9, 133
Wilenski, Peter   187, 192
Wilford, KM   249
Willesee, Don (Senator)   173, 179, 195, 198, 199, 205, 211, 213, 219–20, 261, 262, 265, 279
Williams, MS   84, 87, 88, 89
Winant, John (US Ambassador, Portugal)   64–5
wolfram   40, 43, 48, 89, 90, 91
Woolcott, Richard   170, 188, 212, 221–2, 229, 232–3, 234, 235–6, 250, 252, 254, 261, 263, 265, 267, 269, 272, 274, 278–9, 296, 297